ANTHROPOSOPHY IN THE LIGHT OF GOETHE'S *FAUST*

Writings and Lectures from mid-1880s to 1916

RUDOLF STEINER (1905)

ANTHROPOSOPHY IN THE LIGHT OF GOETHE'S *FAUST*

Writings and Lectures from mid-1880s to 1916

VOLUME ONE
of Spiritual-Scientific Commentaries on Goethe's Faust

TRANSLATED BY BURLEY CHANNER
INTRODUCTION AND COMMENTARY BY FREDERICK AMRINE

RUDOLF STEINER

SteinerBooks

CW 272

SteinerBooks
Anthropsophic Press

610 Main Street
Great Barrington, Massachusetts 01230
www.steinerbooks.org

Original translation from the German by Burley Channer.
Introduction and commentary by Frederick Amrine.

This book is volume 272 in the Collected Works (CW) of Rudolf Steiner, published by SteinerBooks, 2014. It is a translation of the German (GA 272) *Geisteswissenschaftliche Erläuterungen zu Goethes Faust. Band I Faust der Strebende Mensch,* published by Novalis-Verlag Verlag, Freiburg im Breisgau, 1955.

Library of Congress Cataloging-in-Publication Data is available on request.

Print ISBN: 978-0-88010-639-9
eBook ISBN: 978-0-88010-664-1

CONTENTS

GA = Rudolf Steiner Gesamtausgabe (the complete works in German)
BSG = Beiträge zur Rudolf Steiner Gesamtausgabe (supplements to the GA)

EXTRACTS

LECTURES

TRANSLATOR'S NOTE

A few brief remarks are in order to clarify some possibly puzzling conventions of the present text. First, all citations from Goethe's *Faust* have been freshly translated for inclusion in these lectures, except as noted in the accompanying notes and commentaries. No attempt has been made to imitate the many end rhymes throughout Goethe's poetic drama. On the other hand, great effort has been made, as far as possible, to preserve the rhythmic quality of the original German in order to salvage something of its poetry. Second, all citations from the text of *Faust* have been indicated by line numbers in parentheses, e.g., (2038), for easy reference to any standard edition of the work. The same device is used to highlight several allusions Rudolf Steiner made to the text without citing it specifically. Occasionally he would simply incorporate in the flow of his speech certain key phrases that were quite familiar to his German-speaking audience but might not be immediately recognizable to the English reader. Finally, information has occasionally been provided in square brackets […] by the translator for explanation of a text or clarification of some reference. Such information may consist of an italicized German word or phrase that provided more than usual resistance to translation and may be of some special interest to the reader on that account.

INTRODUCTION

Rudolf Steiner's *Faust*

FREDERICK AMRINE

Bringing the Right Expectations to Bear

Rudolf Steiner was an important contributor to mainstream scholarship on Goethe. Although he had only just graduated from the university, Steiner was given the honor and the responsibility of editing Goethe's scientific writings for two major editions, including the definitive critical edition known as the *Weimarer or Sophien-Ausgabe*. His introductions from the other, earlier edition were eventually published separately as *Goethe the Scientist.*[1] Steiner's first monograph, *Goethe's Theory of Knowledge* (1886),[2] sought to make explicit and defend the unstated epistemological foundations of Goethe's alternative scientific method. In 1897 he published another monograph that sought to justify Goethe's unorthodox approach to science in the context of then-ongoing philosophical debates.[3] Unlike the writings of his contemporaries, which are now of historical interest only, Steiner's introductions and commentaries on Goethe's scientific works from the late nineteenth century can be and still are read with profit today.

The story is entirely different with regard to these lectures and essays on Goethe's *Faust,* however, and it is not surprising that they have remained untranslated for nearly a century. As Steiner himself repeatedly warns, his various lectures on *Faust* make no attempt to mount a comprehensive interpretation of Goethe's masterpiece. Indeed, in many places they will seem to be only peripherally about *Faust.* If Steiner were trying to interpret Goethe's drama in any conventional sense, his way of proceeding would be outrageous. But that is not what he was trying to do, and anyone coming to these lectures with that understandable but unjustified expectation can only come away disappointed.

Steiner was himself the author of four dramas, and he worked for several years as a theater critic and the editor of a literary journal after moving from Weimar to Berlin in 1897. He directed the staging of scenes from Goethe's *Faust* himself. Steiner even devised two new art forms, eurythmy and *Sprachgestaltung* or "creative speech," that became integral to the performances, which continue at intervals to this day in their original location, the Goetheanum in Dornach, Switzerland. Indeed, these lectures often function as *Ansprachen* or "addresses," occasional pieces meant to introduce and accompany performances of Goethe's *Faust* showcasing Steiner's new art forms. But he never was, or tried to be, anything like a literary scholar. Steiner was a scientist by training, and it was, after all, Goethe's *scientific* works that he was engaged to edit.

More important, Steiner was himself a philosopher and an artist of tremendous stature, who had his own ideas about the profound questions Goethe had engaged.[4] These lectures and other texts are mostly about central ideas in Steiner's own philosophy, which he delivered initially under the aegis and in the idiom of the Theosophical Society, and to which he later gave the name "anthroposophy." So it is that, as my title of this introduction suggests, I have come to see these various lectures and essays not so much as Steiner's interpretations of Goethe, but rather as his own version of *Faust.*

Steiner's take on Goethe is what the great critic Harold Bloom would call a "strong reading," which is to say a more or less conscious and intentional *misreading* of Goethe's text. Just as Goethe "misread" the chapbook of 1587, Steiner "misreads" Goethe. And Steiner himself makes no bones about it. In the lecture of April 11, 1915, for example, he argues that "in our time we must understand Faust differently from the way even Goethe himself understood him" (p. 120), and in the following lecture, he quotes Goethe's own admissions of the shortcomings of his drama.

Many times in these lectures Steiner claims that he is not so much interpreting Goethe's *Faust* as making explicit ideas that could only remain germinal and unconscious in Goethe's day. In that sense, Steiner often saw Goethe as a kind of proto-anthroposophist. For example, at the beginning of the lecture of September 10, 1916, Steiner warns:

> If we speak about these figures in Goethe's *Faust* the way we wish to here, we have to understand as we do so that Goethe knew them face to face, as it were, and characterized them as well as he could, whereas spiritual science [anthroposophy] can go into the matter even more deeply and is fully justified in doing so…you shouldn't imagine that Goethe had in mind any of the ideas I will develop for you in speaking about Mephistopheles. Goethe simply characterized Mephistopheles as he knew him; but this is just why Mephistopheles, as he really is, remains a definite figure that can also be characterized using spiritual-scientific ideas. The significant thing is that with this spiritual-scientific characterization we can look more deeply into the individuality of Mephistopheles or of other figures that appear in *Faust.*

Note Steiner's explicit claim to justification, and especially the word "also" in the penultimate sentence, which are telling. What we have here is not Steiner looking at Goethe and hence indirectly at Mephisto (Mephistopheles), but rather Steiner and Goethe both looking at Mephisto directly. What Steiner is attempting is not so much an interpretation of Goethe as a kind of triangulation of a spiritual reality: Goethe and Steiner are each looking at the same metaphysical object from a different angle, and by working together they can get a fix on it.[5] But Steiner also claims to see clearly what Goethe saw only dimly. That might sound arrogant, but however one feels about it, one needs to acknowledge that Steiner backed up his claim with some 400 volumes of other lectures and writings, many of which he references explicitly here. Fairness requires that a final judgment be made only within that much larger context.

Reading these texts as Steiner's own version of *Faust* immediately solves certain puzzles, for example how it was that a great champion of Goethe came to criticize him so roundly on multiple issues, above all on his depiction of Mephistopheles. Steiner would have done it differently, and indeed he had already done it differently in his own *Mystery Dramas.*[6] The sequence of lectures does not follow the sequence of Goethe's text, but rather the sequence in which Steiner rehearsed and staged his own interpretations of individual scenes. The focus is primarily on Steiner's ideas rather than Goethe's.

Now another word of caution is in order: the approach to the present volume I am advocating should not awaken an unjustified expectation on this other side either, which likewise can only lead to disappointment. These lectures do not attempt to provide a systematic introduction to anthroposophy. They were mostly private communications to experienced anthroposophists, the great majority of whom had studied his basic and introductory writings for many years, and they were given mostly at the headquarters of the international movement. Much remains unspoken here, and many assertions go unexplained, because Steiner presumes a certain level of background knowledge and commitment.[7] For those who seek it, a much more appropriate introduction to Steiner would be one of his four "basic books" (as they have come to be called), such as *How to Know Higher Worlds*, or the texts selected and introduced by Robert McDermott in his outstanding collection, *The New Essential Steiner*.[8]

Selection and Sequence of Texts

Steiner's immense *oeuvre* divides quite distinctly into "public" and "private" material. The former consists of 28 monographs, eight collections of essays, and 33 volumes of public lectures, delivered mostly in Berlin between 1903 and 1918. The latter consists almost entirely of the private lectures he gave to members of the Theosophical Society and (later) Anthroposophical Society. The "private" lectures run into the thousands, and they fill hundreds of volumes in the German *Gesamtausgabe* [GA] or *Complete Works* [CW]. Contrary to expectation, the distinction is not neatly between exoteric and esoteric: much in the published books is highly esoteric, and much in the private lectures could easily have been spoken before any well-educated audience. And in any case, the so-called "private" lectures have been publicly available for decades, so they have long since ceased to be private in any real sense.

The current volume corresponds to GA 272, the first of two collecting Steiner's various lectures on *Faust*. GA 272 and GA 273 were originally assembled in 1931 (six years after Steiner's death), with a view to the Goethe Centennial in 1932. Most of the private lectures in the GA are "cycles," meaning they were delivered in a single location as an internally coherent sequence, often on successive days, each building on the previous lectures. In addition, these cycles are often highly artistic in their composition. But none of that is the case here. GA 272 was from its inception quite an arbitrary assemblage of lectures given on many different kinds of occasions, spread out over seven years in three different cities. The collection is not an organic cycle, and the lectures seldom refer to or build upon one another. Moreover, other volumes of the GA contain several significant texts that discuss *Faust* directly. In light of the vast scope of the edition, it makes sense that the editors of the GA would not want to publish the same pieces in multiple volumes. But the editor and translator of the present volume decided that this good practical consideration was outweighed by the importance of collecting in one place as much important material on *Faust* as possible, especially since the Complete Works in English [CW] will not be complete for many years to come. Hence we have decided to supplement the original configuration of GA 272 by including several short texts and relevant excerpts from longer texts. In keeping with usual GA and CW practice, but also for the sake of rendering transparent Steiner's evolving relationship with *Faust*, we offer them in strict chronological order.

The volume you are holding, both as originally configured in the GA and as we have supplemented that configuration, straddles the aforementioned divide between "public" and "private." The majority of the lectures in GA 272 were originally private, but one (January 23, 1910, in Strassburg) was a public lecture, and many of the supplemental texts are from books or collections of essays published by Steiner during his lifetime.

A further complicating factor is that Steiner's relationship to Goethe's *Faust* changed subtly but unmistakably over the ten years of lectures collected in GA 272 and GA 273. Early on, Steiner uses *Faust* very much as a vehicle, a means to the end of conveying his own anthroposophical ideas. But toward the end of GA 272, and certainly throughout most of GA 273, *Faust* is treated ever more extensively and carefully as an end in itself, if not quite a literary work to be interpreted as literature. A symptomatic example would be the discussion of Mephistopheles at the beginning of the penultimate lecture (September 10, 1916), which qualifies Steiner's earlier assertions and offers a more nuanced reading that hovers much closer to Goethe's text. Partly—perhaps largely—because by that point many more scenes, including the two "Walpurgis Nights," were ready to perform, Steiner's lectures in GA 273 discuss much more of the drama. While still not a comprehensive interpretation, what had begun as a series of occasional lectures on anthroposophical topics begins to looks more like scholarship on *Faust*.

Two different relationships suggest two different introductions, and the publication of GA 273 as a separate volume will make this possible. Hence, the present introduction is devoted to Rudolf Steiner's *Faust* as an occasion for conveying anthroposophical ideas, and many topics that are broached in GA 272 will be saved and covered by the introduction to GA 273: Steiner as an interpreter of *Faust*; his relationship to his mentor, the Goethe scholar Karl Julius Schröer; his place within the history of *Germanistik* more generally; and a bit about a subsequent line of what might be called "anthroposophical" scholarship on *Faust*, notably the work in English by Alan Cottrell.

As is readily apparent from the chronology appended to this introduction, thirteen of the fifteen lectures collected in GA 272 were presented in Dornach in conjunction with the staging of one or more scenes from *Faust*, a eurythmy performance, or both, beginning on April 4, 1915. These can be identified as the core of the volume, and their purpose was, again, to take Goethe's *Faust* as an occasion to discuss key anthroposophical concepts. Viewed within the larger context of Steiner's career as a spiritual teacher, however, they can be seen as the fifth in a series of six such vehicles. Their place in this larger context will be characterized more fully below.

The texts included in this volume from the period prior to April 4, 1915 vary greatly. "On the Idea of Faust" is an early, incomplete manuscript of uncertain date that was discovered in the archives and first appeared in vol. 77 (Summer 1982) of the *Beiträge zur Rudolf Steiner Gesamtausgabe*, a series of supplements to GA. It looks to be the start of an essay about the methodology of literary interpretation and intellectual history. "*Faust* Explained According to Goethe's Own Method" (1888) and "A New Book on Goethe's *Faust*" (1894) are book reviews, the former of an important edition of *Faust* by Steiner's mentor, Karl Julius Schröer. "*Faust*: A Tragedy by J. W. Goethe" (1897) is Steiner's acidic review of a performance of *Faust* in Berlin. "Goethe's *Faust* as a Picture of His Esoteric View of Life" (1899, rpt. 1902) is a short, freestanding essay. All five of these pieces are best viewed against the backdrop of the early history of Goethe scholarship, so further discussion will be deferred to the introduction to CW 273.

"Goethe's Gospel" (1905) is one of a series of 23 public lectures given in Berlin between September 1904 and June 1905. It is a good example of Steiner's early activity as the recently appointed General Secretary of the German branch of the Theosophical Society. "The Esoteric Foundation of Goethe's Creative Work" (1905) is likewise theosophical; it is Steiner's own written summary of a lecture he gave in London. "Goethe's Secret Revelation—Esoteric" (1908), "The Riddles in Goethe's *Faust*—Exoteric" (1909), and "The Riddles in Goethe's *Faust*—Esoteric" (1909) were all part of a series of 18 public lectures held in Berlin between October 1908 and May 1909 under the overarching title, "Where and How Can One Find the Spirit?" For many years Steiner rented a large hall and gave such a lecture series every winter in Berlin: the lectures were well attended, and they are the main reason why Steiner can be counted among the most important public intellectuals of that time in Germany. His influence extended far beyond the narrow confines of the Theosophical Society. In light of his fame, it is not surprising that he was invited to give the major public lecture in Strassburg, "Goethe's *Faust* from the Standpoint of Spiritual Science" (1910), which was included in the original constellation of GA 272. Of all the lectures in the volume, this is the most carefully crafted, and it is otherwise reminiscent of the public lectures he held over the years in Berlin. Steiner's opening remarks in "The Relationship of Goethe's *Faust* to Goethe" (Berlin, 1911) suggest that he was standing in for another speaker who had to cancel, and his lecture does sound a bit extemporaneous. It blends together material recognizable from his other public lectures with a few esoteric asides about karma and cosmic evolution; and a reference to "Blavatsky" by her last name alone, confirms that this must have been a private lecture to an established group of theosophists. This piece was also included in GA 272, but it is more reminiscent of his earlier theosophical lecture in London than his later lectures in Dornach.

The excerpt from GA 139 (pp. 83-88) is our most daring addition to the volume. In this highly esoteric excerpt from the opening lecture of Steiner's private cycle on the Gospel of St. Mark (Basel, 1912) he claims that the historical Dr. Faustus and the historical Hamlet really lived and that they were the reincarnations of Empedocles and Hector respectively. Steiner offers no evidence for this claim other than the results of his own clairvoyant research, so it is highly problematical from any conventional perspective. But many will find it illuminating, and it is for those who are open to the possibility that it is offered.

"Goethe and the Worldview of German Idealism" (1915) and "Faust's Journey through the World and His Rebirth in German Intellectual History" (1916) take us back to Berlin where Steiner is again holding regular public lectures before large audiences throughout the winter. The public lectures Steiner gave in Germany during World War I have many admirable qualities, and they deserve to be better known: during a time of bitter, propagandistic distortion on both sides, Steiner took it upon himself to appeal publicly to the "better angels" of German culture, focusing on Goethe, the German Idealists, and other great, cosmopolitan figures, offering them as an antidote to the rampant jingoism that infected even such figures as Thomas Mann.[9]

The Fifth of Six Vehicles

If one steps back from these lectures on *Faust* and views them against the background of Steiner's mature career, a remarkable progression emerges, within which they represent the fifth of six different vehicles for the teaching of theosophy and, then later, anthroposophy. Steiner's first choice for conveying these ideas was Goethe's cryptic and atypical *Fairy Tale of the Green Snake and the Beautiful Lily.*[10] Some of Steiner's earliest esoteric writings are devoted to interpretation of this distinctly minor piece, which is initially puzzling for anyone who is well acquainted with Goethe's works as a whole.[11] Goethe's *Faust* is occasionally mentioned in these earliest esoteric writings, but usually just in passing, and almost always by way of elucidating the *Fairy Tale*, rather than as an end in itself. As we shall see, important themes inaugurated here would echo throughout Steiner's later career.

Having been given responsibility for organizing the Theosophical Society's Munich Congress in 1907, Steiner and his future wife, Marie von Sivers, collaborated to translate and stage there Edouard Schuré's *Sacred Drama of Eleusis*.[12] Steiner worried that theosophy had remained too one-sidedly intellectual, so he now began to seek artistic means of embodying his teachings concretely. Hence the appeal of Schuré's attempt to reconstruct the ritual drama performed as the final revelation to the neophytes in the Eleusinian mysteries, which had long been considered the ultimate origin of Greek tragedy. Steiner also transformed the rented hall with red drapes, artistic representations of the seals from the Apocalypse, and painted columns recalling Solomon's Temple. Steiner must have been dissatisfied with something about Schuré's drama, because he seems never to have performed it again. Nevertheless, many seeds of his future activity both as a dramatist and as an architect were planted at the Congress of 1907, which must be regarded as a major turning-point in the history of anthroposophy. Hella Wiesberger has summarized its importance admirably: "In Munich in 1907 the threefold unity [of Steiner's cultural mission] appeared mightily for the first time: the nurturing of supersensible knowledge in connection with a mystery drama as a ritual element in an artistic space, designed and decorated in accordance with these three elements. From the event of the Munich Congress there is a straight line to the First Goetheanum in Dornach" (CW 284, xlv).

By 1910, the focus of Steiner's activity had shifted from Berlin to Munich, which had become the capital of the artistic *avant garde* in Germany. Beginning that summer, Steiner wrote and staged four of his own *Mystery Dramas*, performing one each year through 1913. The first of these, *The Portal of Initiation*, alludes systematically and transparently to Goethe's *Fairy Tale*, recalling Steiner's earliest esoteric writings. These became the third vehicle for conveying anthroposophical insights, and the summer conferences during which the dramas were performed were also the site of several key lecture cycles, notably the three courses over consecutive summers that have been published as GA 115 under the English title *A Psychology of Body, Soul & Spirit*.[13] It is not clear why Steiner not only ceased writing, but also performing his own dramas in full after 1913. He often refers to them in his lectures, but Steiner apparently chose to direct his artistic energies into new areas. The outbreak of World War I surely had a devastating effect on all his plans, as it did for other contemporary groups such as The Blue Rider, but this alone does not explain why Steiner would not have returned to his *Mystery Dramas* once he had reestablished himself in Switzerland.

The constant after 1907 is architecture, but the development of this fourth vehicle was a slow and gradual incarnation. Karl Stockmeyer has described this progression succinctly: "It proceeded out of the Munich Congress—where only 'abstract' construction elements were described—to the model building in Malsch, then on to the lower hall in Stuttgart, and finally to the Johannes Building designed for Munich and the First Goetheanum in Dornach."[14] It is as though the subterranean temple of Goethe's *Fairy Tale* were slowly rising up from beneath the earth to become a site of ritual and artistic transformation. Paradoxically, the local authorities' refusal to allow Steiner to build in Munich provided a significant impetus, because it led him to accept a generous offer of land at Dornach, then in the countryside, near Basel, Switzerland. There Steiner constructed what has come to be called the First Goetheanum, a unique building hovering somewhere between theater and temple, sculpted entirely out of wood, that is widely considered one of the great architectural masterpieces of the twentieth century.[15]

Most of the lectures in the present volume were given during the building of the First Goetheanum, in the so-called *Schreinerei* or carpenters' shed, where the sculpting of the organic forms was being carried out. Thus, even though it was not yet physically complete, the First Goetheanum as ideal and ongoing collaborative project was the omnipresent background of these lectures. Sadly, only one performance of *Faust* was ever staged *in* the Goetheanum—the "Prologue in Heaven" on December 31, 1922—because later that same night an arsonist burned the First Goetheanum to the ground.

And the fifth vehicle, Goethe's *Faust,* must also have been constantly on Steiner's mind as he sculpted the forms of the First Goetheanum. There are even passages in some of his talks about it that describe the building itself as "Faustian." On October 10, 1914, for example, Steiner averred that the truth reveals itself only to those who strive mightily to penetrate superficial appearances and see into the depths of things, and that the harmony of the columns and their motifs in the First Goetheanum sought to give human souls what they need to transcend superficial appearances. The forms were a language that pointed beyond themselves to a direct experience of the spirit [GA 287, untranslated]. Steiner describes repeatedly his intention to create living walls that will become transparent, in the way that the individual letters of a word are transparent to the meaning they embody: it is as though the building itself were responding to Faust's lament in the opening scene of Goethe's drama, where he feels entombed by an abstract knowledge that he cannot feel and experience as real.

As the First Goetheanum moved toward completion, Steiner turned his attention to performances of scenes from Goethe's *Faust*. Clearly these were meant to become the ritual and artistic soul animating the body of the building. Goethe's *Faust* emerged as the fifth vehicle for the teaching of spiritual science and, as the appended chronology shows, Steiner allowed it to supplant his own *Mystery Dramas* almost completely.[16]

And yet *Faust* does not have the last word. That is reserved for Steiner's new art of movement, eurythmy, initially framed for the performance of living speech, and then later expanded to include the performance of music. Thus, Steiner's attention soon shifted to the further development and promotion of eurythmy. By 1915, performances of eurythmy accompany nearly every anthroposophical event, and Steiner never misses an opportunity to introduce it: the volume of the GA containing only a fraction of his brief "addresses" on eurythmy runs to over 600 pages.[17] After the burning of the First Goetheanum, *Faust* was never again performed during Steiner's lifetime: it was supplanted entirely by the sixth vehicle, eurythmy.

Some Esoteric Themes

The lectures and essays collected in the present volume are not Steiner's best work. Mostly, these are occasional pieces, and he has a great deal of business to conduct with the assembled members of the Society. We hear Steiner exhorting them to work harder for the cause, to resist dogmatism, and to understand how spiritual science or anthroposophy is different from theosophy, from which the group had recently split.

Yet, even so, we see many flashes of Steiner's brilliance, and many tokens of his extraordinary range and intellectual foresight. He shows himself to be *au courant* in several emerging disciplines, such as neuro-anatomy (Edinger) and neo-Darwinian evolutionary theory (Hertwig, who would exert a major influence on Stephen Jay Gould). He understands the importance of Franz Brentano, who inspired not only Steiner, but also, directly or indirectly, the founders of phenomenology, psychoanalysis, Gestalt psychology, existentialism, and ecology. There even seems to be a veiled reference to Einstein's recently published theory of relativity.

And Steiner is recognizably himself here in that he delivers a thoroughly esoteric account. He rightly saw, respected, and drew out esoteric dimensions of *Faust* that Goethe had carefully veiled. After all, Steiner called the building that he erected to be the center of the anthroposophical movement "the Goetheanum," and he said that he would have been just as happy to call the movement itself "Goetheanism." From Steiner's perspective, Goethe intuited more than he knew, and knew much more than he could say. Goethe hints at this within the text of his drama, but he displaces the admission by putting it into the mouth of Mephisto, who tells Faust: "Your deepest insights are the things / You can't just tell the boys out loud" (1840-1841). Freud was on to Goethe as well: he famously quotes the same lines in chapter four of *The Interpretation of Dreams*, right where he first introduces the concept of the unconscious. And Goethe intimated the spiritual dimensions of *Faust* to his secretary Eckermann near the end of his life, comparing it to Mozart's *Magic Flute*, and expressing confidence that "the initiate will not fail to see the higher meaning."[18] Steiner saw clearly—indeed, clairvoyantly—what Goethe had seen only darkly, and Steiner had the courage to speak about it openly. Where Goethe censors himself, Steiner speaks freely about spirituality.

Thus it should not surprise us that Steiner moves so quickly and so easily from Goethe's drama to any number of esoteric themes that recur within anthroposophy. Let us just touch upon a few of them briefly, and then consider one of them at greater length. The world of the senses is maya, a "great illusion," and the perspective of wisdom is to see through that world to a higher level of meaning, as with a symbol or a parable. Steiner reminds us repeatedly that Goethe offered up the same wisdom at the end of *Faust*, in the "Chorus Mysticus." And *Faust* confirms Steiner's teaching that the path to higher knowledge consists of a series of trials leading finally to illumination, an inner light breaking forth amid outer darkness. Another important thread woven through nearly all of these lectures is the idea of reincarnation; indeed, Steiner goes so far as to imagine the "Doctor Marianus" at the end of Goethe's drama as a future incarnation of Faust. Like many of his contemporaries, Goethe believed in reincarnation, so there is nothing far-fetched about this interpretation.[19] But the esoteric theme that recurs most frequently in this volume is that of the dual nature of evil. This central topic will be considered at length in the introduction to CW 273, in conjunction with the book by Alan Cottrell that is focused on that issue.

What might surprise and trouble contemporary readers most are Steiner's many references to Christian concepts and festivals such as Whitsun and Easter. By now it should be clear that Steiner was an iconoclastic thinker, and that the last thing we should expect from him is an evocation of religious orthodoxies. In many places Steiner may seem to be doing this, but here we are in danger of being misled by our habitual associations. Steiner had little use for the religious traditions of the established Christian churches, and they had little use for him. They preached openly against him from their pulpits, and Steiner's writings were placed upon the Index by the Catholic Church. Steiner was raised by freethinkers, so he had no traditional religious experience or schooling as a child. As an adult, Steiner strove to develop a free spirituality that has little to do with established religion. And yet he employs that language. It is difficult indeed to resolve this paradox, but I propose to address the problem via a systematic comparison with Mahler's *8th Symphony*, a choral symphony like Beethoven's *9th* that sets a Christian hymn from the Middle Ages in its first part and the seemingly orthodox Christian final scene of Goethe's *Faust* in the second.[20]

Nobody would mistake Mahler for an orthodox Christian. Indeed, having been forced to convert as a condition of his being appointed as director of the Vienna Opera, Mahler had good reason to resent

Christianity. And yet he seems also to be participating in orthodox Christian religiosity. Nor should anyone mistake Goethe for a conventional Christian, but the end of *Faust* seems at first glance to be invoking a thoroughly orthodox vision of the afterlife. My contention is that these three difficult cases—Goethe, Mahler and Steiner—are mutually illuminating. And Mahler's *8th Symphony*, which was first performed in September 1910 in Munich, is all the more apposite in that it is exactly contemporary with Steiner's first *Mystery Drama*, and only a few years earlier than Steiner's first stagings of *Faust*.

In composing the *8th*, Mahler felt himself breaking through into an altogether new kind of music, and in retrospect it is clear that he was: the invocation of the Muse with which the *8th* began was answered already in the second movement of the same symphony, *Das Lied von der Erde* [*The Song of the Earth*], and the *9th Symphony*, which Adorno expressly identified as the beginning of "New Music."[21]

The *8th* sets religious texts, but Mahler's religiosity is as problematical as Goethe's, and for the same reasons. Like Goethe, Mahler was deeply spiritual but not pious in any conventional sense. Mahler told Alfred Roller that he would never compose a Mass because he resisted the Credo, but he later called the *8th* his own, intensely personal "Mass." Goethe and Mahler were both put off by traditional rituals and forms; both developed distinctive late styles tending toward (for lack of a better word) "mysticism"; both rejected established religious structures in favor of the kind of open-ended spiritual striving depicted in the final scene of Goethe's *Faust*.

The end of Goethe's *Faust* and Mahler's *8th* might appear conservative at first, but in both cases one would be mistaken. Neither the poet nor the composer is interested in religious orthodoxy: rather, *they both employ forms of pre- and extra-dogmatic religiosity as a means of representing a post-dogmatic spirituality.*[22] And precisely because he understands this all-important point, Mahler's is the first and only musical setting to interpret Goethe's *Faust* in the right spirit. Goethe and Mahler both deploy older languages metaphorically.

The text Mahler chose to set in the first movement, a ninth-century hymn by Hrabanus Maurus, is itself a prime exemplar of a trans-confessional spirituality. Goethe had been drawn to the text, and translated it in 1820, calling it "an appeal to the collective genius of the world"[23] that "resonates strongly with men rich in spirit and creative power."[24] No simple Credo, Maurus' hymn is suffused by a Faustian *libido sciendi*; at its heart is not a profession of faith, but rather the unorthodox plea "Accende lumen sensibus" [Illuminate our senses with your light], which Mahler made the semantic and harmonic keystone of the whole movement. The underlying notion of God granting *lumen de lumine*, "light from His light," has been aptly described as neo-Platonic, but it conforms just as well to many other forms of pagan Gnosis. By representing the invocation and the rush of inspiration, Mahler thematizes esthetic self-consciousness directly, and thereby brings to light one of the profoundest dimensions of Goethe's *Faust*.

Mahler's "New Music" gives us much-needed guidance in appreciating how very unorthodox and open Goethe's ending is. One needs help for a variety of reasons. Goethe borrows an older religious vocabulary and iconography to represent new ideas, and there can be no doubt that Goethe employed this strategy entirely consciously, so as "not to get lost in vagueness."[25] But the result is an almost irresistible temptation to dismiss the final scene as either ironic, or an old man's intellectual capitulation. Mahler overcame this temptation, reading the "Chorus Mysticus" as the apex of a great pyramid, the culminating, earnest epiphany towards which the whole of *Faust* inexorably ascends.

Another reason is the sheer unorthodoxy of the underlying ideas. Most challenging of all is the "dynamic and demanding" notion of reincarnation that Mahler had joined Goethe in embracing by the time he composed the *8th Symphony*. Mahler explained this unorthodox *credo* to Richard Specht by asserting, "I must live in an ethical way so that my Self, when it returns, will be spared part of the journey and will find its existence not so difficult. That is my moral duty." Knowing that the idea of reincarnation hovers in the background of Goethe's *Faust* is key to understanding its utterly different pictures of striving, of Heaven, and of Grace; and it solves the knotty dilemma of Faust's salvation in the most radical way possible: by taking the concept of salvation off the table altogether.

I submit that the parallels between Mahler's interpretation of *Faust* and Steiner's are uncanny, and that Mahler is a welcome guide in helping us to understand Steiner rightly. Like Mahler and Goethe before him, Steiner invokes the language of religion as a means of transcending religious orthodoxy. All three were heralds of a free spirituality.

Notes

1 New York: Anthroposophic Press, 1950. More recent translations are also available: *Goethean Science* (Spring Valley, NY: Mercury Press, 1988); and *Nature's Open Secret* (New York: Anthroposophic Press, 2001). This is volume 1 of Steiner's Collected Works [CW 1].

2 *Goethe's Theory of Knowledge: An Outline of the Epistemology of His Worldview* (Great Barrington, MA: SteinerBooks, 2008) [CW 2].

3 *Goethe's World View* (Spring Valley, NY: Mercury Press, 1985) [CW 6].

4 I have argued the case for Steiner's importance in a piece commissioned by the Anthroposophical Society in America to mark the 150th anniversary of Steiner's birth: "Discovering a Genius: Rudolf Steiner at 150," *being human*, Fall 2011, 7-17 (available online at time of writing).

5 Cf. the beginning of the lecture on September 9, 1916: "On such an occasion we always try not only to find something that will help us understand this particular poetic work, but also to derive something of general significance for spiritual science from the work itself, to broaden our horizons by looking directly into the same true realities Goethe himself was trying to attain by writing his *Faust*" (p. 296).

6 Rudolf Steiner, *Four Mystery Dramas*, trans. Ruth and Hans Pusch (Great Barrington, MA: SteinerBooks, 2007) [GA 14].

7 I have glossed some of the central concepts in the commentary for those who are completely unfamiliar with anthroposophy, but practical considerations have forced me to keep this to a minimum.

8 Rudolf Steiner, *How to Know Higher Worlds: A Modern Path of Initiation* (Great Barrington, MA: Anthroposophic Press, 1994); Robert McDermott, ed. *The New Essential Steiner: An Introduction to Rudolf Steiner for the 21st Century* (Great Barrington, MA: Lindisfarne Books, 2009).

9 See for example Mann's appalling *Reflections of a Nonpolitical Man*, which he never repudiated.

10 See the commentary to p. 20 in Notes at the back of the book.

11 The most important of these writings have been published in GA 22. See the commentary to p. 20 in Notes for an edition of the *Fairy Tale* that includes

Steiner's interpretations, which have also been published in English under the awkward title *Goethe's Standard of the Soul* (1925).

12 Materials related to this event have been published as GA 284; see the splendid English edition published under the title *Rosicrucianism Renewed: The Unity of Art, Science, and Religion* (Great Barrington, MA: SteinerBooks, 2007) as volume 284 of Steiner's Collected Works.

3 Hudson, NY: Anthroposophic Press, 1999. This new translation by Marjorie Spock replaces an earlier version that was entirely inadequate, and Robert Sardello has contributed an outstanding introduction.

14 CW 284, 219-220. The building in Malsch was a small-scale experiment by Stockmeyer that was inspired by the vision Steiner laid out in 1907; it remained incomplete until long after Steiner's death, but he personally laid the foundation stone in a ceremony on April 5-6, 1909 (CW 284, 141ff.). Stuttgart House was the first space actually owned by the Theosophical Society in Germany; Steiner likewise laid the foundation stone for the transformation of the building on January 3, 1911 (CW 284, 183ff.). "Johannes Building" [*Johannesbau*] was the name given to the edifice that Steiner intended, but was ultimately not allowed to build in Munich. It was however an important milestone in Steiner's development as an architect. The name was meant to recall not the apostle, but rather the main protagonist of Steiner's first mystery drama, Johannes Thomasius. Thomasius is a painter who, like Kandinsky and other avant-garde artists in Steiner's orbit during these years, was trying to overcome naturalism. Stockmeyer's essay "Concerning the Unity of Temple and Ritual in Connection with the Goetheanum Building-Idea" (CW 284, 219-228) is illuminating on the connections among these different architectural projects as forerunners of the First Goetheanum.

15 See e.g. Wolfgang Pehnt, *Expressionist Architecture* (Praeger, 1973). Several volumes of Steiner's Complete Works devoted to architecture generally and the First Goetheanum in particular: the most important are CW 284; GA 286, currently published as *Architecture as a Synthesis of the Arts* (London: Rudolf Steiner Press, 1999); GA 287 (untranslated); GA 288 (German edition still in preparation, untranslated), and GA 289/90 (untranslated).

16 Individual scenes were occasionally performed, but none was ever performed again in its entirety during the remainder of Steiner's lifetime.

17 GA 277, *Eurythmie: Die Offenbarung der sprechenden Seele: Eine Fortbildung der Goetheschen Metamorphosenanschauung im Bereich der menschlichen Bewegung*; a small selection has been published in the volume *An Introduction to Eurythmy: Talks Given Before 16 Eurythmy Performances* (Anthroposophic Press, 1984).

18 January 29, 1827. See the commentary to p. 17 at the back of the book.

19 See the commentary to pp. 18 and 19 on Lessing, and to p. 300 on Goethe.

20 The classic recording is Leonard Bernstein's 1966 performance with the London Symphony (Sony Classical SM2K 61837), but I am especially fond of Václav Neumann's with the Czech Philharmonic (1981, Supraphon 2CDD-204-1/2).

21 Theodor W. Adorno, *Mahler: A Musical Physiognomy* (Chicago: University of Chicago Press, 1992), p. 127.

22 Harold Jantz's study of 1951 remains perhaps best succinct account of Goethe's attraction to what I am calling "pre-" and "extra-dogmatic" spirituality: *Goethe's Faust as a Renaissance Man: Parallels and Prototypes* (Princeton: Princeton University Press, 1951).

23 Letter to Zelter, February 18, 1821.

24 *Maxims and Reflections*, No. 762.

25 Goethe to Eckermann, June 6, 1831.

CHRONOLOGY

Mid-1880s through September 1916

This chronology is based in part on the very useful Performance History appended to GA 273 by the editors of the German edition, Edwin Froböse and Hans Erhard Lauer, who list all the performances of scenes from *Faust* during this period. References to the scenes in *Faust* follow Walter Arndt's English translation in the Norton Critical Edition. It has been supplemented with items from a similar chronology published in *Beiträge zur Rudolf Steiner Gesamtausgabe*, 77 (1982), 49-50. The list of eurythmy performances is based on the "Chronological Survey 1911-1925" in GA 277a, *Die Entstehung und Entwickelung der Eurythmie*, which has been well translated into English by Alan Stott as *Eurythmy: Its Birth and Development* (Anastasi, 2002).

Lectures and publications related to FAUST *in this volume are indicated by* **boldface**.
GA = Rudolf Steiner Gesamtausgabe (the complete works in German)
BSG = Beiträge zur Rudolf Steiner Gesamtausgabe (supplements to the GA)

[mid-1880s?]	**BSG 77: "On the Idea of Faust" (1-3)**
1888	**GA 32: "*Faust* Explained According to Goethe's Own Method" (4-7)**
1894	**GA 32: "A New Book on Goethe's *Faust*" (8-10)**
1897	**GA 29: "*Faust*: A Tragedy by J. W. Goethe" (11-13)**
1899/1902	**GA 22: "Goethe's *Faust* as a Picture of His Esoteric View of Life (14-16)**
January 26, 1905	**GA 53: "Goethe's Gospel" (17-22)**
July 10, 1905	**GA 35: "The Esoteric Foundation of Goethe's Creative Work" (23-25)**
[May 19, 1907	Munich Theosophical Congress; artistic transformation of the rented hall; performance of Edouard Schuré's revival of the Eleusinian mystery drama,

	The Sacred Drama of Eleusis ; beginnings of Sprachgestaltung or "creative speech"]
October 24, 1908	**GA 57: "Goethe's Secret Revelation—Esoteric" (26-27)**
March 11, 1909	**GA 57: "The Riddles in Goethe's *Faust*—Exoteric" (28-31)**
March 12, 1909	**GA 57: "The Riddles in Goethe's *Faust*—Esoteric" (32-35)**
[April 5-6, 1909	Laying of the foundation stone of the model building in Malsch]
January 23, 1910	**GA 272 Lecture 1, Strassburg: "Goethe's *Faust* from the Standpoint of Spiritual Science" (36-56)**
[August 15, 1910	Premiere of Steiner's first mystery drama, *The Portal of Initiation* [*Die Pforte der Einweihung*] in the *Schauspielhaus*, Munich; directly inspired by Goethe's *Fairy Tale of the Green Snake and the Beautiful Lily*]
[January 3, 1911	Laying of the foundation stone of the Stuttgart House]
[August 17, 1911	Premiere of Steiner's second mystery drama, *The Soul's Probation* [*Die Prüfung der Seele*] in the *Gärtnerplatz-Theater*, Munich]
[mid-December	First conversation between Rudolf Steiner and Clara Smits regarding a new art of movement. The first lessons for Lory Smits]
December 17, 1911	**GA 272 Lecture 2, Berlin: "The Relationship of Goethe's *Faust* to Goethe" (57-71)**
[July 1912	Rehearsal of eurythmy for scene 6 of Steiner's third mystery drama, *The Guardian of the Threshold* (*Der Hüter der Schwelle*), Munich]
[August 24, 1912	Premiere of *The Guardian of the Threshold* in the Gärtnerplatz-Theater, Munich]
[1912	Performances of first two mystery dramas, plus Schuré's *Sacred Drama of Eleusis*]
September 15, 1912	**GA 139 Lecture 1, Basel: [excerpt on Faust and Hamlet] (72-76)**
[September 16-24, 1912	First eurythmy course: "The Dionysian Element," Bottmingen/Basel (GA 277a); private course for Lori Smits]
[1913	Formal inauguration of the Anthroposophical Society]

[August 22, 1913	Premiere of Steiner's fourth and last mystery drama, *The Souls' Awakening* (*Der Seelen Erwachen*) in the *Volkstheater*, Munich; in scene 2, sylphs and gnomes perform eurythmy]
[August 28, 1913	Rudolf Steiner's first introductory talk on eurythmy]
[January 20-21, 1914	Eurythmy performance at Annual General Meeting; Steiner's second introductory talk on eurythmy]
[Fall 1914	Beginning of regular performances of eurythmy on the stage in the carpenters' shed before lectures in Dornach]
[1915-1918	Performance of a wide range of scenes from Goethe's *Faust I* and *Faust II* with eurythmy; Steiner's lectures for members regularly preceded by performances of eurythmy]
April 4, 1915	**GA 272 Lecture 3, Dornach: "Faust's Struggle for the Christ-Permeated Source of Life" (77-91)**
April 4, 1915 (Easter)	Performance: *Faust I,* "Night" with eurythmy; also Scene 7 of *The Portal of Initiation*
April 11, 1915	**GA 272 Lecture 4, Dornach: "Faust's Forced Entry into the Spiritual World" (92-111)**
April 11, 1915	Performance: *Faust I,* "Night" (with the appearance of the Earth Spirit); also Scene 7 of *The Portal of Initiation*
May 12, 1915 (Whitsun)	Performance: *Faust II,* "Charming Landscape" (scene with Ariel)
May 22, 1915 (Whitsun)	**GA 272 Lecture 5, Dornach: "Pentecost Mood: Faust's Initiation with the Spirits of the Earth" (112-133)**
May 22, 1915 (Whitsun)	Performance: *Faust II,* "Charming Landscape" (scene with Ariel)
[May 23, 1915 (Whitsun)	Eurythmy performance: *Faust II,* "Charming Landscape" (scene with Ariel): earliest eurythmy forms (choreography) for the chorus of elves in that scene]
May 29, 1915	Performance: *Faust I,* "Night"
May 30, 1915	**GA 272 Lecture 6, Dornach: "*Faust,* The World's Greatest Poetic Work of Human Striving: The Classical Phantasmagoria" (134-153)**
[May 30, 1915	Eurythmy performance: *Faust II,* "Charming Landscape" (scene with Ariel): earliest eurythmy forms (choreography) for the chorus of elves in that scene]

[July 18, 1915	Eurythmy performance: poems by Goethe; also Scene 6 of *The Portal of Initiation*]
[July 25, 1915	Eurythmy performance: poems by Goethe; also Scene 6 of *The Portal of Initiation*]
August 14, 1915	**GA 272 Lecture 7, Dornach: "Faust's Ascension" (153-168)**
August 15, 1915	**GA 272 Lecture 8, Dornach: "Mystical Knowledge and Spiritual Revelation of Nature: Perception of Spirits" (169-186)**
August 15, 1915 (Ascension)	Performance: *Faust II*, "Burial"
[August 15, 1915	Eurythmy performance: *Faust II*, "Burial"]
August 16, 1915 (Ascension)	**GA 272 Lecture 9, Dornach: "The Realm of the Mothers: The Mater Gloriosa" (187-201)**
[August 16, 1915	Eurythmy performance: *Faust II*, "Burial"]
[August 18-Sept. 11, 1915	Second eurythmy course, "The Apollonian Element: Shaping the Mobile Forms of Speech with the Soul " (GA 277a), Dornach]
December 2, 1915	**GA 65, Berlin: "Goethe and the Worldview of German Idealism" (202-208)**
[January 6, 1916	Eurythmy performance: *Faust II*, "Burial"]
February 3, 1916	**GA 65, Berlin: "Faust's Journey through the World and His Rebirth in German Intellectual History" (209-213)**
August 6, 1916	Performance: *Faust II*, "Charming Landscape" (Ariel) with eurythmy
August 7, 1916	Performance: *Faust II*, "Charming Landscape" (Ariel) with eurythmy
August 19, 1916	**GA 272 Lecture 10, Dornach: "Wisdom – Beauty – Goodness: Michael – Gabriel – Raphael" (214-232)**
August 19, 1916	Performance: *Faust I*, "Dedication"; "Prologue in Heaven"
August 20, 1916	**GA 272 Lecture 11, Dornach: "The Historical Significance of *Faust*" (233-247)**
August 20, 1916	Performance: *Faust I*, "Dedication"; "Prologue in Heaven"
August 26, 1916	Performance: *Faust I*, "Dedication"; "Prologue in the Theater"; "Prologue in Heaven"
August 28, 1916	Performance: *Faust I*, "Dedication"; "Prologue in the Theater"; (Goethe's birthday) "Prologue in Heaven"

September 4, 1916	**GA 272 Lecture 12, Dornach: "The 'Burial': The Nature of the Lemures, the Fat Devils and the Skinny Devils" (248-267)**
September 9, 1916	**GA 272 Lecture 13, Dornach: "Goethe's Insights into the Secrets of Human Existence" (268-286)**
September 9, 1916	Performance: *Faust II*, "Midnight" and "Burial"
September 10, 1916	**GA 272 Lecture 14, Dornach: "Perspectives on the True Realities Goethe Was Seeking" (287-306)**
September 11, 1916	**GA 272 Lecture 15, Dornach: "Goethe Plumbs the Depths of Evolution and Its Cosmic Secrets in His *Faust*: The Luciferic and the Ahrimanic Temptation" (307-326)**
September 11, 1916	Performance: *Faust II*, "Midnight" and "Burial"
September 16, 1916	Performance: *Faust II*, "Midnight" and "Burial"
September 23, 1916	Performance: *Faust I*, "Dedication"; "Prologue in the Theater"; "Prologue in Heaven"
September 26, 1916	Performance: *Faust II*, "Midnight" and "Burial"*

*[German Editors' note:] Surviving notes from rehearsals on August 20th and 23rd, 1918, suggest that the scenes from the beginning of the "Classical Walpurgis Night" ("Pharsalian Fields") through Faust's encounter with Manto [lines 7471-7494] were presented during the winter of 1917. Work on the next scene, "On the Upper Peneios, as Before" [lines 7495-8033], began in the summer of 1918. Rehearsals of the remaining scenes in the "Classical Walpurgis Night," including "Rocky Inlets of the Aegean Sea," were completed in early 1919.

GA 277, p. 175 (2nd edn.) lists a performance of "Burial" only, on Sept. 25th. I am unsure whether this was a separate event, or merely a discrepancy in the dating and characterization of the same event. (F.A.)

SYNOPSES

by Burley Channer

EXTRACTS

ON THE IDEA OF FAUST

mid-1880s?

Faust's engaging element is not its folkloric content but its underlying, all-encompassing great idea. Hegelian-style idealism regarded as fiction today. This attitude contradicted by undisputed prominence of mathematics. Grandeur of the idea of Faust : the uniquely human striving for the highest known to us, revealing itself in cognition, feeling, and willing.

FAUST EXPLAINED ACCORDING TO GOETHE'S OWN METHOD

1888

Schröer's works are unique in modern secondary literature on Goethe. His approach not pure philology or literary history but search for "pregnant point in the phenomena" from which Goethe derives each new work. Luther, the theologian, versus Faust, the still Protestant, but free, human being. Fresh, living quality of *Faust* due to its concrete images, whose origin Schröer carefully traces. Examples of this. Both Part One and Part Two of *Faust* connected with the totality of Goethean spirit.

A NEW BOOK ON GOETHE'S *FAUST*

1894

Some difficulties in understanding *Faust* are artificial creations of scholars and critics. Valentin's study relates all parts of *Faust*, not to some abstract concept, but to artistic lawfulness and unity of its composition. Why earthly action of the drama is preceded and followed by episodes in heaven. Faust's gradual development from Mephistophelean guidance to greater independence. "Classical Walpurgis Night" as reawakening of primeval forces of natural creativity that bring the archetypal image of female beauty, Helen, to real life. Faust's penetration into secrets of the infinite. Valentin's approach on right track.

FAUST: A TRAGEDY BY J. W. GOETHE

1897

Scathing review of drama's performance in Deutsches Theater, Berlin, on Goethe's birthday, August 28. Comparison with philistine superficiality of physiologist Du Bois-Reymond's view of *Faust.* Josef Kainz's rendering of Faust a masterful example of linguistic virtuosity with no evidence of Faust's inner suffering. Equally shallow, unconvincing performances of Mephistopheles and Gretchen. Art of acting at Deutsches Theater not mature enough for Goethe.

GOETHE'S *FAUST* AS A PICTURE OF HIS ESOTERIC VIEW OF LIFE

1899/1902

Faust as mystic at beginning of Part Two, Act Four. Death of the lower, temporal, becomes a simile for birth of the higher, eternal, springing to new life within the human spirit. Esoteric interpretation of Mephistopheles seeks that figure's true spiritual content, not one given to it by the poet. A figure that can give up its existence in order to exist will be Faustian; one that cannot do this will be Mephistophelean, living only in what is sensory and material. Experience of secret of "key" to Realm of the Mothers most accessible to a life in science. The human spirit is not a purely spiritual being. Human being must have passed through series of incarnations. Homunculus a kind of daemon, not yet darkened and limited by complete incarnation as a human being.

GOETHE'S GOSPEL

Berlin, January 26, 1905

Theosophical roots of Central European culture. Lessing, Schiller, Herder, and Novalis all familiar with the idea of reincarnation. Goethe an ardent theosophical seeker, for whom world not material, but active, creative spirit. *Faust* a hymn to developing human perfection. "Prologue in Heaven" depicts Harmony of the Spheres, spiritual hearing in which consciousness of third, or spiritual, world expresses itself. Earth Spirit a real planetary being with unified consciousness of all creation. *The Mysteries* a poetic fragment expressing this idea in terms of the Rose Cross. Mephistopheles the tempter who guides Faust through all possible errors to the purification and mysticism of old age. Mysteries of body, soul, spirit and human incarnation depicted through Homunculus and Helen in "Classical Walpurgis Night." Separation of sexes and mystical liberation from all sexuality in final scene of *Faust.*

THE ESOTERIC FOUNDATION OF GOETHE'S CREATIVE WORK

July 10, 1905

Part Two of *Faust* depicts the human being's relation to "three worlds" (physical, astral and spiritual). Faust's search for Helen's immortal spirit in the Realm of Mothers portrays his entry into the spiritual world (Devachan). Mephistopheles and the role of evil in the generation of Homunculus. Clairvoyant Homunculus is the astral human being that must pass through all the kingdoms of Nature on the way to incarnation (Proteus). Union of Homunculus and Helen pictures human nature as triadic (Atma-Buddhi-Manas) and gives poem dramatic unity when viewed this way. "Chorus Mysticus": transitoriness of the world the symbol for underlying non-transitoriness of the spirit. Goethe represents higher human nature as something "female," a traditional symbol of mysticism. Only a mystical interpretation can succeed in unifying this poem.

GOETHE'S SECRET REVELATION—ESOTERIC

Berlin, October 24, 1908

Alchemical image of Lily becomes Beautiful Lily in Goethe's Fairy Tale. Its further transformation culminates in Faust's union with "Ever-Feminine" in the "Chorus Mysticus," where it represents purification of conceptual life, feelings, and will and becomes the "indescribable" or the "attainment." Goethe's most profound revelation.

THE RIDDLES IN GOETHE'S *FAUST*—EXOTERIC

Berlin, March 11, 1909

Part One's portrait of Faust's striving soul are infinitely real and true to life, though some parts seem more theoretical than others. Part Two so little understood because it faithfully depicts poet's loftiest experiences of genuinely spiritual world. These experiences much more real and true for spiritual researcher than physical sense experience. Part Two thus not symbolic or allegorical, but one of most realistic works in all world literature. Dangers of unclear upward striving into spiritual world in sixteenth-century age of Faust, a time of major transition. Mephistopheles a real being, but only one of two tempters. Lucifer works on innermost core of human being. Ahriman, recognized already by Zarathustra as spirit of darkness, conjures up illusion of outer world as being purely material and not as true manifestation of spirit. In later Faust tradition the two devils merged into one: Satan. Goethe regarded illusory appearance of outer world as Mephistopheles, manifesting as second "I" in people, including himself. Origin of name Mephistopheles. Helen scene part of first material Goethe wrote for *Faust*, but could not be included in it artistically. Goethe's need to develop spiritually until he could experience and depict stages of his own growth and deepening. What makes Part Two a magnificent proclamation of Western spiritual science.

THE RIDDLES IN GOETHE'S *FAUST*—EXOTERIC

Berlin, March 12, 1909

Faust at the stage of elementary clairvoyance in the scene at the Imperial Palace. Clairvoyance attainable through appropriate exercises of concentration and meditation. Plutarch Goethe's inspiration for realm of archetypal images. Goethe's spiritually realistic portrait of the Realm of the Mothers. First Homunculus scene imagined as taking place entirely in spiritual world. Homunculus as representative of astral body. Faust's out-of-body experience of astral body clothing itself in all elements on way toward incarnation. No symbols here, only realistic pictures of supersensible events.

LECTURES

1

GOETHE'S *FAUST* FROM THE STANDPOINT OF SPIRITUAL SCIENCE

Public Lecture, Strassburg, January 23, 1910

Sources of knowledge and the life of spiritual science were present at all times people sought answers to deepest questions and riddles of existence. Awakening spiritual perception. Repeated earthly lives scientifically demonstrated à la Francesco Redi: We are descended from ourselves. Soul bonds also immortal. Goethe a seeker of spiritual science and *Faust* the record of his spiritual striving. Goethe's scientific and artistic studies. Faust's progress through the Earth Spirit. The small world and the great world. Mephistopheles, Helen of Troy and the Mothers as the spiritual foundation of all physical objects. Natural science has the key to spiritual science. Homunculus is the soul between the body and the reincarnating human spirit. Euphorion is a child of the evolving soul's first brief connection with the spiritual world. Faust, care, and the overcoming of egoism. Rudolf Steiner's wording of the "Chorus Mysticus." The Eternal or Ever-Feminine that is common to both sexes.

2

THE RELATIONSHIP OF GOETHE'S *FAUST* TO GOETHE

Berlin, December 17, 1911

Various versions of *Faust* over Goethe's long lifetime as records of Goethe's own soul development. Goethe's sense of the truth of classical Greek art and the maya of art in the 5th post-Atlantean epoch. Reincarnation: the problem of carrying the 4th cultural epoch over into the 5th cultural epoch. The "Witch's Kitchen" pictures the dangers of entering the spiritual world unprepared. The search for the "I" and the spirit in the 5th cultural epoch. Homunculus as a body of astral forces preparing for Helen's reincarnation.

3

(From GA 139) THE GOSPEL OF ST. MARK

(excerpt on Faust and Hamlet)

Basel, September 15, 1912

Hector and Empedocles as historical personages underlying Shakespeare's "Hamlet" and Goethe's "Faust." The confident Greek warrior's return as Hamlet, the modern doubter, skeptic, and vacillator. Descent of the Greek philosopher and nature-mystic into Mt. Etna compared with Faust's ascent into fire-element of heaven in final tableau of *Faust*. Forces formerly at work must find new way into struggles of our modern age.

4

FAUST'S STRUGGLE FOR THE CHRIST-PERMEATED SOURCE OF LIFE

An Easter contemplation

Dornach, April 4, 1915

Ahrimanic knowledge and Ahrimanic being fill Faust's soul with the thought of death from the play's very beginning. Goethe could only write the "Easter Night" scene after writing *The Fairy Tale*. Premonition of the Jupiter existence gives meaning to the second half of life. Christ's early death makes soul-strength available for the second half of life. *Faust* a very uneven work of art. Atavistic clairvoyance and the historical Dr. Georg Faust. Eyewitness accounts and the literary tradition. Augustine; Erasmus. Goethe unable to disentangle Lucifer from Ahriman. Mephisto an occult impossibility. Goethe senses Faust's need to experience the Mystery of Golgotha in the aura of the earth.

5

FAUST'S FORCED ENTRY INTO THE SPIRITUAL WORLD

Dornach, April 11, 1915

The aim of these lectures: not to explain *Faust* but to deepen knowledge of spiritual science. *Faust* expresses Goethe's own striving to enter the spiritual world. Faust's Nostradamus-meditation. How experiencing the physical becomes a spiritual sense organ in the soul world. Elemental world, the source of human history. Faust's rejection by the Earth Spirit. Mephisto as Lucifer. Wagner is the only spirit that Faust can understand. Events on stage as images of Faust's self-knowledge. Faust translating the Gospel of John. Mohammed and Paradise. Spiritual science counteracts the shallowness of modern thinking.

6

PENTECOST MOOD: FAUST'S INITIATION WITH THE SPIRITS OF THE EARTH

Dornach, May 22, 1915

The Pentecost festival 1915 witnesses 34 nations at war. Spiritual science is a Pentecost proclamation to humanity. Viewing Christ before and after the Mystery of Golgotha. The "Representative of Humanity" compared with Michelangelo's Christ in the *Last Judgment.* Why non-Christian theosophy has no teachings about Lucifer and Ahriman, but spiritual science must distinguish them. Goethe's "Representative of Humanity" could not yet do this. Spiritual science brings something absolutely new. The Faust of Part II is not the Faust of Part I. His guilt at the end of Part I must be carried over to the next incarnation but it serves as a source of higher knowledge in his present one. Faust's higher self is not subject to guilt; its initiation through the four watches of the night. Life as "reflected splendor." The battle between the Christ-impulse and the Ahrimanic-Luciferic powers in the depths of human nature. The wisdom-filled guidance of the world. A verse for Pentecost.

7

FAUST, THE WORLD'S GREATEST POETIC WORK OF HUMAN STRIVING: THE CLASSICAL PHANTASMAGORIA

Dornach, May 30, 1915

These lectures contain an important key to much of spiritual science. Consciousness before and after death is due to processes of destruction. The different lengths of time between incarnations. Earthly circumstances make us who we are. Working spiritually with the destructive stream of time: the urgent task of spiritual science. Reverence for the truth and knowledge we acquire on our own. Objective judgment from a different cultural perspective. Goethe's long-range plan for writing Part II. Creating new forms out of spiritual science. Form becomes empty over time. Wagner and the student as pictures of Faust's development. Overcoming Luciferic subjectivity by going outside oneself in the "enjoyment of deeds." Current catastrophic events can be rightly judged only from a much broader historical perspective.

8

FAUST'S ASCENSION

Dornach, August 14, 1915

Closing scene of Part II. Difficulties of "esoteric" literary interpretation. Examples from Goethe's *Soothsayings of Bakis*. Goethe's struggle not to use straw symbols and allegories for Faust's ascension into heaven. Faust ascends through real, spiritualized consciousness of anchorites and other figures. Words of Chorus and its Echo describe Nature as anchorites perceive it spiritually, not as physical processes. Blessed Boys. Spirits need to use physical organs to experience the physical world. Younger Angels. Doctor Marianus and/as Faust. Chorus of three Penitent Women and Gretchen. The Mater Dolorosa. The Mystical Chorus.

9

MYSTICAL KNOWLEDGE AND SPIRITUAL REVELATION OF NATURE: PERCEPTION OF SPIRITS

Dornach, August 15, 1915

Goethe only able to add Christian element to Easter scene at a ripe old age. Elemental aspect of Nature surrounding Faust's ascension into heaven. Chorus senses outer form becoming spiritual movement. Goethe's Nature-based esotericism healthy for our time. Ascension of Faust's soul through the consciousnesses of the various ranks of figures. Swedenborg, Filippo Neri, Meister Eckhart, as examples. Being Christian as a non-dogmatic way of feeling and relating to the world. Goethe's Christian images as accurate depictions of spiritual realities. Chorus of elemental beings around Helen returns to Nature and reappears as the Blessed Boys. Younger Angels compared with Elohim. Artistic enhancement in the arrangement of the Penitent Women. Macrocosmic and microcosmic aspects of the female and the male: the Mater Gloriosa.

10

THE REALM OF THE MOTHERS: THE MATER GLORIOSA

Dornach, August 16, 1915

Homunculus as Goethe's solution to the problem of Helen's re-embodiment. Why both Helen and Gretchen are "innocently guilty." From the trinity of the Mothers through the Mystery of Golgotha to the threefold unity of the Mater Gloriosa. The human being as microcosmic image of macrocosmic evolution. The four ethers. Substances as expressions of cosmic harmony. Role of Lucifer and Ahriman in the division of the sexes. Luciferic influence on female clairvoyance. Ahriman and the male aura: the Blessed Boys' "choirs of life." Neutralization of male-auric and female-auric images.

11

GOETHE AND THE WORLDVIEW OF GERMAN IDEALISM

Berlin, December 2, 1915

Faust's striving for knowledge, his great enigma. Magic as Faust's path to experiencing creativity in Nature. Poetic transformation of abstract philosophical thinking into living dramatic images. Faust's encounters with a real being of evil. Faust's journey from sensuous depths of soul to supra-consciousness beyond normal world of soul. Continual self-refashioning of Faust's self compared with differing stances of Schelling and Fichte toward the relationship between understanding and creating in Nature. Mystical experience of the Self of the cosmos within one's own lower self is a common striving of both Faust and Hegel.

12

FAUST'S JOURNEY THROUGH THE WORLD AND HIS REBIRTH IN GERMAN INTELLECTUAL HISTORY

Berlin, February 13, 1916

Faust's acquaintance with magic occurs long before his opening monologue. Anthropomorphic character of medieval philosophical worldviews and experience of Nature. Experiments designed to let Nature reveal its secrets through old magic. Evolution of medieval nature-image into one whose abstract concepts Goethe's Faust found so threadbare. Faust's turn from Sign of the Macrocosm to Microcosm and the Earth Spirit. Mephisto a kind of alter ego of Faust. Faust's tragic clairvoyant experiences in Part One due to a mediumism stemming from morally unsublimated lower soul forces. Faust's progress toward a healthy experience of Nature.

13

WISDOM-BEAUTY-GOODNESS. MICHAEL-GABRIEL-RAPHAEL

Dornach, August 19, 1916

Kant's three *Critiques,* as well as most recent thinkers, assign Wisdom to thinking, Beauty to feeling, and the Good to willing. Brentano assigns thinking or conceptualization to Beauty, the power of judgment to Wisdom, and willing to Sympathy and Antipathy. Scholastic thinking was alive in Brentano. His analysis of the soul similar to what archangels would say more completely. In spiritual worlds, validity of concepts and judgments depends on relation to actual spiritual beings. Hebrew names translated as new names for these concepts: "God-beholder," the same as Michael; "God-proclaimer," the same as Gabriel; and "God-willer," the same as Raphael. A god works through these three beings as the human "I" works through its three soul forces. The application of these thoughts to the speeches of the archangels in "Prologue in Heaven." Goethe's confusion of Lucifer and Ahriman in Mephistopheles. Lucifer and Ahriman contrasted. Goethe's mood in writing the "Dedication."

14

THE HISTORICAL SIGNIFICANCE OF *FAUST*

Dornach, August 20, 1916

Luciferic and Ahrimanic aspects of Mephistopheles. The "Group" statue. Copernican calculations and later, more superficial observation of positions of heavenly bodies. From Copernicus, Galilei, and Kepler to Darwin, Lamarck, and Haeckel. Future way of studying heavens will explain earth in terms of heavens and heavens in terms of earth. Astronomical orientation of Goethe's writings on color and morphology. Shift from Luciferic seduction in Middle Ages to Ahrimanic seduction in the more modern age. Adam and Eve: symbols of the Luciferic tempter; Faust and Gretchen: symbols of the Ahrimanic tempter. Biblical references to the Luciferic and Ahrimanic secret. Historical significance of Goethe's *Faust.* Cosmic shaping of the human embryo. Humor and a non-authoritarian approach to understanding *Faust.*

15

THE "BURIAL": THE NATURE OF THE LEMURES, THE FAT DEVILS AND THE SKINNY DEVILS

Dornach, September 4, 1916

Old, blind Faust's land reclamation project; digging a "ditch" versus digging a "grave." Nature of the Lemures. Bones, ligaments, and tendons are the product of Earth evolution. Forces that created them work on within the earth after death. Lemures, purely phantom-beings; the picture of these forces. Mephisto out to get the spiritual aspect of Faust's physical body. His atavistic, Old Moon consciousness views Faust's spirituality as threefold. Power of the "I" keeps the three aspects attuned to each other after death. Faust's contract with Mephisto. The power of Faust's "I" plus Mephisto's "absurd infatuation" lead to Mephisto's loss of Faust's soul. Comparison of Oswald Marbach's poem to Goethe's *Manes*.

16

GOETHE'S INSIGHTS INTO THE SECRETS OF HUMAN EXISTENCE

Dornach, September 9, 1916

The four Gray Women. Faust's experience at the border between life and death. His relationship to magic. The scene with Care as an inner monologue. Care and spiritual knowledge. The dying Faust as a dying Greek. Luciferic quality of Faust's final words. Comparison of these words with the wager in Part One. Why this not the final scene: the rescuing angels as "devils in disguise."

17

PERSPECTIVES ON THE TRUE REALITIES GOETHE WAS SEEKING

Dornach, September 10, 1916

Mephistopheles is a retarded, though highly advanced, Old Moon being in Earth evolution. Comparison with normal human beings, angels and archangels. Human beings' excessive plunge into the material world in Lemurian period caused by "Luciferized" retarded angels. Ahrimanic evolution a counterweight to this. Faust thus facing both Luciferic and Ahrimanic powers. Mephistopheles the enemy of love between the sexes. His role in producing Homunculus, Helen, and Euphorion. His "shameful" scheme to annihilate the human race. Bacon and Berkeley: powerlessness of their materialistic and non-materialistic worldviews to grasp reality. Diagram of this: the red and blue lines. Goethe's sense of this tension. How spiritual-scientific insights can flow into detailed descriptions of the physical, sense-perceptible world. Limitations of Ahrimanic science in understanding embryology. Luciferic restraints on progress of certain religious and sectarian groups. Mephisto's discernment of the rose-strewing angels. Mephisto's contractual agreement and the life-impulses in Faust's blood. Faust's non-dissolution into the Universal All after his death and the further evolution of the Younger Angels. Goethe's connection with all the great ideas of evolution.

18
GOETHE PLUMBS THE DEPTHS OF EVOLUTION AND ITS COSMIC SECRETS IN HIS *FAUST*: THE LUCIFERIC AND THE AHRIMANIC TEMPTATION

Dornach, September 11, 1916

Two basic facts of Earth evolution: human beings became conscious of sexuality in Lemurian period, and Ahrimanic intelligence became active within matter in Atlantean period. Biblical indications of these facts. Human intelligence descended too deeply, yet heavenly love became earthly love. Ability of humans to design instruments of murder. Luciferic and Ahrimanic influences cannot be escaped; they must be balanced out. Blinding by Ahrimanic Care is counterpart of receiving power of sight through Lucifer; spiritualization of Ahrimanic earthly love with heavenly spiritual love. A rejected courtroom scene. Goethe's sense of grace at work in Gretchen's spiritualization. Moral and spiritual realities that have retained a connection with the human being. Goethe's working outlines for *Faust* and the final results. The proposed "Epilogue in Chaos on the Way to Hell." Increased Ahrimanic activity and the proper strengthening of human personality in the fifth post-Atlantean period. Developing a deep sense for the truth of facts. Spiritual science must lead to recognition of Lucifer and Ahriman. The absurd principle of nationalities and the politicization of the life of thought. Herman Grimm. Grillparzer. The great questions of *Faust* and of the Bible. Warnings that must not be forgotten. The comfortable but false path of modern humanity.

The "Faust" motif from the ceiling painting on the small cupola of the first Goetheanum, completed by M.E. Pyle-Waller from a sketch by Rudolf Steiner.

ANTHROPOSOPHY IN THE LIGHT OF GOETHE'S *FAUST*

Writings and Lectures from mid-1880s to 1916

Rudolf Steiner

EXTRACTS

On the Idea of Faust

[Mid-1880s?]

A few years ago, a great authority pronounced that if Goethe were alive today, he would leave his *Faust* unfinished. It would be hard to imagine anything more depressing than an idea such as this gaining currency. We will recoil whenever we see such views arise here and there, and our only consolation is the fact that, in general, both the scholar and the artist, man and woman, the young and the old—all are engaged by Goethe's work with equal love and interest. Recalling this universal interest, and recalling moreover that Schiller† and Schelling† were delighted by the unfinished text, we must ask ourselves: what is it about Goethe's *Faust* that endears it so much to all cultivated people? Surely it is not because Goethe reverts to folklore and connects to an old folk tale. Such things are already so far from our usual way of thinking that it is safer to assume that people know *Faust* better than they know the folklore.

Rather, what engages us in our reading of *Faust* is a great idea that encompasses the entire world. An idea that dwells at the heights of humanity. Schiller noticed this immediately and wrote to Goethe: "Since the folktale borders on the shrill and formless, as it must, one wants to move beyond the narrow subject and let it lead one to ideas. In short, the demands of a *Faust* are both philosophical and poetic" [Jena (June 23, 1797)].

Here we find it clearly expressed that the subject of Faust calls for a philosophical treatment.

And yet, nothing seems more daring than to speak of an "idea of Faust." During the time when Hegel's† philosophy prevailed in Germany, such an idea would not have been repugnant, and nobody would have resisted it. But today it is different. One sees in Hegel nothing but an enthusiast and a dreamer, who "made himself comprehensible enough despite all the jumble." For Hegel, the Absolute is Idea, and Nature is for him just another side of the Idea. Contemporary philosophy finds such an idea fantastical; Hegel is considered an ignoramus, who spoke such nonsense only because he had not occupied himself sufficiently with the sciences.

Without wanting to approve ignorance of scientific data, I nevertheless would say that it was good for the development of Hegelian philosophy that its creator was less occupied with the details of the various scientific disciplines, for this very fact enabled him to retain a certain openness. It has become one of the hallmarks of "modernity" to explain away ideas as fictions—following Heine,[†] for example, in calling everything stupid that humanity has imagined an idea—and then to throw the baby out with the bath water. One simple fact will reveal the extent to which such thoughts lead one, unconsciously, into self-contradiction. I will adduce a fiction that modern science employs unabashedly and in a way that is no different from Hegel's use of ideas. Yet there will be no danger of its being characterized in some textbook of deductive and inductive logic or in some critical history of philosophy as "religious sectarianism" or as philosophizing with "the most unnatural contortions" of "reasonable syntax."

And now for the fiction of which I just spoke. This fiction is *nothing more and nothing less than—mathematics.* Whoever believes that ideas are the excretions of unhealthy human heads must feel the same way about mathematics, which is, after all, in some sense just the same. And the application of mathematics to the objects of the exact sciences is completely identical to the way that Hegel applies his logic to Nature. Just as Hegel terms Nature the other side of the Idea, one could rightly claim that the phenomena studied in mechanics and thermodynamics are the other side of mathematics. One thinker who is a thoroughgoing proponent of contemporary so-called philosophy has declared, in fact, that the world is *in praxi* exactly what mathematics is in theory. And yet at the same time, he contradicts himself by declaring the genuinely philosophical position to be like standing on one foot, and that every kind of nonsense is "Hegeltry." My point is not to try to deprive mathematics of the rights it has enjoyed for many hundreds of years, but rather only to justify the ideal treatment of a complex, given object.

And now that this obstacle has been removed, I can proceed to the idea of Faust itself.

I called this an idea that encompasses the entire world, and I would ask you to understand this claim in a very particular sense. Only if one is so impressed by the grandeur of mathematics that all human deeds seem small and insignificant in comparison can one consider the idea of Faust to be less than all-encompassing. We, on the contrary, value the world of the human soul and spirit much more highly than that of soulless Nature, and that is what allows us to admire the idea of Faust in its full grandeur.

We must never lose sight of what is uniquely human: the striving for the highest that is known to us. This striving reveals itself not only in cognition, but also in feeling and in willing.

I would like initially to [?] the thought...†

Faust Explained According to Goethe's Own Method

Review of: Faust *by Goethe, with introduction and running commentary edited by Karl Julius Schröer. Second, thoroughly revised impression. Heilbronn, 1888.*

... In view of the sheer volume of secondary literature on Goethe in existence today, there is a danger that the true significance of some new appearance will fail to be recognized or will even be completely overlooked. We would especially wish for this not to be the case with Schröer's works on Goethe.[†] Within this body of literature these works have a character all their own, and we will permit ourselves to call attention to this uniqueness on the occasion of the second printing of Schröer's *Faust*-commentary, which has just come out. Schröer's way of looking at Goethe can be briefly characterized as the one most fructified by the level of education attained by Goethe himself. For Schröer, the poet's writings are not simply an object that he comes to with the customary interest of the philologist or literary historian, in order to pick it apart in accordance with the usual method of research. Schröer sought above all to shape his own method using the example of Goethe himself, in order to find the key to an understanding of the poet in the poet himself, according to the principle that if Goethe is truly the high point of German culture, he can only be measured by his own standard. Goethe's great mind becomes most fruitful for us if we first learn from him, and then only afterward approach him with a critical eye.

What makes Goethe appear so great to us is the grand style pervading all he did: his worldview and the elemental power of his originality, which is greater than all his works. He could never exhaust himself because his nature, capable as it was of virtually endless forms, would rejuvenate itself for new work after each creation. This is why we are drawn back to his life and personality again and again by his works, and for this reason it is so important, especially in his case, to know how his works came into being. This is the aim of Schröer's research. Although he, too, never forgets the philological factor, he also never makes it a goal in itself, but only uses it as a means of penetrating more deeply into the workings of Goethe's mind. Schröer always takes the factual details valued so highly by other Goethe researchers and puts them at the service of the idea. Goethe says about his own creative activity: "I do not rest until I find a pregnant point in the phenomena from which much can be derived, or rather, one which freely produces many things from out of itself and offers them to me."[†]

We must find this pregnant point again if we wish to understand the poet. And Schröer's intention is to lead us to it. In referring to the first part of *Faust*, the commentator shows how Goethe is taken hold of by the Faust-idea and how this idea shapes itself anew within his mind. In its original sixteenth-century form, the Faust-saga is Protestant and orthodox.[†] There Faust is conceived of as the polar opposite of Luther. Both men broke with the currently existing church, stepping outside the forms of religion that had come down through history. But they did so in completely opposite ways. Luther holds the Bible in his hand, pointing to the written Word of God. He throws his inkpot at the head of the Devil, who in those days is what worldly erudition was. Faust does something else. Not only does he renounce the church; he renounces theology itself: "afterwards [he] no longer wanted to be called a theologian, but became a man of the world, called himself a Doctor of Medicine who for a time had put the Holy Scriptures away, behind the door and under the bench." But this means nothing less than that Faust has abandoned the pathways of thinking prescribed by higher powers and wants to determine his own goal and direction as a truly free being. This is why, in the eyes of the sixteenth century, he falls prey to the powers of hell.

Now, out of all this, Goethe created the Faust of his own era, the Faust who must *not* perish, because he has become a "man of the world" whom the heavenly host welcomes with warmth because, "ever striving,"[†] he "exerts himself" (11936-41), although he constantly builds on his own personal energy and capacity for work, remaining in line with the principle of genuine Protestantism. Goethe took the

Faust-idea that was Protestant and orthodox and made it into one that was still Protestant, but free.

Schröer was the first to point to this Protestant character of the Faust-saga. In doing so he introduced an important feature into the interpretation of Goethe's *Faust* and set himself the significant goal of evaluating all the details so as to allow the fundamental character of the work, which had thereby been laid bare, to appear in its true light. Schröer's second task is to show how the individual images that constitute the work arose within Goethe's mind, and how they gradually coalesced into a coherent whole under the guidance of this fundamental thought. For, despite the fact that Goethe was always guided by lofty ideal motives, we must not think that he strove for the incorporation of abstract ideas. The ideas fill him, his nature, and his creative activity; but what he offers us in his works are concrete images. He always had to be powerfully gripped by some intuitive observation or other, to which he would then seek to give poetic form. This is why, for all its depth, *Faust* is so fresh and full of life. Everything in it bears the character of the individual; nowhere do we find dry, abstract generality. In many instances Schröer has successfully demonstrated the origin of such images, and often, even the origin of the very moods that find their expression in *Faust*. By this means he has probably done more to further our understanding than can ever be done by merely pointing out when some scene or other was first written down.

We will only single out one example. In the sixth scene of Act Three of *The Fellow Culprits*,† Goethe has Söller say the words: "Poor me! How horrified I am, how full of seething heat. Not Richard the Third, nor Doctor Faust himself, felt half this bad!" We can conclude from this that when he wrote these words in 1769 he had already focused on the figure of Faust in complete earnestness regarding its tragic aspects. To this Schröer adds the thought that after Goethe had returned home to Frankfurt from Leipzig in 1768 in a state of poor health, he occupied himself with the views of Theophrastus Paracelsus† and was happy to find that Nature, even though in a perhaps fantastic manner in the "Golden Chain of Homer"† (the *aurea catena Homeri* of the alchemists), was represented here in a beautiful association that directs us quite clearly to lines 447ff. of *Faust* :

How all combines into one whole,
Each in the other works and lives!
How forces of the heavens rise and fall
And hand each other golden vessels!

In this connection we read in a letter to Friederike Oeser† of February 13, 1769: "I have seen you so seldom—as seldom as an investigating magus hears a mandrake whistling." Within this lies the origin of Faust's first monologue. In this way Schröer makes use of the psychological origin of the individual parts of *Faust*, leading us to its full understanding. In what was cited above we see quite clearly how the figure of Faust emerges in Goethe's mind already in 1769 and what significance it has.

The following is another example: In Act One of the second part, wherein all the goings-on at the Imperial Palace are depicted with such sovereign humor, we are directed to Goethe's reading of Hans Sachs.† Sachs's two poems, "A story about our late, esteemed Emperor Maximilian and an alchemist" and "A wondrous story about our late, esteemed Emperor Maximilian and a necromancer," which Goethe read in 1775, made a living impression on the poet, who found in them a pregnant point out of which many things could be derived. We recognize this living impression in the way the activities at the Imperial Palace are depicted and in the scene in which Helen is conjured up out of the underworld. In a similar way, the splendid scene at the end of the second part came into being, in which the good and evil spirits contend for Faust's soul.

In a letter of Goethe's to the painter, Friedrich Müller,† on June 21, 1781, we see the thought become alive in the poet's power of imagination as he is speaking about a picture that portrays the struggle of the archangel Michael with the Devil "over the corpse of Moses." There he says: "If we wanted to treat this subject, it seems to me it could not be done in any other way than that the Holy One, still filled with the grace of having been shown the Promised Land, passes away enraptured as angels are occupied in lifting him away in a halo. For the statement, "The Lord buried him," gives our most beautiful imaginations ample room for free play. At this point, all Satan could do would be to stand in a corner of the foreground, his black shoulders forming a contrast with the rest of the scene, and, without laying a hand on the anointed one of the Lord, merely look around to see whether he might not get something out of all this for himself." Commenting on this passage, Schröer notes: "Moses dies while looking at the Promised Land, like Faust viewing the completion of his work. From above right the heavenly host descends in a halo to carry Faust off, and as the angels lift him up we see Mephistopheles looking around, literally the way we see Satan doing in the letter to Müller." Just at this point one would most readily believe that Goethe had started with an abstract idea, and it is interesting to see how here, too, the whole thing rests on a concrete image.

Goethe's *Faust* requires a commentary. The natural freshness of the first part and the high culture of the second, which make this poetic work so attractive to us, nevertheless confront our understanding with difficulties of a quite unique nature. Only when we recognize the connection of each individual feature with the totality of the Goethean spirit do we penetrate it fully. This knowledge is what Schröer seeks to make available to us. It is especially necessary for the second part, which has so often been misunderstood and unappreciated. It is our hope that this commentary in particular will contribute much toward spreading the view that Schröer expresses in the words: "In no way is this work a product of declining poetic strength; it is full of life, admirable both in its individual details and as a whole."

A New Book on Goethe's *Faust**

*Goethes Faust-Dichtung in ihrer künstlerischen Einheit, *dargestellt von Veit Valentin (The Artistic Unity of Goethe's* Faust, *by Veit Valentin), Berlin, Verlag von Emil Felber, 1894.*

WHOEVER comes out with a new study of Goethe's *Faust* these days meets with a difficult situation. An immense body of literature on this national drama of the Germans has been created by scholars and writers who have considered it from every imaginable aspect. We need to know only a little of this literature to realize that some of the things that are supposed to make this work difficult to understand are the artificial creations of estheticians, philosophers, and philologists and that many a riddle we think we find in the work are not really there at all but have only been fabricated. If we want to understand and enjoy *Faust* as a work of art in an unprejudiced way, we will have to have the courage to shake off most of the questions that have come to be attached to it in this way. Only someone who keeps this fact in mind will be able to form a correct judgment of the book to which the present lines are devoted and really enjoy reading it.

Among the different ways of looking at poetic works of art, the one currently in vogue is the genetic approach.† This method of investigation traces the gradual origin of a work and tries to put together a picture of how the parts have been fitted together by the artist in the course of time. We do not have to be an enemy of this approach to realize that through it the enjoyment and understanding of a work as an artistic whole can easily get lost. What leads to such understanding is not the kind of scholarship that picks everything to pieces, but the creative imagination of the appreciative observer who is able to grasp the artistic unity of a work and then sense and assess the relationship of the parts to this unity. Among our contemporaries, a paragon of this way of looking at things that takes its start from this creative imagination is Herman Grimm,[†] who has given us a model of it in his book on Goethe.

Veit Valentin, in his book on *Faust*, bases himself on this approach. In doing so, he refers to Goethe himself, who wanted to have his work understood in this sense. In the "Prologue in the Theater," Goethe gives expression to the various moods with which a work of art can be received. The Theater Director, who has practical aims in view and knows that the audience is simply eager to see something, requires the Poet to provide sensational effects and is quite willing to sacrifice the artistic unity of the whole. "If you're going to present a piece, then just piece it together! … What good is it if you bring it as a whole? The public will just pick it all to pieces" (99-103). The Poet indignantly rejects this: "Is it not harmony that wells forth from his breast and hurls the world back down into his heart? … Who calls single details into general consecration, that together they resound in glorious *chords* ? … The power of humankind, within the Poet revealed!" (148-58).

Valentin is fully justified when he maintains that at the time when Goethe was writing the "Prologue in the Theater" (1797) he set himself the task "of taking the scenes of the *Urfaust*,[†] which had been tossed off in a stroke of genius but showed no trace as yet of being part of any overall plan that would go beyond the profound and intensely gripping poetic effect of the characters' individual destinies, and making them into parts of such a plan." "The swaying shapes that arise again from the mist and fog of the days of youth now gain firmness and clarity as elements of a far-reaching plan in which they will need to attain enhanced significance." The purpose of Valentin's book is to demonstrate in detail that the poet was also successful in achieving this goal. But its author does not fall into the same error that many philosophical commentators on *Faust* do, who have presented the matter as though the play were merely the embodiment of an abstract concept, an idea of higher reason. Such commentators do not understand that instead of directing our attention to the lively images and characters that the play is all about, they are directing it to dead skeletons of ideas; these, to be sure, support the work of art, but they will never exhaust its content. Valentin's way of explaining things shows us why a certain event or a certain utterance of a particular character must occur at a specific point in *Faust.* He goes about this in the same way that an esthetician would explain the strict unity and inner harmony of a composition of Raphael.† And one has to admit that from this viewpoint the inner lawfulness and general symmetry of this poetic work does appear in a completely new light.

Valentin gives an ingenious explanation of why the drama proper, which unfolds on the human level, is preceded and followed by a preparatory and a closing episode in heaven, respectively. The author then explains how, within the drama that takes place on earth, the poet first allows the influence of Mephistopheles on Faust to grow and develop in a steady and consistent manner, after which Faust's independence comes more and more to the fore, until in the end Mephistopheles can only play the role of a servant for the fulfillment of plans that are Faust's alone. We cannot go into detail here, but I would like to point out that a number of passages in the First Part which until now have seemed like arbitrary insertions now stand there as necessary and integral members of the unfolding whole when regarded from Valentin's point of view. But what is of fundamental significance is his conception of the "Classical Walpurgis Night" and of the appearance of both Helen and Homunculus.† Until the events at the Imperial Palace, Faust has experienced only the pleasures that the present age can offer him. His higher nature reveals itself in the fact that he does not drown in this life of pleasure. But is this present age not something purely accidental for Faust? Doesn't the question remain unanswered of how things would be if Faust had lived in a completely different time? Couldn't he have found conditions there that would have corresponded to his yearning for pleasure? It must be shown that the finite life can in no way satisfy Faust's striving, because he wants to penetrate into the secrets of the infinite. For this reason, he must also be led into the way things were in long-past ages. For Goethe, ancient Greek culture was the archetypal age of the past. The shades of the Greek world must be reawakened so that they can form a living relationship with Faust, and the "Classical Walpurgis Night" serves this purpose. The primeval forces of Nature that create reality must be unleashed in order to enliven to a new presence the long vanished powers of the former age that have been living on only as Idea. This is why the forces of material creation appear in the "Classical Walpurgis Night." But in order to awaken the archetypal image of female beauty, Helen herself, to real life, not only physical and geological forces are needed, but also a germ of organic life that must merge with a stream of events that are otherwise purely material in Nature. This is Homunculus, who shatters on the conch shell throne of Galatea in order to enliven the material elements so that they may become mature enough to grant bodily existence to the Idea of Helen.

It may be that Valentin has not yet hit upon the right solution. But his way of looking at things seems to me to be well-suited to self-correct, in the course of time, the mistakes it engenders at its first appearance.

Faust: A Tragedy by J.W. Goethe

A Performance in the Deutsches Theater, Berlin, 1897

Several years ago, on assuming the position of Rector at the University of Berlin, a famous scholar, the physiologist Du Bois-Reymond,[†] gave a speech on Goethe's *Faust* in which he said things that betrayed how well, within one and the same person, a sophisticated scientific education can be combined with a philistine attitude and a complete lack of esthetic judgment. This pedantic speaker went so far as to maintain that, instead of yielding to magic and getting involved in all sorts of crazy sorcery with the Devil, Faust would be better off remaining an upstanding professor, inventing the generator and the air pump, marrying Gretchen and legitimizing his child.

Whoever was sitting in the Deutsches Theater on Goethe's birthday with an attitude like this must have experienced a very special pleasure at the way Josef Kainz played Faust. For in this performance there was no trace of Faust's deep yearning for a knowledge of the secrets of the universe, nothing of the fact that the very thought that we cannot know anything is nearly consuming our bold researcher's heart (364-65). This Faust of the Deutsches Theater has not "studied philosophy, legal codes and medicine, and—even worse—theology," giving them his all, as best he could (354-57). He has only read Du Bois-Reymond's elegant speech, "On the Boundaries of Natural Science,"[†] and Fr. A. Lange's *History of Materialism*,[†] along with some other modern books written in the same vein, from all of which he has seen that there are certain "riddles of the universe"[†] that the human being cannot resolve. Of course, such reading material does stir us up somewhat; it makes us "nervous," but it has no power to summon up the unspeakable tortures in the human soul from which Faust is suffering.

We can only understand the profound psychological truth of Goethe's poetic work when we sense the full power of the storms pressing in on Faust. Whoever is capable of such a feeling knows that the only experiences a soul like Faust's can still bear to have are not only on a far higher level than those of a philistine way of life but are also far more elevated than the satisfaction derivable from, say, inventing the air pump.

These experiences will really play themselves out in the human soul; and a dramatist who lacks the ability to portray inner soul processes and psychological development as such will grasp at unreal regions of life. Imagination likes to take off into the unreal realms when feeling says that there are no real processes in harmony with the feelings stirred up in the depths of the soul. The feelings we sense in the soul foundation of the Faust who was enacted here are not of such a nature as to require the exalted regions Goethe leads us into. This Faust could very well marry Gretchen. And if he would even go on to invent the generator he could completely reconcile himself with life. The artistry with which Josef Kainz speaks the great monologues is admirable and demonstrates a speech technique of rare mastery. Anyone with a sense for such surface technicalities must have found Kainz's rendering of every sentence interesting. The way the actor spoke the following lines was a veritable masterpiece of tightrope-walking linguistic virtuosity:

> Come down here now, you vessel of pure crystal!
> Once more emerge from out your ancient case,
> Of which for many years I've had no thought!
> You gleamed at every joyous festival
> And cheered our fathers' serious guests
> When one would raise you to the other in a toast. (720-25)

Kainz totally annihilated any sense we might have that Faust is a man driven by a raging, insatiable urge for knowledge and for life, "to tear those portals open that one would rather quietly sneak by" (710-11). The tones with which Josef Kainz delights our ear [*Sinn*] do not appear to be coming out of a Faustian interiority. Delivery alone assures the artist his success.†

Then, as though desiring to show us how little interest he has in the passionate storms of Faust, the Man of Knowledge, Kainz transforms himself, immediately after drinking the witch's brew, into a charming, flirtatious philanderer to whom Mephistopheles can never say, "You have the doctor in you still" (3277). In the Gretchen tragedy Kainz plays nothing less than a dallying lover, with the consequence that when Faust's serious nature comes to the fore again, those scenes are represented by the artist with an unpardonable indifference that makes them seem completely untrue.

The art that came to meet us in the Deutsches Theater on Goethe's birthday is not able to do justice to the tragedy of Faust. The portrayal of the central figure was interesting at least in its details. As for the other performances, not even this much can be said. A Mephistopheles who behaved more like the merry advisor of a prince than like the devilish seducer of Faust (Müller) bored this reviewer with his dreadful grimacing and his complete inability to imbue the figure of the jester with any trace of the demonic spirit of hell who constantly desires evil[†] (1336). The actress (Elise Steinert) took away all of Gretchen's naivety and replaced it with a little seductive coquetry. The art of nuancing that she unfolded in such rich measure had an obtrusive effect.

After the performance of August 28, we cannot affirm that the art of acting at the Deutsches Theater is mature enough for Goethe, no matter how lenient we would like to be.

Goethe's *Faust* as a Picture of His Esoteric View of Life

1899/1902

... In marrying Helen, Faust has become a mystic. Speaking as a mystic at the beginning of the fourth act of Part Two, he sees the image of a woman—the depths of his own soul.

He says:

> ... So wide and formless, tow'ring up,
> In east it comes to rest, like distant mounts of ice,
> And mirrors meaning grand of dazzling, fleeting days.
> And yet there hovers still around my breast and brow
> A gentle wisp of mist, so cheering, flattering, cool,
> That, light and hesitant, now high and ever higher climbs,
> Coming together. —Does its charming form deceive,
> As highest good of my young years, so long forgone?
> Earliest treasures from the bottom of my heart well up,
> With gentle flourish showing me Aurora's dawning love,
> The quickly felt, first, hardly comprehended glance
> Which, firmly grasped and held, outshone all other gems.
> Like beauty of the soul the fair, sweet form evolves,
> Does not dissolve, but climbs into the ether's heights
> And takes the best part of my inner self along. (10052-66)

Does it not seem, when we experience these words, which depict the bliss of someone who has descended into the depths of his own soul and felt the best part of his inner self wrenched away from him by the "Ever-Feminine" within him, as though we were hearing the philosopher of ancient Greece:

> When you, set free from the body, rise up into the free Ether,
> Then will it [the soul] be an immortal god, having fled from Death's clutches.

For at such a stage, death becomes a "simile."† For the human being dies away for the lower life, in order to come to life again in a higher one. The higher life in the spirit becomes a new stage of transformation; the temporal becomes a "simile" for the eternal, which springs to life in the human being. Within the human being, the connection with the "Ever-Feminine" brings to birth the child that is not transitory because it belongs to the eternal. The higher life is a "giving-up" of something: the death of the lower existence for the birth of the higher. Goethe expresses this in his *West-östlicher Divan* with the words†:

> And so long as this you lack:
> Die and then become!
> You are but a gloomy guest
> Upon the darkened earth.

We read the same thought in his *Sayings in Prose.*† One must give up one's existence in order to exist. Goethe is of the same mind as the mystic, Heraclitus.† In speaking of the Greeks' worship of Dionysus, Heraclitus feels it would be empty, meaningless, indeed even shameful, if this service were offered only to the god that rules Nature's life and all sensual enjoyment. But such, he says, is not the case. All these goings-on are not intended merely for the Dionysus of life and the immediate fertility of the senses, but for Hades, the god of death, as well. Hades and Dionysus, for whom they "put on these boisterous bonfires," are one and the same. In the Greek mysteries, life was celebrated in union with death, this life being the higher one that passes through sense-perceptible death. This is the life the mystics are speaking of when they say: "And so, death is the root of all life." The second part of Goethe's *Faust* represents an awakening, the birth of the "higher human being" from the depths of the soul. From this point of view we can understand Goethe's words: Let "the throngs of spectators" "rejoice at what they see"; the "higher meaning will not be lost on the initiated."† ...

... It cannot be our task at present to go into the various conceptions people have formed of the significance of Mephistopheles. In these conceptions a striving is expressed that is the exact opposite of my own, namely, to transform artistic figures into straw allegories or symbols. For the purpose of an esoteric interpretation, Mephistopheles may absolutely be conceived of as a real human being, in the sense of poetic reality, of course. For the esoteric interpretation does not seek the spiritual content that certain figures only receive through the poet, but the one they already have in life. Thus, the poet can neither take it from them nor give it to them, but only take it from life, just as is done with what is visible to the eye. It belongs to the nature of Mephistopheles that he lives in what is sensory and material. After all, hell, too, is only embodied matter. Someone who lives within the material as Mephistopheles does can regard the eternal in the womb of the Mothers[†] only as something totally and absolutely alien. The human individual must pass through material existence in order to enter again into the eternal, the divine, in which it has its origin. If it finds its way there and gives up "its existence, in order to exist," it has a Faustian nature; if it cannot let go of the material, it is a character like Mephistopheles. Mephistopheles is able to give Faust only the "key" to the realm of the Mothers. A real secret is connected with this "key." One must have experienced it in order to feel it through completely. Whoever lives in science will come to this most easily....

... Only a purely spiritual being, born in a spiritual way, could unite directly with the spiritual. The human spirit is not this kind of being. It must wander through what is material from beginning to end. Without this life-wandering, this human spirit would be a being without inner substance. Without such inner substance, it could not live. If it were to come into being in any way at all, it would have to begin its journey through matter from the very beginning, for the human being is what it is only because it has passed through a series of previous incarnations.[†] Goethe also had to portray this idea in Faust. On December 16, 1829, Goethe said the following to Eckermann about Homunculus: "For, such spiritual beings as Homunculus, not yet darkened and limited by a complete incarnation as a human being, were counted among the ranks of daemons."[†]...

Goethe's Gospel

Berlin, January 26, 1905

My wish in this lecture is to present an image of the theosophical *weltanschauung* that is free of any kind of dogmatism and to try to show what is characteristic of it by a simple consideration of phenomena within our Central European spiritual life. No alien *weltanschauung* shall be imported from the East;[†] rather, I shall attempt to show that theosophy is life, and must be brought to life. Theosophy is not a new gospel, but rather the renewal of perceptions that are deeply rooted in the human soul.

Most telling for us will be the discovery that geniuses from our own culture were thoroughly imbued with what we call the theosophical *weltanschauung*. Lessing,[†] for example, believed in reincarnation. We find ideas on palingenesis in Herder's writings.[†] In Schiller, we find them in his *Philosophical Letters* (1786), in the treatise "The Philosophy of Julius" (where Julius and Raphael stand in for Schiller[†] and his friend Körner), as well as in the epistolary essay "On the Esthetic Education of the Human Being" (1793/1794). Novalis[†] also believed in it. And where we especially find the theosophical *weltanschauung* is in the later works of Goethe. To be sure, this may be surprising at first, but anyone who becomes deeply immersed in the study of Goethe, and especially in his profound treatment of Faust, will enter ever more deeply into the worldview I intend to characterize here. What I am about to narrate became entirely self-evident to me within my own experience.

Goethe was a theosophist in his heart of hearts and with every bone of his body because he refused to accept any limitations to his seeking, his knowing, or his activity. Goethe was entirely disposed to the *weltanschauung* of which we are here speaking. He was convinced that the human being is deeply connected to the world, and that this world is not material, but rather active, creative spirit. His philosophy was no vague pantheism, leading to some kind of indeterminate, incomprehensible Being. He claimed, rather, that we are able to enter into a living relationship with the divine in the cosmos.

As a seven-year-old, Goethe caught the rays of the sun in a magnifying glass and lit a little candle; he wanted to ignite his sacrificial offering with the fire of Nature itself. In his autobiography *Poetry and Truth* † he says: "If we survey the various religions, we find within them a shared nucleus of truth. Throughout the whole of history, sages have shown the oscillation between the higher and the lower human self."

When Goethe returned home after his studies in Leipzig, having fallen gravely ill, he dedicated himself to mystical studies. He resolved to express everything that welled up within him in his version of *Faust*, in the tale that the Middle Ages used to depict the battle between the old and the new worldviews.

The sixteenth century denied that human beings could achieve salvation through the power of their own souls. It let Faust be damned, but Goethe let him be saved. Having depicted Faust in his youth, in his so-called *Urfaust*, as the striving human individual, Goethe laid a new foundation for the story in the '90s of the eighteenth century. In *Faust*, Goethe shows the development of the human being ranging from the lowest to the highest faculties of soul. As we shall see, he does this in his fairy tale, *The Green Snake and the Beautiful Lily*† as well. It was Goethe's view that only someone who has passed through the stages of development, who has felt drawn to the divine and has passed through doubt, has achieved full conviction and found the way from disharmony to harmony. His *Faust* is a hymn to human perfection. The great issue of finding a path of perfection, set out the Bhagavad Gita, we find spelled out in *Faust* as well. In *Faust*, Goethe sets himself the task of solving the riddle of evil.

It is in the "Prologue in Heaven" that Goethe reveals to us what is really at stake in his version of *Faust*. There, the physical world is shown to be a reflection of the interplay of the forces of the supersensory world. In the words of the "Prologue in Heaven," Goethe depicts the world of Devachan,† the realm of spiritual sounding. He couches it in the imagery of the Pythagorean harmony of the spheres† :

> The sun resounds in ancient manner
> In contest with its brother spheres. (243-244)

Anyone who claims that this is only a superficial image is saying something superficial.

> Harken! Hear the storming Horae!
> Spirit ears perceive the sounding
> Of the new day being born (4666-68)

as Goethe has Ariel say near the end of "Charming Landscape." Goethe is always speaking about the resounding of the spiritual world.

In theosophy we speak of three worlds: the world of dreams, the astral† world or world of the soul, and the mental or spiritual world. The awakening of the spiritual eye calls forth powerful alterations, first of all within the life of dreams. As the new clairvoyance, the new world, opens up it attains great regularity. What is then experienced is not yet a valid basis for science. The neophyte or chela must learn to reach through dreams into the consciousness of the second, or astral, world and carry it over into waking life. Later on, experiences are gained within dreamless sleep by means of which the spiritual, or mental, world is perceived.

The consciousness of the astral world expresses itself in images, and the consciousness of the spiritual world expresses itself in spiritual hearing. The Pythagoreans called this the Music of the Spheres.

Yet another important human principle unfolds within the "Prologue in Heaven": the law of karma. Anyone who is aware how intimately Goethe knew the mystics of the Middle Ages will not dismiss it as arbitrary imagery when Goethe says:

> The world of spirits is not locked,
> Your sense is shut, your heart is dead!
> Up, pupil, bathe now, undismayed,
> Your earthly breast in morning's red! (443-446)

"Morning's red" is an expression that was current among the mystics. Jakob Böhme's first work was called *Aurora or the Morning's Red at Sunrise.*†

From the moment we first meet him, Faust strives to transgress the limits of physical life. Goethe's depiction of the Earth Spirit is couched entirely in the technical language of mysticism, a wonderful description of the astral body of the earth, the immortal raiment of the soul woven and embroidered by the spirit using the fruits of life. The Earth Spirit is no symbol: for Goethe, it is a real being. He assumed that the planets were inhabited by planetary beings in the way we inhabit our own bodies of flesh. Goethe's credo was: the Earth Spirit had taught him not only to contemplate, but also to feel and to sense the unified being of stones, plants, and animals all the way up to the level of the human being, the crown of creation. It had taught him that all creatures are our brothers. He expressed the same credo around the age of 35 or 36 in his fragment, *The Mysteries.*† A pilgrim wanders up to a monastery. At the portal he sees the sign of the Rose Cross. The Rose Cross is the sign of the kingdoms of Nature: mineral, plant, animal = cross. Roses = love. Goethe himself would later say that each of the twelve individualities in *The Mysteries* represents one of the world's great confessions or religions. The pilgrim's goal was to seek the kernel of truth at the core of all the world's religions.

In Part One we see the young Faust, full of sensations and disharmony. Guided by the Tempter, Faust must lead his lower self through all possible errors. In the figure of Mephistopheles, Goethe created the image of an ancient idea that is to be found in all spiritual wisdom: he sought to solve the riddle of evil. Evil is the sum of all the forces that oppose the progress of human perfection. If progress implies the truth, then every hindrance is a lie. Hence the name Mephistopheles means "he who destroys through lies": Mephiz, "the destroyer"—Tophel, Hebrew for "liar." Mephisto leads Faust through every kind of experience of the lower self.

Towards the end of Part One, Faust stands in a different way before the Earth Spirit; he gains the insight that it is possible really to know the self. Having made all his mistakes, he arrives in the spiritual world through purification.

Faust lives to a very old age, to the time when one can become a mystic. In Eckermann's *Conversations with Goethe*, Goethe is reported to have said: The initiate will soon see that many profundities can be found in *Faust*.

The Journey to the Mothers: in all forms of mysticism, the highest part of the soul is depicted as something feminine; knowledge is a process of fertilization. The fire in the tripod is primal matter. The realm of the Mothers represents the foundation of all existence; here is the source of the spirit. In order to enter into the realm of the spirit—called Devachan in the language of theosophy—one needs to have attained certain moral qualities. Theosophy strives to lead humanity upward. We must first make ourselves capable, worthy. When Faust first summons forth Helen, he burns with wild passion and that causes Helen to dissolve.

Faust's task is to fathom the deep mystery of human nature: how body, soul, and spirit are conjoined.

Spirit is the eternal; it existed before birth and will continue to exist after death. Soul is the intermediary between spirit and body; in the course of human development it inclines more towards the body at first and later on towards the spirit, which leads it on to the eternal, to that which persists. The development of the spiritual eye helps to accomplish this.

Faust now leads us into the laboratory in which Homunculus is being conceived. This figure becomes comprehensible to us in a wonderful way when we understand him as Soul that has yet to incarnate. Homunculus is to receive a body. Goethe depicts the gradual evolution of the physical body by means of a splendid image in the "Classical Walpurgis Night." Proteus is the wise man who knows how it is that bodily metamorphoses proceed. Homunculus must start with what is mineral; then the realm of plants will follow. Goethe captures the journey through the vegetable kingdom in the expression: "Es grunelt so" ("It smells so fresh and green.") (8266).

Sexuality appears only at a certain stage. Eros unites with Homunculus: the union of the masculine aspect of the soul with the feminine aspect of the soul gives rise to the human being.

Faust's blinding represents the fact that the physical world dies away for him as his powers of inner vision increase. The lines from Goethe's poem "Blessed Yearning" are a magnificent image of this process: "And so long as this you lack, / Die and then become! ..." The mystics express it this way: "Therefore we have in death the root of all our life." And: "Who fails to die before he dies, will decay before he dies."

In the final lines of *Faust* the "Chorus Mysticus" intones:

> All that must pass away
> Is but a simile;
> Here the inadequate
> Becomes an event;
> The indescribable,
> Here it is done;
> The Ever-Feminine
> Draws us upward and on. (12104-11)

In every kind of mysticism, the striving human soul is depicted as something feminine. The union of the soul with the Cosmic Mystery: this spiritual union is described by the mystics as the Marriage of the Lamb. Goethe gave even deeper expression to this concept in his *Fairy Tale of the Green Snake and the Beautiful Lily*.

In his conversations with Eckermann, Goethe himself said about the last part of *Faust* that he had wanted to represent Faust's ascent in the image of Montserrat.[†] There is a hint of this in his fragmentary epic *The Mysteries*. Parsifal,[†] the Wanderer in the Vale.[†] When Faust went blind, he acquired the capacity to accelerate his inner development dramatically. He then entered into the higher regions, or Devachan, as we would say. But Goethe also made use of Catholic ideas. For example, he had Pater Marianus appear in the "purest cell," thereby suggesting his liberation from any trace of sexuality and thus his stance "beyond male and female." This is why Goethe also gave this figure a female name with a masculine ending. At this point the unification of the sexes replaced the duality of the sexes. He had awakened entirely within Buddhi;[†] and Buddhi, the sixth fundamental aspect of our human nature, had gained the upper hand over all the others.

The Esoteric Foundation of Goethe's Creative Work

July 10, 1905

...In Part Two of this dramatic poem one finds in fact what Goethe had to say about the relationship of the human being to the "three worlds": the physical, astral and spiritual. Viewed from this perspective, the drama becomes an expression of human incarnation.

One figure who presents insuperable difficulties to an understanding that refuses to base itself on esotericism is Homunculus. And yet, if one proceeds from this foundation, every feature and every word becomes clear. Homunculus is begotten with the help of Mephistopheles, the representative of the forces of hindrance and destruction in the universe, which manifest within the human realm as evil. Goethe wishes to characterize the part that evil plays in the genesis of Homunculus, who is soon to become a human being himself and hence will soon be led through the lower realms of Nature in the "Classical Walpurgis Night"....

... Goethe's intention is to portray the *astral body* before its incarnation into earthly matter. He makes this absolutely clear by outfitting Homunculus with clairvoyant faculties. This is evident from the fact that the latter is able to see Faust's dream in the laboratory where Mephistopheles is helping with the work.

The actual incarnation of Homunculus, that is, the astral human being, is then depicted in the further course of the "Classical Walpurgis Night." He is directed to Proteus, the spirit of the transformations that takes place on the way through the kingdoms of Nature:

Away to Proteus! Ask the man of wonders
How one can come to be and then evolve. (8152-53)

Proteus then shows the way the astral human being has to take on the journey through the kingdoms of Nature in order to arrive at a physical body in an earthly incarnation....

... But now we also see in *Faust* a representation of the ways in which the immortal human spirit is related to its mortal sheaths. Faust must seek this immortal spirit among the "Mothers." And this leads us to a plausible explanation of this important scene in Part Two of *Faust*. Goethe pictures our actual human nature as triadic [which conforms to the theosophical teaching of Atma-Buddhi-Manas†]. And one can likewise express Faust's descent to the "Mothers" in theosophical language as Faust's entry into the realm of Devachan. There he is to find what there is of Helen. She is supposed to reincarnate, that is, she is supposed to return to earth from the realm of the "Mothers." In Act Three we see her as having in fact reincarnated. For this to happen, the three aspects of human nature needed to unite: the astral, the physical, and the spiritual. At the end of Act Two, the astral [Homunculus] has surrounded itself with the physical sheath, and the union of these two can now take the higher nature into itself. Viewed in this way, the poem acquires dramatic unity, whereas for an interpretation that precludes esoteric insights the drama's individual events can only remain an arbitrary juxtaposition of poetic aggregates....

... Viewed in this way, the remaining plot of *Faust* joins seamlessly with what has preceded it. Faust has been initiated into the mysteries of the "three worlds." Hence he views the world as a mystic throughout the remainder of the drama....

... Goethe's poem, "Blessed Yearning," closes with the words:

> And so long as this you lack:
> Die *and then become*!
> You remain a gloomy guest
> Upon the darkened earth. (17-20)†

The "Chorus Mysticus" at the end of *Faust* is in complete accord with this, for it expresses nothing other than the following: At the root of all passing phenomena of the external world lies the non-transitoriness of spirit, and we attain this when we learn to view the world's transitoriness as a symbol of the spirit, which is hidden:

> All that must pass away
> Is but a simile.

What cannot be attained by a thinking framed for the sensory world and its forms reveals itself in its actual nature to "spiritual sight," and what the abstract intellect cannot describe is a "deed" in the regions of the spirit:

> Here the inadequate
> Becomes an event;
> The indescribable,
> Here it is done ...

And in keeping with all the symbols of mysticism, Goethe represents higher human nature as something "female" that unites with the divine [grammatically masculine] spirit. For it is just such a fructification of the purified human soul tending towards the divine that Goethe is seeking to describe in the final lines:

> The Ever-Feminine
> Draws us upward and on. (12104-11)

Anything short of a mystical interpretation is doomed to failure here.

Goethe's Secret Revelation — Esoteric

Berlin, October 24, 1908

... I would still like to bring you two examples to illustrate how much Goethe's spiritual worldview pervades his entire life and how the work of his final years harmonizes with what he had achieved earlier in everything having to do with knowledge of the spirit. When Goethe wrote *Faust*, he made use of an idea he had borrowed that can be traced back to a symbolic way of expressing a deeper evolutionary pathway of Nature. Faust's father was an alchemist who had accepted all the ancient teachings on faith, even though he had already misunderstood them. In speaking of his father, Faust quotes an example from his teachings:

> ... a Lion red, a suitor bold,
> Wed to the Lily in a lukewarm bath. (1042-43)

Faust says this without having any idea what it means. Such words, however, can become a ladder leading up to high levels of development. In the *Fairy Tale*,† Goethe uses the figure of the Young Man to depict the human being striving for the highest bride, and he calls what this Young Man is to be united with, the Beautiful Lily. As you see, you find this Lily in Part One of *Faust* as well.

We also find this underlying thread of Goethe's approach in Part Two of *Faust*, in the "Chorus Mysticus." This is where Faust stands at the entrance of the spiritual world, and Goethe declares in monumental words his own faith in the spiritual way of viewing the world. There he shows how Faust's ascent takes place along a pathway of knowledge in three successive stages: the purification of conceptual life, the illumination of feelings, and the preparation of the will for the pure deed.

What is achieved through the purification of conceptual life leads to the recognition of the spiritual behind everything. Sensory appearances become a simile for the spirit. One penetrates more deeply in order to grasp what is inaccessible to conceptual life. One then reaches a stage at which one can no longer consider things by means of concepts, but must enter the heart of the thing itself. The essential nature of the thing, which can no longer be described, thereby becomes an "attainment." And what cannot be described but must be conceived of in a different way, as we shall hear in the further course of our lectures this winter, what leads on into the mysteries of the will is called the "indescribable." Whoever has traveled this road through conceptual life, through feelings, and through will, then unites with what in the "Chorus Mysticus" is called the "Ever-Feminine." This is what has passed through its developmental stages in the form of the human soul and is portrayed as the Beautiful Lily.

And so we see that Goethe utters his most profound confession, his secret revelation, at the point where he brings his greatest confessional poem to its close. At this point he has made his way up through conceptual life, through feelings and through will in order to unite with the Beautiful Lily, all the way to the situation that now finds expression in the aforementioned "Chorus Mysticus," where the same thing is said as in Goethe's philosophy and in his spiritual science, as well as in the *Fairy Tale:*

> All that must pass away
> Is but a simile!
> Here the inadequate
> Becomes attainment;
> The indescribable,
> Here it is done;
> The Ever-Feminine
> Draws us upward and on! (12104-11)

The Riddles in Goethe's *Faust*—Exoteric

Berlin, March 11, 1909

...Looking at Part One, we have to say: This portrait of a striving soul is infinitely real and true to life. Everything that comes to meet us in Part One, especially in those parts of it that were written first, rings true in a deeply moving way. And yet some parts of it have a more theoretical ring, as though someone were speaking of things that had not yet been thoroughly experienced in the soul.

Everything in Part Two is experience from the innermost recesses of the poet's own soul: loftiest experiences of a spiritual kind. Through these the human being climbs, onward and upward from one stage of existence to the next, permeating first the physical world, then pressing on into where the soul unites with the spirit of the world—merges with it, but also preserves itself there, with the world in which it finds both space and light and, at the same time, what gives it freedom, dignity and independence. All this is contained in Part Two of Goethe's *Faust* as innermost, personal experience.

The time will come when people will regard Goethe's *Faust* very differently than they do today. They will have a better understanding of what Goethe meant when he said to Eckermann on January 25, 1827: "And yet everything in it appeals to the senses. Imagine how it will look on stage: it will be a delight for everyone's eyes. And I have not wished for any more than this. If the majority of the audience will just take pleasure in the way it looks, the initiate will not fail to grasp its higher meaning."

If Part One still seems somewhat theoretical to us in certain respects, as though not worked down into life quite all the way, Part Two is one of the most realistic works in all of world literature, one that goes most deeply into reality itself. For everything in Part Two of *Faust* has been experienced, not only with physical eyes and physical ears, but also with spiritual eyes and spiritual ears. But that has also been the reason why this second part has so far been so little understood. One has seen symbols and allegories in what, for the spiritual researcher, who can experience these things in the spiritual worlds, is *much more real and true* than what external physical eyes can see and external physical ears can hear....

... The fact is that in a certain respect the journey upward into the spiritual worlds is associated with dangers. Souls whose striving is not clear and pure, whose intellectual life and higher reason have not been purified to the point where they can come to pure, sense-free concepts in their thinking, can all too easily stumble and fall into this abyss. Thus it was that certain souls, who still knew something or were "giving their all" (357) to the study of the mystics' writings, did not manage to find their way; or else, because they could not find it, they fell into charlatanism and fraudulent activity. But the opposite was also possible, namely, that among many misunderstandings then current among the common people this genuine striving was decried as magic, or that Trithemius of Sponheim, Agrippa of Nettesheim† and many others who were serious and honest investigators of spiritual forces in Nature were labeled as black magicians and frauds who had departed from the straight and narrow path prescribed by the old-time religion.

This was the age of the sixteenth-century Faust, an age that in certain respects experienced the evening glow of an ancient stream of spirituality. On the other hand, it was also the dawn of an entirely new age, an age that produced such glowing lights as Giordano Bruno, Galilei, Copernicus,† and so on. Many ages are known as "times of transition." But no other age deserves this name as much as the age of Faust.

... Whoever knows the way that leads into worlds of spirit knows that this Mephistopheles is a real being. He is one of the two tempters that everyone encounters who follows the path into the land of the spirit, or even seeks the way into the spiritual world. Such a seeker will meet two different beings or powers there. One of these we call the Luciferic power.† This is the one that takes hold of the human being in a more inward way, in the very center of the soul, propelling all his or her passions, drives, desires, and so forth, one level downward into the realm of what is purely personal and ignoble. Everything that works on the innermost nature, the very core, of the human being itself constitutes the Luciferic. At one time in the course of our evolutionary development through the world as humans, we were seized by this Luciferic principle, and this fact led to our being handed over to another principle as well. If we had never been seized by this Luciferic principle, the outer world would also never have presented itself to us in a merely material form; the outer world would present itself to us in such a way that we could say to ourselves from the outset that everything external is only an expression, a physiognomy, of the spirit. We would see the spirit behind everything that appears to our senses as a world made up of matter. But because things are the way they are, because everything material has come about through a process of condensation under the influence of the Luciferic power, something became part of this world of external appearance that conjures up in front of us a deceptive picture of an external material world. This is what shows the outer world to us in the form of maya or illusion,† as though it were not the outer physiognomical expression of the spirit.

This power, which shows us the outer world in an untrue form, was first fully recognized in its true depths by Zarathustra.† He was the first to describe this figure which opposes itself to the god of light, calling it by the name of "Ahriman."† Zarathustra calls this opponent of the Godhead "Ahriman"; and for all those who then associated themselves with Zarathustran or Zoroastrian culture, Ahriman became that deceptive figure who suffuses what we would otherwise see with transparent, spiritual clarity with the smoke and fog of illusion. Whenever one wanted to express it especially coarsely, one would call this figure that corrupted or depraved us by forcing us into the chains of matter and then deceived or lied to us as to the true form of what is material, "Mephistopheles." This was the Hebrew name of this figure, from the words "mephiz" meaning "the corrupter" and "topel" meaning "the liar" or "the deceiver." This figure then passed over into Western culture and into the figure of Mephistopheles. In the various books on *Faust*, we see Faust being confronted by this power, which is sometimes also called the "Old Serpent."

Goethe came to know this Mephistopheles quite well. In the later Faust-tradition the two figures of Lucifer and Mephistopheles could no longer be kept apart. The period following the sixteenth century no longer had any clear concept of the differences between them; everything flowed together in the figure of the one devil or Satan. As they flowed together, all their differences disappeared, and since no one knew anything at all about the spiritual world, there was no particular interest in distinguishing between them. Goethe, however, began to regard as Mephistopheles everything that eventually becomes our quite specific way of viewing the external world, depending on what we take in through our outer senses and our human intellect, which is accustomed to using a physical brain as its instrument. As a result, someone who only makes use of this capacity of the ordinary intellect seemed to him like a second "I" or ego-being: the companion, as it were, of one striving upward to reach the spiritual world. ... Goethe himself had such a "second I," and it went so far as to give him serious doubts about the spiritual world. At such times he would feel entrapped in the conflict of what we can call the Mephistophelean power, between this evil power stirring in his soul and his soul's true and honest striving to reach the heights of spirit. He could feel both powers within his soul, but he did not know as yet how to relate to the spiritual world. He was still a long way from having the experience he was finally able to bring to us in such a magnificent way in Part Two of *Faust*....

... The Helen scene[†] was also part of the first material Goethe ever wrote for *Faust*. Nevertheless, this scene was not even included in the *Faust* edition of 1808. Why not? Because there was no way to adapt it artistically to the form of *Faust* as Goethe had managed to finish it by that time. What Goethe wanted to say with the figure of Helen was the expression of such a deep premonition of the most profound enigmas of existence that the whole of Part One was not sufficient to accommodate it. Not until he had reached a ripe old age was Goethe able to give real artistic shape to the actual content of his inner life's work.

And so we see his view opening up all the way to the macrocosmic worlds as he gives expression to them in the "Prologue in Heaven." But we also want to see how Goethe is able to give a detailed picture of the path, the stages of soul experiences that lead the human being from the first stages up to the level of imaginative vision. This is where the soul is able to penetrate more and more deeply until it bursts through the gates of the spiritual world, which Mephistopheles would like to keep closed and locked. Goethe depicts these inner experiences as well. Because what he gives us in Part Two of *Faust* is a realistic portrait of what the soul can experience in spiritual or spiritual-scientific[†] training, we see in this the deepest riddles of existence—something that, once recognized, will be for us nothing less than a magnificent Western proclamation of spiritual science....

THE RIDDLES IN GOETHE'S *FAUST*—ESOTERIC

Berlin, March 12, 1909

... As the scene [at the Imperial Palace] goes on, however, we are taken right out of the world that supersensible forces are shown to be playing into, the world in front of us, and are led into the genuinely spiritual world. After the court has been made wealthy again, it expresses the desire to be entertained by having figures out of a long-gone past paraded around in front of it. The intention is to have Paris and Helen conjured up out of the past. Mephistopheles, who belongs to the powers of the spiritual world that inspired the invention of paper money, is unable to enter the worlds that are the source of all the deeper impulses of human evolution. Faust bears within himself both a soul and a spirit that can penetrate these spiritual worlds. For Faust is the student who has bathed his earthly breast in the morning's red (445-446), and we are shown that Faust has already experienced something that can be considered the first stage of clairvoyance, the stage a clairvoyant experiences who has allowed the appropriate exercises to work upon the soul. These are specific exercises that the student has to work with in meditation, concentration and, so forth, assigned in the form of "spiritual-scientific" or esoteric symbols. Once the student has worked with these exercises in some depth, and the soul slips out of the physical and etheric bodies,[†] it finds itself so transformed during the night by the aftereffects of this meditative work that its first experience is to become clairvoyant in the spiritual world....

... As Goethe was reading this scene [in Plutarch], something became free within his soul that had already been laid into it as a seed of initiation during his time in Frankfurt. At that moment he knew what it meant to enter the spiritual worlds. This is the reason for the words he puts in Faust's mouth. Faust shudders when he hears Mephistopheles mention the "Mothers." He knows what it means to be touching this sacred realm, but also that it is "not to be entered" (6223) by someone who is insufficiently prepared. Of course, what Mephistopheles also knows about this realm is that Faust must not enter it unprepared, which is why he says, "Unwilling, I betray a higher secret" (6212). But Faust must go down into this realm in order to do what has to be done, this realm where things otherwise firm and rigid are all seen as continual, transformative processes of Eternal Being itself. This is where a spiritual sense organ can look behind the physical shapes we see with our ordinary senses and discern what reaches into this sense world in order to receive firm contours within it. And then Mephistopheles says something that perfectly characterizes the way this realm appears to anyone who enters it:

> ... Flee from what has come about
> And go to regions freed from all formations!
> In what's no longer present take your joy;
> Throngs move sinuously there like strips of clouds. (6276-79)

The genuine experience of a true initiate cannot be depicted any more vividly than this. "What's no longer present" is found in this world if it is presented the way it is. The "regions freed from all formations" are the realm in which there are no objects like the ones we find in the world of the senses, because it has been set free from them. Faust is to go where he can find "what's no longer present." Finally, when we read that "throngs move sinuously there like strips of clouds," we immediately recognize something absolutely characteristic of this realm. Imagine the entrance to the world of the supersensible as a large gate or portal. Before you can enter, you must prepare your soul by means of symbols of great dignity. One of these symbols is borrowed straight from the sight of the rising sun, and it supplements the image of bathing the earthly breast in the morning's red (445-446); this symbol is the sun that forms a characteristic triangle around itself. The soul experiences this symbol deeply, and it experiences the aftereffects of such a symbol when it has passed through the gate and is then inside the spiritual world. These are then the aftereffects: "Throngs move sinuously there like strips of clouds" (6279). Every word would thus be living proof of what this scene is supposed to be: Faust's entrance into the first stages of the supersensible world, which, as you know, is called the "imaginative world." When Goethe depicted this, he did not depend on something he had concocted from ancient Indian or Egyptian sources and had intended to be a portrait of the spiritual world. He was able to give a realistic portrait of what he had actually experienced, and this is what he did....

... Much thought has been expended on the topic of Homunculus, but thinking and speculating about these things is of no use at all. The riddle of what Homunculus is can only be solved by delving into the genuine resources of spiritual science. For people who spoke about Homunculus in medieval times, he was nothing other than a specific form of the astral body. We must not imagine this Homunculus scene as taking place within the sphere of the physical senses, but rather as located entirely in the spiritual world. We must follow the entire series of events with the state of consciousness that the sleeping Faust is in. Homunculus is then really characterized in the following scenes as the representative of the astral body....

... Homunculus seeks to find out from both Proteus and Nereus some way in which he can get into the physical world. He is shown how he can clothe himself in the elements of material substance. He is also shown what his spiritual properties are like, that is, how the soul gradually enters into the elements of the physical sense world on its way through everything that has taken place in the kingdoms of Nature. We are shown how the soul again has to pass through all the conditions of the mineral, plant, and animal kingdoms in order to shape itself upward toward the human being:

> The ocean broad is where you must begin! (8260)

In other words, in the mineral realm. Then you have to go through the plant kingdom. Goethe even invents an expression for this that doesn't exist otherwise, as he has Homunculus say:

> It smells so green, the fragrance is so nice![†] (8266)

He is told what he has to do to get to where a physical body will gradually form around him. Finally, the moment for Love arrives, when Eros will bring everything to completion. Thales gives him this advice:

> Yield to the laudable desire
> To do creation from the start!
> Be prepared to work with speed!
> To eternal norms you'll move,
> Through a thousand thousand forms,
> And till you're human there's still time. (8321-26)

Once Homunculus has arrived in the physical world he will have lost his distinctive features. His "I" will become his ruler:

> Just do not strive for higher orders,
> For once you've reached the human stage,
> That's the end of it for you. (8330-32)

Proteus says this, meaning the end of it for you, the astral body, which has not yet made its way into the human kingdom.

The entire Goethean view of Nature, of the interrelation of all beings and their metamorphic development from imperfection to perfection, appears here in picture form. The spirit can be in the world at first only in embryonic form. It has to pour itself out into matter, into the elements, diving down into them in order to assume a higher form only when it again emerges. Homunculus shatters against the conch shell chariot of Galatea and dissolves away in the elements. This is a wonderful depiction of the moment in which the astral body surrounds itself with a body of physical matter and can now live as a human being.

These are all experiences Faust undergoes while in a different state of consciousness outside the physical body....

... Goethe gave a realistic representation of what he knew to be facts of the spiritual world. Part Two of *Faust* is a realistic work of poetic art, closed, of course, to anyone who does not know that the spiritual worlds are realities. We have no symbols here, but only the poetic garments of events represented in an absolutely realistic manner, even though they are supersensible events, supersensible events that the soul experiences when it becomes one with the world that is its original home—when it has a feeling- awareness of itself, not in a kind of knowledge that is only an abstraction, a growing-together or fusion with sensory observations or intellectual abstractions, but a kind of knowledge that is a real fact of the spiritual world....

LECTURES

1
Goethe's *Faust* from the Standpoint of Spiritual Science

Public lecture,† Strassburg, January 23, 1910

The science of the spirit, which is seeking to become a living part of modern culture, has no desire to be anything new. In fact, this is just what distinguishes it from the various worldviews and other ways of thinking that are appearing at the present time and believe they can justify their existence by claiming that they have something new to say about this or that question of spiritual life. In contrast to this, what is here called spiritual science emphasizes that the sources of its knowledge and its life were present in the same way at all times when people strove for answers to the deepest questions and riddles of existence. I have often stressed this point in the earlier lectures† that I have also had the honor of giving in this city.

Now it must be especially interesting to examine from this viewpoint not only the various religious denominations and worldviews which have appeared in the course of human history, but also those personalities for whom we have a certain sympathy. For if something is supposed to be true in spiritual science, at least a grain of this truth must be found in all those personalities who have striven honestly and energetically for knowledge and an existence worthy of the human being.

When people speak of spiritual science today, they judge it in many different ways. People who have not penetrated more deeply into a particular field of knowledge, but have only gleaned a superficial idea of it from a few lectures or brochures, will, depending on their point of view, regard this spiritual science as a bunch of fantastic delusions on the part of a few people who are very out of touch with reality and have the weirdest ideas about life and its deeper meaning. Admittedly, if we do not take a closer look, a judgment of this sort can seem perfectly understandable. Even though these things cannot be spoken about today, since we have a special topic to deal with, some of the principal insights of this spiritual science will still need to be pointed out. But even just mentioning and characterizing these insights will arouse in our contemporaries the honest feeling that this is all pretty weird stuff.

Serious spiritual science is based on the general premise that what surrounds us in the material world, what we can perceive with our senses and understand with our intellect—which in turn is bound to our senses—is not the whole world, but that behind everything sense-perceptible there lies a spiritual world. And this spiritual world is not located in some vague afterlife, but is always around us, just as light and color phenomena are always around someone who has been born blind. Now the only way we can know anything about the world around us is if we have an organ with which to perceive it. And just as people born blind cannot see light and color, people living in our times also cannot use their normal faculties to perceive the spiritual facts and beings around us. However, if we have the good fortune to be able to operate on a man who was born blind, and restore his sight, the moment comes for him when his eye awakens, and what was not there for him—light and color—now flow into his inner being. As soon as his sight is restored, the world of light and color becomes for him a world he can perceive. In the same way there is a higher awakening in the realm of the spirit, an awakening through which a person becomes an initiate into the world of the spirit.

Using Goethe's words, we might say: There are such things as spiritual eyes and ears;[†] only, as a rule, human souls have not advanced far enough in their development to be able to use them. But if we apply the means and methods by which these forces come into being, what takes place in us on a higher level parallels what happens for the person born blind who finds himself flooded with a world of light and color after his sight has been restored. Those whose eyes and ears are opened awaken. A new world is around them, a world that has always been there but that they can perceive only from the moment of their awakening on. Whoever has come this far now learns to acquire different kinds of knowledge: knowledge that can enlighten life, knowledge that can give us strength and confidence for our work and enable us to see into the nature of what determines us as human beings and into the mysteries of human destiny.

Let us take one of these insights as a preparation for the actual theme of today's lecture. It is one of those insights that often seems at least strange and dreamy to people today, if not downright insane. This insight is nothing but an enlivening of an ancient process of knowing, its continuation on a higher level; it is a truth that on a lower level has been discovered only relatively recently. People generally have a short memory for great events in spiritual history. This is why people today so rarely think of the fact that in the seventeenth century not only laypeople but scholars as well believed that lower animals, even worms and fish, could develop out of river mud. It was the great scientist Francesco Redi[†] who first pointed out that no fish or earthworm ever grows out of dead river mud unless the germ of an earthworm or a fish is in it first. He stated the principle that what is living can only come from what is living. We see from this that it is merely an inaccurate observation to believe that a living being, such as a fish or a worm, can grow out of lifeless river mud. Closer observation shows that we have to go back to the living germ and that this living germ can only draw the forces out of its environment that are there in order to allow what is living in the germ to unfold and develop to its fullest extent.

Redi's principle that what is living can only develop out of what is living is taken for granted in modern science. Yet when Redi stated this principle in his own time, he barely escaped the fate of Giordano Bruno. This is the way the evolution of humanity proceeds. For a fact of such importance to be established, those who first proclaim it must be declared heretics; only then does it become a self-evident truth and a part of our general human heritage. What Redi did for science must be done today for the spirit by spiritual science. The task is to take the principle he stated for the natural sciences and carry it over to the realm of the soul, using what we have learned through our awakened spiritual eyes and our awakened spiritual ears. The new form of this principle will then be: What is soul-spiritual can only come from what is soul-spiritual.

In other words: it is a mistake to believe that a human being entering life is descended only from his or her father and mother and other ancestors. Just as we have to go back to the living germ of the earthworm to explain how the earthworm comes into existence, we also have to go back to an earlier spiritual existence when we see a human being developing out of the germ and becoming a specific individual. We must also be clear that this individual, as it comes into existence through birth, takes from its bodily ancestors only the forces it needs for its own development, just as the earthworm draws upon the forces of its own lifeless environment. Accordingly, the principle that what is living can only come from what is living can be extended to the other principle: that the life now present, which has come into the world through birth, goes back not only to physical ancestors, but back through the centuries to something that was once of a soul-spiritual nature.

If you go into this matter more deeply, you will see it is shown absolutely scientifically[†] that there is not just one, but repeated earthly lives; that what lives in us between birth and death is the repetition of something soul-spiritual that was already present in earlier stages of existence; and that our present life is once again the point of departure for our following lives. What is soul-spiritual comes from what is soul-spiritual; it can be traced back to something soul-spiritual that existed before birth, comes down out of the spiritual world, and realizes itself in physical incarnations. Equipped with this knowledge, we see something quite different if, for example, as parents and teachers we look at a child whose capacities are gradually unfolding. We see the indefiniteness of the child's face and features at birth and how something gradually unfolds out of its inner nature and becomes more and more definite. This "something" does not come from heredity, but from the child's previous lives. We see how this core of the soul-spiritual element unfolds more and more from birth on through the child's developing talents.

That is what spiritual science has to say about repeated earthly lives. Today it may seem only daydreams, just as what Francesco Redi said in the seventeenth century seemed to be only a daydream. But what seems to be a dream today will be a matter of course in the not so distant future, and the principle that what is soul-spiritual comes from what is soul-spiritual will become common knowledge for all humanity.

Nowadays heretics are not dealt with the way they used to be. They no longer end up being burned at the stake, but are looked at instead as fools and dreamers whose words are only the product of a capricious imagination. They are ridiculed, and from the high court of scientific judgment they are told that what they have to say cannot be harmonized with genuine science. But the people who do all this are not aware that true, genuine science is precisely what demands this truth. And now we can cite hundreds and hundreds of such truths that would show us how spiritual science can illuminate life by showing there is an immortal core in human beings that passes through death into the spiritual world; when it has fulfilled its mission there it returns to physical existence to gather new experiences that are then carried up through death into spiritual worlds. We would see how the bonds established from one person to another, from soul to soul in all areas of life, those attractions of the heart that pass from soul to soul and for which there is otherwise no explanation, can be explained by the fact that they were formed through relationships in former lives. We would also see that the inner spiritual bonds we form today also do not come to an end when death moves over the face of our earthly existence. Instead, what moves from soul to soul as a bond of life is as immortal as the human soul itself; it continues to live with the soul as the latter passes through the spiritual world, and it will come to life again in other, future earthly relationships and new incarnations. It is only a question of evolution until people will remember their earlier earthly experiences and what they lived through in former earth lives and conditions of existence.

Such truths will become a necessary and integral part of human life in the not too distant future; and people will gain strength, hope, and confidence from them. Today we can see that only a few individuals are drawn by their healthy sense for truth to what spiritual scientists have to say on the basis of their experiences in the spiritual world. But spiritual-scientific knowledge will become the common property of humanity as a result of this serious search for truth. And those who have followed the path of being serious seekers of truth have always, in everything they offered humanity, given form to the great wisdom and knowledge that spiritual science is bringing again today.

Let us allow an example of such a seeker to pass before our souls today in a personality who is close to the life of our times. We mean, of course, Goethe and the greatest and most comprehensive of his works, with which he occupied himself his whole life long: his *Faust*.

When we approach Goethe and try to illuminate his striving with what spiritual science can give, we can actually begin rather early in his life. We can say that the way soul and spirit were constituted in him was evident from his whole predisposition. Everything that urges a person to search for a spiritual element behind the phenomena of the sensory world was already present in him as an early tendency. We see Goethe as a seven-year-old boy who should have been able to take in normal pictures from his environment and use them for his first soul-pictures like any other boy. But he is not satisfied with that, and he tells us so himself in his autobiography: *Poetry and Truth*. There we read how the seven-year-old boy starts something very peculiar in order to express his longing for the divine. He takes a music stand from his father's collection and makes an altar out of it by placing on it all kinds of minerals and plants and other natural products of out of which the spirit of Nature is speaking. Intuitively the boyish soul erects an altar, places a scented candle on it, picks up a magnifying glass, waits until the morning sun rises, focuses the first rays of the rising sun with the glass and beams them at the candle so that smoke begins to rise from it. Then in his ripe old age Goethe remembers how as a boy he had wanted to send his pious feelings up to the great God of Nature who speaks through minerals and plants and sends us his fire in the rays of the sun. That all grows as Goethe grows. Later on, he is called to Weimar to become the Duke's advisor, and there we see how, at a more mature stage and yet out of a yearning soul, this feeling for the spirit that speaks out of all beings of Nature lives in Goethe and eventually finds expression in his beautiful prose hymn.[†] There he writes:

> Nature, we are surrounded and embraced by her, unable to step out of her and unable to go into her any more deeply. Unwarned and unbidden she takes us up into the whirl of her dance and carries us off with her until we are exhausted and fall away from her arm....We have not done what we do; she has done it all. It is she who continually ponders and thinks and looks out into the world with a thousand eyes.

Later on, in the section called "Antiquity" in his beautiful book on Winckelmann,[†] he writes:

> When the healthy nature of human beings is active as a whole; when they feels themselves in the world as though in one great, beautiful, noble and meaningful totality; when the harmonious comfort of it all grants them pure and free delight: at that moment, the universe, if it could feel its own existence, would give a shout, as though it had attained its goal, and admire the summit of its own being and becoming.

This is the way Goethe felt about how everything that lives and weaves in outer nature celebrates a resurrection out of the human soul and how a higher nature, a spiritual nature, is born out of the human soul and the human spirit. But Goethe's struggle for complete clarity in his spiritual understanding of Nature was a slow process. Throughout his long life, Goethe strove ceaselessly to transform his knowledge again and again in order to come to a higher stage of development; nowhere do we see this better and more clearly than in his life-poem, *Faust*.

Very early in his youth he had begun to put into this poem everything that filled his soul, which was yearning with anticipation. He finished the poem only shortly before his death as an old, old man. By then he had been working on it for over fifty years and had put into it the very best part of his life. At the time of his death, Part Two lay sealed as the great last will and testament he had given to humanity. It is an eloquent document. But we can understand this document only if we pay a little attention to the way Goethe himself struggled to attain his insight.

We find Goethe, for example, as a student at the University of Leipzig. He is supposed to be studying law, but that is only a side issue for him. Already in the young student there lives an unconquerable impulse to understand the secrets of the world, a thirst for the spiritual. So he explores everything Leipzig has to offer in the way of knowledge about Nature. He seeks to listen in on what Nature has to say to us in her phenomena, to cull from the world the riddles of its existence. In order to transform what natural science could offer him, to re-form it in his soul into that impulse that lives and weaves through all the forcefulness of his innermost being and does not seek abstract knowledge but knowledge warmed by the heart, Goethe needed a great experience, an experience that really leads the human being to the insight that is the gateway we look toward with foreboding, the gateway that closes off what is invisible and supersensible for the normal person of today: the portal of death. At the end of his study time in Leipzig, death passed him by. A serious illness had laid him low and brought him close to death. He had lived through hours and days when he had to say to himself that he might pass through that mysterious portal at any moment. And the mysterious, impetuous impulse to know demanded from him the utmost seriousness in his striving for knowledge. It was in this mood of knowledge that Goethe returned to his hometown of Frankfurt. There he met a group of people headed by a woman of great and profound gifts: Susanne von Klettenberg.† Goethe left her a wondrous memorial in his "Confessions of a Beautiful Soul."† He showed there how it was that in this personality, with whom he developed such a close spiritual affinity at that time, something lived that cannot be described in any other way than this: In Susanne von Klettenberg there lived a soul that was seeking to grasp the divine within itself in order to find through the divine in itself the spiritual that permeates the world with its life.

Through the circle this lady belonged to, Goethe was introduced at that time to certain studies that any modern person who spent some time with them would find quite insane. These were medieval writings that Goethe immersed himself in. People looking at them today could not make head nor tail of them. They would find strange signs and symbols there, and simply wonder what any of this has to do with the modern scientific striving for truth. One book had a special effect; it was called *Aurea catena Homeri* or *The Golden Chain of Homer*. When you open it you find a strange symbolic illustration: in a semicircle across the top, a dragon full of life, bordering on another dragon that is withering and dying away into itself. All kinds of signs are connected with this: symbolic keys, two interconnected triangles, and the signs of the planets.

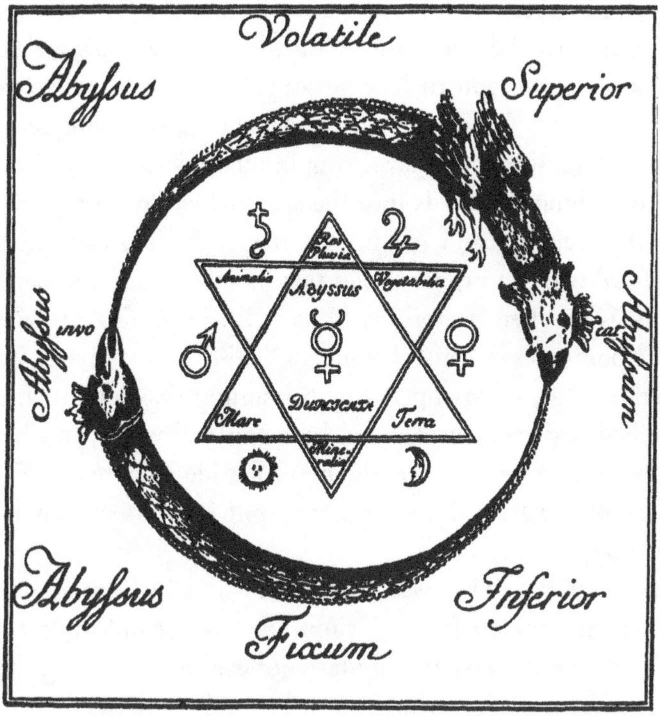

For our contemporaries, in the face of present-day science, this is pure fantasy, because no one has any idea what these signs are supposed to mean.[†] Goethe had a premonition that they do express something and that a person can find meaning in them through sustained contemplation. They do not express something directly that can be found here or there in the world. But if we allow these signs to work on us by taking them in so deeply that we become, so to speak, blind and deaf toward our physical environment, allowing only these signs to work in us, we have a very peculiar experience. We sense how the soul begins to feel something within itself that has formerly been asleep, like a spiritual eye beginning to open. And if we have enough persistence, then we take hold of something that can be called meditation or concentration. In this process our soul becomes so developed that we actually undergo something like an operation on our spiritual eyes, and a new world opens up.

At that time Goethe was not far enough along for a new world to open up. But what did come alive within his soul was the feeling that there are keys to this spiritual world and that one can penetrate into this spiritual world. We must imagine this mood; the living sensation, the living feeling: something is stirring in me now, coming alive; there must be something that leads into the spiritual world. But at the same time Goethe feels he can't get in yet. If Goethe had ever in his life been identical with Faust, we would say: Goethe was in the same situation Faust is in when he appears to us at the beginning of Part One. This is the point where Faust, having studied the most diverse areas of human knowledge, opens up books containing drawings such as the one described and feels surrounded by a spiritual world; but he can't get into the spiritual world. Goethe never felt identical to this Faust to such an extent; a part of him was Faust, but he himself grew beyond what was only a part of him.

And so it was that what was more than Faust in Goethe grew and grew in that he kept on striving, shunning no discomfort and saying to himself: We never grasp the mysteries of existence in a single leap or with magic formulas and incantations, but only if we really penetrate with our soul and spirit whatever comes to meet us in the physical world, gradually, step by step, with patient, energetic awareness.

It is easy to say that higher knowledge must dawn in the human soul. It must dawn, but it will only dawn in its true form when we strive patiently and persistently to acquaint ourselves more and more thoroughly with the actual phenomena of the physical world and then seek the spiritual behind them. Armed with what he took with him from his stay in Frankfurt, however, Goethe was able to tie everything else together and see it all in a new light.

Goethe came from Frankfurt to your city, to Strassburg. We could mention many things that led him to a higher level here. But especially characteristic is the way he took into his soul something that is of such great significance in this city, namely, the cathedral.[†] At that time the idea of that wonderful structure presented itself to Goethe's soul, and he understood why each individual line is the way it is. With the spiritualized way of looking that he had acquired through his deepening in Frankfurt, he saw every triangle, indeed every individual angle of this significant building, as belonging to the whole. Within his soul the great idea of the architect was resurrected, and Goethe felt that he could recognize again what had flowed into this structure as thought and as idea.

We could mention many things that show the marriage in Goethe's soul between what this soul had attained as an inner way of viewing and what it took in as processes and events of the external world. It is therefore not surprising that when Goethe went to Weimar later on he took in the natural sciences—botany, zoology, anatomy, and so on—from a whole new direction, regarding everything as letters of an alphabet that, taken all together, would constitute the Book of Nature and thus lead directly into the mysteries of existence. This is how his studies on the metamorphosis of plants and the animal kingdom came about, which he carried on later as though he were still a student, the only difference being that everywhere he looked he sought the spirit behind the sensory phenomena of existence.

We see how, particularly during his Italian journey, Goethe regarded art, on the one hand, and the works of Nature, especially the plant world, on the other, in order to recognize the spirit holding sway in them both. Great and beautiful are the words he wrote to his friends as he carried on this kind of spiritualized science of Nature. Oh, he [Goethe] said,[†] everything I encounter here looks new to me; how I would like to visit India to look in my own way at what has already been discovered! In the way, that is, in which his own development, insofar as we have been able to indicate it, was demanding of him.

We also see how he regarded the art works he found there. In one letter[†] he writes: "This much is certain: the ancient artists had just as great a knowledge of Nature and just as sure a concept of what can be portrayed and how to portray it as Homer did. Unfortunately, the number of art works of the first class that remain is all too small. But when one sees these, one desires only to recognize them in their true nature and then depart in peace. These high works of art have been produced by human beings in harmony with true and natural laws just as the highest works of Nature have been. Everything arbitrary and purely imagined falls away; here is necessity, here is God." Just as the great God of Nature spoke to the seven-year-old boy from his homemade altar, so did the Great Spirit of the existence of the spiritual world speak to him out of these works of art, which he regarded as a unity. In this way, Goethe came to regard each individual thing with energetic, devoted effort. Then he was able to quietly await the moment when a genuine recognition of the spiritual world would emerge from his observations. This was to be a true science of the spirit as we then encounter it, reworked and transformed in an artistic fashion, in his *Faust*.

This is why the very first parts of *Faust* he wrote are filled with the mood of a man who has a premonition of the mysteries of existence, but is not yet able to find his way into them. We see there how Faust lets certain signs work on him that cause him to be surrounded by a spiritual element, but also that he is not yet mature enough to truly feel this spiritual element. These are the lines in which Faust lets the signs of the Macrocosm and of the Earth Spirit work on him as the Nostradamus-aura,[†] when the spirit of the Earth appears before him. The Earth Spirit is characterized by Faust in wondrously beautiful words. We see how he senses that the planet Earth is not simply the physical globe science considers it to be, but that just as the human physical body has a soul, the body of the earth has a spirit.

> In floods of life, in storm of deeds
> Up and down I well,
> Back and forth I weave!
> Birth and grave,
> An eternal sea,
> A changing weaving,
> A glowing living,
> I weave at the buzzing loom of time
> And work at God's living garment sublime. (501-09)

This is what lives in the earth as the spirit of the Earth, just as our spirit lives in us. But Goethe characterizes Faust as not yet mature, his spirit as still imperfect. He has to turn away from the fearsome sign like a worm shriveled up in fear. The Earth Spirit answers: "You resemble the spirit you comprehend, not me!" (512-13). In Goethe's soul the knowledge lived—albeit still only as a premonition—that we must never say at any stage of our development that we are satisfied or have attained anything, but must continually strive to reach ever higher stages. Goethe was led into these mysteries from phenomenon to phenomenon by his own enthusiastic studies. And now we see him grow.

After Goethe himself had attained a higher stage following his Italian journey,† which I have characterized by saying that he wanted to penetrate all Nature and all art with his own way of looking, Goethe has Faust address the same spirit he had first called up and which he could only speak of then as: "Dreadful apparition!" (482). Faust is now in the same mood as Goethe himself. Standing before the same spirit, he now addresses him quite differently:

> Exalted Spirit, you gave me, gave me all
> Of what I asked for. It was not in vain
> That in the fire you turned your face to me.
> You gave me glorious Nature for my kingdom
> And strength to feel her, to enjoy her. Not
> Cold staring in amazement give you only;
> To gaze into her breast so deep you grant me
> As into the deep bosom of a friend.
> You lead the rank and file of living creatures
> Past my eyes, and teach me to perceive
> My brothers in quiet bush, in air and water.
> And when the storm in forest roars and crackles,
> The giant spruce in falling strips down, crushing,
> Crunching, nearby trunks and nearby branches,
> And hill responds to fall with hollow thunder;
> You lead me then to this safe cavern, show
> Me then myself, and then to my own breast
> Profound and secret wonders are revealed.
> And when before my gaze the pure, clear moon
> Arises, gently calming: then there waft
> From cliff walls, from dew-damp bush
> Silver shapes of former worlds upon me,
> And ease the austere joy of my beholding. (3217-39)

Goethe, and with him Faust, has arrived at the pinnacle of no longer having to turn away from the spirit he once wished to reach in a single leap. The spirit now comes to meet him in a form from which he no longer needs to turn away. Now he can recognize it in all living creatures, in all kingdoms of Nature: in forest and water, in the quiet bush, in the giant spruce, in storm and thunder. And not only there. After it has appeared to him in great, grand outer Nature, he recognizes it also in his own heart: the spirit's profound and secret wonders are revealed.

That is a step forward in Goethe's recognition of the spirit, but Goethe never rested in his attempts to go even further. We see how he then, probably urged on by Schiller, seeks to deepen himself, especially during the last decade of the eighteenth century. These years brought what he needed in order to get beyond the still vague type of spiritual awareness that there is spirit living in everything. It now became possible for him to grasp this spirit as a concrete entity. But Goethe needed much preparation before he was able to depict the life of the human spirit in the sense that "the soul-spiritual can only be descended from the soul-spiritual." But many a work he created before he finished *Faust* shows that he never shunned the attempt to come into the spirit more and more deeply. The second part of *Faust* shows what heights he managed to attain.

Many people already turned away from him when they met the deepened Goethe in his drama *Pandora*.† Even today we hear people say the first part of *Faust* is full of life and breathes with an immediate naturalness, while the second part is a product of Goethe's old age, full of symbols and artificialities. Such people have no idea what infinite wisdom is to be found in this second part of *Faust*, wisdom to which a life as rich as Goethe's could come only in the evening of his life, to be left behind as his last will and testament. We can therefore also understand it when, referring to certain works that already breathe the spirit of *Faust*, Goethe writes the lines that make it clear that he represents Faust as a struggling soul upon whom something completely new has dawned. We recognize this in the anger he poured out over those who had called *Faust* an inferior work of his old age. As he says of them:

They say Faust's pretty good†
And also find
Things in my other works
That suit their mind;

The same old stuff is what
They really like;
The lousy bums believe
I've gone on strike!

These are the words Goethe finds for his attitude toward those among his readers who believe that it is only what he accomplished in his younger years that is worth anything and who are not willing to follow him to the heights of the more mature achievements in his later life.

Having led his Faust into the everyday life of our immediate surroundings and allowed him to experience that marvelous tragedy with Gretchen, Goethe then leads him outward, at first into the world that is the great one in an external sense: the world of the "Imperial Palace." Goethe wants to show us here that it is now time for Faust to enter into the mysteries of this world in a genuinely spiritual way as well. But for this to happen, Faust would need to be guided into the world that is really spiritual, the world beyond the senses.

Right at the beginning of Part Two, we see how Goethe has Faust surrounded by all sorts of spiritual beings. This expresses Goethe's intention not only to lead Faust into an external physical world but to have him undergo the experiences of someone whose spiritual eyes have been opened and whose spiritual ears have learned to hear. This is why in Part Two Goethe unfolds for us the essential nature of the human soul and of human development, step by step. What is Faust supposed to experience? The knowledge of the supersensible world. He is to be initiated into the mysteries of the supersensible world. Where is this supersensible world?

If we take the spiritual content of *Faust* into account, it is only now that we can begin to consider the question of Mephistopheles, that spirit who is around Faust from the very beginning and who plays a role in everything Faust undertakes. But it is not until Part Two, where Faust is to be led into the spiritual world, that we see what sort of role Mephistopheles plays. After Faust has experienced the events at the Imperial Palace, he begins to see something that is no longer in the world of the physical senses: the spirit of Helen of Troy, who lived centuries and centuries before. She is to be found for Faust, but she cannot be found in the physical world. Faust must descend into the spiritual world. Mephistopheles has the key to this world, but he is unable to enter it himself; he can only describe it intellectually. He can say, for example, "You will descend." One could just as well say, "You will ascend." (6275).

But then he actually does describe the spiritual world that Faust is to plunge down into in order to get to know it in a supersensible way and to find the spirit in it, the immortal, eternal part of Helen that has been left behind. Then a word resounds, a marvelous word: Faust is to descend to the Mothers.† What are these "Mothers"? We could speak for hours if we wanted to characterize exactly what the Mothers are. Here we need only say that for spiritual science the Mothers have always been what people come to know when their spiritual eyes are opened. When people look into the physical world, everything seems to have a boundary. When they enter the spiritual world, they come into something that all physical things emerge from, the way ice emerges from water in a pond. Just as someone who could not see the water would say, "There's nothing here but ice, piling itself up out of nothingness," someone who does not know the spirit says, "There's nothing here but physical objects." People don't see the spirit between and behind the physically perceptible objects, out of which all these objects form just as ice forms out of water. The very foundation of physical objects is no longer visible through physical eyes, but where it is, is where the Mothers are.

Mephistopheles is the being whose task it is to portray a kind of intellectuality that only knows what has external form in space; to be sure, he is aware that there is a spiritual world, but also that he cannot get into it. Mephistopheles stands there, next to Faust, just like a materialistic thinker that stands next to a spiritual investigator and says, "Oh, you spiritual scientist, you theosophist, you want to see into a spiritual world, do you? Well, there's nothing in there at all. It is all just a dream. There's nothing to it."

To this materialist, who wants to build firmly on what the microscope and the telescope reveal, but at the same time deny everything that lies behind all physical phenomena, the spiritual investigator calls out: "In your nothingness I hope to find the All" (6256). This is the materialistic thinker's way of confronting a spiritually oriented person who hopes to find the spirit in the very place where the materialist sees nothing. These two forces will confront each other forever. This is how Mephisto confronts Faust from the very beginning as the spirit who can lead up to the door, but cannot pass through it. Neither the theosophist nor the spiritual scientist says, "There's nothing to material science; we don't need it." What they say is: "We must take this science seriously and study it, but it only has the key. It leads to where true spiritual life can first be found."

Faust then descends into the realm of the Mothers, into the spiritual world, where he is able to find the spirit of Helen and bring her to the physical world with him. But he is not yet mature enough to actually unite this spirit with his own soul. Therefore we have the scene in which sensual passion stirs in Faust and he tries to embrace the archetypal image of Helen with it. This is why he is thrust back, as anyone will be who tries to approach the spiritual world out of personal, egoistic feelings. Such a person is thrust back, as Faust is thrust back when he has retrieved Helen's spirit from the realm of the Mothers. Faust has first to mature and learn to recognize how the three members of the human being truly come together: the immortal spirit that goes from life to life, from incarnation to incarnation; the body that lives its life between birth and death; and the soul that stands between them. Body, soul, and spirit: how they interconnect and belong together is what Faust is to learn about. Helen's archetypal image, the immortal, eternal element that goes from incarnation to incarnation, from life to life, is what Faust has already sought, but in an immature way. His task now is to mature in order to become worthy to really enter the spiritual world. For Faust must also learn that this immortal element approaches the human individual only when it is again able to incarnate in a physical existence in a new life between birth and death. Goethe therefore has to show how the soul inserts itself and lives between the spirit and the body, which in turn stands between birth and death. This is precisely what he does show us in the second part of *Faust.*

Goethe conceals the soul in that wondrous creature that the Goethe scholars have little to say about, but in whom experienced spiritual investigators recognize the archetypal image of the soul. This wonderful creature is none other than Homunculus, the "little human being." He is a picture of the human soul. What does this soul have to do? As the mediator between the body and the spirit, its function is to attract the elements of the body from all the kingdoms of Nature in order to establish a connection with them. Only then can it be united with the immortal spirit. This is why we see how Faust is led by this Homunculus into the "Classical Walpurgis Night" and to Anaxagoras and Thales,† the philosophers of Nature, who have thought about how Nature and all that is living come into being.

Here the true theory of evolution is shown that goes back to the fact that not only something animal-like is at the root of human evolution, but something soul-like as well that gathers the elements from Nature and builds up the body with them bit by bit. This is why Homunculus receives the advice: You must start with the lowest kingdom in order to ascend from it to higher and higher ones.

At first the human soul is directed to the mineral kingdom. Then Homunculus is told†: You have to pass through the kingdom of the plants. What a wonderful expression it is to say, "It smells so green" (8266), in order to record the passage through the lush green plant world. This is where the soul gathers all the elements of the kingdoms of Nature in order to then make its ascent. It is expressly stated: "And till you're human there's still time" (8326). Then we see how Eros, the spirit of love, approaches after the soul has shaped the body for itself out of all the kingdoms of Nature. At this moment the soul connects itself with the spirit, and body, soul and spirit are united. The soul of Homunculus, along with what it is organizing into a body for itself, connect themselves here with Helen's spirit. This is why, in the third act of Part Two, Helen can appear before us in the flesh. We see the doctrine of reincarnation secretly woven into the second part of *Faust* in a poetic and artistic way. The way to connect with Helen is not by drawing her close in a storm of passion, but by really living through the mysteries of existence and experiencing the reality of reincarnation.

Goethe could not yet express the idea of repeated earthly lives in harmony with the thinking of his time, as we can today. But he did put it into the second part of his *Faust.* This is why he was able to say to Eckermann†: I have written my *Faust* in such a way that it suits the theater and that, in an externally sense-perceptible way, the scenes it offers are interesting to someone who wants only to see in an externally sense-perceptible way. To the initiates, however, it will be apparent that the deepest things have been woven secretly into this second part of *Faust.* Thus, Goethe expressly pointed out that his view of life and of the spirit can be found in this poetic work. And so we now understand as well that in this reunification of Faust with Helen, Goethe was able to make clear to us what true mysticism is.

Faust connects himself with the spiritual world. The child who then appears is not your everyday child, but Euphorion, who is just as true as he is poetic. Just as truly he represents for us what comes to life in our soul when it joins with the spiritual world. When the soul finds its way into the mysteries of the spiritual world, there comes a moment of development in the soul that is of extremely deep significance for this soul. Before the soul goes any further, it comes to see this connection with the spiritual for a few moments and to know what the spiritual world is. For this brief span of time it is as though a spiritual child were being born out of spiritual knowledge. But then that moment in life comes when this spiritual child disappears again as though into the spiritual world. If you grasp this with the full life of your heart, you will feel how, despite all the truth of his poetic life, Euphorion, the spiritual child of the mystic, sinks down again into the spiritual world that Faust cannot yet fully enter, but how he also takes something else along with him. This is an experience of the spiritual investigator, the spiritual seeker, when the moment comes to our soul in which it truly feels its relationship to the spiritual world, and this knowledge makes its appearance as a child born of a marriage with the spiritual world. Then the soul experiences deeply its own sinking down again into everyday reality, and it seems as though the child takes the best that we have away with it. It is as though our own soul were escaping and being drawn along with it into the spiritual world. When you have felt that, you feel the echo of the spiritual words of Euphorion who has sunk down and is calling out of the dark depths: "Do not leave me, Mother, in this gloomy realm alone" (9905-06). The true mystic knows this voice; it is that of the spiritual child calling to our soul as though to its mother.

But this soul must go further. It must free itself from all purely personal passion. We must be able to devote ourselves to the spiritual world in an impersonal way. As long as the slightest trace of self-interest or self-will is still present, we cannot take hold of the spiritual world. We will be able to do this only when everything personal has been scoured away before the higher standard of the spiritual world. Only then can we enter the spiritual world in a really lasting way. But then, even when we have already experienced that moment that thrusts us back again into the physical world, other moments come that rob us of all mystical experience for a long time to come. We have to say about such moments that, even when we have overcome all self-interest and all self-will, there is still something left, just as there was still something left in Faust even after he had said: Here on free ground I stand; my one desire is to work, to reclaim everything from Nature and to do things only for others.

Faust has not gotten this far as yet. As long as looking at the cottage of Philemon and Baucis continues to disturb his gaze, he shows that he is not yet free of that brand of egoism that wants to take pleasure in what it looks at. His desire has been to create an estate, selflessly, but he cannot yet endure what spoils it: the cottage of Philemon and Baucis. The Spirit of Evil draws near to him once more, and the cottage is burned down. Now something shows itself to him that shows itself to everyone who is evolving. This is Care, who comes to those whose strivings are still tinged with self-interest and who keeps them from ascending into the spiritual world. Care stands there before us, and we come to know her in her true form; at that moment she is something that can lead us to the ultimate in the way of true spiritual knowledge.

The point here is not that we should become unworldly, hostile to the world, but that we should stay in the world and get to know what keeps us from becoming free of it. In wise self-knowledge we should allow Care to come before us so that we may become free from Care's egoistic aspect, not from Care herself. This is pictured by Care's saying that she will slip in through the keyhole. When we come to know this Care and not just learn to feel her but to bear up under her weight, we attain that degree of human development that opens our spiritual eyes. This is pictured by Faust's becoming blind as a very old man, so that he can no longer see with his physical eyes, but is able to see into the spiritual world. "The night seems deeper, deeply to press in" (11499). Outwardly all is dark, but bright inner light, the light that can illuminate the world, flashes up; it is the light that the soul is in between death and birth: the realm of the Mothers. Now at last Faust can begin his journey into the spiritual world, at the point where his ascension is so beautifully depicted.

Goethe is then able to summarize what has become of Faust, from his first premonitory striving as a human being who despairs of all scientific knowledge and turns away from it to the stage in his life when he reaches his highest knowledge of the spirit. This summary is the Chorus Mysticus, which shows by its very name that it is supposed to signify something deeper. The purpose of this Chorus Mysticus is to bring together once more, paradigmatically and in a few words, what offers the key to all the mysteries of the world, namely, the idea that everything transitory is only a simile for what is everlasting. What our physical eyes can see is only a simile for what is spiritual and immortal, and Goethe has shown that when he entered into this spiritual element he even attained to the knowledge of reincarnation. The purpose of this closing is to show that when a person enters the spiritual realm, everything that has only been a premonition or a hope in the physical world, now becomes a truth. What is striven for only in the physical world becomes something actually attained [*ein Erreichnis*] in the spiritual world.

It might seem almost pedantic for me to mention something at this point that we need to know to properly understand these closing words.† In his old age, Goethe's speech was rather indistinct because he had no teeth. He dictated the second part of his *Faust* to a secretary. Since he still had something of his Frankfurt dialect, some of his words and sounds came out a bit indistinctly. So quite a few times the secretary wrote a "g" where there should have been a "ch." For example, for the word *"Erreichnis"* [something attained] he wrote *"Ereignis"* [an event] instead. But what Goethe said when he dictated the closing words of *Faust* was *"Erreichnis."* What is insufficient or inadequate[†] [*das Unzulängliche*] becomes something here that can be attained, an *"Erreichnis,"* with two "r's" and a "ch." In all the Goethe editions you will find the word *"Ereignis."* This is how little the Goethe scholars know about how to penetrate the true meaning. What is insufficient or inadequate in the physical world becomes something attained in the spiritual world. What cannot be described in the physical world is done in the spiritual world. There it becomes a living deed.

Finally, we experience that magnificent concept that Goethe is allowed to express in the closing words of the second part of *Faust* : the "Ever-Feminine." It is a sin against Goethe to say that he uses this expression to mean the female sex. What Goethe has in mind is the profound essence of what the human soul represents as it stands face to face with the mystery of the universe. It is what yearns as the eternal element in the human being: the eternal feminine that draws the soul onward and upward to the eternally immortal, the eternal wisdom, and that surrenders itself to the eternal masculine. The eternal feminine draws us onward and upward to what is eternally masculine. It does not refer to anything feminine or female in the usual sense. For this reason we are quite within our rights to look for this eternal feminine in both the man and the woman: the eternal feminine that strives toward the eternal masculine in the cosmos in order to unite, to become one, with the divine-spiritual that works and weaves through the universe and toward which Faust is striving.

This mystery of the human being in all the ages, which Faust is striving to understand from the very beginning and to which spiritual science in a modern sense is to help us find our way, this mystery is what Goethe expresses monumentally and paradigmatically in the beautiful words that he places at the end of the second part of *Faust* in the form of the mystical spirit chorus: the fact that everything physical that surrounds us in the world of the senses is maya, illusion and deception, a simile or picture of the spiritual. This spiritual element, however, is what we see when we push through to what covers it as a veil. In this spiritual element we see something attained that cannot be attained here on earth. We see what is indescribable for the intellect bound to the physical senses transformed into actual deed when the spirit of the human being unites with the spiritual world. "The indescribable, here it is done" (12108-09). And we see that significant event in which the soul unites and lives together with the eternal masculine of the great world that weaves through and enlivens this world. This is the great mystery that Goethe expresses with the words:

Alles Vergängliche	All that must pass away
Ist nur ein Gleichnis;	Is but a simile;
Das Unzulängliche	Here the inadequate
Hier wird's Erreichnis / Ereignis;	Becomes attainment / an event;
Das Unbeschreibliche,	The indescribable,
Hier ist's getan;	Here it is done;
Das Ewig-Weibliche	The Ever-Feminine
Zieht uns hinan.	Draws us upward and on.

(12104-11)

Goethe could well say to himself: "Now I have done my life's work. It really doesn't matter what I do with the rest of the time I have yet to live on the earth." So Goethe sealed up the second part of his *Faust*, and this second part was not given to humanity until after his death. It will be our task to garner all the resources of spiritual science in order to penetrate into the mysteries of this mighty work.

Today's remarks had to be in a very sketchy form. With all the knowledge and wisdom at our disposal, we could spend hours and even weeks trying to illuminate what Goethe bequeathed to humanity as his last will and testament. May humanity open up this testament more and more! Seal after seal will fall away, the more people find the will to penetrate into the mysteries of the second part. Some will say, "You are looking for something that Goethe had no intention of putting into his work," but their voices will fall silent.

Whoever speaks this way has never experienced the true depth of Goethe's soul. Those alone who can recognize this depth see the very highest in this work and in what Goethe distilled into the Mystical Chorus, which can serve as a fitting closing to so many remarks whose purpose it is to lead us to the spirit.

2
The Relationship of Goethe's *Faust* to Goethe

Berlin, December 17, 1911

Since Frau Wandrey's† illness has prevented her from giving her *Faust* lectures during our gathering here in Berlin, I would like to use this morning to offer a somewhat disconnected series of remarks of a more extemporaneous nature on Goethe's *Faust* myself. I have often spoken on *Faust* and hope to write a little monograph† some day that will bring together what has been said on these various occasions.

The Faust theme is a very broad one, and at the same time it is extremely difficult to treat; difficult, because not many works of world literature have as peculiar and intimate a relationship to their author as Goethe's *Faust* does to Goethe himself. We only have to consider the external fact that when Goethe went to Weimar he took along a first version of *Faust* that had already taken shape in him as a poetic work, so that in this relatively early period in Weimar he only needed to add a bit to it and rework it a little to be able to present it as a reading. This is the version that was discovered later on in the form of a handwritten copy and published at the end of the nineteenth century. It goes by the rather tasteless name of Goethe's *Urfaust*. What we have here, in other words, is the form of *Faust* that Goethe had in his possession very early on.

Then we have a version of *Faust*, the so-called *Faust Fragment* that Goethe published in 1790 as a result of certain feelings. I say "as a result of certain feelings" intentionally, because people have connected the fact that he published it at all with the idea that at that time he was actually in a state of despair at not being able to finish writing it. It was thus a matter of his putting everything he had thought about it until then behind him because he could see no possibility of continuing his work on it any further.

Next, we have the version of *Faust* that appeared before the reading public at the beginning of the nineteenth century. This is more or less the same as our present *Faust*, Part I, with the "Dedication," the "Prologue in Heaven," and so on. But it is still not the whole picture, because at that time Goethe had already finished writing the "Helen of Troy" scene that today constitutes Act Three of the second part. This means that at the very time Goethe had this version of *Faust*, the connection of the Faust-figure with the figure of Helen was already very much alive in his thoughts and feelings.

Finally, we see Goethe in 1824, at the age of 75, going at the second part with renewed vigor to round it out and polish it into a complete poetic work, which he would then leave behind after his death as a last will and testament.

So you see, we are dealing here with a work of poetry that not only accompanied Goethe as he worked away at it his whole life long but was continually changing its entire inner configuration, its content, its form, its overall concept—in fact, everything about it—over this long period of time. Now we must add that *Faust* is just where Goethe shows himself to be one of the most sincere poets in world literature. For as he was writing *Faust* it was never Goethe's concern to produce something that was merely beautiful or perfect in an outward sense, but simply to give what he was able to give out of the deepest, innermost recesses of his honesty, to give in plain and unvarnished form the truth that his soul had grasped at any given moment. Goethe's life was first and foremost a continual striving, and we can follow how it develops and becomes more and more sublime from decade to decade as he himself thinks and comes to see new things and establish relationships with one new world after another. Taking these things into account, we see how important it was that Goethe always let what was living in him flow into his poetic work. So, it was quite reasonable for Goethe himself to find this or that spot in his *Faust* text quite problematic when he went back to work on what he had written in earlier decades. By now, he himself had moved on, but the work from those former years had to be continued.

Now we want to look at something that will allow us to use *Faust* to see into Goethe's soul a little. If you take the *Urfaust*, you will see that what is in it is more or less what Goethe brought along with him to Weimar and rounded off in his first years there. We could call it the work of an extraordinarily gifted young poet who had not yet been able to unearth for himself very much of what was still lying buried in his soul. In this form of his *Faust* poem, all the connections that Goethe in his later life would have called connections with the spiritual world are still missing. The scenes we have here are really only the ones set in the world of human beings, representing what Goethe had been able to grasp and portray with such youthful freshness in an external and completely realistic way. People who prefer to remain at this level in their relationship to the spiritual world their whole life long, closing their eyes to any change or development on Goethe's part, will obviously find contradictions. Goethe once said of such people:

> They say Faust's pretty good†
> And also find
> Things in my other works
> That suit their mind.
>
> The same old stuff is what
> They really like;
> The lousy bums believe
> I've gone on strike!

But we can also look at the situation from the standpoint of Goethe's soul. Let us look back at that period from 1787 to 1788, in the second half of the next-to-last decade of the eighteenth century, when Goethe was in Rome during his trip to Italy. Something had been going on in Goethe's soul between the time he wrote what we find brought together in the *Urfaust* and the time he spent later on in Italy when the form of art he provided in his *Tasso* and his *Iphigenie* was what he regarded as the most suitable one for him at that time. What had been going on? Think for a moment what it means that the same personality who produced the curious, chaotic first version of *Götz von Berlichingen*† was able to fashion such a wonderfully harmonious form later on in *Tasso* and *Iphigenie*. It was the very same person. Some day, when people no longer know that all these works are by the same poet, it will be possible to prove on the basis of internal evidence that the same person could not possibly have written them. We can say that in the truest sense of the word Goethe himself was a combination of several different individuals. Goethe had overcome the Goethe of 1775, and in 1788 it was this later Goethe who wrote the "Witch's Kitchen" (2337 ff.) and the marvelous scene beginning, "Exalted Spirit, you gave me, gave me all of what I asked for"† (3217-28) in the Villa Borghese in Rome. A very significant fact for our understanding of Goethe's soul is that the images of the *Urfaust*, which he had written down in the titanism of his early years in rebellion against the prevailing intellectual currents, rose up before his inner spiritual vision out of the same mood that had given birth to his *Götz von Berlichingen*. The same Goethe felt impelled to bring moderation and harmony into his way of looking at things and to take up the work on these old characters again in Rome. He had to make an honest and forthright effort to add something to *Faust* out of his own time and to try to develop *Faust* further in the same way he himself had developed. It was a very difficult situation. The earlier time was long since gone, but the working poet still had to confront it. He had two choices: to rewrite everything written up to that time or to take the manuscripts in front of him at the age of forty as actual copies of the way he had been at the ages of seventeen, twenty-five, thirty, and so on. On the other hand, if he had rewritten the whole of *Faust*, he would not have been true to himself, for then he would not have been able to express the same mood that had been present in him when he first became interested in writing these scenes. This is why Goethe's *Faust* is so immensely important and at the same time so inaccessible to the philistinism of our life today. But something else was present in Goethe's soul while he was writing the "Witch's Kitchen" and the "Exalted Spirit" scene ["Forest and Cavern," (3217 ff.)].

What had he experienced in the meantime? Everything in his soul had drawn him closer and closer to the fourth post-Atlantean cultural epoch,† the Greco-Roman era, and by this time his enthusiasm for it was very great. "I suspect," he wrote from Italy,† "that I am on the trail of the laws of Greek art and that those artists created their works in accordance with the same laws as Nature herself."

In his search for the God in Nature, Goethe had become a deep student of the writings of Spinoza.† Now, in front of those works of art in Italy, he seemed to be standing in the presence of Art itself as he said†: "Here is Necessity, here is God." He now felt the inner challenge of what he had absorbed from his own culture in the North. Its essential features were what had played into it as the first morning rays of the fifth post-Atlantean cultural epoch.† From the thirteenth to the seventeenth centuries, some peculiar things had been very much alive in it, such as the strange belief in the Devil, the legends, and everything having to do with the origin of the Faust saga. But no matter how strange some of these things that first appeared with the dawning of the Middle Ages may seem to us today, they are all connected with the cultural epoch that gradually superseded the Greco-Roman era. Now, however, what came to stand before Goethe's inner spiritual vision in a most remarkable way was the perfection of the human being in Greco-Roman times. Such perfection had been brought about by the fact that the Greco-Roman period was the middle one of the post-Atlantean epoch, preceded by three others that will manifest again in a certain way later on. This fourth period was the focal point of the post-Atlantean epoch, the era in which human beings came out of themselves and penetrated most deeply into the physical world. We can see in all these things the origin of the isolated, finished quality and calm perfection of Greek art† that had impressed Goethe so strongly. He felt that when you have an art work of this kind in front of you, you have no need to go out into space; everything has flowed into the work of art itself. It was this total outflow into the form, the "how" of the work,† that Goethe found so appealing.

In the culture of Northern Europe there was an element that one part of his being had loved deeply in earlier years but to which he was now totally opposed. Let us take a Gothic cathedral or any art work by Dürer or Holbein,† for example: all things that pave the way for the fifth cultural epoch. In themselves, these works of art are incomplete; their true content only reveals itself to our patient searching. A Greek temple is complete, so much so that there do not need to be any people in it at all. A Gothic cathedral, on the other hand, is not; it only becomes a finished work of art when it has pious people in it, absorbed in their devotions. In Greece, right on into the period of its cultural decline, we always have the spiritual in the outer form of the art work itself. But everywhere in Dürer we have the striving to go more deeply than what the outer form expresses. Sometimes, in the Greek sense, these forms are not beautiful at all, because a powerful will is trying to express itself in them. In his youth Goethe was a great admirer of this kind of art, of Shakespeare's art, for example, which is the exact opposite of Greek art. What we find opposed here in Goethe's soul like two conflicting elements would hardly have generated such an inner uproar in anyone else's soul. Goethe wanted nothing less than to have the supersensible, the spiritual itself, as an integral part of whatever came toward him directly in the outer world. He was not one of those who find satisfaction in the outer form alone; it was rather the case that he treasured the form he saw in Greco-Roman art so highly because the supersensible was actually present in it. The form itself was something supersensible. Goethe saw that whatever is given to us in Nature, or comes to us from the surrounding world in any other way, is maya, the great illusion. But he demanded from art that into this maya it should place the True: the Greek temple or the Greek god, for example, both of which are the True, from the standpoint of the supersensible. So we see Goethe, athirst for the truth of the supersensible within the sensory, intoxicated with a yearning for Greco-Roman art because it was through the medium of art that he wanted to insert the realm of truth into the realm of maya. Art was to be purged of everything untrue.

On the other hand, he saw how dangerous it is to demand this sort of thing from art. Spiritual science tells us why it is dangerous: each art form is connected with a specific historical epoch and cannot reappear at a later time. Here was something for the fourth period, not for the fifth. Human destiny in the fifth period requires us to direct our attention to the supersensible, which cannot express itself in form. Hence that struggle in the cultures of the North to wrest oneself away from everything external and to view the spiritual in everything in such a grotesque way. As he sat in the Villa Borghese, Goethe was already saying to himself that we are not really being true as long as we are only talking about these things, as he had done when he was young. For the only way to avoid speaking in empty phrases is to saturate our everyday speech with inner soul being. It seemed to Goethe that all the works he had created to date were something untrue in the light of the plan he now had of inserting truth into maya in the form of art. And so the urge arose in him to bring over into the new age what it was from the Greco-Roman period that could live on in any period as something eternal. Please grasp this clearly. We are not consciously aware of what carries over from one cultural period to the next, for each epoch rests on the one that precedes it. The fourth cultural epoch was living on unconsciously in the fifth one. All this was alive in Goethe as an urgent question: How can it be brought over in a conscious way? How can something of eternal value be made to stream over from its life in a former time into the present one? What would some living element of the Greco-Roman culture look like if we could bring it over into our present-day awareness consciously? Furthermore, how would a person who had lived fully in the Greco-Roman age and were now to bring his or her conscious awareness over into the later age consciously, have to look?

With this thought a chord was struck in Goethe's soul, which for that time could not have resounded any more profoundly: the whole problem of reincarnation or re-embodiment. It resounded in such a way that he asked himself how it might be possible to consciously bring the contents of a previous culture over into those of a later one. This lived in him in such a way that he did not know how to get hold of it in his own soul. For there now lay buried in the subconscious soul something that had transformed his own soul in such a way that in the transition from the fourth to the fifth cultural period such a peculiar figure as that of Faust was able to make its appearance.

Faust was an actual person; he registered for courses at the University of Heidelberg. What kind of a character was he anyway? As a contemporary of Nostradamus, in a certain sense, he was a person who felt a certain longing to bring up more or less consciously, from the hidden depths of the soul, something that had to be brought forth again at that time. Now the fourth cultural epoch is what had to be brought up again, and it was Faust's task to do just this. Goethe never doubted the justification of such a modern spirit alongside the other one that had arisen as an ideal in Goethe's soul out of the Greco-Roman age. But now, he said to himself, this spirit must dive down into its own soul-depths and acquaint itself with everything that splits us apart as human beings whenever we enter the higher worlds. Goethe could feel that hardly have we met the "Guardian of the Threshold"† when we are immediately approached by a multitude of figures. And so Faust became a highly questionable figure for him, but one he could not simply ignore: How is the spirit I have brought over from the fourth cultural epoch contained in a justifiable way in a spirit in transition from the fourth to the fifth epochs?

It is contained in such a way that there must play into its striving every danger that a person encounters who passes by the Guardian of the Threshold and goes on into the supersensible world. The fact that Faust enters the supersensible world is evident from his longing and his feeling-filled contemplation. Goethe knew this from the very beginning, but he only gradually became aware of the dangers still connected with it in those days. Today these dangers are no longer present, since they can be avoided by following the principles outlined in my book *How to Know Higher Worlds*. But Faust still had to face these dangers. The way Faust enters the supersensible world is of such a nature that the moment a certain form of Imaginative knowledge lights up, the life of the lower passions is also stimulated, ignited, and inflamed. These two things cannot be separated unless the pupil decides to follow a regular path of spiritual development. You can read about this in Blavatsky's[†] works too. We need only note, she says, how the karma of people who want to penetrate into the spiritual world changes, how they can bring misfortune to the world around them if they do not enter the higher worlds in a regular way, how they spread the circles of the impulses in them over their whole environment. On the other hand, their own drives and passions also intermingle with the higher world, surrounding them with whole worlds of figures.

Goethe had to imagine such real spiritual seekers, standing as he did on his firm sense of the absolute truth of the Greco-Roman culture. In particular, he had to imagine the spiritual seekers of the fifth cultural epoch with all their attendant difficulties. What do such people find around them? What dangers are they exposed to? Nothing in the whole world of the senses is remotely similar to what they experience. They must enter the world of the spirit. But first they have to know how the experiences of people who do this differ from those in the world of the senses. This is why Goethe wrote the "Witch's Kitchen." His intention was to portray the whole supersensible milieu that Faust would have to enter, because people needed to be shown what the supersensible worlds look like in view of all the factors we have now dealt with. We have to take what this "Witch's Kitchen" offers us literally as an integral part of the spiritual world. We have to know that Goethe was so familiar with certain secrets of the supersensible world that he was able to give an accurate depiction of how things are actually perceived by clairvoyant consciousness. This whole description of the bubbling-up of human passions at the moment the spiritual world is entered, which at that time was still a fearful undertaking, is an extraordinarily accurate depiction of that world. All the passions that bubble up here are reflected even in the names of the "She-Apes" (Meerkatzen) and the "He-Apes" (Meerkater), as well as in everything else that is so appropriately portrayed in the "Witch's Kitchen."

Now, however, Goethe's concern is not to just stop short at this world of the untrue, but to get Faust up to the level of truth. To be sure, this world is absolutely true in terms of the facts it depicts, but it is still more of an illusion than the usual sense-perceptible world is maya for the senses. This is how Goethe has to strive to approach the truth. He has to depict how the outer world that Mephistopheles belongs to surrounds the supersensible one represented in the "Witch's Kitchen." Goethe wants to show that Faust can get out of the world that Mephisto can find so stimulating. Imagine being placed into the supersensible world as Faust is in the "Witch's Kitchen." If you can no longer find your way around in this world, then not even the laws of our everyday numeric system can make any sense either. It is not important to work out some ingenious interpretation of the witch's multiplication table; what matters is to feel what it is really like to be faced with what is written in this table:

You have to see
From one make ten
And two let go,
Make three alike
And then you're rich.
Then lose the four!
From five and six,

So says the witch,
Make seven and eight,
That's how it's done:
And nine is one,
And ten is none.
This is how witches multiply. (2540-52)

What matters is that you place yourself in the soul of a person who suddenly finds him- or herself in a world where everything is different, after learning the normal number system. Explaining these things in a more or less ingenious way only ruins the poetry; it makes it seem as though the poet himself had merely dreamed up a bunch of symbols. That was not the case here; our poet was faced with a real-life situation. If we call Goethe a symbol maker or an abstract thinker, we show how little understanding we have for what is real and significant about this situation. What had to happen to Faust if he was not to ruin either his own karma or that of those around him, at Gretchen's house, for example? It was a long way from this Faust to the one who, out of his inner perception of the fourth cultural epoch, would speak the words: Oh, the human heart is the source of imaginations that spin the whole world of illusion up into a net:

Exalted Spirit, you gave me, gave me all
Of what I asked for. It was not in vain
That in the fire you turned your face to me.
You gave me glorious Nature for my kingdom
And strength to feel her, to enjoy her. Not
Cold staring in amazement give you only;
To gaze into her breast so deep you grant me
As into the deep bosom of a friend.
You lead the rank and file of living creatures
Past my eyes, and teach me to perceive
My brothers in quiet bush, in air and water.
And when the storm in forest roars and crackles,
The giant spruce in falling strips down, crushing,
Crunching, nearby trunks and nearby branches,

And hill responds to fall with hollow thunder;
You lead me then to this safe cavern, show
Me then myself, and then to my own breast
Profound and secret wonders are revealed. (3217-34)

This is the Faust who speaks with Nature by merging his own world of imaginations with the maya or illusion of the world around him, a different Faust from the one to whom Mephistopheles is allowed to say so strangely:

How would you, poor son of earth,
Have led your life without me?
Of such nonsensical imaginations
I've cured you for a long time yet to be. (3266-69)

How has he managed to cure him? By guiding him into the supersensible world. But this is not how Faust is to be cured of Imagination. His task is to recognize Imagination as encompassing the great maya or illusion itself. What is needed for Faust to be able to say:

And when the storm in forest roars and crackles,
The giant spruce in falling strips down, crushing,
Crunching, nearby trunks and nearby branches,
And hill responds to fall with hollow thunder;
You lead me then to this safe cavern, show
Me then myself, and then to my own breast
Profound and secret wonders are revealed. (3228-34)

What must Faust develop so that he can open himself to the world with such classic calmness? If he does not develop something quite specific, he will lose himself completely as he faces what goes on in the "Witch's Kitchen." He does not have to proceed like some theosophical theoretician but must come to himself as a person with a very specific way of experiencing things. He must view himself objectively. While he is confronting the events of the "Witch's Kitchen" something has to approach him in which he can view himself. Something of higher truth must appear to him in Imagination, but it must be something that has a higher reality than the "Witch's Kitchen." Now, as we know, a man's higher self is female. This is depicted in a very real way in the appearance of "Helen" in the "Witch's Kitchen." It is the appearance of the etheric body, which can only be viewed from a certain distance. Because Mephisto does not understand this etheric form, all he can say about it is:

> Once you have this drink in you
> You'll see Helen in every girl you meet. (2603-04)

A truly poetic impulse is at work here, portraying a striving for something that, from its surface appearance alone, people will not be able to appreciate for a long time to come. For people of the fifth epoch a question will long resound as to just what it is they need. This question could easily appear ambiguous, but once we have its true answer, we find it easy enough to understand. What could we say in the face of the most important human concern of the fifth epoch?

> What is cursed, yet always welcome?
> What longed for, and yet chased away?
> What is all the time defended?
> What chided sorely and then sued?
> Whom do you not dare to summon?
> Whom do all love to hear named?
> What's approaching your throne's dais?
> What has sent itself away? (4743-50)

Goethe presents us with this strange passage full of riddles near the beginning of the second part. We could find words enough to solve these riddles, but for our time we will find the best solution by answering them all with a single word. That word is: spirit. Goethe did not mean for the solution to be so easy, and he certainly did not intend to lay it on so thick himself. But the spirit is cursed in the most varied ways, and yet it is also always welcome. We have only to look at many people's spiritual development to know "what is longed for, and yet chased away." In Goethe's time, the spirit could only show itself in the form of the court jester; it was rarely welcome in any other form.

This is the big question: How, using what it has and knows, is the fifth post-Atlantean civilization ever to arrive at true knowledge of the spirit? How can it come to grasp the being that is the actual foundation of the world? Actually, there has never been a cultural epoch in which humankind was better suited to finding the spirit in the form of the ego than our own. But how was it first possible to find the true nature of the human being by grasping this ego in terms of the astral body? Let us assume that a person of the nineteenth or even of the sixteenth century wanted to go about finding the astral body. We do not have Imagination at first in our process of knowing the external world. The astral body, the factor that has been the basis of external ego-development ever since the period of the Old Moon,† had first to be sought.

Now, because all energies can go everywhere, we can of course arrive at something even when we apply our intellect to things or objects. But what will we get out of the astral body if we do this? Let us assume what will arise out of the astral body when we apply to it what is very well suited to external maya. We cannot express this any more fittingly than by calling what emerges in this way a "Homunculus." The Homunculus has something to do with the astral body, as the latter organizes itself around what constitutes the ego. Since we have to do here with the realm of the supersensible, Goethe was quite justified in coining a word that by its very nature points to something produced in the supersensible world. Wagner himself says—for, after all, the philistine intellect is what produces the Homunculus in the laboratory:

> It's coming! The moving mass grows clearer!
> The higher product [*Überzeugung*] ever truer, truer!
> What formerly was praised as mysterious in Nature
> We dare to undertake with understanding,
> And what She organized in other ways,
> We've managed here to crystallize ourselves. (6855-60)

Commentators have sought to interpret this word "Überzeugung" (6856) in the most peculiar ways because they could never understand that its proper pronunciation here is not "Über*zeug*ung" [a "conviction"], but that Goethe is speaking here of an "*Überz*eugung" [a "higher product" or "product from on high"], in the same sense as he speaks of an "*Über*mensch"[†] ["higher type of human being"]. But then the second part of *Faust* has been interpreted in such a peculiar way that even the spelling mistakes have been interpreted. For example, when Goethe dictated, and his secretary wrote: "Nun strebe nicht nach höheren Orden," etc. ["Now do not strive for higher orders/ranks"], "Orden" was really not what was meant here. The man Goethe was dictating to wrote "Orden" instead of "Orten" ["places"].

These things all show us that once Goethe had managed to envision Faust's spiritual striving in its totality, one question became an especially burning one for him: How can a consciousness be recuperated consciously? How can one, for example, recuperate the consciousness that lived in Helen, who now appeared before his spirit? That was the burning question. In this connection I have to mention that 1797 was the year the great soul who was Goethe underwent the most profound change that he ever experienced. At the very time when the Faust figure within him made him think of it as having come from something more than his own private soul processes, and when he had no choice but to write the "Prologue in Heaven," everything in his inner being changed. From now on he felt the need to give more and more concrete shape to the conscious carry-over of consciousness from the fourth post-Atlantean epoch into the fifth. This is also the origin of his striving to somehow resolve the question.

I have often indicated that Goethe sought to resolve the question of reincarnation poetically by showing us that what is eternal about Helen can be found at rest in the spiritual world of the "Mothers." But it will not do to force our way into the spiritual world unprepared. If we do, what paralyzed Faust when he looked at Helen's image will paralyze us as well. Before it can take on a body of physical nature, the spirit must first surround itself with a soul. Helen is surrounding herself with soul at the moment when, in the astral world, soul-material is being placed at her disposal in the form of Homunculus. What we see in Homunculus are the forces of the astral body of a human being who is entering into earthly existence.

He isn't missing any spiritual features,
But sorely lacks a body one could touch. (8249-50)

Everything is properly depicted, even to the final enshrouding of the spirit by external Nature, where we are shown how the spirit actually takes on its external corporeality. For this to happen, Homunculus has to pass through all the elements of Nature. Starting with the mineral world, he goes on through the world of plants. Goethe found the wonderful expression: "Things are greening so" (8266), in order to indicate what can pass over into human nature from the greening world of plants. And so it goes, on through all the kingdoms. "You have time until you're human" (8326).

But then you can't go any farther.
For once you have become a human,
There's nothing else for you to do. (8331-32)

But things do go on and on until, as so wonderfully depicted here, the human being enters earthly existence through the mystery of love, the mystery of the opposition of the sexes. After Goethe has depicted everything that precedes this mystery, he has the Sirens announce the miracle itself:

What fiery wonder transfigures the waves
That shatter each other in sparkling array?
It glistens and gleams as it wavering approaches,
The bodies aglow in their passage through night,
And fire all around them is flowing in rings;
So rule then, dear Eros, from whom all began! (8474-79)

And here the human being enters earthly existence.

Hail to the gently rocking breezes!
Hail to the crevasses, rich in their secrets!
Praises high to all you four,
Elements, forever more! (8484-87)

We turn the page. The third act begins, and there is Helen. We must not touch these things with clumsy fingers or entrust them to merely superficial interpretations. They can only be depicted in such a way that we are able to pursue and follow up their content delicately by dissolving them in ever-changing water,† just as Goethe did. But this is all there. Goethe was filled with the urgency to raise to the level of conscious awareness something that had once lived unconsciously in human beings of the fourth cultural epoch and must now become part of modern consciousness.

Finally, we see how Goethe retains the use of the moral-religious-mystical element so characteristic of the northern cultural world to show how something that had appeared without justification in the "Witch's Kitchen" could in fact develop into something fully justified after all. How splendidly he shows us this in the closing scene, in which we experience not only the wonderful interplay of spiritual science and mystery drama but also the "Chorus Mysticus," which is such a marvelous concentration of everything living in Goethe that it can actually serve as a symbol of spiritual science itself. This had already been indicated earlier by the roses strewn down from heaven. So when we hear:

> All that must pass away
> Is but a simile;
> Here the inadequate
> Becomes attainment;
> The indescribable,
> Here it is done;
> The Ever-Feminine
> Draws us upward and on;† (12104-11)

what we find expressed in these few lines is everything we acknowledge as spiritual-scientific truth.

3
The Gospel of St. Mark

Basel, September 15, 1912

[From GA 139: Excerpt on Faust and Hamlet][†]

... I should like to turn your attention to the first millennium of human evolution, as it was thought to be in earlier times. There, in the remotest period of this first millennium, stands the towering figure of Homer, the Greek poet and singer. Hardly more than the name remains of this man to whom are ascribed those two great poems that are among the greatest of human accomplishments: The Iliad and the Odyssey. Scarcely more than his name is known, and in the nineteenth century doubts were cast even on that—but we need not dwell any further on that now. The more we know of the figure of Homer, the more we admire him. For a person who studies such things, the characters created by Homer whom we meet in the Iliad and the Odyssey seem more alive than all the purely political figures of Greece. Many different people who have studied Homer over and over again have said that because of the precision of his descriptions and his manner of presentation he must have been a doctor. Others say he must have been an artist, a sculptor, or a craftsman. Napoleon admired the way Homer described tactics and strategy; still others think he must have been a beggar wandering through the land.

However all this may be, it certainly does demonstrate the unique individuality of Homer. Consider one of his characters, Hector. Some time, when you have the time, I would ask you to study the figure of Hector in the Iliad—how vividly he is described so that he stands as a complete personality before us. Notice his affection for his paternal city, Troy, and for his wife, Andromache; notice his relationships to Achilles and to his army, and the way he commands it. Try to call up this man before your minds, this man who possessed all the tenderness of a husband, who clung in the ancient way to his home city of Troy, and who suffered such disillusions as only really great human beings can—remember his relationship to Achilles. Hector, as presented by Homer, is a towering figure from very ancient times, a man of great all-embracing humanity, for of course what Homer is describing belongs to a period well before his own, in the darkness of the past. Hector stands out above all the others, all those figures who seem mythical enough to our modern eyes.

Now take this one figure. Skeptics of all kinds and philologists may indeed doubt there ever was a Hector at all, in the same way as they doubt the existence of Homer. But anyone who takes into consideration what may be understood from a purely human viewpoint will be convinced that Homer describes only facts that actually occurred. Hector was a living person who strode through Troy, and Achilles and the other figures were equally real. They still stand before us as personages of real earthly life. We look back to them as people of a different kind from ourselves, who are difficult to understand but whom the poet is able to bring before our souls in every detail. Now let us place before our souls a figure such as Hector, one of the chief Trojan commanders, who is defeated by Achilles. In such a personage we have something that belongs to the old pre-Christian age, something by which we can measure what people were like before the time when Christ lived on earth.

I will now draw your attention to another figure, a remarkable figure of the fifth century B.C.: the great philosopher Empedocles,[†] who spent a large part of his life in Sicily. Not only was he the first to speak of the four elements, fire, water, air, and earth, maintaining that everything that happens in the material realm caused by the mingling and separating out again of these four elements results from the principles of love and hate ruling in them. Mainly, he left his mark on Sicily by calling important political institutions into being, and he went about trying to lead the people into a life of spirituality. When we look back to Empedocles we find that he lived an adventurous life, as well as a deeply spiritual one. Perhaps others will doubt the truth of what I am about to say, but spiritual science knows that Empedocles went about in Sicily not only as a statesman, but also as an initiate and a magician, just as Hector, as depicted by Homer, walked in Troy. And in order to characterize Empedocles' remarkable attitude toward the world, the fact confronts us—which is not an invention, but really true—that in order, as it were, to unite himself with all existence around him, he ended by throwing himself into Mount Etna and was consumed by its fire. This is how a second figure of the pre-Christian era appears to us.

Now let us consider such figures as these with the methods of modern spiritual science. First of all, we know that these individualities will appear again, will return to life. We shall disregard their intermediate incarnations and look for them somehow in the post-Christian era. We then see something of the change brought about by time, something that can help us to understand how the Mystery of Golgotha[†] intervened in human evolution. If we can say: Such figures as Hector and Empedocles have appeared again; how do they move among other human beings in the post-Christian era?—then we will have illustrated the impact of the Mystery of Golgotha, the fulfillment and beginning of a new age, by means of these souls themselves. As serious anthroposophists who have come together here, we no longer need to recoil from the communications of genuine spiritual science, which can be verified by means of external observations.

I should now like to turn your attention to something that took place in the post-Christian era, and perhaps again it may be said that the person concerned was a fictional personage. But this fictional personage can be traced back to a real individuality that was once alive. I direct your attention to the character created by Shakespeare in his *Hamlet.* Anyone who knows the development of Shakespeare, insofar as it can be known externally, and especially someone who is acquainted with it through spiritual science, will know that Shakespeare's Hamlet is none other than the transformed real Prince of Denmark, who also lived at one time. I cannot go into everything underlying the historical prototype of the fictional figure of Hamlet, but through the research of spiritual science I can offer you a striking example of how a man, a spirit of ancient times, reappears in the post-Christian era. The real figure underlying Hamlet, as presented by Shakespeare, is Hector. The same soul that lived in Hamlet lived in Hector. It is just by such a characteristic example as this, and the striking way the two different souls manifest themselves, that we can interpret what happened in the intervening time. A personality such as that of Hector stands before us in the pre-Christian age. Then comes the intervention of the Mystery of Golgotha in human evolution, and the spark it kindled in Hector's soul causes a figure, a prototype of Hamlet, to arise, of whom Goethe said, "This is a soul that is unable to deal with any situation and is not equal to its position, who is assigned a task but is unable to fulfill it." We may ask why Shakespeare expressed it in this way. He did not know. But anyone who can investigate the connections through spiritual science knows what forces were at work behind these things. The poet creates in the unconscious; before him stands, so to speak, first the figure that he creates, and then, as in a tableau of which he himself knows nothing, the whole individuality with which the figure is connected. Why does Shakespeare choose particular qualities in Hamlet and sharply emphasize them, qualities that perhaps Hamlet's own contemporaries would not have noticed? Because he observes them against the background of the era: he feels how different a soul has become in its transition from the old life to the new. Hamlet the doubter, the skeptic who has lost the ability to cope with the situations he meets in life, the vacillator: this is what Hector, once so sure of himself, has become.

Let me direct your attention to another figure of modern times, who was also first presented to humanity in a poetic picture, in a poem whose protagonist will certainly live on in humanity for a long time to come when for posterity the poet—such as Homer or Shakespeare—is no longer in existence. About Homer we know nothing at all, and about Shakespeare we know very little indeed. What the various compilers of notes and biographers of Goethe have written will long since have been forgotten. In spite of the printing press and other modern inventions, what interests people about Goethe at the present time will likewise have been long forgotten. But large as life, and modeled from life, there will stand the figure of Faust that Goethe has created. Just as people today know nothing of Homer, but a great deal about Hector and Achilles, they will some day not know much about the personality of Goethe either—and that will be a good thing—but they will always know a lot about Faust.

Faust, you see, as he comes down to us in literary form and is then reshaped and brought to a certain conclusion by Goethe, is a figure who can be traced back to a real historical personage living in the sixteenth century.† He actually existed, but not as Goethe portrayed him in his *Faust*. Why then did Goethe portray him as he did? Goethe himself did not know. But when he directed his attention to the traditional Faust that had been handed down to him, a Faust he had known ever since the puppet play of his boyhood days, forces stemming from what stood behind Faust worked within him, the forces of Faust's previous incarnation, the forces of Empedocles, the old Greek philosopher. All these streamed into the figure of Faust. And one could say: Empedocles throws himself into Mount Etna and unites himself with the fire-element of the Earth, whereby what we could call pre-Christian Nature mysticism becomes a fact. What a wonderful spiritualization of this mysticism it then is, we can say, when Faust ascends through Pater Seraphicus and the others into the fire-element of heaven in the final tableau of Goethe's *Faust* ! Slowly and gradually a totally new spiritual direction enters into what humanity is striving for in a deeper way. Already some time ago it began to dawn on the most profound minds of humanity that, although they had no knowledge whatsoever of reincarnation or karma, when they were considering a great and comprehensive soul whom they wished to portray out of the firm foundations of their inner life, they found themselves portraying the gleam that came over to them from earlier incarnations. Although Shakespeare did not know that Hamlet was Hector, he nevertheless portrayed him the way we know him, unaware that the same soul had lived in both of them. In the same way, Goethe portrayed Faust as though Empedocles were standing behind him with all his peculiarities, because Faust was the very person in whom the soul of Empedocles had lived. But it is characteristic that this is the way the human race progresses and develops.

I have mentioned two characteristic figures, in both of whom we can perceive that when great figures of earlier times reappear in a modern post-Christian age, they are so shaken in the very depths of their souls that they can hardly find their way through life. Everything that was within them in the past is still within them. For example, when we allow Hamlet to work upon us, we feel that all of Hector's might is within him. But we also feel that this might cannot come forth in the post-Christian era; that it meets with obstacles at first; that something now works upon the soul that is the beginning of something new, whereas in the figures of antiquity something was coming to an end. Both Hector and Empedocles, as they stand there before us in full sculptural relief, represent a conclusion. But what is working on further in humanity must find new pathways into new incarnations. This is how it stands with Hector in Hamlet, as well as with Empedocles in Faust, who had within him the whole Empedoclean urge to plumb the deepest depths of Nature and could therefore say, "I will lay aside the Bible for a time and study Nature and medicine. I will no longer be a theologian." He felt the need to have dealings with demonic beings, which made him wander through the world, much marveled at but misunderstood. The Empedoclean element works on in him, but it cannot find its way to what the human being must be, now that a new age has dawned....

4

Faust's Struggle for the Christ-permeated Source of Life

An Easter contemplation. Dornach, April 4, 1915

(After a dramatic performance of the "Easter Night" scene with eurythmy†)

Among the Easter performances we have just been privileged to witness were also the ones that show us how the soul of a man who comes very close to passing through the portal of death of his own free will is pulled back to the world of earthly life at the very last moment by the message of Easter. It seems to me that of all the impressions Goethe's *Faust* can leave us with, the one we have of this scene must surely be one of the most profound.

Now, so to speak, *after* the transformation of the scenery† signifying the world and its evolution, try to connect what you have taken into your souls as a future prospect within the *Faust*-drama itself with what I told you yesterday, *before* the transformation, about the momentous and real vision that can arise before the human soul when it stands before the symbolic representation of Christ Jesus at rest within the grave.

Think about what could be said yesterday†: that the sight of what has become part of human life in the course of earthly evolution in connection with the worlds of Lucifer and Ahriman† is awakened through a corresponding act of spiritual seeing or spiritual feeling. Remember also that in *Faust* we have to do with a soul that tells us quite openly from the very beginning how deeply steeped it is in Ahrimanic knowledge and Ahrimanic insights.

Let us look into this soul as it struggles in its bondage to Ahrimanic wisdom to make its way to what we may call from our particular point of view the Christ-permeated wellspring of life. What a significant moment this is in the history of a human soul! Let us contemplate this human soul with all the powers of our spiritual understanding. There it stands before us, with all the knowledge it has acquired in its observations of the external material world and its interconnected activities, all the knowledge this soul has been able to garner with the instruments a physical scientist uses to penetrate Nature's inner secrets.

But how far has this soul really come with all the research associated with these various instruments, as well as with the vial of juices that for earthly life "make us drunk without delay" (732)? We can feel Ahrimanic influence already working at this Faust-soul's side, and that this Ahrimanic being has a connection with earthly death. Isn't it as though this human soul, filled as it is with Ahrimanic influence, were simply harvesting the fruits of its Ahrimanic knowledge? The result of the knowledge Ahriman can give to human beings on the earth is summarized in the words:

> I greet you, one and only precious vial!
> As now I take you down with reverence,
> In you I honor human wit and art.
> Quintessence of the juices of sweet slumber
> And extract of all death's finest forces,
> I see you, and my pain is lessened,
> I grasp you, and my striving's eased,
> My spirit's flooding stream begins to ebb,
> The high sea's channel opens out to me,
> The glassy waters shimmer at my feet,
> A new day lures me on to newer shores. (690-701)

Already this soul has the vision of arriving at the other shore where it may be able to find what it has been forced to believe it cannot find on this earth through its Ahrimanic entanglement. It already sees itself as passing over to that other shore:

> A fiery chariot, on air-light wings,
> Is floating up to me! I feel I'm ready
> To follow this new path through ether worlds
> To new, high spheres of pure activity.
> This noble life, this godly exaltation!

Still but a worm, you think you're worthy of it?
Make up your mind, be resolute, and turn
Your back upon the bright, sweet sun of earth!
Be bold and tear the daunting portals open
That others only wish to slither past.
The time has come to show the world through deeds
That manly worth is equal to the gods' on high,
To never quake before that somber cavern
In which the mind condemns itself to its own pain,
To strive to reach that passageway
Around whose narrow mouth the fires of hell are burning;
To cheerfully decide to take this step
And flow, no matter what the peril, out into the Void. (702-19)

Now, holding the other Ahrimanic instrument, he is ready to make his way over into those regions that Ahriman's school has taught him he will never have any knowledge of as long as his soul remains imprisoned in its earthly body. The soul is then torn out of this frame of mind by the sound of the Easter bells and the voices of the Easter choir. Faust's soul has its earthly life again, so that now, in the earthly body, this human soul will search for what it is meant to carry with it as the fruits of its lengthy seeking within the earthly body, through the portal of death and up into the fields of spirit where these fruits will be needed for the soul's further development.

What you have heard today from the first part of Goethe's *Faust*, as well as many other things that belong to this first part and this particular scene, originally appeared as the completed Part One of the poem in 1808. But a previous version, entitled *Faust, a Fragment*, had already been published in 1790. This fragment still did not have the final Gretchen scene, nor did it have the scene in which the events so significant for Faust's soul were brought before our souls today. Goethe published his fragment in 1790, still without the Easter scene ["Night," 606-807] and the monologue that leads us into the deepest layers of human soul-experience.

Toward the end of the nineteenth century another manuscript of the work was discovered that contained all the text that Goethe had written in the 1780s and even in the 1770s, as well as in the 1790s. We know it by the insipid title of *Urfaust*, or *"Original Faust,"* under which it was first published. This Easter scene was also not in the *Urfaust*, and we could easily say, "of course not." But why was it not there? Well, Goethe was a child of his time. In order for him to be able to depict the effect of the Christ-impulse[†] on Faust's soul, from his own standpoint and in harmony with his own soul-nature, Goethe would need to reach a certain degree of maturity. By 1790 he was not yet at that level.

Then in the 1790s that expansion of Goethe's soul took place that is reflected in the *Fairy Tale of the Green Snake and the Beautiful Lily*, a work we all know so well. This occurred in the time between the first publication of *Faust* without the Easter scene and the second one, which included it. What led to the infinitely profound expansion of Goethe's soul was what he had given form to in writing the *Fairy Tale of the Green Snake and the Beautiful Lily*. And not until he had had this experience was he able to understand how he could allow the Easter Resurrection scene to have such a profound effect on Faust's soul.

Let us now turn our attention to this soul itself, as we look deeply into it and try to find our way into the atmosphere of the poem's opening scene. This scene is pretty much the same in the various editions. As we know, it goes like this:

> So, now I've studied philosophy,
> Legal codes and medicine,
> And — even worse — theology!
> I gave them my all, as best I could.
> Now here I stand, poor fool that I am,
> No smarter than I was before.
> Got a Master's and even a Doctor's hood,
> But all I've done for the past ten years
> Is lead my students around by the nose,
> Up and down and back and forth –
> And see that we can't know one single thing! (354-64)

As we see, Faust has been at the university for the past ten years. Let us say he followed the normal career pathway; that means he must have started teaching there around his early thirties, so he has been leading his students around by the nose since he was about thirty! Now remember what I told you yesterday. Between the ages of thirty and forty we will be faced with the image of the Jupiter existence,† and the temptation I told you about yesterday will rise up before us. And when we stand before Christ Jesus lying in the grave, we have a vision, a prophetic vision, of that very temptation. Isn't this the vision presented to us in dramatic form in *Faust* ? Don't we plainly see Faust standing before the Easter Mystery? And don't we see him doing this just near the end of his thirties? May we not take it for granted that something is stirring in his feelings that every human being must feel arising from the Easter Mystery† as a premonition of the Jupiter-experience with Lucifer and Ahriman?

In Goethe's time it was impossible to represent this the way we can today. But Goethe was able to represent the feelings that had awakened in his heart as he contemplated the Easter Mystery, and those feelings were also stirring in Faust's soul. And at the moment when Mephisto-Ahriman approaches him, doesn't Faust seem to be feeling how completely his soul has fallen prey to the Ahrimanic forces? And as if he has to save himself from something? Yes, but from what? What does he have to save himself from? Can't we say that something of this kind had been Goethe's own experience when, as a mature adult, he had allowed the Faust-mood of his own youth to work on him again; and that as a mature soul he then felt, as far as he was able to in his own time, something of the Easter mood as we have experienced it here in the past few days? We can see from this how the need arose for him to include the Easter scene in *Faust*, which had not had such a scene in it before. The insertion of the Easter scene between 1790 and 1800 was what transformed *Faust* into a poem of genuine Christian spirit.

So what were the years that Faust still had to live through? What years was he shrinking back from with such reluctance that he was even willing to reach for the vial of poison? Well, they were the years of the second, the declining, half of his life, that part of life about which we have said that when we come to stand before the image of the Jupiter existence, we know we will have to carry on to Jupiter what Christ can give us as food for the journey, because otherwise we would not have any nourishment in the second half of life.

What is Faust looking for? He is looking for soul-nourishment for the second half of life. As a matter of fact, we are all looking for this, and have been ever since the Mystery of Golgotha entered Earth evolution. For what will assume physical-soul form during Jupiter existence is already living in the depths of our souls, and all of us must have some sense of this Faustian mood. We need a kind of strength that we can't have through what merely gives us freedom as human beings and leads us straight to Ahriman and Lucifer as a result. We need the strength to deal with the impulses within ourselves that are connected with the declining half of life. This is the Christ-power, the power that Christ possessed after he had passed through the portal of death without experiencing the second half of human life in an earthly body. Why did he not have this experience? Because this power needed to be made available to human beings in the second half of their life; and therefore it had to flow out into the aura of the earth, so that we as human beings could find it there in the course of the earth's evolution. Something resurrects through the Easter Mystery that we as human beings need so that we can go with our soul on its pilgrimage throughout the whole of our life on earth.

And now imagine the deep significance of this in Goethe's *Faust*. Faust had acquired—and Goethe knew by what means, for he had said so without using the Easter Mystery, when he published the *Fragment* without the Easter scene—Faust had acquired what can be learned by anyone through a connection with Lucifer and Ahriman, namely, what makes it possible for the soul to become truly free. Faust, however, who had fathomed the depths of his soul, knew full well that he would not be able to keep on living if this was all he had, that in order to keep on living he would need something else. Then Goethe matured to the point of being able to show that Faust needed the impulse of the Easter Mystery. Does not the Easter Mystery stand there before us in all its profundity in what Goethe was finally able to make his *Faust* into after he had reached full maturity, but which as yet had had no place in the *Faust* of 1790, because at that time he hadn't understood it yet?

How did the idea arise in the young Goethe's mind of writing this poetic drama that leads us into such immeasurable depths? We know that as a young man Goethe was deeply impressed by two different sources from the popular culture of his day. One was a puppet play, a simple reenactment of Faust's destiny by means of puppets; the other was a folk drama, *Doctor Faust.* Goethe's first contacts with the Faust theme were thus tinged by a strong folk element that sank so deeply into his soul that he had to ask himself, "Who is this Faust, anyway?" And the answer that came immediately was clear: this Faust must be the image of struggling humanity in general, a man who in his striving can explore all the hidden paths of the life of the human soul and who must find the way up into the clear heights of the spirit. As a young man, Goethe could already see that this human soul would have to follow a path of inner development. For what else does Faust in fact experience burning in his soul at the sight of the different signs but a meditation?—a meditation that eventually leads him to the vision of the Earth Spirit flooding through the earth with its waves of activity. As its response, the meditation receives these words:

> In floods of life, in storm of deeds
> Up and down I well,
> Back and forth I weave!
> Birth and grave
> An eternal sea,
> A changing weaving,
> A glowing living,
> I weave at the buzzing loom of time
> And work at God's living garment sublime. (501-09)

A meditation and a counter-meditation! This leads Faust at once into the very depths of life, but what about the way out? How is he led up into the spiritual heights?

When we consider the greatness of Goethe's conception of the striving Faust that owed its origin to the puppet play and the folk drama, and then consider what form this powerful conception took after Goethe had realized the Easter Mystery within the depths of his own soul, we may well ask what then became of *Faust* as Goethe continued to work with it in the further course of his life. And when we consider the power of the creative potential stirring in Goethe's soul under the influence of the Faust-impulse, we may well also ask: How did Goethe treat these impressions from an artistic and poetic point of view?

Well, one thing I just said can help satisfy our inclination to want to understand *Faust* from an esthetic, artistic point of view as well. In 1790 Goethe published a fragment that ended, more or less, with the cathedral scene. But the scene that makes *Faust* seem so wonderful for us today was not there. Goethe composed it later and added it when he was in Rome. It was the scene he added in 1787, and that we know today as the "Witch's Kitchen." From time to time he would add other scenes to the original manuscript, so that by the time the later scenes were added, the original had been written over and recopied so much that Goethe himself described it as a "yellowed, time-stained manuscript."† When at the end of the eighteenth century Schiller urged Goethe to get back to work on *Faust* and really finish it, Goethe told him how hard it would be for him to take up the threads of the old monster *Faust*† again and bring what had been lying around for so long to a fitting and consistent conclusion. The real problem was that for Goethe, *Faust* represented everything he was and appeared to be up to 1790, and he was afraid to add any new material to it that was the product of experiences he had undergone since then and that he had only later become mature enough to write.

So now, when we consider this first part of *Faust* in general, don't we see from a close study that it really is a patchwork of material that came about and was woven together at many different times? If people did not cling so strongly to traditional criticism, they would see in *Faust* the most powerful poetic conception of isolated human nature that has ever been given to the world. At the same time they would have to admit that, from the artistic and poetic point of view, *Faust* is also a very uneven and inharmonious work, never actually completed and so full of cracks and gaps that many things could be added to it that are still missing. Goethe's great genius was of such a nature that he could only ever bring what he had in mind to a satisfactory conclusion in fragmentary form. And as much as we admire the intense beauty of individual scenes, if we are impartial and do not rely solely on the traditional judgments of literary historians we can hardly fail to see that the *Faust* we have today is not a harmonious work of art but is patchy in many places, with many cracks and gaps that are still quite evident. Why is this?

When he was a very old man, Goethe once more undertook to complete the second part of his *Faust* ; isolated scenes of it were already in existence, and to these he added what new material he was able to add in his extreme old age. For example, the beginning of "The Classical-Romantic Phantasmagoria," "The Helen Interlude," was already complete by the turn of the century, and some other parts had been finished earlier. Again, we have every reason not to say, as some literary historians maintain nevertheless, that the second part of *Faust* can't be understood, or, as one man who is by no means stupid† but really very clever has said, that *Faust* is "a bungled, sorry piece of work thrown together by Goethe in his old age." That it certainly is not! On the other hand, it is a work the scope of which was so tremendous that even Goethe's rich life experience was not equal to the task of working it out to the last detail. Everyone may have an opinion about what is greatest in the world. But why is this so?

In a series of lectures I once gave in The Hague,† I pointed out that *Faust* is by no means anything new in the history of the world. Faust, as he lived in the puppet play that Goethe saw and in the folk drama as well, represents the human being who descends into the depths of spiritual experience in order to raise himself to the light-filled heights of knowledge. This representation was so realistic that it moved the greatest poet of modern times to invoke the aid of the Easter Mystery to save Faust's soul.

The Faust of the folk drama was taken almost directly from real life, from Dr. Georg Faustus,† in fact, who lived as a vagrant scholar in the second half of the Middle Ages. We learn this from Trithemius of Sponheim and other celebrated men who had met him and even had a certain respect for him—the respect commanded by a striking personality who seems quite endowed with intellectual knowledge and some spiritual power. And it was not without reason that the real Doctor Faust had all those titles I mentioned here once before: "Master Georg Sabellicus,the younger Faustus, inspiring source of necromancers, Second Magian, Chiromancer, Aeromancer, Pyromancer, second in the art of divination by water."†

This is how he styled himself. Now mind you, it was customary at that time to have as many titles as possible; we could make a long list of similarly high-sounding titles from the ones that Giordano Bruno and many other luminaries of the Middle Ages had. Nowadays very clever people may find it strange that Trithemius of Sponheim and other scholars who knew of Faust's existence actually thought that he was in communication with the daemonic world[†] and with secret forces of the earth and that he could use them to accomplish certain things. But we must remember that even in Luther's time such tales were nothing out of the ordinary. We know that Luther himself wrestled with the Devil and that in those days such tales and notions were a normal part of everyday life. Nevertheless, a feeling was alive in all this that contributed significantly to Faust's becoming a prominent folk figure in the popular consciousness. I say "a feeling," not "a conception" or "an idea." It was the feeling that natural science was on the advance, a natural science that brings the Ahrimanic part of everyday reality to the attention of the human soul. And through this the feeling arose that Faust was, and always had been, a personality in league with these Ahrimanic powers. It was as though one could see the secret spiritual threads passing from Faust's soul to the Ahrimanic powers, and that Faust's fate was inevitable after his surrender to these powers. Enough remained of the ancient clairvoyance and of ancient clairvoyant knowledge that people could still sense and feel something of how Luciferic and Ahrimanic elements have to do with the whole evolution of the human soul. And so the figure of Faust became connected with this feeling that human beings are dependent on the Luciferic and Ahrimanic powers. At the same time it was an age in which this feeling-perception was already fading away into the twilight, and such things had already become confused and indistinct. And yet the feeling arose that with all the dangers and temptations that beset his soul the figure of Faust could become an adequate representation of the striving human being.

But the exact nature of the relationship of Lucifer and Ahriman to what the human soul is striving for was no longer clearly understood. That had long since vanished in a fog, and the resulting haze gave rise to the immense lack of clarity that makes such a strong impression on us when we pick up the medieval "Faust Book."[†] What we find in this book is one tale after another of everything this popular folk figure was supposed to have been through, all jumbled together in a bizarre ragout of every possible adventure a human soul can have in the course of its earthly striving and well seasoned with all kinds of demonic and elemental spirits, even Ahriman and Lucifer. Once these latter two could no longer be visualized in their full, clear forms, since by that time they had been dismembered and ground into a pulp along with all the elementary spirits of Nature, the figure of Doctor Faust was added to the resulting brew in this chapbook. Goethe's keen insight and wide sympathies alone were finally capable of rescuing the powerful root idea from the depths of this terrible mixture and bringing it up to where it could meet the light of the Easter Mystery.

I would like to say it is actually very interesting to observe how, over time, Lucifer and Ahriman were broken up bit by bit into little pieces to be made into ingredients for stews like these. If we go back to earlier times to look for a prototype of Faust, we can look in the books that appeared then as the so-called chapbooks that everyone had who was at all interested in such things.

Augustine was a great favorite at the time this "Faust Book" was written. Patched, cobbled, and glued together, it seemed more as though the book was compiled by a book dealer whose main aim was the fattest book he could get than that it was written by a man of letters or even a real author. But whoever wrote it must have known his Augustine, particularly Augustine's autobiography. Now Augustine's whole development seems very remarkable to us. At first he can't understand what the essence of Christianity is. Then, by degrees, he works his way through a secret antagonism to Christianity that develops with the evolution of his soul, turning first to what the Manichean doctrine has to teach him. Then, from one of the most important men in the Manichean sect, he hears about the Manichean Bishop Faustus. We can almost guess now who Faustus Senior was, as distinguished from that other Faust who, as I just mentioned, styled himself as Faustus Junior, or the "younger Faustus." It was the man Augustine had once come across in olden times and who, as Faustus, Bishop of the Manicheans, had preserved something of the earlier Manichaean doctrine.

And what was this? It was what has since been eaten away by Ahriman, so that as human beings we can no longer understand how our souls are connected with the whole cosmos, with all the impulses from the stars. We can say that the ribbon of knowledge leading to cosmic enlightenment, which shows how the human soul was born out of the whole cosmos, and the enlightenment we must attain if we would truly understand the Easter Mystery, was already broken at the time of the Manichean Bishop Faustus. It was therefore possible for the compiler of the chapbook of Doctor Faustus to make Faustus, as Ahriman's prisoner, arise out of the figure Augustine had depicted as the Manichean Bishop Faustus. But since all these matters had become so confused, he did not realize that the real adversary was Ahriman. We see traces of Ahrimanic danger glimmering through the plot of the folk play, but they are very faint. Nevertheless, it arouses in us a distinct feeling that Faust is the figure that represents striving humanity and that he is to be depicted as threatened with danger from the Ahrimanic powers.

By the time Goethe received the Faust-figure, much had been added to it from that Manichean Bishop Faustus, Faustus Senior. Moreover, many chapters of the "Faust Book" appear to have been copied, albeit very badly, straight out of the book in which Augustine described his own development and his meeting with Bishop Faustus. So we can clearly prove that this is the source of the Faust-figure's Ahrimanic features, the result being that when the "Faust Book" came to be written down, only a last, faint impulse remained to represent the Ahrimanic elements now present in human nature by means of the Faust-figure in particular.

Now what about the Luciferic element? How have the Luciferic elements been chopped up into those bits of ragout and cooked into the hash of elemental spirits and the bits and pieces of Lucifer and Ahriman, as I said before? Well, we will have to do some hunting if we wish to find Faust's connection with Lucifer. Here, too, we can look around in history, but we don't need to go all that far. We only need to go as far as Basel, where we can find some clues as to how Lucifer was chopped up in pieces for the ragout. As the story goes, Erasmus of Rotterdam† and Faust once met in Basel, where they attempted to have a meal together in the College. Erasmus didn't see anything he thought would taste good, and he said that to Faust, who was sitting with him and wanted to eat with him. Nothing suited their fancy. Then the Faust-saga tells us that Faustus suddenly managed to produce some strange birds – where from, nobody knew – that were not to be had in any of the markets around Basel, but there they were on the table, all cooked, baked and ready to eat. So here we have a scene between Erasmus of Rotterdam and Faust, in which Faust shows his ability to set birds before Erasmus that could not be bought at any of the markets in or anywhere around Basel at the time. What does this mean? As it stands in the saga, it is not comprehensible at all; in fact, we can say it is completely incomprehensible.

But the matter becomes more comprehensible when we pursue it somewhat and bring together what we can find in some of Erasmus's writings. He himself tells us that in Paris he had made the acquaintance of a certain Faustus Andrelinus. Now this Faustus Andrelinus was not only an extraordinarily learned man, but an extraordinarily sensuous man as well. Erasmus soon became well acquainted with this Faustus, but he had no real liking for the sensuous side of his character. However, he also speaks of a meal the two are supposed to have had together. Now we must certainly not expect that of two such learned gentlemen of that time, such as Erasmus of Rotterdam and Faustus Andrelinus were, one would set birds before the other one of the sort and in the way that Faustus is supposed to have done with Erasmus in Basel. The tale we find there probably originated from some kind of joke the two men exchanged during the meal. But we can see a little behind these joking words if we remember that Faust—and this time it really is Faust—had declared that he did not really like what he had been served but would especially enjoy ordering something else, such as strange birds and young rabbits. Yes, strange birds and young rabbits. At first Erasmus had the idea that this must have some hidden meaning. He was behaving just like some theosophists who are always meditating on the meaning of things and think that everything must have a meaning. But then the other man said: All right, I will do without the young rabbits. Erasmus thought to himself: Couldn't that mean flies and ants? He is willing to forego the rabbits. But the birds must really be flies, and he would especially relish flies. Now we are getting somewhere. The birds have become flies through an astral transformation. And in

Goethe we find the figure of Mephisto as the god of flies. All it would take to conjure up these beings is the presence of the spirit who rules them. And so we have found the connection between the incomprehensible Legend of Basel with its strange birds and the flies that simply come from the Devil. And, after all, we shouldn't be surprised that the Devil would serve flies to his table guests.

If we now follow Erasmus a little further along his way in Paris, the particular quality and true nature of Faustus Andrelinus's soul soon becomes clear. In Paris, Erasmus was not especially willing to fall in with Faustus Andrelinus's views and general way of being. But then he has to go to London, and from there he writes—just imagine Erasmus writing this!—that he has now learned how to comport himself in a salon, whereas before now his manners were as crude as a peasant's, and that he has also learned to bow and even move around on the polished floors of the Court. And—yes, Erasmus writes this himself—that in the atmosphere in which he is now living people are always kissing each other, both when they come and when they go. We can see by the way he writes this, that he wants to appeal to the taste of his friend in Paris. He also writes: "Come on over here. And if your gout is keeping you from coming, just fly over in the chariot of your thoughts [*Geisteswagen*], through the air. That's the element for you!" There we have it: a clear reference to the Luciferic tendencies of Faust's soul.

In Goethe's account we see Lucifer at work in everything Faust does to seduce Gretchen. By this time, Lucifer's influence in the Faust-figure's environment has receded so far into the background that we have to make these kinds of literary investigations if we want to prove the connection between Lucifer and the Faust in Paris. But in the chapbook we plainly see Faust standing there with Lucifer and Ahriman at his side, even if they are only faintly visible in the confusion of the times and all cooked up together into one big stew. Need we be surprised to find in the folk puppet play and the folk drama, and even in Marlowe's *Faust*,[†] a remnant of ancient intuitions from those times when the connection of humanity with Lucifer and Ahriman was still recognized by means of atavistic clairvoyance?[†] But all that had become very confused, and in the literary productions of which I have just been speaking it was represented in a thoroughly confusing way.

Goethe sensed this deep connection, but what could he not do? What he could not do was separate Lucifer from Ahriman. In Goethe's poetic imagination, these two still coalesced to meld into that composite figure of Mephisto about whom it is so hard for us to know whether he really is the Devil or Ahriman or the real Mephisto, because he has taken on so much of Lucifer's nature as well. Goethe simply received the mixture as he found it, so to speak, sensing both Ahriman and Lucifer at work there. But he was still not able to pick the two apart; instead he entwined them even more tightly into the figure of Mephisto who as a crossbreed of Ahriman and Lucifer is actually an occult impossibility.

We can call the period of time that Goethe looked into when he first became acquainted with the "Faust Book" the fading twilight or final darkening of an ancient knowledge of these things concerning Ahriman and Lucifer. And Goethe's *Faust* is the first dawning of the new knowledge of Ahriman and Lucifer: still below the horizon, still dim and confused by the chaotic mixture of Ahriman and Lucifer in the figure of Mephisto. But already the need had arisen to portray how much the human soul can profit from allowing itself to be worked on by what flowed into the earth's aura when the Christ Being passed through the Mystery of Golgotha!

The Easter Mystery itself in Goethe's *Faust* appears to us as the beginning of a new era in the spiritual life of humanity. Nevertheless, in spite of the masterly way in which the theme is handled, there is still a feeling of confusion about this work, something of that dim, misty morning twilight we see below us if we climb a mountain to experience the sun rise earlier than we could if we remained below.

If we allow Goethe's *Faust* to work upon our minds, we will feel how one of the greatest of human beings, through his efforts to revive the ancient knowledge, turns his soul to the Easter Mystery. And if we let it work on our souls in the right sense, my dear friends, we will feel what takes place in the heart of a really great man, when that man's heart is moved by the Easter Mystery—as was that of Goethe himself. We will also see in this early perception by Goethe of the Easter Mystery there is something that also demonstrates that after the red dawn into which the first faint, clear rays of the Easter Mystery are already streaming, the sun of a new spiritual experience will rise. The human soul itself will rise from the grave of the darkened perception into which it too had to descend.

In the course of its evolution the human soul will itself experience the Easter Mystery, the resurrection of the Christ-impulse, which lies buried in the deep underworld of its being, if it unites itself with the force gained by a contemplation of the Christ-Easter-Mystery.

So would we sense the meaning of Goethe's call; and then, after we have allowed the tragedy of the Easter Mystery to affect us deeply, we would transform it into a new call: for the resurrection in human hearts and human souls of a spiritual knowledge in full accord with the needs of future times. May human hearts and human souls, after sensing the deepest of all tragedies, receive the fullness of the Easter Mystery with holy joy in their inmost being and experience the Resurrection within themselves through the Christ within them!

May you, my dear friends, experience in your souls through the words I have permitted myself to speak to you today something of the perception that the reason you are here—the reason why we are gathered together around our building, dedicated as it is to spiritual investigation,[†] —is that through the strength drawn into your souls you may carry away into the future something of the Resurrection-impulse that has appeared so plainly to us in the Easter Mystery, toward which, as we have seen, the greatest minds of that past era were so eagerly pressing.

May the magic ringing of the Easter bells, resounding in your spirits, echo on within your souls in your further work with *Faust*.

5
Faust's Forced Entry into the Spiritual World

Dornach, April 11, 1915

After a dramatic performance with eurythmy

We have preceded today's performance of the Easter scene in *Faust* by a performance of the scene in which the Earth Spirit appears to Faust. A week ago we were able to develop some ideas in connection with *Faust* that can be highly meaningful to anyone wishing to approach the laws and life of the universe in the light of spiritual science. My reason for taking this particular poetic work of Goethe's as the subject of my last lecture on Easter Sunday and the one today is not to give you explanations of Goethe's *Faust.* The reason is to show you that the human soul, by exposing itself to the artistic images that come before it in a performance of *Faust,* is really able to perceive something of what we can and must call the development or the actual living immersion of this soul into the spiritual worlds. The extent to which we can deepen our knowledge of *Faust* from the standpoint of spiritual science will permit us to develop further observations in connection with this poetic work.

Faust is, after all, the expression of Goethe's own efforts to enter the spiritual world, the expression, in other words, of the fact that at a significant turning point in modern history a mind as great as his was striving to enter the same world we are seeking access to today as we continue to deepen our knowledge of spiritual science.

In the last lecture we saw that Goethe lived at a time when it was really not yet possible to find the true path into the spiritual worlds in a clear and consistent way. We were able to show that such truths as that of the meaning of Lucifer and Ahriman were still only hovering before Goethe's soul as indistinct conceptions; like an unclear inkling, as it were, of the spiritual world. We were also able to conclude that the two figures of Lucifer and Ahriman had flowed together in the single figure of Mephisto, so that in Mephisto Goethe was working with the unclear image of a figure he was not able to grasp at all with the unambiguous clarity now possible through spiritual science. And so, precisely in this striving of Goethe's that expresses itself so well in *Faust*, we can see with what earnestness, intense conscientiousness and sense of responsibility to our own soul we have the task of working as we carry on with what the continual deepening of spiritual science has yet to reveal to us.

When a mind of such depth runs into difficulties of this sort on the path to what many, many people are trying to reach today, there is a real opportunity here to learn a great deal from Goethe's searching and striving in particular. I would wish that everyone who has taken even a little interest in the results of spiritual science go back to Goethe's *Faust* again, this document from the early dawn of modern spiritual-scientific striving, not yet from the time after its sun had risen.

In my last lecture I showed that Goethe needed the maturity of his later years to get out of the state his soul was in in his youth. Goethe's soul could never content itself with seeing in the world only what his physical eyes could see and what his brain-bound intellect could perceive. He took what was living and seething in his soul as it strove to understand the deeper spiritual foundations of life and gave it form in his figure of the striving Faust, who is not an actual copy of Goethe but does represent certain sides of Goethe's life and striving in a way both absolutely real and genuinely artistic. We can see from all this that in the scene with the Earth Spirit we have something belonging to the very earliest parts of *Faust* that Goethe ever wrote.

In my last lecture I spoke of *Faust* in such a way that if I were misunderstood (as I so often am), people might go away and say that I had described *Faust* as a poor work of art and had in fact had some rather harsh words to say about it. And anybody who was particularly ingenious might say that I had changed my views on Goethe; that at one time I was one of his great admirers but had now proved to be one of his detractors. Well, I should not have to mention that I do not honor Goethe any less now than I ever did, nor that as far as I am concerned he is still the greatest mind of modern times. The fact that we honor and respect a great personality should never make us into blind worshippers of authority but always keep our vision clear for what we ourselves have recognized to be the truth.

Faust was put together—one can say patched together—at different times out of various parts. And one can say that when Goethe wrote the earliest parts of *Faust* in 1770, he was really not capable of writing the later ones, but had to mature before he could move on from his ardent desire for the spiritual world to what we can call his "understanding of Christianity." Only further life experience could give Goethe the maturity he needed in order to continue his artistic work on Faust, the great seeker of the spiritual world, so that this Faust is brought to the point of being preserved for life through the memory of Easter, even to the point of his taking up the Gospels and beginning a translation of the Gospel of St. John. When we hear many people say today that they have no need of spiritual knowledge in order to plumb the depths of Christianity, that this spiritual science is unnecessary anyway because Christianity can be understood well enough from what every priest or preacher proclaims from the pulpit, and that the only thing of any avail, especially in this Christianity, is faith alone; and we then compare such an attitude with what must be said of Goethe, who as one of the very greatest minds took decades to become mature enough to arrive at his understanding of Christianity, we can then get some idea of the huge conceit and arrogance of these people, especially of the ones who are always talking in an arrogant and conceited way about the simplicity of their hearts and minds, dismissing what they have no need for—the contents of spiritual science—for which, as they see it, they have no use.

In the scene with the Earth Spirit (454-513) we see something of what occupied Goethe in his youth, in his thirties, and also in the last twenty years of his life. From this scene with the Earth Spirit, as well as from Faust's so-called first monologue that precedes it, we gather that Goethe steeped himself in so-called occult-mystical literature and tried to use what this literature gave him to find the spiritual world in meditation, in meditative devotion. In the very scene that was performed for us today we see Faust absorbed in a meditation based on indications he tells us he has discovered in an ancient occult-mystical book by Nostradamus, by means of which he hopes to swing himself up into the spiritual worlds.

Let us try to form a picture of the worlds into which Faust—and therefore Goethe as well—actually wants to ascend. When the human soul has succeeded in strengthening its inner power to such an extent that the soul-spiritual core of the human being is freed from the instrument of the physical body; when the soul, so to speak, with all its own forces, which are completely imperceptible to it during normal everyday life, has slipped out of the physical body, we can ask what this experiencing of the physical then becomes for the human soul. What we mean by this is not the physical body itself as a thing enclosed in a limited form in space, but rather physical life, with which the human being is after all always spiritually connected because a ray or current goes to this physical life. Also in the life between death and a new birth there is a ray or stream of spiritual life going back through time to what we have lived through on earth, as you can gather from what I have said in earlier lectures. In other words, it is as though the spirit were always stretching out its hand, or even doing something more than this, reaching back to connect us with what constitutes our physical experiencing. What does this physical experiencing then become for the human soul that has freed itself from having to use the instrument of the physical body? When we are outside our physical experiencing, this whole activity of experiencing physically becomes, so to speak, an organ of the soul. The entirety of our physical experiencing becomes, as it were, an eye or an ear. The whole human individual becomes a sense organ, a spiritual sense organ—an organ, so to speak, of the whole earth that now looks out into cosmic space. For our eye to be able to see physical objects we have to be outside of it; like a kind of independent organ the eye has to be imbedded in the socket, which even closes it off with walls of bone. The ear too is closed off in a similar way. Furthermore, the whole physical apparatus of the brain is enclosed in the cavity of the skull and closed off from the rest of the human body. Our experiencing of the physical must be isolated in the same way, so that it becomes a kind of sense organ, a sort of eye or ear, by means of which we can gaze out into the whole wide worlds of space, once we are outside our physical experiencing.

What we then experience can also be described as follows. We can say we are now in the world described as the "Soul World" in my book, *Theosophy*.[†] This is the world we first enter when we have the experience of being outside the body with our now independent soul and have our own experiencing of the physical outside ourselves. In the Vienna lecture cycle of April, 1914,[†] I described the fact that also during our life between death and a new birth we have a soul-spiritual sense organ derived from our previous earthly life with which to perceive the rest of the world. That is to say, through this earthly life we perceive the rest of the world. In this world we also find our deceased friends for a rather long time after death, until they move on up to another world, which can then only be reached through a further stage of soul development, even by initiates. There are a number of things about this world we are now in that we cannot fail to notice. We can only mention a few details, of course; you will have to collect others from the various lectures that characterize this supersensible world. What the soul immediately notices above all else when it has left the body and begins to live in a new world is that first of all it sees, and even feels, the light of the stars go out. The soul begins to live in an elemental world, so that from now on it weaves with the sea of air, flows along through the world with the undulating warmth itself and rays out with the light; and since the soul is now raying out with the light, it can't see any external objects by means of that light. This is why the lights of the sun and the stars go out, along with the light of the moon. It is no longer a viewing of things from the outside, but a co-experiencing of the elemental world. And at the same time it is a co-experiencing of what we call the driving force of historical events, of historical evolution. In this world we can see something going on that is the actual source of human history.

In its further meditative development the soul can wrestle its way upward to an even higher kind of experiencing. At this stage, more than just its own experiencing becomes a soul-spiritual sense organ; the whole earth becomes a sense organ. Speaking paradoxically—but you will understand me—the human soul must now move on ahead to a way of experiencing, about which we can say: the human being is now something the whole ball of the earth is set into, as the eye and the ear are otherwise inserted into our body, and just as we see with the eye and hear with the ear, so do we perceive the worlds of space with the whole earth and its experiencing. We now become aware that what the physicists tell us about the sun and stars is nothing but a materialistic dream. The stars had already gone out and the sun and the moonlight had already disappeared in the world previous to this state. Now, however, we become aware that what we thought was the sun is really a community of spirits, and that wherever we assumed a star to be, there is a spiritual world. And as we look back upon our earthly existence we become aware that what the physicists are speaking about is only a fantastic, materialistic dream. For what looks like a star or a sun is really the seat of a spiritual community somewhere in the spiritual world, just as the earth is the seat of a human community. Just as from a distant star it would not be possible to see any physical bodies but only human souls, just as little can one say that anything can interest us up there in the sphere of the stars that is not of a spiritual or soul nature. But what we do see may be described as the vapor of the earth's atmosphere that collides with what it meets coming in from outer space. The physical eye cannot perceive what the star really is. It only sees the vapor the earth itself sheds out into cosmic space. All that appears to us as the starry heavens is nothing but what is woven out of the material substance of the earth itself, although that substance is an etheric one, a curtain drawn by the earth over the reality behind it. But when the soul extends its life into this world, it learns that what exists out there are not the stars the physicists speak of with their materialistically colored imaginations, but rather living beings, actual communities of living beings, soaring upward and downward and weaving back and forth in cosmic space, handing down gifts from the upper spheres to the lower, and again passing gifts upward from below. If we read the following words in their spiritual sense:

> Into the Whole how all things weave,
> One in another work and live!
> What heavenly forces up and down are ranging,
> The golden buckets interchanging. (447-50)

—forces, but now in the sense in which we speak of primal forces,

> With wafted benison winging,
> From heaven through the earth are springing,
> All through the All harmonious ringing! (451-53)

But with all this pictured in a soul-spiritual way, we then have, more or less, the world into which the soul's life now extends.

Now what exactly did Faust get from everything just described, during the time in which we see him here? He has opened an old book written by someone who recorded an ancient spiritual perception in it in symbolic form: the sign of the macrocosm. But Faust is of course not able to reach out with his soul life into spheres where the great beings of the universe unfold their cosmic activity. He is not able to soar so high. He only sees the sign written down by someone who had managed to reach these regions—the sign of the macrocosm. But a dream is aroused in him, a dim presentiment that this sign means something. Now suppose for a moment that you had never heard anything about spiritual science and that you had this sign in front of you, but also that you had a feeling that someone had once seen something similar that you would also like to see. Now you know what it is like to be in Faust's soul. At first you can dream your way into these symbols, which are really the signs of the zodiac, the signs of the elements, the signs of the planets, and imagine that something in them stirs some chord in your imagination so deeply that suddenly, overcome by emotion, you burst out with the words:

> "What a show!" (454)

But this strikes back at you, and suddenly you realize that all you have is the sign in the book, an imagination...

> "But just a show, that's all!" (454))

What's more, this pageant is your own inner imagination! And now you're back on earth. The sign hasn't led you anywhere at all. On the contrary, it has rejected you and left you with the feeling that you are indeed standing before the spiritual world, but you can't find any way to get in.

> Where can I grasp you, endless Nature?
> Where, you breasts? You sources of all life,

On which both earth and heaven hang,
And for which yearns my withered breast— (455-58)

Nothing but the feeling of being in the elements again: in the light and the air, as I said, in the whole subordinate world, and expressed now with absolute clarity. Faust has forced his way up into the spiritual world but has then fallen back into the world I described earlier as the supersensible world closest to us. This living with the light and the air is clearly indicated in the line:

You gush and quench, and yet in vain I languish? (459)

Faust has sunk back into himself again; he has fallen out of the spiritual world and back into the elemental one. But he is not able to recognize even this world as yet. At this moment help arrives, in that he opens the book again and sees the sign of the Earth Spirit. This sign was also written down by someone who had experienced the nether or elemental world as his own inner world as well. Faust now feels as though he is within it too. He has an intuitive sensation of having entered it.

How different is this sign's effect upon me! (460)

Why is it so different? Because Faust feels something when he sees it; because he has turned away from the experience of the senses and feels something of his actual presence within this world. This is actually the world he is always talking about now:

Already I feel my powers heightened, (462)

—what we experience when we live in warmth and light—,

I glow, as if with new made wine. (463)

Imagine feeling warmth in your soul, living and weaving in the world as a wave of warmth!

I feel the strength to bravely meet the world. (464)

It is really like moving within the elements. As I said before, the very process of experiencing life on earth becomes a sense organ, and just as you formerly felt your eye and your ear within yourself, so now you feel your sense organs within the earth.

Strength to bear the woes and joys of earth,
To battle with its raging storms— (465-66)

when you're in the air as a wave of air.

Clouds gather overhead—
The moon withdraws her light— (468-69)

No wonder! I have just described how the stars and moon go out, and why. For Faust the light disappears, because he himself becomes part of the streaming light.

Vapors rise!—Red rays of light are darting
About my head— (471-72)

This is now an inward perception.

A shudder
Down-wafted from the vaulted gloom
Lays hold of me!
I feel you hovering round me, conjured Spirit.
Reveal yourself!
Ah! What a spasm racks my heart!
With what new feelings
All my broodings now are reeling! (472-79)

Can you see how this expresses life in the elements?

I feel my whole self given now to you.
You must, you must! Although it cost my life! (480-81)

And now, out of his meditation, Faust speaks the invocation he has found written next to the sign of the Earth Spirit, a meditative, suggestive mantra that really does lead him to the face of the spirit who is the master of the spirits whose domain we enter the moment we come into the elemental world. But right away we notice that Faust is really not mature enough for this world, that he is especially incapable of even *feeling* mature enough for it. What's missing here? What does he need? Self-knowledge is what he needs, in the sense that this is truly the highest form of world-knowledge that all of us acquire as we experience what can be experienced as we swim and weave and flow and have our being in the elemental world. But Faust is unable to recognize anything in that world that takes on individualized existence.

The ensuing spiritual conversation between Faust and the Earth Spirit is very characteristic of the stage of maturity attained by Goethe himself at the time he wrote this scene,[†] representing as it does his own tremendous endeavor to penetrate the spiritual world.

> *Spirit*: Who calls to me? (482)

Faust is already turning away. Of course, this doesn't sound like something we would normally hear with physical ears, coming from a long way off, but rather as though we were living in the sounding itself. It sounds different from what we can hear on earth, quite different. Just as one sees what one sees, not *through* the light, but by oneself raying out along with it. Everything looks different. Faust wanted to become a super-man.[†] That is to say, he wanted to enter the spiritual world. But now he is terrified of this spiritual world. This encounter with the Earth Spirit makes it clear to Faust that to gain entrance into the spiritual world one must become a very different being from what one was as a human being beforehand, that it is impossible to enter this spiritual world encumbered with one's normal powers, sensations and passions. Faust has to feel in his innermost being how at first he fell back, or was thrown back, from the higher spiritual world into the elemental world, and how now in the elemental world he is rejected in his knowledge, because he has only remained the "I" that he was before. He has not developed a fitness for this elemental world, which he was brought to by the suggestive meditation he carried out with the aid of the invocation ascribed to the Earth Spirit. For a moment he has been able to see what kind of beings inhabit this world. But then the spirit says to him:

> Where are you, Faust, whose voice so clear I heard,
> Who pressed himself upon me with such power? (494-95)

I have already pointed out that this voice resounded from the subconsciousness of the Faust that the external Faust himself does not even really know.

> Is it you, who by my breath surrounded,
> Trembles to your very core... (496-97)

This "you" refers to the ordinary Faust, whereas the struggling, striving Faust was Faust's higher self.

> A lily-livered, cringing worm? (498)

But now Faust becomes defiant. He is ready to plunge into the very world for which he is so unripe.

> I, yield to you, O form of flame?
> I'm Faust, your equal, I am he! (499-500)

Now he can still hear how the spirits of the elemental world that he has thrust himself into accompany human history, how they live in everything that takes place on the earth through the activity of the various races and civilizations. And the secret of the Elemental World is uttered by the Earth Spirit, who never speaks of "being," but only of "becoming" and of what "happens."

> *Spirit*: In floods of life, in actions' storm,
> Up and down I wave,
> To and fro I weave!
> Birth and grave,
> An eternal sea,

A changing weaving,
A glowing living,
So do I work at the loom of time
On the living garment of Godhead sublime. (501-09)

Not in space, but in time. — Read the lectures given in the Hague![†]

This much at least Faust can understand: this is the spirit that passes through history:

You who roam the wide, wide world,
O restless spirit, how close I feel to you! (510-11)

You who roam the wide, wide world! You spirit who belongs to the spirits of time! How close I feel to you!—This is what his presumptuous attitude has driven him to say. But then the spirit says something to him that Faust himself will later on call words of thunder. Like thunder indeed they strike into his soul and dash him back to the ordinary world in which he dwells, because he is not yet mature enough. His task is to seek knowledge of the self, and then, in the self that has expanded to include the world, the spiritual world itself. But as yet he can't find it, and so the words of thunder must resound to him from the Earth Spirit:

You're like the spirit you comprehend,
You're not like me! (512-13)

Who is this spirit that Faust can comprehend? What spirit *does* Faust comprehend, this image of the Godhead who *cannot* comprehend the Earth Spirit? How can he now advance in self-knowledge? What does the human spirit look like that Faust *can* comprehend? Well, at just this moment in he walks in nightshirt and nightcap, this other Faust: Wagner! That's the spirit you comprehend! You've only come as far as Wagner; everything else that's alive in you is only passion and defiance!

With this, Faust has taken an important step forward on the road to self-knowledge. In fact, it is particularly characteristic of Goethe's *Faust* and of its fine artistic structure that what we see portrayed on the stage in concrete form is basically always a piece of self-knowledge. Wagner is a piece of self-knowledge that Faust has attained, just as Mephisto is. Wagner is Faust himself. And it would not be wrong at all to have a performance of *Faust* sometime[†] in which this figure of Wagner in nightshirt and nightcap that Faust has such an aversion to were made to look like Faust. Then people would see right away why Wagner comes in at just this moment. What Wagner says is basically all that Faust can comprehend. Everything else Faust says is only empty rhetoric. He thinks he is lifting himself up into realms of highest spiritual truths, but he can only declaim them in empty phrases without experiencing their real meaning in his soul. And now we see him acquiring a new piece of self-knowledge. Wagner speaks the truth. Faust hasn't really been expressing the innermost experiences of his soul at all. He has only been declaiming.

> I beg your pardon—I hear your voice declaiming! (522)

That's true. He has only been declaiming. And it is an act of self-reflection for Faust to realize that this is not the way to approach the Spirit of the World, but at best only a way to recite from a Greek tragedy. So many people, when they first meet spiritual science, have a great urge to hold forth on the deepest of truths, even if they're often proclaiming these deepest of truths only to themselves. All they really want is to proclaim elements of this spiritual science to themselves, fooling themselves into believing they will somehow "profit from this art." As far as our own time is concerned, we can say that in some circles this certainly is the case. Many people are very interesting when they hold forth about all the visions they've had. In former times one heard a lot of this from the priests. Now, however, the actors have learned to do this even better, so much better, in fact, that the priests could learn a thing or two from them. Now if Faust could confine himself to what he fully understands, he would have to speak the words of Wagner, who is his reflection. Instead, he speaks out of his passion, out of what is Luciferic in him, not out of the genuine, fully human core of his soul, but out of its Luciferic core. Now Faust answers Wagner; not Faust himself, however, but Lucifer in him, speaking to what Faust is as he stands there in front of us in Wagner's form:

Yes, if your preacher is by chance an actor,
As that from time to time may be the case. (528-29)

This scorn, this pride comes from what is Luciferic in Faust. For if Faust were not in Lucifer's clutches, he would speak the same way Wagner does, if, that is, he would only say what he can honestly admit he has understood. The other part is a faint foreshadowing of what Faust hopes to attain. But in this conversation with himself—which is really what it is — Faust nevertheless takes a step forward. We do take a step forward in life when we meet ourselves this way in others. We don't like to admit to ourselves that we possess some characteristic or other, but we're more willing to study it when we encounter it in other people. By considering one of our own characteristics as it appears in the personality of someone else, we gain self-knowledge, even as Faust does through the personality of Wagner. Faust, however, is not yet far enough along to be able to say when Wagner leaves, "Yes! That's the way I really am." If he had managed to understand himself completely, he would have said, "So far I'm only a Wagner! What's thinking in me is still just Wagner!"

How that man's head does not lose all its hope
That spends its whole time stuck to shallow nonsense,
That digs for treasures with a greedy hand
And is in ecstasy when all it finds is worms! (602-05)

For until now Faust's way of searching for the spirits has been no different from the one depicted here. Self-knowledge is what Faust meets in Wagner. But who sent Wagner to Faust in the first place? It was the Earth Spirit who sent him:

You're like the spirit you comprehend,
You're not like me! (512-13)

So now Faust is to see what spirits he resembles. Clearly he does not resemble the Earth Spirit, the ruler of the earth. But at some point he is meant to see one of the figures that dwells within him: "There you have him! This Wagner is part of you!'

But there is more in Faust than Wagner alone. The Luciferic element is there too, striving against Wagner: in other words, against Faust himself. But there is another element in him, too.

If we look into the earliest edition of *Faust*, we find that the scenes immediately following the one in which the Earth Spirit appears are missing because they had not yet been finished. In the earlier edition we find the conversation with Wagner; followed by the one between the student and Mephisto.... When Mephisto enters the circle of Faust and his students, Goethe is not quite sure whether he is really Lucifer or Ahriman. Had he been acquainted with spiritual science, he would have had Lucifer appear at this point. In Mephisto we have the other spirit sent by the Earth Spirit to Faust. The Earth Spirit has already sent Wagner; now he sends Mephisto, or, as we would say, Lucifer. Little by little Faust is to learn what is really living within him. Mephisto has been sent by the Earth Spirit. "Look!" he says. "Here is another of those spirits that you can comprehend. Try to understand the Luciferic element within yourself, instead of starting right away with the Spirit of the Earth!"

How uncertain Goethe was about the matter is evident from four lines in the original manuscript that were omitted in the later edition. They occur in the original manuscript of 1775, after the scene in which Mephisto has led Faust to Gretchen, and in which Faust is burning to make her acquaintance. These four lines are no longer in the *Fragment* published in 1790. After Faust has asked Mephisto, who is really Lucifer—only Goethe confuses the two—to provide the jewelry for Gretchen, he goes away. And Mephisto, left alone, says, in the old manuscript:

> He acts as though he were a prince's son.
> If Lucifer had a dozen of such princes,
> They'd have to pay him well for what he does.
> He'd even end up earning a commission. (*Urfaust*: 526-29)

There it is: Mephisto gives himself the name of Lucifer. As I have said, these lines were omitted from the later editions.

Now what exactly was it Goethe's concern to accomplish in his later years as he strove, we might say, to express his own self in his Faust ?

Well, his real concern was to show how we human beings are supposed to attain self-knowledge. But in this first scene, which Goethe had already written as a young man, something was foreshadowed, we might say, that you can now read so clearly described in *How to know Higher Worlds*† as the meeting with the Guardian of the Threshold. In the way Faust divides up into Wagner and Lucifer-Mephisto we see a premonition of how we ourselves do this as we gradually come to realize that we are composed of various beings. Faust gradually comes to know himself in his different parts, first as Wagner, then as Lucifer-Mephisto. But, as I said before, Goethe had to wait until he was more mature before he could fully understand the tremendous import of the Christ-impulse for humanity, as far as this was possible at the time in which he lived. This is why we do not see Goethe finishing the work he had begun as a young man until he was more advanced in years. That work had depicted Faust's struggles up to the point where he met himself face to face in various self-reflections, including his Luciferic reflection, as every human being can. Goethe's greater maturity enabled him to supplement his former work by bringing Faust in touch with what had been poured out by Christ into the aura of earthly evolution. We could say that Faust is now confronted by the symbols of Christianity. We thereby see in *Faust* the document that indicates to us how Goethe himself brought esotericism to Christianity, that is to say, to the Christ-impulse. This same document shows that today we too are working our way farther along the same road on which Goethe took his first pioneering steps. In Goethe's time it was only possible to get an inkling of this.

Today, the time has come when spiritual science has made it possible for us to enter the full reality of those regions of spiritual life that Goethe's lifelong struggles were directed toward. In our time we must understand Faust differently from the way even Goethe himself understood him. You see, the world progresses, and if we don't fully acknowledge this fact, we aren't taking the world seriously enough. But experiences such as these, in which we split up into different parts and actually approach ourselves in our true form, in Luciferic form, such experiences do help us progress, but always only a little bit. We must give up the belief that we can command a view of the whole spiritual world when we've only taken a few steps forward, as we can do through meditation. We only advance a little at a time.

There are two natures in Faust: the Wagner-nature and the other one that is continually striving forward. Goethe worked this point out very beautifully in the revision he made in his mature years. As soon as Faust had come to Christianity, Goethe felt that he had to show how the Wagner-nature was at work in him. This is why he has Faust and Wagner take their walk together on Easter Day. The struggle going on in Faust's soul is really being shown to us here in the form of two distinct persons in a way that is perfectly natural for the dramatic form of representation. The higher man in Faust strives forward; the Wagner-nature holds him back. A spark of comprehension of the spiritual world has been enkindled in Faust, so that when the poodle meets him, what he perceives is more than the merely physical poodle. It is really something like a soul force in Faust that expresses itself in his conversation with Wagner:

> *Faust*: Do you see that black dog prowling through the stubble? (1147)

Now the Wagner-nature wakes up again in Faust:

> *Wagner*: I saw him long ago. He did not seem important.
> *The higher nature*: Look at him more closely! What do you take him for?
> *Wagner-nature*: Just a poodle, who, in his own way is working hard to follow up his master's scent. (1148-51)

These words of Wagner's are actually objections Faust is making to himself. And now it continues. Faust is beginning to perceive the invisible behind the visible. He has already become aware of its existence. It is an intuitive awareness created by his experiences, a spark from the spiritual world that has descended into him. And it is beautiful to see Goethe's honesty and infinite loyalty to his artistic principles; only, we must understand him correctly. Faust now feels the Luciferic in himself. As you know, the Luciferic is connected with stubbornness, with a secret egoism. Faust allows himself to be deeply affected by this Luciferic attribute even as the Christ-impulse permeates his very soul. It is a Luciferic attribute that makes the Gospel of St. John seem incomplete to him when he feels the urge to translate it. To someone who really understands the matter, the commentators on Goethe seem somewhat peculiar. They certainly follow him, because they always go along with their poet, even when he divides the things he wants to say up among his various characters. Faust really doesn't understand the Gospel text at all as yet. If he did, he would be satisfied with the wording: "In the beginning was the Word." But he hesitates because he doesn't understand it yet. The professors present it as though Faust were developing an ever deeper understanding of these words. But he doesn't understand them yet. Thinking of "the Power" and then "the Deed," he introduces a rationalistic, intellectual element into the Gospel text. This method now produces an effect that is the exact opposite. Whereas formerly Faust was thrust back into the world of the senses, he is now led up into the world of the spirit. By asserting his limitations so strongly in writing "Thought" and "Power" and finally "Deed," he is thrust up into the spiritual world, because there is a spark of spiritual power in his soul. At that moment the spirits come, followed in turn by Mephisto as a messenger of the Earth Spirit.... Mephisto, that unclear, nebulous blend of Lucifer and Ahriman. As you see, we have to understand Faust's efforts to force his way into the spiritual world in the light of Goethe's own struggles; and just at the present time there is an infinite amount that we can learn from this.

Both in this lecture and in the last one on Easter Sunday, my special concern has been to make it clear to you that it is a more difficult affair for a mind that really desires to deepen itself to approach the Christ-impulse than it is for a mind that can't get beyond its own pride and arrogance and has no interest in anything spiritual science is able to offer it. On the other hand, I also wanted to use the example of *Faust* to illustrate the power of what it was that came into the world through the Christ-impulse. The time will come when people will learn to understand the inner nature of the Christ-impulse better and better, precisely through what spiritual science is able to give. The fact remains, that centuries after the Christ-impulse entered the stream of earthly human evolution, something else appeared in this stream that is also not properly understood. But the moment we begin to understand it properly, this very understanding will bring us to a deeper feeling for the Christ-event. This new factor is a kind of illustration of what the Christ-impulse really is, an illustration afforded by world history for the earthly evolution of humanity.

As you know, six hundred years after the Christ-impulse entered the evolution of humanity a prophet arose in a certain community who at first rejected what the Christ-impulse had brought. This prophet was Mohammed. Now we really must no longer give our allegiance to the superstition of the nineteenth century that aims to give detailed explanations of matters from the rationalistic standpoint that can only be explained from the standpoint of the spirit. It must seem ridiculous to any genuinely serious student of spiritual science that an especially learned and clever man has made the following comments about Mohammed: "Mohammed," he said, "declared that an angel had come to him in the form of doves and whispered into his ear what he later wrote down in the Koran! But Mohammed was an imposter," said the learned rationalist. "He put some grains in his ears that doves like to eat. Then the doves flew to him, got the grains and then flew away again!" Yes, there were such explanations in that clever nineteenth century of ours, both within and outside Christianity!

The time will come when we'll just laugh at such explanations, even though they may be able to fully satisfy the materialist. But we need to take Mohammed more seriously. We have to realize that what was living in his soul was an actual relationship with the spiritual world such as the one Goethe was seeking for his Faust. But what did Mohammed feel? What did he find? Today I am only able to touch on this; some other time I will describe it in more detail. What did Mohammed find? Well, as you know, he was striving first of all for a world for which he had an expression that consisted of just one word: God. For him the world became a "monon," a monistic expression of the one God. This world contained nothing of the essence of Christianity, of course. But Mohammed did see into the spiritual world, all the same; he came into the very elemental world I have been speaking of today. And he promised his followers that they too would enter this spiritual world after passing through the gate of death. But he could only describe to them the spiritual world he himself had come to know. What kind of a spiritual world is this? This spiritual world that Mohammed described to his followers as the very world they are to strive to attain is the Luciferic world, which he himself regarded as Paradise. And if we come down from the abstract to the concrete and add to this, by way of interpretation, the essential meaning of the Islamic striving to enter the spiritual world, we will recognize what spiritual science also proclaims. But this spiritual world is the world in which Lucifer has his dominion. Reinterpreted, the Luciferic world has become Paradise: that world toward which all human striving should be directed.

It has to make a deep and lasting impression on our souls whenever we can work our way into the nature of historical evolution in this manner by means of such an important phenomenon. But certain questions arise the moment we experience that in the course of religious life a great prophet once appeared and promulgated the error that the Luciferic world was identical with Paradise. I would not wish for this idea to enter your souls like one more abstract truth. I believe it can already shatter the soul if one allows such a thing to work upon it. Nevertheless, we have to ask: what does a Muslim do in order to enter the spiritual world? It would be interesting to count the number of our dear friends sitting here today who have read the Koran from beginning to end. It is not easy to read the whole Koran, with its endless repetitions and a style that seems so tedious to the Western mind. But there are Muslims who claim they have read the Koran from beginning to end, no less than seventy thousand times. That means they have taken this written word and impressed it so deeply upon their souls that it has become a living reality in them! As far as the contents of Christianity are concerned, there is certainly nothing we can learn from such a religious community. Nevertheless, it can still be our experience that within that human community, even with its spiritual error, there is a completely different way of doing things than there is in ours, with all that we are called upon to recognize as spiritual truths. As Europeans, the most we do is read our *Faust*. Then, when we've forgotten what it is about, we read it again. And when we've forgotten it again, we read it again. But people who have read *Faust* a hundred times would be hard to find. This is understandable in the context of modern Western culture. How could we possibly read everything printed in the Western world seventy thousand times? It is very understandable. But one thing we should learn at least is that it is one thing merely to inform ourselves about something of great significance for the life of the soul, but something quite different to live with this content so deeply that we make it an integral part of ourselves by constant repetition. It will take some time for us to gain a real understanding of this; we can't even begin to understand it with the thinking habits of our current national community. But we should think about such things. Words spoken in these lectures have not been spoken just to tell you something, but to stimulate you to think and reflect, to heighten our sense of responsibility toward ourselves and toward the world in terms of everything spiritual science can and should become for us.

In many respects we are living in a difficult age. The terrible events going on all around us are only the outer signs of how difficult our whole age is. It is not good to think of this difficult time as an illness, in the way we often refer to an ordinary sickness as an illness. The sickness itself is often a healing process, with the true illness having worked at a deeper level long before it manifested physically as a sickness. In the same way, something unhealthy has preceded the tragic events now sweeping over the world, and to understand this we need to look much more deeply into things than people today are at all inclined to do.

Oh, my dear friends! What a load of grief can weigh down our souls when we contemplate not only our present time and all its tasks but also how small the amount of understanding is that so many people bring to bear on these tasks! And when we also see how people today arrive at their opinions of world affairs—the way they think and feel and sense; how their thinking, feeling, and sensing leads to certain external events, and how people then learn so little from these external events—the anguish of our souls becomes well-nigh intolerable. This is the sense of pain that must often come over us now. Look at what we have gone through in the last few months, to take only our most recent experiences. What have people learned during this months-long ordeal? Compare their opinions today with what they were just eight months ago.† What is the result? The same sort of judging, the same sort of sensing. People still believe in what they thought they were right about eight months ago. These particular people even claim that these terrible events have taken place just to prove how right they were then.

I can't tell you how infinitely painful it is to know that human souls have hardly changed at all during the past few months, in terms of what was needed to make such a change so that our time might really be one of testing and one of learning. But we may hope that students of spiritual science will take to heart some of the things that can be learned from observations such as the ones we have been making in connection with our study of *Faust*. Again and again we would like to direct people's attention to the deep earnestness and the sacred striving for truth that must be connected with our spiritual-scientific way of viewing the world. In a movement such as ours, any motive not arising out of profound honesty and a deep feeling for truth will exact its revenge. Everything about which we can say, "Pardon—I heard your voice declaiming!" (522) to the person who said it, is something we must really try to overcome.

Isn't it strange to see Wagner appearing so often on stages these days as he is traditionally portrayed, at the very same time as our learned scholars, rationalists, and intellectuals are so busy scoffing at what Wagner really is instead of searching their souls and recognizing themselves in him, as they should be doing? This Wagner is everywhere today, in the academic chairs and in the laboratories, and our scientific and philosophical literature would contain a much greater degree of truthfulness if as many authors as possible would simply adopt the name "Wagner" as their pseudonym. For "Wagner" is the real author of our present-day philosophies.

I am afraid there are many even in the ranks of spiritual science who have sufficient reason to do some very serious soul-searching to see how much of what they find there is merely a product of pedantic declaiming—even if only to themselves—and how much is based on absolute honesty and the purest feeling for truth! I will end my remarks today with this note of warning addressed to your hearts and to the innermost forces of your souls.

6
Pentecost Mood: Faust's Initiation with the Spirits of the Earth

Dornach, May 22, 1915

Following a performance of the first scene of Faust, Part II, with eurythmy

You will understand that this year, just at this point in time, it is hardly possible for me to give a Pentecost lecture in the usual meaning of that term. Think for a moment how the time of Pentecost is characterized in that document of Christianity we call the New Testament. We will find the most significant characteristic of Pentecost to be that the Spirit is poured out over those people who are called apostles. And the consequence of this outpouring is that, as we see from Chapter 2 of the Acts of the Apostles, although the people who have come together for the Feast of Pentecost, ten days after the so-called Ascension, all speak the most different languages. Each one perceives what is to be proclaimed to them in such a way that it sounds perfectly familiar, in spite of their assertions that the only language they know is their mother tongue.

And so, the outpouring of the Spirit at the Feast of Pentecost manifests as the outpouring of the spirit of the love, concord and harmony among those who speak the most different languages all over the world. Or, we could look at the matter in a slightly different way in order to catch the flavor of the biblical wording a little more accurately. We could say that something is given in the proclamation of Pentecost that is so in tune with the human heart that everyone can understand it, even if the only language we understand is our mother tongue.

Now if the only thing given here today is an interpretation of the possible meaning of the message of Pentecost, nearly everyone will feel how contradictory this is in terms of what we find going on all around us this year at the Feast of Pentecost. We need only consider that today, nineteen hundred years after the original proclamation of Pentecost, the world has finally managed to observe the content of that proclamation in such a way that our Pentecost festival must be the witness of how thirty-four nations, all speaking different languages, can be at war with each other, in complete contradiction to the true meaning of the Feast of Pentecost. Perhaps this language spoken by the facts themselves will show at least a few people that the first Pentecost proclamation has not yet managed to spread over the whole earth in a sufficiently penetrating and convincing manner; and that, in fact, it will have to speak to the minds and hearts of people in a whole new form, more urgently and more meaningfully than ever before, so that in the future people will be able to understand it in the way in which it must be understood.

This year's observations on Pentecost will therefore be of a general nature. Coming from a particular direction, they can make it clear to us that we understand spiritual science itself to be the new proclamation of Pentecost. For we have no other course than to regard the spiritual science presented in these lectures as a Pentecost proclamation to humanity as a whole.

Let us review what we have learned about the Mystery of Golgotha.[†] What is the essential feature of this Mystery of Golgotha? Its essential feature is that a spiritual being, who as we know belongs to the cosmic spheres, came down to the earth where, as the Christ Being, he lived in the body of Jesus of Nazareth for three years, undergoing earthly fortunes and experiencing earthly sorrow in a physical human body. Since the Mystery of Golgotha, as a result of what the Christ Being went through in the body of Jesus of Nazareth, this being has been united with what we can call the Spirit of the Earth, or the earth's auric aspect. For this reason we can divide the whole of our earthly evolution into two great periods: the time before and the time after the Mystery of Golgotha. In the first of these periods, what the Christ Being is can only be faintly hinted at by those individuals whose initiations have enabled them to rise above the earthly sphere and perceive in those realms, not something that lies within the earthly sphere itself, but rather something in which the earth does not as yet participate, although predestined to do so in a distant future. As I said, the other period is the time after the Mystery of Golgotha. We know that since the Mystery of Golgotha human beings have not needed to leave the earth with their soul-spiritual nature, but have been able to remain within the earthly sphere and perceive, within this earthly sphere, the inspirations of the Christ Being.

Now we must be clear that throughout the centuries on into our own time part of humanity has become aware that the Christ-impulse has connected itself with Earth-existence. A great change has taken place in the consciousness of human beings as a whole, especially in the consciousness of those people who have sensed something of the inspiration of the Christ. This change of consciousness in people as a whole has filled the soul with the belief that Christ is with all human beings; that the heart and mind can unite with Christ and that within Earth-existence itself the human soul can consciously experience something that is pervaded by the inspiration of Christ in a living way. But a comprehension of what the Christ-impulse means in the evolution of humanity throughout the whole of Earth-existence can only really be brought home to human souls by spiritual science. For this to happen, a clear recognition is necessary of how this inspiration of Christ works in the human soul, so that two other spiritual impulses are, so to speak, kept in balance.

The task of representing this balance will fall to a statue that we intend to erect in the east end of our building.† This statue will be the representative of all humanity, the representative of the human being as such, insofar as this human being can experience the most profound thing possible: the total permeation of the soul by the living inspiration of the Christ. As far as I am concerned, the main figure of the Group at the east end of the building can be called the Christ, but it can also be called, generally, "the Representative of the Human Being [Humanity]," whose inner nature has undergone an immeasurable deepening. But this spirit who speaks through a human body will have to be viewed in connection with two other spiritual beings, Lucifer and Ahriman. The standing figure of the Representative of Humanity will have to express the relationship to Lucifer and Ahriman. Everything about this figure will have to be merely characteristic. Once this figure has been set up, you will be able to notice in particular that the gestures of the raised left hand and the lowered right hand are very special ones. Their meaning will become evident the moment you see that the left hand of the Representative of Humanity is raised up toward the top of a rock and that Lucifer is plunging down from the top of this rock because he has broken his wings.

Now it will be easy to believe that Lucifer's wings are broken by the power streaming out of the arm of the Representative of Humanity, as though this power were breaking them by radiating out in his direction. But that would be a misconception. We hope to be able to model the statue in such a way that it will avoid giving this impression. The point here is not that something streams out of the Christ-permeated human being that then breaks Lucifer's wings; but rather that Lucifer experiences something within himself when he feels the presence of the Christ, and this is what causes his wings to break. They break because Lucifer is not able to bear the power of the Christ-impulse. Christ has not initiated a battle with Lucifer in order to bring this process about. It is a process within the inner life of Lucifer himself, something that he himself must experience, and there must not be a moment's doubt that it would be impossible for Christ to harbor any feelings of hatred or animosity toward Lucifer. Christ is, after all, Christ. He does not do battle against any worldly power; He only fills the being of the world with positivity! But the power that comes into his presence as the power of Lucifer must do battle against itself. For this reason the raised left hand must not work aggressively in any way. The left half of the face must not work aggressively with this strange gesture either; it is a kind of indication that within the context of the whole world Christ has something to do with Lucifer. But this relationship is not a conflict of any kind. The conflict arises within the soul of Lucifer himself. He breaks his own wings; they are not broken by Christ.

The same thing is true for Ahriman, cowering in a cave underneath the right side of the Christ-permeated human being. Underneath this cave the earth is being forced upward, giving us a picture of the material substance that is being driven, so to speak, into human beings but is kept from becoming strong there by the presence of the power of Christ, and so grows weak.

As before, the power streaming and surging through Christ's arm and into his hand must also not betray any hatred toward Ahriman. On the contrary, Ahriman grows weak all by himself. Driven by the urgings within his soul, he takes the gold hidden in the veins of the earth and wraps it around himself like chains, fettering himself in the chains he himself has made out of the gold of the earth. He is not put in chains by Christ, but does this to himself while feeling the presence of Christ so strongly.

All this lays bare for the first time what I would like to call the "original" or "fundamental" relationship that must be recognized before the true nature of the Christ-impulse can really be understood by human souls.

A simple comparison can make this Christ-impulse clear, at least abstractly. Imagine a pendulum. It swings out to one side, then returns to the lowest point by virtue of its own weight. Then it swings out just as far to the other side until there is a point on this other side that we call the point of equilibrium. This point would be a dead one, or a resting point, if the pendulum did not then swing back out to the other side. The pendulum has life in it because it swings out to both sides and has a point of rest in the middle.

We can imagine the evolution of the earth ever since the Mystery of Golgotha by using this image: a swing of the pendulum toward one side, the Luciferic one, and a swing toward the other side, the Ahrimanic one. And the point of equilibrium is the Christ in the middle.

You may be able to tell from a significant historical fact that this has yet to be recognized. We all admire Michelangelo's painting of the *Last Judgment*.† You know it from reproductions of the original, which is located in the Sistine Chapel. There we see the Christ, painted by Michelangelo with such magnificent mastery, triumphantly sending one group of souls to hell, to the evil spirits, and the others, the good ones, to Heaven. But if we once really look into this Christ's face, what we see in it is cosmic anger. And if we have taken up spiritual science and really united everything we have been able to absorb from it until now with our hearts and minds in love, we say today, despite our admiration for what Michelangelo accomplished: "This is no Christ, for Christ does not judge!" Human beings judge themselves, just as Lucifer and Ahriman experience inner processes of their own, not something brought about by any kind of battle against them on the part of the Christ.

When Michelangelo created his Christ, the time had not yet come to recognize the Christ in his true perfection. Lack of clarity still clouded human minds. In those days, people saw in the Christ himself something of what we now know must be ascribed to Lucifer or Ahriman.

And today we can somewhat understand how people could have found something of Lucifer or Ahriman in Michelangelo's Christ, because the Christ as Michelangelo represents him is not yet free of that from which the Christ himself is completely free.

Let us form for a moment a very clear picture of what this means: that from the way of viewing things out of which Michelangelo himself had grown and developed, it was not possible for a picture of the Christ to come into being that would correspond to a real understanding of the Mystery of Golgotha, because what has to be known had not yet been made clear, namely, the relationship between Christ, Lucifer and Ahriman.

We have often stressed among ourselves how misguided it is to point to Lucifer and say, "I want to run away from him," or to point to Ahriman and say, "I want to run away from him." Doing that would only mean wanting to make a pact with weakness. It would be the same as telling the pendulum not to swing out to the right or to the left at all, but just to stay in one place so it would always be in a state of equilibrium. We can't run away from the worldly forces we call Lucifer and Ahriman. All we have to do is find the right relationship to them. And we find this right relationship when we understand the Christ-impulse in the right way, when we see the Christ Being as the leader who can bring us into the right relationship to the Luciferic and Ahrimanic powers, who now have the task of being powers in the world.

Look at what Lucifer brings into our lives as human beings: everything having to do with our sensing, our passions, with the whole feeling life of our souls. How dry and sober and abstract our lives would be if it were not for the living flood of sensations and feelings continually surging through them! Look at what human passion has brought about in human history, that passion which is often, and with good reason, called noble passion. Look at what these feelings and sensations have brought about. But the only way we can ever harbor feelings and sensations of any kind at all is by entering the sphere of Lucifer. The important thing is never to enter this sphere without the guidance of the Christ-impulse.

Now look at the other aspect of things and notice how necessary it has become, especially in recent times, to understand the world in more and more depth by extending scientific knowledge and mastering the forces of external Nature. Now, the lord of everything that has to do with external science and of what lives in the forces of external Nature is Ahriman. And it would be pretty stupid and foolish of us to want to run away from this Ahrimanic element. Again, it is not a matter of running away from this element, but of making sure that when we enter the sphere in which Ahriman holds sway in the world we do so under the guidance of the Christ-impulse. And so, we must not merely look for a resting point in some sluggish fashion, but rather seek to experience the living movement of the world-pendulum in such a way that we never take a step without the guidance of the Christ-impulse. Christ-knowledge is only possible when the human soul has a clear idea of the relationship of the Christ-impulse to the Luciferic and Ahrimanic forces. This is why the proclamation of the Luciferic and Ahrimanic aspect of the world is such an important part of what our spiritual-scientific movement had to take on, since it knew that it had to establish itself on the firm foundation of the Christ-impulse. The fact is that nothing of these Ahrimanic and Luciferic elements can be found in any of the teachings of the non-Christian kind of theosophy,[†] precisely because this Luciferic and Ahrimanic element had to make its appearance at the very moment the spiritual-scientific movement had to take the Christ-impulse into account in a serious way.

I think it is extraordinarily important for the human soul to feel that spiritual science has the task of bringing something absolutely new to people's awareness. This is something so new that we may well measure it against such great creations of humanity as Michelangelo's Christ in the *Last Judgment.* And so we should regard the picture given to us by spiritual science as the new Pentecost proclamation in the truest sense of the word.

Around Easter time we saw how Goethe, one of the great geniuses of modern times, struggled to bring Faust, *his* Representative of Humanity, into a relationship with the Christ-impulse. We also saw that Goethe had not been able to do this as a young man, but had had to wait until he was more mature before that became possible for him. In this way, as it has continued to develop up to the present time, the life of the spirit presents itself to us in many ways as a struggle, a ceaseless struggle. It truly seems that it must make us modest to the highest degree to witness how the best spirits of humanity have striven to find concepts and feelings for what the Christ-impulse actually means. We get the feeling of how modest we ourselves must be in our own human striving for this understanding of the Christ-impulse.

As we saw, Goethe felt at first that it was important to have what works actively around the human being as the Luciferic and the Ahrimanic element step up to his Representative of Humanity, Faust, in human form. We also saw how Goethe mixed the Luciferic and Ahrimanic elements together in the figure of Mephisto in a way that makes it hard to tell them apart. We showed in our Easter lectures that the Luciferic and Ahrimanic elements are all mixed together in the figure of Mephisto because it was not yet possible for Goethe to have a clear picture of the true situation. Throughout his whole life Goethe had the feeling that something was stirring deep within his soul, striving to arrive at a clear understanding of how the human being is related to Lucifer and Ahriman. When at the end of the eighteenth century he was approached as a mature man by Schiller to continue working on *Faust*, he took another look at what he'd written in his youth and called what he'd put together at various times a "tragelaph"†—something half animal and half human. This is what his *Faust* seemed to be. And in order to indicate how hard it would be to continue his work on it, he called his *Faust* "a barbaric composition."† So this judgment about his work comes from Goethe himself, who really ought to know his work better than other people do: *Faust* is a tragelaph, something "half animal and half human," as well as "a barbaric composition"! What I wanted to present at Easter, which can so easily be misunderstood, ultimately goes back to a judgment made by Goethe himself. Certainly, some very clever people see in *Faust* a perfect work of art that can never be surpassed. But this was not Goethe's opinion, and it must also not be our opinion any longer. Even though we see that in *Faust* something has been raised to its highest level, we must nevertheless be clear that, especially in its inner composition, this *Faust* suffers from the fact that in its figure of Mephistopheles, Lucifer and Ahriman are mixed together in a completely non-organic way.

In spite of all this intermixing, Goethe always had the dim feeling that Lucifer and Ahriman should have appeared as separate characters. But

Goethe mixed everything together and called it all "Mephistopheles," so that in some scenes of *Faust* Lucifer is often Lucifer, whereas in other parts he is Mephistopheles or Ahriman. But one thing was absolutely clear to Goethe: something is going on in the human being that happens under the influence of Lucifer and Ahriman, of Lucifer and Mephistopheles. This is really going on in us.

Now look at the end of Part I of Goethe's *Faust*. How does it end? Faust has burdened himself with the heaviest guilt imaginable. He has a human life on his conscience; he has deceived a human being; he has taken on this heavy guilt, with regard to both himself and others. And the last words of Part I are: "Here to me!" spoken at the same moment as a fading voice resounds, as though coming down from heaven: "Henry! Henry!" From this closing of Part I we know where Faust has ended up: He has ended up with Mephistopheles. Mephistopheles has him. About that there can be absolutely no doubt.

And now we see how the second part begins. The opening of Part II presents us with a pleasant landscape: "Faust, lying on a flowery meadow, tired and restless, seeking sleep." Spirits appear, and from what they say we get the impression that we have to do with Nature, really, with Nature—we only have to go outdoors right now, at this time of year, to find this Nature. Pentecost-Nature, more or less! The mood of Pentecost! This Pentecost mood has its effect on Faust. And afterward he is ready to get on with the rest of his life.

A scholar once said something about what Goethe did here, and we can say there was something to what he said, even though it was philistine and pedantic. This scholar said that if you are carrying a heavy burden of guilt, as Faust was carrying with respect to Gretchen, just go out into some pleasant landscape, lie down on a flowery meadow, take a hike through the mountains; then your soul will be well again and ready for new activities. As we have said, viewed in a realistic, Ahrimanic way, what this scholar (Rieger)† said has something to it. Actually, anyone who looks at the world in the purely materialistic way normal for our times today could hardly endure the effect of the second part of *Faust* after seeing how the great and powerful guilt that Faust has burdened himself with has been characterized at the end of Part I. But unfortunately, people don't take this great work literally enough, despite the fact that *Faust*, although its first part is a barbaric composition and a tragelaph, is still the greatest poetic work of human nature, insofar as what is humanly personal comes into consideration. If we would take it literally enough, we would understand that "Here to me!" is absolutely true: Mephisto has Faust in his clutches. And just as he has him, Faust is lying on a flowery meadow, restlessly seeking sleep. We must not imagine that Faust, as we see him at the beginning of Part II, is in any way set free from these hellish powers. Goethe, however, was wrestling his way toward genuine spiritual understanding. We may see how close he was to spiritual understanding from a passage he wrote in a letter to his musician friend, Zelter.† A significant passage!† Goethe writes: "Let us consider that with every breath of air we breathe, an etheric Lethe-stream† flows through our whole being, so that we have only a faint remembrance of our joy and hardly any of our sorrows." It is a fact that with every breath we breathe, an etheric stream of life permeates our inner being, but this can only mean that Goethe was quite well informed about the etheric body that every human being has. Of course, in his day he only spoke about this in his circle of intimate friends.

Goethe looked at the whole human being, and as he looked at its essential nature he said to himself, "This essential nature of the human being can become guilty because something living in it is subject to the influence of Mephistopheles and actually even belongs to him." And as Goethe continued to contemplate the human being who belongs to this sphere of Mephistophelean influence, he was also quite clear that something else lives in human nature as well that can never succumb to this influence. In fact, it can be kept safe from the influence of both Ahriman and Lucifer. And this part of the human being that can be kept safe from the Ahrimanic-Luciferic influence is just the part of Faust we're dealing with at the beginning of Part II. The Faust that could incur guilt, the Faust that allowed Mephisto to entice him into the most trivial, banal pleasures of life, the Faust that then seduced Gretchen: this is the Faust that succumbed to guilt. In our spiritual-scientific language we would say that this element in Faust will have to wait until its next incarnation.

However, there is something in human nature—the higher human self—that maintains its connection with the spiritual powers of the world. This is why the spiritual powers of the world come face to face with this eternal principle in Faust. We must not imagine the Faust we see at the beginning of Part II in any realistic sense, as though he were so and so many years older than the one in Part I. At first he is really only the representative of the higher self in Faust. Outwardly he still looks the same, but inwardly he is the representative of something in Faust that has not been able to fall prey to guilt. This principle in Faust that has not incurred guilt now forms a relationship to the servants of the Earth Spirit.

Ever since his youth, Goethe had longed to arrive at a view of just how it is with human guilt and with the evil in the world, as well as of how, in the final analysis, something is hovering over it all that must have a reconciling effect in the face of both guilt and evil. And so, since Goethe had had to abandon one side of Faust's nature to Mephisto, as it were—"Here to me!"—he now ventured to approach Faust's other nature. We must be absolutely clear that the Faust speaking at the beginning of Part II is first of all not the same one we know from Part I, but that a different, or second, nature is speaking that only looks like Faust in an external sense and is actually able to live its way into what permeates the external world as spirit. But what must find its way into this spirit is something that at first has no connection with Faust's external physical body. For, as long as we remain in the same incarnation the physical body retains by its very nature all the signs of any guilt we have incurred. The only thing in us that can make a proper connection with our higher self is what frees itself from the physical body. And so, Faust has to undergo a special transformation that we can call the transformation of guilt into a higher kind of knowledge.

What he is carrying now as guilt he will carry with him over into his next incarnation. For his present earthly incarnation, the guilt he carries will be the source of a higher and more precise knowledge of life which is gradually dawning on him. And so, despite the fact that he bears such an enormous burden of guilt upon his soul, the possibility is opening up for him to be embraced by what lives, moves and weaves through the world as spirit.

Faust's higher self enters into a relationship with a spirit of the earth's aura. Goethe wanted to portray, as it were, that what is highest in the human being was never able to be seized by Mephistopheles—or as we would say, by Lucifer-Ahriman. It must have been protected; it must be able to enter other spheres. And so Goethe is to be taken very seriously when he shows this higher self in Faust now finding a relationship to what the elemental world contains as actual spiritual Being.

We will see later on how all this is connected with what was said here during the Easter lectures. But for now we want to consider how these spiritual beings work under the guidance of the Air Spirit—for that is what Ariel is, and the group as a whole can therefore be called air spirits—we want to consider how these spirits are connected with the processes of external Nature and yet reveal themselves as a different spiritual world with respect to the self, which in supra-earthly nature is not exposed to the influence of Lucifer and Ahriman:

> When in spring the blossoms' raining
> Gently floats down over all,
> When green blessings of the meadows
> Sparkle for all born on earth, (4613-16)

in other words, when everything in Nature is budding and sprouting in the spring-time of Pentecost, that's when the elemental spirits are also coming out. As far as everything external and material is concerned, they are small; but as spirits they are large, exalted above everything in the human heart that can fall prey to good or evil.

> Tiny elves with spirit-greatness
> Rush to help where'er they can;
> Be he holy, or so evil... (4617-19)

—but this has to be left to the next incarnation; to these spirits it is of no concern at all—

> Be he holy, or so evil,
> They pity the ill-fated man. (4619-20)

What these spirits *are* concerned with is Goethe's higher self, and it remains protected from everything that has to run its course in the karma or incarnation process. However, these spirits are only able to work in their own element, and we are only in their element with our own true nature when we have entered it as soul-spiritual beings, having left our external bodily sheaths behind. And now Goethe explains what these elves have to bring about with their spirit-greatness:

> You float about this head in airy circles;
> Display your nature now as noble elves,
> Assuage the vicious struggle in this breast;
> Remove reproach's painful, burning arrows
> And purify his inner self from horror lived. (4621-25)

This could never happen with a Faust exposed to Ahriman-Lucifer. This purification means: Take Faust's higher self and make it pure. And now something is taken very seriously, running its course like an initiation performed on Faust while he is outside his body:

> Four are the watches of the night, (4626)

—from six o'clock in the evening until six o'clock in the morning, from the time Faust goes to sleep until the time he wakes up, the elves fulfill their duties, bringing his soul together with what moves and weaves through earthly existence.

> Now go, and fill them in your friendly way. (4627)

—the four watches that the soul lives through from the moment of going to sleep to the moment of waking up.

> First lay his head down on the cool, soft pillow,
> Then bathe him in the dew from Lethe's stream;
> His limbs, cramp-stiffened, shortly will be supple,
> As resting, strengthened, he prepares for day; (4628-31)

—when he has absorbed what the world-permeating spirit has offered him, and when this spirit has entered into what has been preserved in Faust's being as a higher self.

Fulfill now, elves, your finest task,
Return him to the sacred light. (4632-33)

The events that happen outwardly between going to sleep and waking up are real, and the whole process is analogous to an initiation. And now we see what happens in each of these three-hour periods: from six till nine, from nine till twelve, from twelve till three, and from three till six.

First we have the watch from six till nine:

When the breezes gently fill
All around the greening plain,
Sheaths of mist and sweetest fragrance
Drape the world as twilight nears:
Whisp'ring softly sweetest quiet,
Lulling childlike heart to sleep,
As, for his exhausted vision,
Closes now the door of day. (4634-41)

The soul is gone now, out of the body. Now the second part:

Now has night descended fully,
Star joins star in rev'rent move;
Nearby glisten greater lights, while
Smaller sparks gleam from afar;
Glisten here in lake's reflection,
Gleam above in clearest night;
Moon's full splendor now confirms
The happiness of deepest rest. (4642-49)

Something is being absorbed here: the harmony of the spheres, the wisdom of the spheres, coming in from the greater lights and the smaller sparks. And also, the secrets of the moon—everything, in fact, that we learn from spiritual science about the secrets of the spheres—all this is being immersed in Faust's higher self as well.

Then the third part of Faust's sleep:

> All extinguished are the hours,
> Gone the pain and happiness;
> Feel ahead! You will recover;
> Trust the new-found sight of day.
> Dales are greening, hills are swelling,
> Bushes thrive for shady rest;
> And in swaying waves of silver
> Fields of grain toward harvest crest. (4650-57)

Connecting inwardly with the Being of Nature; we have already spoken about this. Read my last cycle of lectures given in the Hague,† where I talked about how the human soul becomes one with the moving and weaving of outer existence when it lifts itself out of the body. But this also signifies the process of becoming that is also taking place in the soul of Faust:

> And in swaying waves of silver
> Fields of grain—(the soul of Faust)—
> toward harvest crest. (4656-57)

Now recall my saying that the sleeping human being desires to come back into the body. This is the last part of the night:

> To attain desires abundant,
> Look upon the radiance there! (4658-59)

Already there is a hint of the coming sun.

> Sleep embraces you but gently,
> Sleep's a shell, so cast it off! (4660-61)

An important sentence! A great poet does not write empty words. "Sleep's a shell, so cast it off!" What does that mean? For someone that sleeps a normal sleep, sleep is not a shell. But sleep is a shell for someone for whom this period between going to sleep and waking up becomes a receptive organ for assimilating cosmic mysteries.

> Dally not in taking courage
> When the crowd has lost its aim;
> Nothing noble man can't do, if
> Quick to see and lay his claim. (4662-65)

And now we have the monstrous din that announces the approach of the sun, this now reminding us of what Goethe has already told us about the sun's resounding in the "Prologue in Heaven" in *Faust*, Part I.

> The sun resounds in ancient manner
> In contest with its brother spheres,
> And firmly its predestined journey
> It carries out with thunderous course.
> Its sight gives strength to all the angels,
> Though none of them may fathom it;
> The works, inscrutable and lofty,
> Are glorious, as when first performed. (243-50)

If a soul is outside its body when the sun is rising and light is pouring out over the physical plane, this soul hears the sun's approach as music of the spheres, as a special element in the music of the spheres. Spirits hear it by their very nature. Human beings do not hear it because they can hear only with their physical bodies. But the physical body is an integral part of the physical plane, and when the sun is together with the physical plane, that is the time when human beings can be awake. This is why spirits have to withdraw. What Ariel, the Air Spirit, now says to his servants is a sign that the music of the spheres is drawing near. These spirits can hear it. Anyone outside the body can hear it, which is why Faust can still hear it. But then he goes back into his body, and at this point Ariel is faced with the task of disappearing and of instructing his servants to do the same, that is, disappear from the physical plane. The sun must be allowed to find them only as a resounding sun, for if its light falls on them, it will make them deaf.

But they have no problem tolerating the resounding sun because they themselves live in its tones:

> Harken! Hear the storming Horae!
> Spirit ears perceive the sounding
> Of the new day being born.
> Rattling, rocky gates creak open,
> Clatt'ring roll the wheels of Phoebus;
> What a din comes with the light.
> Trumpets blasting, brasses blaring,
> Eyes all blink and ears are stunned,
> Unheard then is unheard now.
> Slip into the crowns of flowers,
> Deeper, deeper, there to dwell,
> Under leaves and into cliff sides;
> If it strikes you, deaf you'll be. (4666-78)

Now the elves disappear, and Faust goes back into his body. But the guilt-laden Faust remains unconscious: not standing there bodily in front of us, but lying deeply buried in Faust's subconscious for safekeeping until his next incarnation. The Faust who has just experienced being together with the entire spiritual cosmos has now to form a clear idea of how everything he has gone through during the four watches of his sleep relates to the way he now perceives the world around him. He now lives in his body as higher self. Now, if we were to sleep through a night and then wake up without having everything in us that Faust had in himself when he woke up, it would be pretty foolish for us to say, "You, earth, were also steadfast all this night." After all, no one would expect the earth to be anything but steadfast all the night through. On the other hand, if we had experienced what Faust did as his initiation with the spirits of the earth, we could very easily believe that the whole earth had changed. If we had become new human beings, or rather, if the new human being had been awakened in each of us, we would be justified in saying, "You, earth, were also steadfast all the night—in spite of what I have just experienced." The world would seem completely new, because it would actually be being given to a new human being.

Life's pulses fresh and lively now are beating,
Etheric light of dawn so gently greeting;
You, earth, were also steadfast all the night
And breathe now, newly quickened, at my feet;
With pleasure you are starting to surround me,
You stir in me a powerful decision
To strive for highest being evermore.— (4679-85)

Even now, when the spirit has freed itself from what has to be preserved until the next incarnation!

In dawn's revealing light the world lies open,
The forest rings with scores of living voices,
From valley into valley mists are streaming;
And yet, see heaven's clarity descending
And boughs and branches into new life springing
In fragrant gorges where they once were sleeping,
And color upon color now outstanding
Where flower and leaf with trembling pearl were dripping,
The world around me paradise becoming. (4686-94)

This is what we human beings see if we, I will not say, have been initiated, but rather if the initiation is alive in us. Faust has every reason to see the world anew. All the words he now speaks he would never speak if he were nothing but that other, guilty human being, living, as it were, in this incarnation under the impression of this guilt.

Look up and see!—Gigantic mountain peaks
Proclaim already this most solemn hour;
'Tis they who first enjoy the light eternal,
Which later finds its way to us down here.
Now to the sloped and greening mountain pastures
New glow and sheen and clarity are granted,
As step by step it downward makes its way;—
It comes!—(he means the sun)—and I, alas, already blinded
Must turn myself away, with pain-racked eyes. (4695-703)

The higher self is not able to behold the sun, which the sensory self was able to do. Nevertheless, Faust has experienced enough to recognize that the sun is something essentially different for him now. And now, something is stirring within his inner being that is closely related to powers of human cognition:

> So this is how it is, when ardent hoping,
> Its highest wish in tender struggle winning,
> Finds portals of fulfillment opened wide. (4704-06)

What are these "portals of fulfillment?" At first, only the ones that had opened for him while he was asleep. Now, however, even the ordinary world seems to be sending forth huge masses of flames from the depths of its eternal foundations:

> But now a monstrous mass of flames breaks forth
> From those eternal grounds; we stand confounded;
> We wanted to ignite the torch of life,
> Instead, a sea of fire surrounds us, what a fire!
> Is't love? Is't hate?... (4707-11)

We know that from before, but what we are experiencing now is more than love or hate.

> Is't love? Is't hate? that, glowing, now surround us,
> Exchanging pain and joy in mighty alternation,
> So that again we turn our gaze to earth,
> To seek safe shelter in a youthful veil. (4711-14)

At this moment he can't look into the sun at all; he looks toward the waterfall, which reflects the sun and shows him the colors of the rainbow in the form of an arc. In this way, by turning away from the sun, he becomes an observer of the world, as this world shines in, reflecting the splendor of the spirit's life. This is the world of which we can say: "All that is transitory is but a symbol of what is eternal" (12104-05).

So may the sun remain behind my back! (4715)

Earlier he did look at it. Now he turns away from it to look at the waterfall.

The waterfall, now roaring through the rocky rift,
I gaze at it with growing fascination.
In thousand, then a hundred thousand streams
It pours and hurls itself from fall to fall,
As clouds of mist and foam on high it sends.
Then from this storm how gloriously emerges
The colored bow in ever-changing permanence... (4716-22)

—which reflects in seven colors what is unified in the sun.

Now clearly drawn, now into air dispersing,
Around, its cool and hazy showers spreading.
It forms a picture of our human striving.
Consider it, and then you'll see more clearly:
In this reflected splendor we have life. (4723-27)

In this reflected splendor we have life!—After this night, Faust has come to the point of no longer wanting, as the Faust of Part I still did, to fling himself into life the way it threw him into guilt and evil deeds. He turns instead to its colored reflection. It is the same colored reflection we call spiritual science, which he can only see as reflected splendor, but which we gradually wind our way up through in order to experience reality.

What follows now, that is Part II, is at first a reflection of life's splendor. But it would be nonsense to think of this second part in merely realistic terms. Here we have Faust contemplating with his higher self the life he sees through his physical body as a colored reflection. But he is carrying this body along through life only as something he is preserving so that something else can develop in him that, as his higher self, will protect him from what is coming in later incarnations.

Goethe found it very hard to go on writing his *Faust* after Mephisto's final words, "Here to me!" had sounded. But then we see how Goethe approaches the mysteries we recognize today as the mysteries of spiritual science, and strives to penetrate them. Look closely at this second part and notice how Mephisto really has Faust in his grip at first, how he really is at work in everything that goes on at the Imperial Palace, and so on. Then notice how, under the influence of the initiation living within him, Faust gradually manages to disentangle himself from Mephisto's clutches in the course of the second part. These are but some of the additional secrets contained in this second part; Goethe himself told us that he had woven many secrets into it! —People have not taken this remark of his seriously enough, but we will learn to take such words more and more seriously through spiritual science.

One thing you will have understood from today's reflections is that in *Faust*, Goethe was striving to go beyond what he had achieved in Part I by expressing in his *Faust* something of the mood that is really being hinted at here symbolically in the course of the seasons.

When Pentecost approaches, and when the spirits of the elemental world draw near to us in such a way that we can say of them:

> When in spring the blossoms' raining
> Gently floats down over all,
> When green blessings of the meadows
> Sparkle for all born on earth,
> Tiny elves with spirit-greatness
> Rush to help where'er they can;
> Be he holy, or so evil,
> They pity the ill-fated man. (4613-20)

This is the mood of Pentecost! The outpouring of the Spirit in the next sentences that the chorus speaks, in the four time periods of sleep between going to sleep and waking up again!

And so from a certain perspective we can show, by means of this *Faust* as well, how urgent it will be for humanity to receive, as time goes on, what spiritual science wants to proclaim to us as a new message of

Pentecost. This *Faust* is a perfect example of how complicated things really are in the depths of human nature. Something living in those depths is continually being exposed to the Ahrimanic-Luciferic powers of the world, but something else is living there as well that can be found by every human being who gives him- or herself over to the guidance of the Christ-impulse.

Why do we speak about a threshold? Why do we speak about a Guardian of the Threshold? Because it really is the case that what is rumbling and fighting and waging war in our everyday life in the very depths of the human soul was at first withdrawn from the human soul as though by an act of grace on the part of the wisdom-filled guidance of the world. Life goes on as if on a sort of surface, while all that rumbling and fighting and warring are going on down below. But even the life we experience on a daily basis is a continual victory. It is just that this victory has to be achieved over and over again. And in the future it will only be achieved anew when people know how it is that a benevolent, wisdom-filled world guidance has been leading them all along without their being aware of it. We must really find in the very foundations of our soul what we know nothing at all about from our everyday life of the senses, but what the spiritual in us can nevertheless experience. It is in these human depths that our essential nature is connected with those powers of the world that transcend both good and evil with their spirit-greatness.

I would like to express this in a special Pentecost verse, in which I have brought the idea of how we have these elemental powers constantly fighting with each other in the innermost core of our soul-nature together with the idea that what lives in our conscious awareness is victorious over what is waging war down there in the depths of our life of soul.

Tomorrow, or perhaps the day after tomorrow, we will be speaking about how all these things are related in the context of human life in general. Today, however, I would like to close with this Pentecost verse, which expresses the essence of the ever-living, innermost nerve of our spiritual science, to which we have directed our attention today:

Where senses' knowledge ends:
There first the portal stands
That opens to the soul
Realities of life;
The soul creates the key
When she herself grows strong
In the struggle that world powers
Upon their own foundation
Wage with human forces,
When she herself dispels
The sleep at senses' borders
That shrouds our knowledge-forces
In spirit's darkest night.

7
Faust, The World's Greatest Poetic Work of Human Striving: The Classical Phantasmagoria

Dornach, May 30, 1915

If you take the remarks I made here yesterday together with the other lectures I gave here a week ago,† you will find in them, in a certain way, an important key to much of the content of spiritual science. So that we may find our way more easily into today's topic, I would like to begin with the main ideas we will need for our further considerations.

A week or so ago, I drew your attention to the significance of processes that from the point of view of the physical world we call processes of destruction. I said that from the viewpoint of the physical world we actually only speak of something as being real when we see it coming into being, arising out of nothing, so to speak, and entering into a state of existence that we can notice. For example, we say that something real is going on when a plant works its way up out of its root, adds one leaf after another, and finally puts forth a blossom, and so on. But we do not speak in the same way about something real when we look at processes of destruction: at wilting, for example, or a gradual process of dissolution and an ultimate streaming back into nothingness. But if we want to understand the world, it is eminently necessary that we also pay attention to what we call destruction, the processes of dissolution that, as far as the physical world is concerned, end up flowing away into nothingness. For the fact is that conscious awareness within the physical world can never come about where processes of sprouting and growth are taking place, but only where what has sprouted into being in the physical world is dismantled again and carried away, annihilated.

I have pointed out how the processes called forth in us by life itself have to be destroyed by our soul-spiritual nature if consciousness is to arise in the physical world. It is so, in fact, that for us to perceive something outside ourselves, our soul-spiritual nature, working within our nervous system, has to bring about processes of destruction, and these processes of destruction then make it possible for us to be conscious. Whenever we become aware of something, our processes of consciousness have to originate from processes of destruction. I have also indicated that the process of destruction most significant for all of human life, the process of death, is precisely what creates the consciousness we then have in the time we spend after our death. The fact that our soul-spiritual nature experiences the complete dissolution and separation of the physical and etheric bodies and their absorption into the general physical and etheric worlds is what enables our soul-spiritual nature to create—out of the death process itself—the strength to also experience processes of perception between death and a new earthly birth.[†] In view of all this, the saying of Jakob Böhme that death is the root of all life can be understood on a much deeper level within the context of world-phenomena as a whole.

You have probably often asked yourselves: What are things like, anyway, during the period of time the human soul passes through between death and a new birth? It has often been pointed out that for a normal human life this period of time is relatively long compared to the time we spend here in the physical body between birth and death. It is brief only in the case of people who have lived their lives in a manner contrary to the interests of the world, in other words, those who have managed to do things of a truly criminal nature. In these cases we find them spending only a brief period of time between death and a new birth. But there are also people who did not succumb to egoism in their lives between birth and death; in their case, we usually find a relatively long duration of time between death and a new birth.

Nevertheless, the burning question must still confront us: By what does a human soul let itself be guided when the time has arrived for it to embark on a new physical incarnation? The answer to this question is intimately connected with everything we can know about the significance of the processes of destruction I have referred to. Just imagine how we are born into quite specific circumstances when our souls enter upon a new physical existence. We are born into a particular historical age, brought together with specific people, and so on—quite specific circumstances. Sometime you must ponder very deeply the fact that our life between birth and death is filled with everything into which we have been born. What we think, what we feel, what we sense—in short, the entire content of our life depends on the particular period of time into which we have been born.

But now you will also easily understand that what surrounds us when we are born into a physical existence is dependent on preceding causes, on something else that has taken place earlier. Let us assume—if I may make a picture of this for you—that we are born at a particular point in time and then pass through life between birth and death. Now when you add to this picture what is all around you, you will see that this is not just standing there all by itself but is there as the effect of something that comes from an earlier time. What I mean is that you have been brought together with something earlier, namely, with people. These people are the children of other people, and these of other people, and so on. Now if we take only the relationships resulting from this series of generations into consideration, you will say: By entering into physical existence I take on something from all these people; in the process of being educated I absorb a great deal from the people around me. But these people in turn have absorbed a great deal from their ancestors, the friends and relatives of their ancestors, and so on. We could say that people have to go back farther and farther in order to look for the causes of what they themselves are.

Continuing this line of thought, we can say that in this way we can follow a certain stream back beyond our birth. This stream, as it were, has brought us everything that surrounds us in our life between birth and death. And if we follow this stream back farther and farther, we come to a point somewhere in time where we find our own former incarnation. By following backward the time before our birth, we would thus see a long period of time that we had actually spent in the spiritual world. Now during this time a great deal has taken place on earth, and everything that has taken place has brought about the conditions into which we have been born and in which we now are living. Then, in the spiritual world, we finally come to the time when we were on earth in an earlier incarnation. When we speak about these things, we are talking about what is absolutely true as a general rule. Of course, there are numerous exceptions, but they all lie along the line I have indicated for souls who return to an earthly incarnation more rapidly.

Now what are the determining factors that cause us to be born again, right here, after a certain period of time has elapsed? Well, when we look back to our earlier incarnations, we also find certain circumstances that surrounded us during that period of time on earth and have had their corresponding effects. There were people all around us, and these people had children whom they passed their feelings and ideas to; then their children did the same thing with their children, and so on. But if you follow the course of this life history, you will find that there finally comes a time when it is no longer possible to notice in any of these progeny anything like or even remotely similar to what their ancestors were like. Everything is passed on, but the fundamental character of any particular era itself appears in its children in a weakened form, and even weaker in their grandchildren, and so on, until a time comes when there is nothing left of the fundamental character of the environment from the previous incarnation. You can see from this how the stream of time itself works away at the destruction of what had formerly been present in the environment as its fundamental character. This process of annihilation is something we watch in the period between death and a new birth. And when the character of the previous age has been completely done away with, when no trace of it is left, when everything that was of any concern or importance to us in an earlier incarnation has been completely annihilated, the moment arrives in which we again enter upon an earthly existence. Just as the second half of our life is a sort of dismantling of our physical existence, a similar kind of dismantling of earthly circumstances—again, a process of annihilation or destruction—also has to take place between death and a new birth. A new set of circumstances and relationships has to be present into which we are then born. In other words, we are born again when everything for the sake of which we were born the previous time has been annihilated and destroyed. This is how the idea of being destroyed[†] is connected with the successive recurrences of our earthly incarnations. And when we see our body fall away from our soul-spiritual nature, what creates our conscious awareness in the moment of death strengthens itself by virtue of this moment of death. By virtue of watching something being destroyed, we develop the very capacity to watch the process of destruction that has to run its course in the midst of earthly circumstances between our death and a new birth.

You will also understand now that if we have no interest at all in our earthly surroundings, such as in other people or other beings, but only in what suits us, so that we just slip through life from one day to the next, we will not have a very strong connection with earthly things and circumstances. We will also have no interest in pursuing their gradual dismantlement, but then will very soon be back again in order to correct this state of affairs so that we can really live with the circumstances we have to live with in order to learn to understand their gradual destruction. Someone who has never lived with earthly circumstances doesn't understand their destruction, their dissolution. For this reason, those who have experienced the fundamental character of some particular age most intensively by completely immersing themselves in it will have the special tendency, if nothing prevents this, of bringing about the destruction of what they have been born into, and then of reappearing when something completely new has come into being. To be sure, there are exceptions "in an upward direction," as I would like to call them, and it is essential that we give special consideration to these exceptions.

Let us say a person finds the way into a movement such as the one our spiritual-scientific movement is today, at a time when this movement is not only at odds with everything in its environment but is, in fact, something totally alien to it. Now this spiritual-scientific movement is not something we were born into, but rather something we have to work on first because we want it to become an integral part of the evolution of spiritual culture on the earth. Our task, above all else, is to live with the circumstances that offer so much resistance to everything spiritual-scientific and then to come back to the earth again when it has changed to such an extent that spiritual-scientific principles can really take hold in the life of culture. This is an example of an exception "upward." There are exceptions in both a "downward" and an "upward" direction. It is a fact that the most serious co-workers of spiritual science are preparing themselves for another earthly existence as soon as possible by using their present one to work at the disappearance of the circumstances they were born into. You see, therefore, that if you take hold of this last thought, you are then, to a certain extent, helping the spiritual beings guide the world by devoting yourselves to the innermost intentions of these spiritual beings.

If we really look at the state of the world today, we have to say that on the one hand something is heading straight into decadence and decline. People who have the heart and the soul for spiritual science were placed, as it were, into this very age in order to witness how ripe it is for decline. Here on earth, people are becoming acquainted with what they can get to know only on earth. But then they will carry that up into the spiritual worlds. There they will witness the decline of our age and then come again when what lies at the very heart of the innermost impulses of spiritual-scientific striving will have the task of calling forth a new age. This, we might say, is how the aims of the spiritual leaders and guides of earthly evolution are furthered by what people take up who are concerned with things that in a sense are really not part of the culture of their time.

Perhaps you are familiar with the objections people nowadays very often make to adherents of spiritual science, complaining that the latter are occupying themselves with something that often seems fruitless in an external sense, since it has no external influence on contemporary affairs. Well, there really is a need for people in a given earthly incarnation to occupy themselves also with something that has significance for future evolution but no direct significance for the present age. Whoever objects to this should take the following into consideration. Imagine this series of consecutive years: 1915, 1914, 1913, 1912.

We could go on with these. Imagine that these are consecutive years and that these signs (center) are the grain crops of the succeeding years. What I am drawing here (on the right) represents the mouths that eat these grains of cereal. Now someone can say: The only arrow

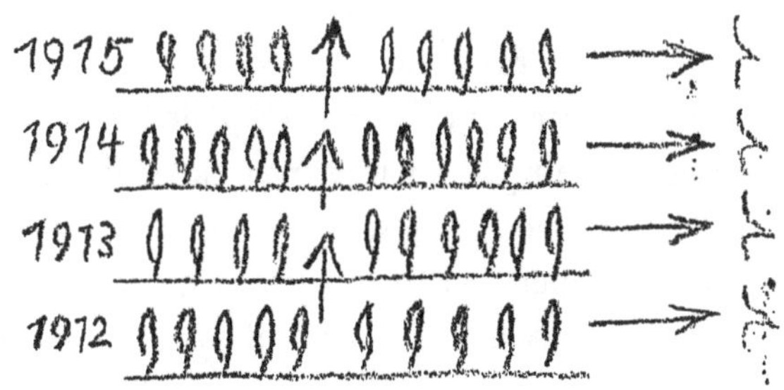

that means anything here is the one that goes from the grains into the mouths, →, because that is what feeds people in the following years. And that person can also say: Whoever thinks in accordance with reality will only look at these arrows that go from the grains into mouths. But the grain crops themselves are not very interested in this arrow. In fact, they don't care about it at all because their only intention is to develop every seed of grain on into the following year. They only care about this arrow ↑ and not at all about being eaten, which is just a side issue for them. Each grain, if I may put it this way, has the will, the impulse, to pass over into the next year and turn into another grain. And it is good for mouths that the grains follow this arrow ↑, because if all the grains would follow this one →, this mouth here wouldn't have anything more to eat next year! If all the grains from 1913 had followed this arrow →, the mouths in 1914 wouldn't have had anything to eat. If we wanted to be completely consistent in thinking this through materialistically, we would investigate the chemical composition of the grains to make sure their products would have the highest possible nutritional value. But this wouldn't be a very good observation because this is not the grains' intention; all they want to do is make sure they develop into next year's grain crop.

Now the same is true for the course of world development. People who genuinely follow the course of world development are the ones who see to it that evolution itself goes on, whereas the ones that become materialists follow the mouths that are only looking at this arrow here →. But there is just as little need to divert the ones from their striving to prepare for the following ages of world evolution as there is to divert the grains of cereal from their task of preparing for next year's crop, even though the mouths here demand that they pay attention to arrows pointing in a completely different direction.

I dealt with this way of thinking at the close of my book, *Riddles of Philosophy*.† There I pointed out that what is called materialistic knowledge can absolutely be compared with eating these grains of cereal, and that what is really going on in the world can be compared with reproduction: with what happens when this year's grain of cereal becomes next year's grain. This is why what we call scientific knowledge is of so little significance for the inner nature of things, just as eating is of so little importance for the continued growth of grain crops. Modern science, which is only concerned with how to get what we can learn from things into the human intellect, does the same thing as someone who uses grain for eating. What grains are when they're being eaten has nothing to do with their inner nature, just as little as external knowledge has to do with what goes on in the inner nature of things.

I have tried in this way to put an idea out into the bustling world of philosophical thinking to see whether it would be understood for once, or whether such a plausible idea would be met over and over again only by the foolish one—which Kant,[†] after all, has already proved—that our knowledge can never reach as far as the things themselves. But he has proved this only for the kind of knowledge that can be compared with eating grains, not for the kind that arises with the progressive development inherent in things.

We have to learn how to repeat in every possible way—just not in ways that are rash, fanatic, or inflammatory—the nature and essential principles of spiritual science over and over again to people of our present age, as well as of the coming one, until it has been drummed into them and they have gotten the message. For the characteristic of our age is that Ahriman has made people's skulls so hard and dense that they can only be softened up gradually. None of us should shrink back from the necessity of finding every possible way to stress the essential nature and impulse of spiritual science.

Now, however, we will look at another conclusion that we came to yesterday on the basis of various presuppositions, namely, that our age must experience an increase in the growth of reverence for truth and in reverence for knowledge, not for authoritative knowledge but for the kind of knowledge we acquire on our own. The attitude must become more widespread that people should not form judgments out of nothingness but on the basis of knowledge they have acquired about what actually happens in the world.

As we have seen, being born into a specific age makes us completely dependent on our environment and everything in it. But we have also seen that this connection is part of the whole stream of evolution or striving that leads in an "upward" direction, namely, the fact that the circumstances we are born into are dependent on the previous ones.

Think how we get into these circumstances. Of course we are placed there by our karma, but these circumstances are always quite specific and have a definite character. And now consider how derivative our entire way of judging things becomes as a result. This fact is not always readily apparent, but it is nevertheless how things are. So that, even if karmic connections are at work in all this, we still have to ask ourselves: What would things be like if we had not been born at this such and such a time and in this such and such a place, but fifty years earlier in some other place? How would everything be then? Wouldn't we have received the form and inner direction of our judgments from the different conditions of that other environment in the same way we received the ones we have now by being born where we are?

So you see that when we observe ourselves more closely, we really have to conclude that being born into a specific milieu or set of surroundings makes us so dependent on this milieu in our feelings and in how we judge things that whenever we make a judgment, the whole milieu reappears. Just think how different things would be, for example, if Luther had been born in the tenth century and at some other place! Even in the case of a personality who has such a strong influence on his surroundings, we can see how he absorbs what comes from his times into his own judgments, with the result that what he then actually does is to give these impulses back, as a child of his era.

This is the case for everyone; it is just that the ones for whom it is the strongest are the ones who notice it the least. As a rule, the people it is strongest for, those who only reflect back the impulses of their era, are the ones who talk the most about their freeness, their independent judgment, their lack of prejudice, and so on. On the other hand, when we come across those who are not as dependent on their environment as most others are, we see that these people are the very ones who become the most aware of what makes them dependent on their environment at all.

Among those who never lost the sense of how dependent they were on their environment was the great soul, Goethe, another of whose plays we have been privileged to see performed today. He was eminently aware that he would not have been the way he was if he had not been born in Frankfurt am Main in 1749, and so on. He knew that his era was expressing itself through him, as it were, and his whole attitude toward life was warmed and stimulated by this knowledge in quite an extraordinary way. He knew, for example, that his way of thinking had been formed by the fact that he had experienced certain events and situations in his father's house, as well as by the time he had spent studying in Leipzig and by his eventually going to Strasburg. This was why he wanted to get out of certain circumstances and into very different ones, so much so, in fact, that one time in the 1780s he suddenly disappeared in the dead of night[†] and only notified his friends of his disappearance after he was so far away that—as things stood at the time—they had no way to get him back. He wanted out so that something else would be able to express itself through him. If we take many of the things Goethe said, especially during his developmental years, we will notice everywhere this feeling or sense he had for how very dependent he was on his milieu.

What would Goethe have had to strive for if, at the moment it really dawned on him how totally dependent we actually are on our environment, he had connected his feelings and sense for this dependency with the ideas we have been exploring today? He would have had to say, "Well, yes, I have to admit that what makes up my environment is dependent on the whole stream that goes back to my ancestors. I will always be a product of this. I would have to go back in my thoughts and in my soul-experience to another time when conditions were very different from the way they are today. If I could place myself back into those other conditions, I would come to a way of thinking independently and no longer just form judgments in the way my own era does about itself, but in the way I am able to when I lift myself entirely out of my own era."

Now the success of the matter cannot of course depend on whether or not the people who feel the necessity of doing this would end up precisely in their own former incarnation. But it would be essential for them to reach a point in time connected with a former incarnation where they had lived in quite different circumstances. And if they go back to this incarnation, they are no longer dependent on it the way they were then, because in the meantime the circumstances have become completely different, in that the former ones have been destroyed, have perished. Of course, it is a very different matter if I go back to a time of which the whole surrounding milieu has disappeared. What are we dealing with here? Well, we have to say: Earlier, we lived in that life; we were bound up in it and enjoyed its benefits. But we can no longer be bound up with a life of an earlier time that has all passed away. We can only experience that life now in a soul-spiritual way. In such a case we could say, "In this reflected splendor we have life." (4727)

What would have to happen if a man who felt this way wanted to depict his exit from the circumstances of the present and his entrance into a way of making objective judgments from a point of view that is not possible today? He would have to depict it by showing how he was actually placed back into completely different circumstances. What matters here is not whether this incarnation is his own previous one or not, but that the circumstances on earth are completely different. And then he would have to strive to fill his soul with the impulses that were present at that time. He would have to place himself into a sort of phantasmagoria, as it were, identifying with this phantasmagoria and living in it as in a sort of phantasmagoria representing a former era.

This is what Goethe was striving for as he continued writing the second part of his *Faust*. Remember that he had first brought Faust out into the conditions and circumstances of the modern world, where he allowed him to experience everything one can today. But all the while, he was plagued by the feeling that *this* life could not guide him to judgments that are true in any way. "I'm always at the mercy of my environment," he said to himself; "I've got to get out of here and go back in time to circumstances that by now have completely changed and will therefore not be able to affect how I look at things." This is why Goethe has Faust go all the way back to the time of classical Greece, where he brings him together with everything that happens in the "Classical Walpurgis Night."

What Goethe depicted in the northern Walpurgis Night is what Faust could experience most deeply in the present. Now he has to go back to the classical Walpurgis Night, because from the northern Walpurgis Night to the classical Walpurgis Night all conditions have changed. The essential nature of the Classical Walpurgis Night has disappeared and has been replaced by new circumstances symbolized by the northern Walpurgis Night. This is his justification for having Faust go back to the time of ancient Greece. The whole second part of *Faust* is the realization of what we can designate by the phrase: "In this reflected splendor we have life." (4727)

The first thing that happens is that Faust passes through the circumstances of the present day, but these very circumstances are preparing their own destruction. Soon we see what unfolds at the "Imperial Palace," where the Devil takes the place of the Fool, and so on.

In the creation of Homunculus we see the striving to escape from the present, and at last, in Act III, how the whole classical scene appears. Goethe had already written the beginning of this scene around the turn of the eighteenth century. The most important scenes were not added until 1825, but the Helen scene had already been written by 1800. Goethe called it a "Classical Phantasmagoria" in order to imply that what he had in mind was a transfer or transposition backward into circumstances that are not the real, physical ones of the present-day world.

I would like to say that the most significant thing about Goethe's *Faust* is that it is a work of striving and of struggle. I think I have managed to stress sufficiently clearly in recent times how nonsensical it would be to think of Goethe's *Faust* as a finished work of art. I have done enough to show that this is not even a question. But as a work of striving and struggle, Goethe's *Faust* is all the more significant. When we step into the light that can shine from our spiritual science onto a composition of this sort and see how Faust gazes into the classical age, that ancient Greek milieu of the fourth post-Atlantean era when quite different conditions were present than now in our fifth post-Atlantean one, we can understand for the first time what Goethe managed to achieve in his intuitive way. We feel the deepest reverence for what he was struggling to achieve when we see how he began his work on *Faust* as a young man, literally giving himself over to all the resources available to him at that time without really understanding very well what he was doing. It really is true that in approaching *Faust* we have to come at it from the viewpoint of spiritual science, for the judgments the outer world sometimes comes up with in regard to *Faust* are really quite foolish.

How, for example, could someone familiar with spiritual science not be struck by the fact that people who consider themselves especially clever insist on pointing out again and again how wonderfully this Faust succeeds in affirming his faith in God, and how they go on to say, "Indeed, compared to all the things so many people say about some creed or other, we should be increasingly reminded of the conversation between Faust and Gretchen:

> ...It's all just feeling;
> Name is but noise and smoke,
> Beclouding Heaven's glow." (3456-58)

Well, you know very well what Faust is deliberating about here with Gretchen, which people cite again and again whenever they think it especially necessary to emphasize what should not be regarded as religious deepening and what should be regarded as religious feeling. They just fail to consider that in this instance Faust was giving a form to his views on religion for the benefit of a sixteen-year-old Gretchen and that what all the clever professors are actually demanding is that people should never get beyond this Gretchen-standpoint in the development of their religious views. The moment Faust's religious confession to Gretchen is presented as though it were something especially sublime the demand is being made that humanity never elevate itself above the Gretchen-level. That is really a very comfortable position to be in and an easy one to attain. But while it is also very easy to make a great show of how everything is only feeling and so forth, it nevertheless goes unnoticed that this is only looking at things from Gretchen's standpoint.

Goethe, for his part, was striving in a very different way to make his Faust the bearer of an ongoing struggle, as I have indicated by referring even to this self-placement back into an earlier and completely different incarnation in order to come to an understanding of the truth. Perhaps at the very same time, or possibly a little earlier, when Goethe was writing this "Classical-Romantic Phantasmagoria" as a picture of Faust's transportation back into the world of ancient Greece, Goethe wanted once more to get a clearer idea of how things should run their course in this *Faust* of his and what all he wanted to represent in it. And so he wrote down a plan for himself. At that time, what there was of his *Faust* consisted of a number of scenes that constituted the basis of Part I, and probably also the Helen scene. This is what he wrote:

> "Ideal striving for working and feeling one's way into the whole of Nature."†

And so, as the century was coming to a close, and under Schiller's incessant urging, Goethe got back to work on what he called "the old tragelaph, the barbaric composition."† He had good reason at the end of the century to refer to his *Faust* this way because it really had been written scene after scene. Now he asked himself: "What have I done here, anyway?" And he imagined Faust striving to make his way out of the world of scholarship and more and more deeply into the world of Nature.

Here are some notes he wrote as a part of a sketch for the appearance of the Earth Spirit:

> "What I wanted to put there was:
>
> 1. Ideal striving for working and feeling one's way into the whole of Nature.
> 2. Appearance of the Spirit as genius of the world and deeds."

Now I have already explained to you how Wagner, who comes in just after Faust's encounter with the Earth Spirit, is really meant to be a part of Faust. He is only a means by which Faust can come to an understanding of himself and what he really is. Something is at war in Faust, and we can ask what this is and what Faust does while this battle is raging within him. First of all he realizes: "So far you have only been living in your surroundings, in what the outer world has offered you." He can see this most clearly in Wagner, who, as an externalized piece of Faust himself, is so totally at home in his pedantic world. Whereas Faust is just on the brink of attaining something that will set him free from what one is simply born into, Wagner is content to remain what he is and within what the outer world has made of him. But what is it that lives on in the outside world, from generation to generation and epoch to epoch? We can call it Form: the bearer of the stamp of all human striving. The Spirits of Form are working away at this outside of us, and we are intended to become an integral part of it. But as human beings we must always be striving to get beyond this Form if we really want to make progress and not die out within it. Goethe makes a note of this as well: "Battle between Form and formlessness."

3. "Battle between Form and formlessness."

But now Faust takes a really good look at this Form: at the Faust he sees out there in Wagner. This Form is something he wants to get free of, and his desire to do this is itself a striving for the inner content of this Form, a new content that can come into being out of his own inner nature.

We too, after all, once we had decided to erect a building for spiritual science here in Dornach, could have looked around at all the available forms and stylistic possibilities and then chosen one of them as the basis for our new building, as many architects evidently did in the nineteenth century. But then we would not have created anything new out of the Form that has come down to us in the process of world evolution; that would have been mere Wagner-nature. Instead we chose to seek a "formless content." We have tried to take spiritual science, experienced in a living way, out of what at first is only pure, formless content and then pour it into new forms.

Faust does the same thing when he dismisses Wagner with the words:

> Don't be a fool's cap-wearing fool!
> Reason and good common sense
> Speak for themselves without much art. (549-51)

4. "Preference for formless content" is what Goethe writes next.

And this is the scene in which Faust dismisses Wagner: "Preference for formless content over empty form." But form becomes empty as time goes on. If someone were to build a building just like the one we're building a hundred years from now, that would again be just an empty form. This is what we have to consider. So the next thing Goethe writes is:

> 5. "Content brings its form along."

This is what I so wish we could all experience! This is something we want to achieve with our building: Content brings its form along. For "Form," as Goethe then writes, "is never without content." Of course it is never without content, but the world's "Wagners" don't see the content in it, which is why they are so accepting of what is only empty form. Form is as justified as it can possibly be. But all progress consists precisely in the fact that old form is overcome by new content.

> 6. "Form is never without content."

> 1. Ideal striving for working and feeling one's way into the whole of Nature.
> 2. Appearance of the Spirit as genius of the world and deeds.
> 4. Battle between Form and formlessness.
> 5. Preference for formless content over empty form.
> 6. Content brings its form along.
> 7. Form is never without content. (Paralipomena, 5)

And now we have a sentence that Goethe writes in order to give his *Faust* a certain impulse, a highly characteristic sentence. Wagner-natures, you see, think about such questions: Hm… form, content… how can I bring that all together…mix it all up? You can very well imagine some person nowadays who wants to be an artist saying: "Well, O.K., spiritual science…fine. But it is no concern of mine what all these complicated minds are coming up with in the way of spiritual science. But now they want to build a hall. I thought it was supposed to have some Greek, or Renaissance or Gothic elements in it. But now that I see the hall, I can see what they're thinking into it, how the content of the hall they're building matches the form." We can imagine that things will eventually come to this. They will have to, when people start thinking about getting rid of contradictions, even though the world is basically made up of contradictions and everything depends on our being able to place all the contradictions side by side. And so Goethe writes:

7. "These contradictions, instead of being united, are to be made more disparate."

This means that in *Faust* he wants to present them in such a way that they stand out as strongly as possible: "These contradictions, instead of being united, are to be made more disparate." In order to do this, he once again puts two figures opposite each other, one of whom lives completely in Form and is quite content to adhere to this Form, greedily digging for treasures of knowledge and is happy to find earthworms (604-05). In our time we could say: greedily striving for the secret of human evolution and happy when he discovers, for instance, that humanity has evolved from an animal species similar to our hedgehogs and rabbits. Edinger, one of the most significant philosophers of our time,[†] recently gave a lecture on the subject of how the human being originated from a primitive form similar to our hedgehog and rabbit. Science has long since gone beyond the concept that the world of humans is descended from monkeys (simians), prosimians-on-the-way-to-becoming-monkeys, and the like, hasn't it? Now it is time to go back even farther to the point where the animal species as such splits off even earlier. At that time there were ancestors that resembled the modern hedgehog or rabbit, and on the other hand we have the human being as our ancestor. Now, since we modern humans are most similar to the hedgehog and the rabbit with respect to certain features of our brain formation, we have to be descended from something similar, don't we? These animal species have been preserved, but the other has naturally died out entirely. So, we go on greedily digging for treasures and are happy when we find rabbits and hedgehogs. That's the one kind of striving—a striving within nothing but pure form. Goethe wanted to show us this in the figure of Wagner, and he well knew that this is a very clever kind of striving. People are not stupid; they're clever. Goethe calls it "Bright, cold, scientific striving." And then he adds, "Wagner."

8. "Bright, cold, scientific striving: Wagner."

The other, disparate thing is what we desire to work up from within ourselves with every fiber of our souls, after not finding it anywhere in the outer forms. "Dull, warm, scientific striving" is what Goethe calls it. He opposes this statement to the one he had written just before, and then he adds the word, "Student." At this point, after Faust has been approached by Wagner, he is also approached by the student. Faust remembers what it had been like when he was a student and had to absorb all he did in the way of philosophy, jurisprudence, medicine and, unfortunately, theology as well. (354-57) He also remembers what he had said to all of that, back in the days when he was just like this student: "I feel so stupid from all this that it is as though a mill wheel were turning in my head." (1946-47) But that's all behind him now. He also can't go back to looking at things this way any more. And yet all of this has had its effect on him, so Goethe writes:

9. "Dull, warm scientific striving: Student."

And this is how it goes on. From now on we see Faust actually becoming a student and getting back into everything that enables a person to take in the life of the present.

Goethe now characterizes the remainder of Part I, to the extent that it had already been completed or would ever be, as:

10. "Enjoyment of life by the person, seen from outside; in dullness and passion, Part I."

This shows how precise Goethe is in making it clear to himself what he has created here. Now he wants to say, "How do we go on from here? How is Faust supposed to get out of this one-sided way of enjoying life as a single person and into an objective way of viewing the world?" To do this, he must get as far as Form itself, but then he must grasp Form with his whole essential nature. We have seen how far he has to go back: to the point where quite other conditions prevail. Then Form will approach him as reflected splendor. It will come toward him in such a way that he will absorb it by becoming one with the truth that was entirely justified at that time and by stripping off everything which, in the process, had to happen in that age. In other words, he tries to place himself into that time, insofar as it was not permeated by the influence of Lucifer. He tries to go back to the divine standpoint of ancient Greece.

Now if we immerse ourselves in the external world in such a way that we enter it with our whole essential nature, leaving behind all of the circumstances we have grown into, we arrive at what Goethe calls beauty in the highest sense. This is why he no longer speaks of "enjoyment by the person, enjoyment of life," but of "enjoyment of deeds." "Enjoyment of deeds" is a process of going out, gradually growing more and more distant from oneself. Living one's way into the world is an enjoyment of deeds in an outward direction and an enjoyment with conscious awareness.

> 11. "Enjoyment of deeds in an outward direction and enjoyment with conscious awareness: Beauty, Part II."

What Goethe himself was no longer able to achieve through his own personal struggles, since his era was not yet the era of spiritual science, he nevertheless sketched out for himself at the turn of the eighteenth to the nineteenth century. We can see this from the highly significant words he has at the end of the outline he wrote then, the first part of which was a recapitulation of what he had done. He was already planning to write a kind of third part to his *Faust*; but he only got as far as the two parts we have, which do not fully express all he had in mind, since for this he would have needed spiritual science.

What Goethe wanted to depict is our experience of the whole of creation outside ourselves once we have managed to get free of our own personal life. What Goethe, in what I would call stammering words, outlines for himself as: "Enjoyment of creation from within," is this: We can experience the whole of creation objectively in the world outside ourselves by carrying outside ourselves what is truly inward, thereby experiencing creation from within outward. In other words, not from our own personal, subjective standpoint, but from the one we have attained by stepping outside ourselves.

12. "Enjoyment of creation from within."

With this "enjoyment of creation from within," Faust had not only entered the classical world, but the world of the spiritual itself.

The outline ends with a very peculiar statement that refers to a scene Goethe did not write, but wanted to, and certainly would have written if he had already been living in our age—a scene he could already envision. What he wrote was:

13. "Epilogue in Chaos on the way to hell."

I have heard very clever people speak about what these final words: "Epilogue in Chaos on the way to hell" could possibly mean. What they said was, "So, in 1800 Goethe really still had the idea of having Faust go to hell, but having him hold an epilogue in Chaos before he got there? It was only much, much later that he got the idea of having Faust not go to hell!" As I said, I have probably heard many more scholarly conversations on this topic than I can count! The consensus seems to be that in 1800 Goethe was still not free of the idea of having Faust go to hell after all. But these people were all missing the point: obviously, it was not Faust holding the epilogue, but Mephistopheles, after Faust had escaped his clutches and gone to Heaven!

Today we would say that Lucifer and Ahriman hold the epilogue on their way to hell; along the way they would be talking about their experiences with Faust and all his striving.

I wanted to call your attention to this outline and recapitulation, because once again it really shows in an outstanding way how Goethe used every means he could acquire in his era to strive for the way that leads straight upward into the region of spiritual science.

We will be viewing *Faust* in the right way only if we ask ourselves the following questions: Why did *Faust* remain an incomplete work of art, as far as its innermost core is concerned, in spite of the fact that (1) it is the greatest poetic work of human striving in the world, and (2) Faust is the representative of all humanity because he is striving to escape from his own milieu, and is even carried back into an earlier time? Why did this *Faust* nevertheless remain such an unsatisfying work of poetic art? Because it represented only a preliminary striving for what spiritual science is ultimately to incorporate into the evolution of human culture.

It is good to direct our attention to this fact and to consider that at the turn of the eighteenth to the nineteenth century a poetic work came into being in which its central figure, Faust, was to be lifted out of all the limitations a human being must be surrounded by while passing through life in repeated earthly incarnations. The significant thing about Faust is that, although he is such an intense product of his own folk culture, he has nevertheless grown beyond this folk culture and into the realm of what is generally human. He has nothing of the narrow limitations of a folk culture about him. Instead, he strives upward to the generally human in such a way that we not only find him as the Faust of our more modern age, but in Part II as a Faust who stands as a Greek among Greeks. It is a monstrous relapse in our time that in the course of the nineteenth century people have again begun to put the greatest weight on the limitations of human evolution and even to see in the "national idea" an idea that could somehow still be a culture-bearing factor in our present epoch. Humanity could work itself up in a most marvelous way to an understanding of what spiritual science is intended to become if people were willing to understand such a thing in the way it has been secretly inserted into *Faust*.

It was not for nothing that when Goethe had finished writing the second part of *Faust*, he told Eckermann he had hidden many secrets in it that would only gradually come to light.[†]

Herman Grimm,[†] about whom I have often spoken to you, also pointed out that it will take a full thousand years to understand Goethe completely. I have to say that I think so too. Once people have experienced an even greater deepening than they have in our time, they will understand more and more of what is really to be found in Goethe, especially of what he struggled and strove for but was never quite able to express. If you would ask Goethe whether what he put into the second part of *Faust* was really all that he had wanted to say, he would answer, "No!" But if we would ask him today, "Are we, with our spiritual science, on the same path you were striving for in the way it was possible at that time?" we may be sure he would reply without reserve, "The paths of spiritual science are the same as mine."

Since Goethe had his Faust go back as far as Greece in order to be allowed to portray him as someone who understands the present, so may we be allowed to say that what we must acquire is reverence for truth—reverence for the knowledge that struggles to find its way out of the knowledge of the milieu, out of the limitations of the surrounding world. The events of our time are warning us that humanity is heading toward exactly the opposite extreme, judging things in the most shortsighted way possible and desiring to go back no farther than the events of 1914 in order to explain what we are experiencing in such a horrible way today.

But anyone wishing to understand the present age will need to look at it from a more elevated standpoint than the one of this present age itself.

This is what in these days I again wished to lay into your souls in the form of a feeling. I wanted to show you how this feeling follows from a really inward, living understanding of spiritual science and how it has been striven for by the greatest minds of the past, of whom Goethe was one.

Only when we take such considerations into our hearts, not merely as something theoretical, but as something we work on there, allowing it to live in our meditative life, will spiritual science become alive. May we do this with everything that passes through our souls as spiritual science!

8
Faust's Ascension

Dornach, August 14, 1915

Tomorrow we are scheduled to undertake the challenging task of performing the final scene of Goethe's *Faust* in eurythmy. It will therefore make sense if today's and tomorrow's lectures are devoted to this scene. The whole second part of *Faust*, and especially this closing scene, must be regarded as one of the very greatest poetic efforts in all of world evolution, based as it is on spiritual truths of the highest significance. Nevertheless, as true as it may be that Goethe's *Faust* can be understood on many levels, it is also true that there is no end to how far we can go in pursuing what flowed into it from the infinite richness of Goethe's soul life, particularly into its second part.

In addition, when we look at the fine points of what is depicted in the closing scene of Part II, we will find more esoteric truths in this scene than hardly any other writer of world stature has ever attempted to reveal. We will also see that these truths have been secretly inserted into the second part of *Faust* with a marvelously esoteric-scientific character, if I may use such an apparently pedantic expression: a scientific character totally in harmony with its esoteric subject.

Now I have to confess that I would not dare speak about *Faust* in the way I intend to if I were not able to look back on a problem with Faust and Goethe that I have been working on ever since 1884.[†] I hope you will allow me to hint at certain things in an aphoristic way for which someone not coming from a background in spiritual science would require a much more solid basis. It is also not without a certain hesitation that I find myself about to link some observations of an esoteric nature to Goethe's *Faust*, and indeed to a work of poetry at all. In undertaking this I am reminded of all sorts of deplorable things that have been achieved by esotericists and non-esotericists alike in their interpretations of literary works.

We really have to be somewhat wary of discussing literature from an esoteric point of view when we think of all the crimes committed with respect to such interpretations, both by literary scholars and by so-called theosophists! And so, I ask your permission to precede my remarks with a kind of introduction so that you can see from it just how little inclined I am to blithely dream esoteric truths and knowledge into some poetic work or other that has to do with the spiritual evolution of humanity and how concerned I am to bring forth only what is solidly based in reality.

Now when I have to speak on some particular topic, my usual practice is to immerse myself beforehand somewhat more deeply in its various aspects. Just taking esoteric observations seriously already requires us to feel our way into the whole atmosphere in which the topic is being dealt with. And so, in this case I made a special effort to get back into Goetheanism.

For this purpose I had to review a number of literary aids I had dealt with decades earlier. This is how I came to take another look at Goethe's *Soothsayings of Bakis.*† These consist of thirty-two verses clothed in the form of riddles—thirty-two riddles, you could say. Now you can imagine that an endless amount has been written about what Goethe went on to call *Soothsayings* and over which he poured a kind of orientalizing wisdom. Of course, this was a real feast for literary historians, and all kinds of people have discovered the most colossal mysteries in these thirty-two rhymed riddles.

Let me begin with a characteristic example: the twenty-ninth and thirtieth riddles that Goethe cast into this verse form. It will be very good for us to immerse ourselves in this kind of riddle-verse before we move on to the final scene of *Faust.*

> One thing I know which is honored, indeed on the foot even worshipped;
> Placed on the part of one's hair, it is by everyone cursed.
> One thing I know that firmly is pressed by the lip so contented;
> Yet in the moment that's next it is the scourge of the world.
>
> (# 29)

We have to admit this sounds very mysterious! The thirtieth riddle-verse goes like this:

> This is the highest of all, at the very same time the most common,
> Now the peak of all joy, now most repugnant to all.
> Savor it only in sipping while tasting it never more deeply:
> Under the charms of the froth, dregs to the bottom will sink.
>
> (#30)

Before we see how a theosophist of this ilk goes about "interpreting" these mysterious verses, let us take a look at one of the exoteric attempts. Of course, we can't make head or tail of what he says, but that doesn't hurt; we can still see from the example what so-called "science" looks like: "A very peculiar turn of phrase! Just in this instance, Goethe chose the riddle—the most capricious of all forms—in order to conceal his meaning and reveal it at the same time." Another Goethe-interpreter epitomized these verses as referring to "freedom and love." This good man accuses the other one of being at a loss, and then proceeds to offer his own interpretation. "The highest and, at the same time, the most repugnant thing there is." This is supposed to be youth. Youth enjoys the highest as well as the most repugnant. This, he tells us, is how the riddle solves itself.

There's an exoteric commentator for you! An esotericist could say we have to look at things like this on an infinitely deeper level!

> One thing I know which is honored, indeed on the foot even worshipped;*
> Placed on the part of one's hair,** it is by everyone cursed.
> One thing I know that firmly is pressed by the lip so contented;
> Yet in the moment that's next it is the scourge of the world.
>
> [*or: worshipped (when it is) on foot]
> [**or: placed on the part of its hair, i.e., stood on its head] (#29)

This refers to a plant, we could say, since the plant is an upside-down picture of the human being. We can also connect it with the Logos and

Lucifer, or with white and black magic, and so on! Theosophical literature abounds in explanations of this sort.

However, living our way into spiritual science is not just a matter of taking what we have learned there and applying it to anything at all, but rather of finding the right relationship—as in our present case, for instance, to Goethe. Spiritual science should not mislead us into spinning all sorts of fantasies but should take us to the source of truth. Then we will find that what is meant in the first two lines of the first verse is a slipper, and in the last two, a cigar! Goethe hated cigar smoke. That is the truth; it is not very deep, but it is what he meant. And the solution to the second verse is "Spiritus" or "spirit(s)." [The German word *Spiritus* means both "spirit" and "alcohol."] As the spirit, it is the highest thing there is; in alcohol, as drunkenness, it is the most disgusting. Going through a process like this at least once is a very good thing to do. We should really not allow ourselves to be blinded by the art of interpretation and other such profound arts, but should let ourselves be guided to the truth.

Goethe has also been made into a national chauvinist, which he was not, in any sense of the word. Let us take the fifth verse as an example:

> Two things I see! The great one! I see the greater one! Each
> Grinding the other to bits, clashing as enemies do.
> Here we have rocks and the land, there we have cliffs and the water!
> Which one the greater one is, only the Parca[†] can say. (#5)

This was said to refer to the Continental Powers, the battle between France and England. The commentator cited above rejects this, however, saying that what it means are the French Revolution and the German people. Now this is really foolish! What it actually means is life and death!

This is not a matter to be taken lightly. The fact that something can be proved is no proof at all that it is correct.

I wanted to say these things first so that you will not think I intend to succumb to the same error in explaining the closing scene of *Faust*. What this last scene depicts could be called "Faust's Ascension."[†] As we know, Faust has gone seriously astray, passing through all possible trials and tribulations in the wider, greater world. We are to be shown how Faust is led through all these tribulations and brought under the influence of Ahriman-Mephistopheles. But the deepest element in him, which lies as an eternal element within the human breast, is not to be nibbled at by any influence coming from Mephisto-Ahriman. In the final analysis, Faust is to be capable of being taken up into the good spiritual worlds. That is what Goethe undertook as the aim of his *Faust*.

Someone who has learned something about spiritual worlds from a study of spiritual science but doesn't have much of an artistic sense can generally form an idea of how to put this knowledge into poetic form. For Goethe, who was an artist through and through, this was not such a simple matter. He could not simply come up with some abstract, allegorical structure and use it to depict Faust's ascension into heaven. For him that would have been nothing but straw, empty symbols, something he did not want. What he wanted was art, something that could hold its own in the face of true reality. And so he began to think about the matter somewhat like this: How am I going to show on stage that Faust is being taken up into heaven? The most I can do is to put objects from the physical plane there that can only hint at something symbolic. But again, that would only be straw, not art! Even the most elaborate stage machinery could only depict straw. First Goethe had to look around for some worldly medium through which Faust could penetrate upward as a soul into the spiritual worlds. It is not possible to make one's way up into the spiritual worlds by going through the air or any other external physical element. Where then is something real that can provide the medium through which Faust is able to make his way upward? That can only be something that already represents the spiritual on earth. Well, where is that on earth? What absorbs the spiritual into itself is consciousness! This means that Goethe's first task was to create a reality of consciousness or conscious awareness that takes in the spiritual. He did this by placing into this setting human beings who can be assumed to have the spiritual already living in their consciousness. These are the monks, or anchorites, whom he arranges on different levels. Now one can say that the ascent of a soul into the spiritual worlds is a real process. It would not be real to depict a purely spiritual process in front of an ordinary audience, because this process has no roots in them; but it does have roots in the souls Goethe presents us with. In them, he was seeking first of all to depict the various consciousnesses who witness the spiritual process. This is why he also puts in both the Chorus and its Echo, since they can perceive the elemental world of the spirit within what is physical and sensory. They have prepared themselves to see, within the physical plane, not only external physical Nature but also the spiritual world into which the soul of Faust must enter.

And now things are depicted in such a way as only these monks can sense them. For if you just look at the words themselves, you will see that they are really not depictions of physical processes:

> Woodlands come swaying up. (11844)

This is what it is like to feel the elemental world emerging from the objects in Nature.

> Woodlands come swaying up,
> Cliff sides weigh heavily,
> Roots, how they tightly clutch,
> Trunk next to trunk so close,
> Wave upon wave, they spray,
> Cavern, the deepest, guards,
> Lions slink, friendly, but
> Mute in their circling round,
> Honor this sacred place,
> Love's holy safe retreat. (11844-53)

This chorus has an echo, which is not without significance. Its aim is to show us that what comes out of elemental Nature really comes from all sides.

At the same time we are now led to something that undergoes a marvelous intensification in Goethe's hands. Three anchorites come before us who have made some progress in their spiritual development: Pater Ecstaticus, Pater Profundus and Pater Seraphicus. These three have attained higher stages than the others, who as anchorites can only describe the events that have just been portrayed.

In moving from Pater Ecstaticus through Pater Profundus to Pater Seraphicus, we experience a marvelous progression. Pater Ecstaticus has to do with the lower stages of perfection—with sensory experiences and being within the self. Pater Profundus has progressed to the point where he goes from within himself outward, experiencing what pervades Nature as living spirit and yet at the same time is also the human spirit. From a spiritual point of view, he stands higher than Pater Ecstaticus. We can say that Pater Profundus sees the spirit in the cosmos, which at the same time becomes for him the spirit in the human being. Pater Seraphicus looks directly into the world of the spirit; this world does not have to reveal itself to him through Nature since he is in direct contact with the spirit itself.

This is why we see Pater Ecstaticus becoming mystical as a result of inner development. What he now says refers to purely inner states of being:

> Infinite fire of bliss,
> Luminous bond of love,
> Turbulent pain in my breast,
> Feverish joy in God,
> Arrows, tear through my flesh,
> Lances, restrain my flesh,
> Cudgels, now batter me,
> Lightning bolts, shatter me;
> So that the All dissolve
> All that is trivial,
> Gleam the fixed star on high,
> Core of eternal love. (11654-65)

We have already gone through how Pater Profundus passes over to the stage of being able to feel the spirit through Nature.

> As rocks weigh down, on others resting,
> A deeper chasm at my feet,
> As radiant flow a thousand rivers
> Together toward their fateful plunge,

As straight, with mighty impulse towering,
The tree trunk thrusts itself aloft—
In all this works, creating, tending,
Its miracles all-powerful Love.
All around me wild confusion,
Like heaving of the rocks and woods!
And yet, so full of love in roaring,
The ample waters downward plunge
To irrigate the vale below them;
The lightning that struck down aflame,
The former atmosphere reviving
That harbored poisons in its breast:
Love's messengers are these, proclaiming
Creative life's unceasing surge.
May it inflame my inner being,
Where Spirit, all confused and cold,
Endures within dull senses' limits
The torments of their tight-drawn chains.
Oh God! Appease this tortured thinking,
Illuminate my needful heart. (11866-89)

Finally, we see in Pater Seraphicus the direct, conscious comprehending of the spiritual world into which Faust is to be received, that is, the direct, conscious comprehending of the spirits into whose midst Faust is now to first enter. Once again, a consciousness must first be put on stage for this to happen. This consciousness is Pater Seraphicus; he provides the medium through which the Blessed Boys can appear. And again, I must emphasize in what a wonderfully accurate way this has all been observed:

What little morning cloud is floating
Through the pine trees' weaving hair?
Do I sense what's living in it?
Children's spirits feel I there. (11890-93)

Goethe has children appear who have died immediately after birth. They are commonly called "those born at midnight." The first souls

Faust meets are the ones of those "born at midnight"; their former consciousness has been dimmed by birth, and they don't know anything about the new world as yet. This is an integral part of Faust's ascension. Just as in the physical world lightning is always followed by thunder, in the spiritual world an ascension such as Faust's is followed by a Blessed Boy's dawning self-awareness.

> Draw near now, for you can feel that
> One who loves you is at hand;
> But of earth's steep, dusty pathways
> —Lucky ones!—you have no trace. (11902-05)

It is only by looking through our eyes and listening through our ears that spiritual beings can become aware of the physical aspect of the physical plane at all; otherwise they only see its spiritual aspect. When a spiritual being sees a hand, what it sees is actually the will that moves the hand, as well as the form. If it wants to see the physical aspect of the hand it has to make use of a physical eye.

> Welcome organs are my eyes,
> Suited well to see the world,
> Look through them to see this region;
> You can use them as your own!
> *(He takes them into himself.)*
> Those are trees and that's a cliff side,
> Waterfall, now thundering down
> And with its tremendous tumbling
> Shortening its path so steep. (11906-13)

Now the Blessed Boys are inside Pater Seraphicus. He gives them as much of his own spiritual power as they need to rise up into higher spheres. From this we see again how the spiritual world and the physical world are connected. Whenever we meditate, the spirits benefit from it. This is why we should read to the dead. Pater Seraphicus gives the Blessed Boys the fruits of his meditation, and by means of this they rise to a higher level.

Rise to ever higher regions
As, unnoticed in your growth,
You are strengthened by God's presence
In a pure and ceaseless way.
This, you see, is food for spirits,
Holding sway in freest ether:
Love unceasing, self-revealing,
To eternal bliss unfolding. (11918-25)

If we know *Faust* well enough to recognize how in Goethe's case an esoteric truth of such depth has been incorporated into a major work of world literature, we are already closer to esotericism than any number of "esoteric" explanations could ever bring us.

Now the Blessed Boys are in their own regions. They have passed out of the sphere of the Spirits of Form and on into the sphere of the Spirits of Movement.†

Now the angels come, bringing Faust's entelechy, or immortal part, with them. They have torn this member of the world of spirits away from Mephistopheles and carry it upward as they speak the words:

This noble part of spirits' world
Is rescued now from evil:
Whoever strives and never quits
Is worthy of our saving.
And if, from on high, Love itself
Has granted him its favor,
The blessed host will welcome him
With joyful, heartfelt greeting. (11934-41)

The younger angels say:

Roses from the lovely hands of
Loving, holy penitents
Helped us gain the victory
And carry out the noble deed of
Capturing this treasured soul.

Evil ones escaped our strewing,
Devils fled when roses struck them.
In the place of hellish tortures
Spirits felt the pangs of love;
Even the old devil-master
Had to suffer from his piercing. (11942-52)

It is an esoteric principle that for Mephisto-Ahriman love is an all-devouring fire and a dreadful gift of darkness.

Shout for joy! We have succeeded. (11953)

Now the more perfect angels:

To bear remains of earth
We find distasteful;
And were it of asbestos,
It's still not clean.†
If spirit power, strong,
The elements
Unto itself had drawn ... (11954-60)

What kind of earthly remains are these, anyway? When our soul lives on the earth, it takes in what happens there through perceptions, mental pictures and feelings. In this way it gathers to itself, so to speak, what is living in the elements of the physical plane. That cannot be separated again right away. Just as in earlier times corpses were wrapped in an asbestos cloth so that the ashes would hold together, in the same way Faust's soul has in it a remnant from the world of the senses, and this remnant is not clean, even if it were like asbestos, which can resist fire.

No angel could divide
The dual-nature, fused,
Of this tight bond.
Naught but eternal Love
Could ever part them. (11961-65)

Angels veil their faces before the fact of human incarnation. That is a mystery that can only be witnessed by those beings that can descend more deeply than angels can, who themselves have never experienced human incarnation. Only love can separate this bond.

The angels now become aware of the Blessed Boys, who receive what is being led up to them:

> Take off the floccae now. (11985)

Here Goethe again connects up with physical processes in order to characterize spiritual ones. When Benedictine monks die, they are wrapped and buried in a special brown-colored garment or robe called a "flocca," which is the origin of this word "Flocken."

At this point I have tried to allow myself a little freedom with respect to what is really happening around Faust. As I said earlier, if we are to become aware of all of this, it must first pass through some sort of consciousness. Until now everything has passed through the consciousness of the chorus of anchorites. Now Faust himself must rise through a consciousness, but one that is fully conscious. He must completely fill out a new consciousness: new, but at the same time identical with him, for he arrives at a higher state as a human being in the fullest sense.

Many things in *Faust* are still incomplete, and one of these is certainly the figure of Pater Marianus, whom Goethe later called Doctor Marianus. Now, this Doctor Marianus is present so that Faust can appear through his consciousness, and for this reason I have Doctor Marianus simply be Faust himself. Doctor Marianus, the anchorite, is both Doctor Marianus and Faust at the same time.

The stage is now set for the approach of the profound mystery of Love, permeating the world as it does in the fullest Christian sense.

As we know, and speaking in a profane sense, Faust has led Gretchen astray, so far astray that she has even been executed. But she has become guilty in an innocent way. The innocence she harbors within herself is the same innocence lying enclosed within the mystery of the human being, and her love is the "eternal fixed star." If one wants to express this in an imagination, one comes to the figure of the Mater Dolorosa-Gloriosa. She brings three penitent women with her, not looking upon their guilt as such, but rather upon what is guilty in them in an innocent way. Doctor Marianus comes to understand this mystery.

> From here the view is free,
> The spirit lifted.
> Women are passing by,
> Upwards are wafting;
> Among them the Glorious One
> In starry halo,
> High Queen of Heaven, as
> Her radiance shows me.
> *(Enraptured)*
> Highest ruler of the world!
> Reveal to me your secret
> Woven in the outstretched blue
> Canopy of heaven.
> Stern, yet tender: a man's breast –
> Sanction what thus moves it
> And with holiest joy of love
> Up to you now bears it.
>
> Under your august command:
> Invincible our spirit.
> Suddenly the glow is milder
> As you then appease us.
> Virgin, pure in finest sense,
> Mother honor-worthy,
> Queen elected for our sex,
> Of equal rank with gods.
>
> Winding around her,
> Cloudlets so gentle ... (11989-12014)

Goethe's way of letting her soul come forth out of weaving mists—cloudlets—before shaping itself into a finished form could not have been more appropriate.

This is followed by the Chorus of Penitent Women. It is splendid, the way Goethe took love in its sensuous form and transfigured it in a religious sense—for the second time; the first time this happened was in the Bible. Mary Magdalene loved much in the real sense, but the main thing is that she loved, and Christ saw only her love and not her sin. This is why she also belongs to Him. Then come Maria Aegyptiaca and Una Poenitentium (One of the Penitents), "otherwise known as Gretchen." In the same way, it could also have said in the text: "Doctor Marianus, otherwise known as Faust."

Now the Blessed Boys take Faust up into their own circle. Faust seeks the Maria-like in Gretchen through the Queen of Heaven, and for this reason what has taken place may be expressed by a Mystical Chorus, which then speaks the grandiose, yet succinct words:

> All that must pass away
> Is but a simile,
> Here the inadequate
> Becomes attainment.
> The indescribable,
> Here it is done;
> The Ever-Feminine
> Draws us upward and on. (12104-12111)

With this skeletal presentation I wanted to show you that Goethe's spiritual knowledge enabled him to depict everything in this final scene in an absolutely appropriate way, showing everywhere that he knew how to create real foundations for it: foundations consisting of consciousness.

Goethe portrayed everything the way anyone familiar with the subject matter would, who knows it and truly understands it. Of course, we have to live our way into what he intended. We must be within his intentions, as though the dead Goethe were standing there before us in a living way. For many of these things are not so easy to understand.

9
Mystical Knowledge and Spiritual Revelation of Nature: Perception of Spirits

Dornach, August 15, 1915

After a performance of "Faust's Ascension" with eurythmy

We have made the effort to give eurythmy performances in connection with Goethe's *Faust* at Easter, at Pentecost and at the Feast of the Assumption.† In one respect, it was a kind of necessity for us to finish this work by the Feast of the Assumption. You will remember that in linking my remarks to our previous presentations of scenes from *Faust* I have tried to show how the nature of Goethe's spiritual development can serve as a highly effective model. This is so because we can see by his example that whereas a lesser individual often feels able to grasp something fairly quickly, the great individual, the genius, works at assimilating it slowly and gradually before arriving at a view of the matter that is ultimately satisfying. How many people there are who believe they are good Christians and really understand Christianity! We have had to point out that when Goethe wrote the first scenes of his *Faust* the underlying manner of his feeling, although not anti-Christian, was nevertheless what we could call a-Christian.

Sometime you should look through what has come down to us as the so-called *Urfaust*—please forgive me for calling it by a title of such poor taste, but this is how the work is generally known today—and compare what you find there with what was later published under the much better title of *Faust, A Fragment* [1790]. Such a comparison can show us that Goethe had to attain a rather advanced age before he was able to incorporate a Christian element into these things in such a meaningful way when expressing the most secret urgings of his soul. What this soul needed was an infinite deepening of what it knew and could feel about the world. And yet, when this fragment of *Faust* came out in 1790, it still did not have the scene in it that Goethe was not able to write until a much more mature stage of his life: the scene in which the ringing of the Easter bells pulls Faust back from the step into suicide he is on the point of taking. Not until ripe old age did Goethe feel moved to insert this Christian element into the first part of his *Faust.* A genius of this sort has to experience much, much more before it can feel mature enough to do what many others would feel mature enough to do much sooner. As we see, Goethe really was of this mind, and this made it possible for him to add something Christian, something of Christianity, to the *Faust* he had started writing in his youth—in the latter years of his youth, to be sure—and of which, at that time, he had already worked out several scenes.

Now it is characteristic of Goethe that he needed another new start, so that with his sensitivity and the inner way his feelings dealt with the world he would then be able to work through what I would like to call a region of the world out of which the Christian impulses had been torn. This would also have to happen before he would be able to approach Christianity through his poetic activity in the new way that would satisfy the needs of his later years.

Yesterday I called your attention to how professionally appropriate (to use a pedantic expression for it) the whole structure of the last scene is—the one depicting Faust's ascension. We look even more deeply into the matter when we make one more aspect clear to ourselves with the help of spiritual observations.

Let us imagine a landscape: a mountain wilderness with cliffs, a gorge, and everything that can possibly give an impression of a mystical nature. Within this especially appropriate landscape, a chorus of monks appears who take up what is going on around them into their consciousness. We have heard why this chorus of monks is present. In order to place the whole affair on a solid footing of reality, Goethe needed this consciousness out there as a receptive medium for the events connected with the ascension of Faust's soul into the spiritual world.

What is happening? The chorus begins by drawing our attention to this. We can say: This chorus senses what is otherwise at rest as movement. The world of the Spirits of Form is gradually beginning to pass over into the world of the Spirits of Movement. It becomes permeated with spirit as it begins to be moved. What appears to us in an elemental way is at first all in motion:

Woodlands come swaying up,
Cliff sides weigh heavily,
Roots, how they tightly clutch,
Trunk next to trunk so close,
Wave upon wave, they spray ... (11844-48)

Why is this? It is so that we can be shown how a soul can raise itself up from its earthly existence on the physical plane into the spiritual world. A soul is to be wrested away from the physical plane—the physical plane is also Nature, and this soul is to be wrested away from Nature. Now, we know that Nature is permeated by the elemental world, and that the moment we pass from a rigid state of existence within Nature into an elemental state of existence, everything is actually in motion. We can't imagine a depiction of the ascension of Faust's soul into the spiritual worlds being conjured up in front of us in such a way that we could not at the same time imagine in a living way the enlivening of Nature and Faust's gradual release from this life of Nature. For it must be stated once and for all that, in comparison to so much of an unhealthy nature that is asserted in mystical-esoteric movements, we have, in everything we may readily connect with Goethe's esotericism, something that is healthy through and through because it rests on the solid ground of worldly reality. This is why Goethe would not have been able to give us a picture of the spiritual world in any other way than by connecting it with what we encounter on the physical plane—in other words, with Nature: showing how Nature appears to the healthy senses when permeated with spirit. Goethe would never have advocated an esotericism that failed to nurture a deep and genuine love for the knowledge and thorough penetration of Nature's mysteries.

We can do an enormous amount for the healing of our spiritual-scientific worldview if we strive for an overview of the mysteries of Nature. This is hard to do in our time because people go about investigating Nature in such a foolish way. This had to be pointed out yesterday with reference to research into the wisdom of Bakis and other things we come across in our spiritual growth. What does this foolishness look like? A lot of what science says about Nature today is really the same thing as that apparently infinitely profound explanation of Goethe's eight lines that are supposed to refer to everything in the world but actually refer to slippers and cigars. You see how a great deal of what passes for natural science today is related to truth in exactly the same way as what I presented yesterday as philological science is. You also see how Goethe's wisdom relates to what really is the case. This is why it is hard in our time to start from science and acquire the relationship to Nature that Goethe actually had. But we must strive without ceasing to shape our esotericism in a thoroughly healthy way. And for our time there is no better or more worthy starting point than the contribution that Goethe has made to esotericism in particular.

We see how, within the consciousness of the Chorus, the spiritual aspect of Nature wrests itself free as this consciousness now actually inserts itself into the impersonal aspect of Nature, in that the Echo resounds along with the Chorus's words. And we can now immediately hope that this same consciousness, which is able to see through Nature in such a way that everything rises up out of Nature's depths, is also watching the ascending soul. By simply seeing it at all at first [i.e., the spiritual in Nature], one sees it with the soul that is ascending in the spirit, entirely inserted into real life. But how does one then arrive at an actual view of this spiritual world? I already mentioned this yesterday. It is presented to us in a dignified way in three stages. The consciousness of the Chorus has a general awareness of the fact that Nature has a spiritual essence concealed within it, and up to this consciousness there steps, first of all, the consciousness of Pater Ecstaticus, then the consciousness of Pater Profundus, and finally the consciousness of Pater Seraphicus. These are successive stages of soul development. In the transition from Pater Ecstaticus to Pater Profundus we are shown how mystical development rises from a level of pure self-absorption and the self to the visionary penetration of a broader spirituality of Nature than the Chorus itself can achieve. This is shown in the transition from Pater Ecstaticus to Pater Profundus. Then, in the transition from Pater Profundus to Pater Seraphicus we see how the soul can develop in a healthy way on into the actual spiritual world to where the very depths of this spiritual world lie open to its gaze.

Goethe had already received the direction for this line of thinking in his youth, when he first learned what sort of communication Swedenborg† had with the world of spirits. We should not value Swedenborg all that highly, but his work was a powerful stimulus for Goethe. Swedenborg relates that he associated with spiritual beings in such a way that they would come quite close to his head, take possession of his sense organs, and see the world under the guidance of his eyes. They were able of course to communicate what they heard and saw quite differently than the human soul can. In this way, Swedenborg was able to experience the spiritual world through the angelic beings that would come into his sensory organs. This entry of the spirits into the human organism made such a big impression on Goethe that in a certain respect he became quite familiar with how a mind of this sort deals with the spiritual world. Goethe knew these things quite well. What we haven't been able to show here yet—but once our building is finished,[†] we will show it—is the fact that Pater Ecstaticus floats up and down. On May 26, 1787, Goethe writes about Filippo Neri[†]: "In the course of his life the highest gifts of religious enthusiasm developed within him: the gift of tears, of ecstasy, and at last even of rising from the ground and floating above it, which is considered by everyone to be the highest gift of all."

I mention this expressly because I have to tell you that Goethe did not write this out of any lack of conscious awareness or as a mere poetic fancy. He was well-versed in these things and deeply aware of them. In other words, he doesn't have Pater Ecstaticus float up and down just because it occurs to him to do this. We have to consider the fact that Goethe was a man who spoke about Filippo Neri in the way he did. This deepens our feeling immensely. In these matters it is much less important to have ingenious explanations of everything than to immerse ourselves in Goethe's soul, which was so deeply connected with this ascent of the human being on this path of mystical knowledge. Then we see Pater Ecstaticus showing us how the soul receives the working of divinity into its innermost nature, in the manner of, say, Meister Eckart, Johannes Tauler, or Suso,[†] so that the soul comes to the point of admitting to itself, along with Meister Eckart: "Not I, but the god in me wills and thinks and feels." For if the soul rises even higher, the spirit within Nature begins to reveal itself to it out of the elemental world; this is clearly evident in the figure of Pater Profundus, whose inner life extends out over the whole, all-dominating life of Nature.

Once the human soul has experienced all this, it ascends even higher, up to a level of direct communication with the spiritual world. We witness this level of spiritual activity in Pater Seraphicus, who now really takes into his consciousness the perceptual activity of spirits like the Blessed Boys, "the ones born at midnight," who live as spiritual beings in all the weaving spiritual life that develops here between the "cells," or dwelling places, of the anchorites and the monks.

It makes quite a living impression on us—and everything depends on the representation of this living element—that Goethe escorts Faust's soul up into the spiritual world, but needs some spiritual "scenery" that will enable him to do this. We can surmise how Nature first of all begins to move, how the elemental life in Nature emerges, and how the beings of Nature then pass over into the consciousnesses that stand at ever higher levels. Later, moving along with the soul, they enter the embracing activity of spiritual beings such as the Blessed Boys, as well as of others who can soon be the souls of the Penitent Women, and even the soul of Faust himself. All this is an integral part of the whole spiritual scenery. Then there comes the series of wonderful enhancements that continues on to the very end, where the Chorus Mysticus voices the secret of the world, and we see how the eye of our spirit is lifted up into a spiritual world. We ourselves take part in this ascent from standing within Nature on the firm ground of the physical plane to the spiritual worlds into which the soul of Faust is received.

In Goethe's lifetime, all that was published of *Faust* was the first part, as we have it today. Later on came the scene, "Charming Landscape," Faust reclining on a flowery turf. Then individual parts of the scene at the Imperial Palace from the first act of Part Two. Within this part there was a transitional scene leading to the journey to the "Classical Walpurgis Night," although not this scene itself, and finally the "Helen Scene."

During Goethe's lifetime many people were already thinking about how *Faust* could be completed. Some of these thoughts appeared in print, and if we follow them up we find everywhere that people already knew Faust's soul had to be saved by ascending into the spiritual world. But all the ideas they came up with have something about them that can only be characterized as being extremely vague and abstract. At one point Goethe made a remark to Eckermann† that he had to look to

Christian images for assistance in escaping from vagueness and getting into what he wanted to place before his audiences as a spiritual reality.

And so we meet this wonder once again, this time in Goethe's very advanced old age. Keep in mind that by now Goethe had already written all the pagan, pre-Christian material of *Faust* for those parts of it in which he brings Faust together with Helen, as well as another part, which is certainly not anti-Christian in character, namely, the fourth act. Only after he had once again plunged into something in which Christian impulses were not directly at work, and had wound his way through this, was he faced with the task of placing before us the riddle of Faust in its highest sense. Only when he had put the entire pagan culture behind him did he feel the need in his most advanced years to implant Christianity into *Faust*. Goethe had to turn eighty before he could say to himself that he was in a position to make use of Christian ideas and images in such a way that they would be an appropriate garment for the path Faust's soul would have to take.

Goethe walked the very paths that we in spiritual science designate as pathways for broadening our understanding of the Christ-impulse more and more. In a future time, many others will come to the small beginnings we were able to make in this direction now, when we ourselves will no longer be able to be there with them or will only be able to in following incarnations. Goethe initiated what spiritual science itself has to undergo, namely, taking what streams in our soul as a result of the Christ-impulse and connecting it with the permeation of reality. Goethe illustrated this for us in concrete, vivid depictions of tremendous depth that were always in line with spiritual reality.

From somewhere in a natural setting the chorus of monks appears, indicating by their first words the presence of the spiritual. They see the elementals emerging from Nature, and these elementals are soon joined by soul-spiritual beings. All of this is coming out of Nature. Goethe already sensed this as a specifically Christian way of looking at things. Being Christian is not a matter of saying "Christ, Christ, and again Christ!" all the time and repeating Christian dogmas over and over. It is a way of feeling, of relating to the world. And this feeling, this way of relating to the world comes out in a wonderful way from what Goethe depicted here. The way this feeling lives and weaves throughout the final scenes of *Faust* is Christian in the most eminent sense. And we become aware of its Christian quality especially through the fact that even though some parts of the work remained fragmentary and incomplete, *Faust* as a whole is artistically so grandiose and so powerfully conceived that its powerful artistic conception only dawns on us gradually, over a period of time.

As we look at the physical plane spread out before us in the form of Nature, we first see it passing over in a genuinely Christian sense into the elemental state of existence and then into the genuinely spiritual state. Faust is led into all this now that his experience of being connected with Helen and the spiritual world of antiquity is behind him. That experience was also one of being confronted by spiritual beings. There we see Helen being led up out of the underworld and Faust meeting these beings. There are twelve of them in the chorus around her, and when she returns to the underworld at the end of the third act we see them still standing there, showing themselves as elemental beings that have not yet matured to a level of fully human existence. Now how does this chorus disappear at the end of the third act? This is very interesting! Remember that we have to do here with elemental beings and that as Helen disappears, the chorus of elemental beings also disappears. The chorus divides into four parts, and the three persons in each quarter describe how their respective quarter disappears, namely, into Nature. So, at the point where Goethe is depicting the pagan aspect, he shows us the elemental beings standing around Helen in the form of a chorus of twelve, who now disappear into Nature. Try to feel how the first part of the chorus goes into Nature:

> We, in many thousand branches whisp'ring, trembling, rustling,
> floating,
> Beckon gently, mincing charming, up the root the springs of life
> To the branches; where with foliage, then with blossoms all effusive
> Fluttering hair for airy thriving freely wafting we adorn. (9992-95)

What this means is that these beings of the chorus are turning into trees as they become part of Nature. This permits them to approach us again out of Christian impulses when we see them approaching later on as:

Woodlands come swaying up. (11844)

The pagan elemental spirits disappear into Nature, only to emerge again after the Christ-impulse has connected with the earth in a living way. How wonderful it is to see this chorus disappear along with Helen and then, as we know from the final scene, emerge again from Nature as the beings who, as Blessed Boys, have received the Christ-impulse. Now take the second part of the chorus with this:

> We, in gentle waves now moving, nestle, flattering, up close to
> Smooth and glistening walls of cliffs that far into the distance
> gleam;
> Listening, hearing every sound of birds a-singing, reeds
> a-piping, (9999-10001)

Truly, these are the same cliffs into which those elemental beings once slipped who now are "tightly clutching Euphorion" (11846), and out of which the beings of the spiritual world come later on, who come out of the earth after receiving the Christ-impulse.

You see here how deeply felt this *Faust* poem is, and how there are other connections in it besides the ones usually observed. But these connections are what makes all the difference. Goethe was aware of this, as we can tell from a very specific indication he intended to give before finishing the third act of the second part of *Faust*. He had more or less completed it up to the point where Helen disappears and the chorus of elemental beings goes into Nature, in other words, about as far as the scene I have just read to you. What he then wanted to do here, which he did in a certain way at the end of the third act, was to have Mephisto arise out of the form of Phorkyas. At that point at the close of his *Faust*, Mephisto was supposed to say what Goethe actually had in mind with Faust. The fact that he gave these words to Mephisto was due to production reasons, because in a certain sense Mephisto is the one who actually brings the third act about. The third act is incorporated into *Faust* as a "classical-romantic phantasmagoria." In a certain sense, Mephisto is the one who introduces the third act with a sort of spiritualistic laboratory-magic; and so it is his task to let us know what Goethe has in mind by having his *Faust* continue on through Mephisto's efforts. At a time when Goethe already understands that he has to incorporate the Christ-impulse into it, he wants to speak through Mephistopheles and say that, certainly, there have always been times that recognized the fact that spiritual existence rests on the foundation of sensory existence. We can go back into the mysticism of ancient India and of ancient Egypt; there we see that people knew and portrayed the fact that what is spiritual rests on the foundation of natural existence. But Goethe wished to say that it is no longer proper for us today to picture the spiritual as it was conceived in the ancient mysteries.† In comparison to all the ancient mysteries and ancient wisdom, the Christ-impulse has brought something completely new into the world. The old can no longer be of use to us—this is what Goethe wanted to say. And I am not just claiming that he wanted to say it. The passage itself has been preserved; it is just not included in *Faust*. We have it in the form as first conceived by Goethe and later altered by corrections he gave to his secretary. There, at the end of the third act, it is stated how Goethe demands the newer Christ-impulse expressly for his *Faust* : how he does not want anything there in the way of ancient wisdom, but rather something entirely new in the sense of the Christ-impulse. For Mephisto was supposed to step before the public and speak the following words†:

> Enough, you see him,

(he means Euphorion)

> although it's much worse here
> Than on a British stage, as a little child
> Who by and by grows up to be a hero.
> But here it's even crazier. Hardly conceived,
> Right away he's born.
> He leaps and dances, speaks a dainty word.
> Though many censure that,
> Others think it wrong to take it in so crude
> And unrefined a way; something is behind it.
> It smells like ancient mysteries, and maybe even

Mystifications, Indian and even some
Egyptian stuff, and if you pinch it right
And brew it up and have fun running back and forth
In etymologies, you're the right man for the job.

(Paralipomena 196: 7-18)

Goethe is already anticipating something of those doctrines that have since appeared and made an etymological brew[†] of everything. But he doesn't want to have anything to do with them, for at this point he has Mephisto say:

We say it as well, and of our view profound
Will be the newer symbolism's faithful pupil too.

(Paralipomena 196: 19-20)

Goethe actually says this: Don't be Egyptian or Indian; be "the newer symbolism's faithful pupil"!

Then he came to the point of integrating the Christ-impulse into his *Faust*, not just by adding a trace of something Christian here and there, but by secretly integrating the whole way his soul had of taking a stand on something into the stream of his creative activity. And as we see, he does that. We can tell how well he really knows the mystical process when we experience, on the one hand, the enhancement exhibited by the three Patres, and observe, on the other hand, how wonderfully he divides the unified choir of angels into the two choruses of younger and of more perfected angels, respectively. And when we read what the younger angels say and what the more perfected angels say, we again notice something quite peculiar. Take what the younger angels say when they begin to speak:

Roses from the lovely hands of
Loving, holy penitents

(we have to remember the previous scene)

Helped us gain the victory
And carry out the noble deed of

Capturing this treasured soul.
Evil ones escaped our strewing,
Devils fled when roses struck them.
In the place of hellish tortures
Spirits felt the pangs of love;
Even the old devil-master
Had to suffer from his piercing.
Shout for joy! We have succeeded. (11942-53)

But the angels can already be perceived in the previous scenes. The ones we see now are the younger angels. We can hardly say how deeply touched we are when we allow the accuracy of this representation to work on in us. Why, for instance, are the younger angels called "younger"? It means they *are* younger and have very little connection with the earthly world as yet.

In pre-Christian times the angels are those beings whose nature it is to hide their faces from human incarnation on earth. As yet they don't mingle in affairs down on earth but stay entirely above the earth in spiritual spheres.

Just think how much in character these younger angels are who have not yet found a connection with the Christian sphere but have stayed above instead of descending during the Christian era…how in character they are! Then think of how the Elohim are characterized at the creation of the world. At the conclusion of each day's creative work it is stated: "And they saw that it was good," or "beautiful." This last word is difficult to translate.† It means that the Elohim are spiritual beings whose nature is to create things first and then see that what they have done is beautiful. That is the point. The other kind of beings attained their perfection on Old Moon and are now passing over spiritually into Earth-existence. First they act, then they look and perceive that what they did has been successful. These younger angels must have the perception of these spiritual beings [i.e., the Elohim]; they must first say what they have done. Now they become aware that they have strewn roses from the hands of the penitents and that they themselves have been the cause of the old devil-master's pain.

Goethe's writing is so in accord with spiritual reality that he knows that beings who have not come into contact with the Christian world can only recognize the beauty and goodness of what they have done after the fact:

> Roses from the lovely hands of
> Loving, holy penitents
> Helped us gain the victory.... (11942-44)

The fact of the victory comes later. As you see, I am not making this up:

> Wafting in mists around
> These rocky heights,
> I sense a spirit life
> Stirring nearby.
> The little clouds turn clear;
> Of blessed boys I see
> A host in motion,
> Free from the weight of earth,
> All in a circle,
> Finding refreshment
> In the new spring and joy
> Of higher worlds.
> From the beginning
> May he for steady gain
> Be joined with these. (11966-80)

The Blessed Boys have already been there for some time, and they have something to do with the appearance of these angels, but the angels only notice that they are there after the performance has gotten underway. Goethe is fully aware of all this. They are not carrying Faust's soul element, which is connected with the earth. That must be carried by those who are somewhat older and more perfect, who have come down with the Mystery of Golgotha and have come in contact with what is earthly.

> To bear remains of earth

(the more perfect angels say this, not the younger ones)

We find distasteful;
And were it of asbestos,
It's still not clean. (11954-57)

And then they explain that through the Mystery of Golgotha they have attained the insight, before which the other angels hide their faces, about how spirit strength connects itself with the elementals, which are mixed in with the nature of earthly life. It is powerful to perceive how accurately Goethe depicts all this, how correctly he can characterize the individual members of the spiritual world. If we compare what others who also wanted to represent spirits managed to put together as a bunch of stuff that was full of color but completely lacked character, it sometimes seems as though someone wanted to depict external Nature and would try to do this by saying: Oh, I went out for a walk in the woods and the meadow and in the meadows I saw such wonderful blue roses and such wonderful yellow chicory flowers and such gorgeous red and yellow violets, and things like that. None of it fits. Someone who knows the spiritual world feels many a depiction of it to be impossibly clumsy because it is all inaccurate. Everything Goethe writes is correct! The essential thing is not to perceive some made-up interpretation, but to see the way this soul is rooted in the spiritual world at the very moment it undertakes to depict a spiritual event out of itself, such as Faust's ascent into the spiritual world. And then there is the compositional aspect within the spiritual itself that is artistic to the highest degree!

I once tried to show you how, quite apart from everything else that the Gospel of St. John may be, there is something to be found simply in the whole mood or atmosphere of this Gospel that at the same time makes it into one of the greatest works of art. Think back to the Kassel cycle on the Gospel of St. John.† We really find artistic strivings of this sort everywhere in *Faust*, ones that strive to accomplish something artistically perfect within the realm of the spiritual, but do this in such a way that while being artistic, the artistic element in it is spiritually correct at the same time. This is the significant thing. For everything depends on the world's coming to see more and more that what is really cognized and experienced out of the spirit is what is correct, even when placed into the world. What is simply made up out of the spiritual usually looks like a house of cards when it is in the world. But what has been cognized out of the spiritual can be placed into the world.

This is what we were striving for in the whole architecture of our building,[†] namely, that it would be conceived entirely out of the spiritual. This is why everything can also be implemented. We need not be concerned if people come by now and then and say they do not like this or that about it. There are such people who find fault with various things about our building. But if you know the world a little, as well as the extent to which people belong to the chorus of those who interpret Goethe like the gentleman I told you about, you will not pay any attention to this fault-finding. That gentleman, for example, could say whatever he wants to about our building, our way of thinking, and so on, without necessarily impressing anyone. And people do think this way, after all. You just have to know life a little. But what is born out of the spirit becomes possible, since it is both spirit and artistry at the same time.

And now I would like to point out at least one more thing today. Three penitent women appear, in conjunction with the penitent woman otherwise known as Gretchen. Now, an artist—a real, true artist, that is—doesn't work by saying: "O.K., now I want three penitent women to appear. Where can I find three penitent women?" Of course, in life you can meet all kinds of people. There really are people who pick up a rhyming dictionary and use it to write poetry with; they look up a word to see what rhymes with it, then they write the next line, and so on. I knew people like this. But the true poet, who is an artist, would never take just any three penitent women and arrange them in some arbitrary way. Instead, as an especially characteristic instance of wonderful inner composition, Goethe brings us another of those marvelous enhancements of his which is both correct and perfectly suited to the subject matter at the same time. What are the three penitent women there for: Mary Magdalene first, then the Samaritan woman at the well, and finally the Egyptian Mary?[†] What are they supposed to show us? I have already hinted at it. They are supposed to show us that there is something eternal in the nature of woman—"the fixed star of eternal love"—that can't be nibbled away at, as Goethe would say, when love—the love that Christ brought—unites with the female soul, and also with this soul's guilt. Despite the fact that these women were not model human beings in their external lives, their souls were of such a nature that they could understand love. To think this thought in the right way we have to say: Something that spreads out in the world the way the Christ-impulse does has to start by taking hold of what is nearest to it, then what is farther away, and finally what is the farthest of all. And now it would be beautiful to see the impulse of Christian love spreading out like a wave, taking hold of the guilty ones and spreading its rays over them in greater and ever greater circles. And so we have, first of all, Mary Magdalene, the Jewish, Hebrew woman, directly from the country most deeply bound up with Christ Jesus through its Judaism. The nearest surrounding area is taken hold of by Christian love. Then Christ goes out beyond the boundaries of Judaism as such, but still into the closest area next to it. He goes to the Samaritans, who have no dealings with the Jews at all. This is the second circle. Then he comes to the third circle. You know that what is considered to be very far away from Christianity is depicted as the Egyptian culture: the Egyptian Mary. She comes from a culture out there in the pagan world that is far more alien and is now being taken hold of by the Christian impulse from a far distance. It is as if she is pressed back from touching the cross by an invisible hand because of her sin, only atoning for her guilt by a forty-year penance. How far the waves of love travel!

We really see how far the waves of love spread out, and we understand something of what gradually crystallized into Goethe's concept of what he termed the "Ever-Feminine" or the "Eternal Feminine" at the close of this work. Our understanding of this term must include absolutely no trace of baseness.

There is an exact correspondence between what spreads out here as love and what I would like to call the intonation, the whole manner in which Goethe formulated these words. Try to discover the wonderful enhancement contained in the very feeling and rhythmic structure of these words:

> By the love that let the tears flow,
> Soothing with their healing balm
> The feet of your transfigured Son,
> Despite the scorn of Pharisees;

By the vessel that so amply
Dripped the fragrance drop by drop;
By the locks that then so softly
Dried again the sacred limbs— (12037-44)
It feels to us like a gentle rain close by.
By the well to which of old
Father Abram led his herds,
By the vessel that through grace
Cool the Savior's lips did touch;
By the pure, abundant fountain
Pouring now from out that source,
Flowing over, ever brightly,
Flowing round through all the worlds— (12045-52)

Think how that spreads out! With the whole presentation we are really in the immediate presence of the person of Christ. Additional whole worlds are absorbed in this depiction of Nature. Then, coming to the figure of St. Mary of Egypt:

By the place most sanctified,
Where the Lord was taken down,
By the arm, that from the portal
Thrust me away in warning sign; (12053-56)

At last, the invisible, the spiritual, is being spoken of directly. Another enhancement! We do not need to use our intellect to find out that these circles are really there. Speaking the words is enough in itself to make us feel their presence. That is the significant thing.

Let us now consider the following. We have spent many years reflecting on the fact that our Earth evolution† was preceded by a Saturn period, then a Sun period, then a Moon period, and that we are now living in the Earth period. As human beings, we have experienced everything that has gone on during these different evolutionary stages. What is the essential feature of these evolutionary stages? It is that they have all come and gone and we are now in the Earth period. But before the Earth period we ourselves passed through the Saturn, Sun, and

Moon periods, and now we bear the effects of these ages of experience within us. If we now investigate modern human beings with the aid of spiritual science, we find that by acquiring its first predisposition during Saturn, the physical body was then able to develop further through Sun and Moon. Finally, during the Earth period, it has more recently united with cosmic powers in order to take on something new. Here we touch the hem of a significant mystery. The most evident effect of everything the human physical body as such experienced in the course of these three stages is what has found its expression here on the earth in the constitution of the inner female organs. The interior of the female organization—what is bodily and physical as well as what expresses itself as soul in connection with the physical body—all this bears the marks of Saturn, Sun, and Moon periods in the most eminent sense. It is not for nothing that the Bible tells us how the Elohim took dust and used it to form the "Adam," the Man—"dust" here meaning the earthly element, which only appeared on the earth for the first time, such as air and water. The first thing that happens is that the male aspect, coming out of the cosmos [i.e., the earth], is added to the macrocosmic aspect that the woman brings over from Saturn, Sun, and Moon evolutions. This earthly polarity of maleness and femaleness is shrouded in a deep mystery. Of course, what has just been said refers only to what brings the masculine and the feminine to expression within the human organization. And this mystery is connected with the whole world of the earth; with the capacities that the woman possesses only as woman during Earth evolution; with the fact that the macrocosmic aspect of the Saturn, Sun, and Moon evolutions is carried over within the woman and is taken up into the microcosm of the woman, whereas the macrocosm of the immediately preceding part of Earth evolution is taken up into the microcosm of the man. What is female and what is male carry the whole cosmos within themselves in quite a special way. And if I have often said here that we human beings in general bear the whole macrocosm within ourselves, this means that the female and the male organizations each bear it within themselves in a different way.

A cosmic thought dawns on Goethe as he brings the Penitent Women to the Mater Gloriosa. For what is the Mater Gloriosa for him? She is the one who has carried the everlasting effects of the Saturn,

Sun, and Moon periods over into the Earth period in the purest way, has left them untouched by what is earthly and united herself with the macrocosm by being allowed to prepare the Christ for the earth. The macrocosmic aspect—the eternal within the feminine—draws upward and on. What draws upward and on? What could we say to answer this question? We could only answer it by repeating the words of the Chorus Mysticus.

That is what Goethe had in mind—he just didn't want to use a general expression for it—this is what he meant:

> All that must pass away
> Is but a simile,
> Here the inadequate
> Becomes attainment;
> The indescribable,
> Here it is done;
> *The Mater Gloriosa*
> Draws us upward and on. (12104-12111)

All that has been done, all that has taken place in the time preceding our own, is at the same time drawing the whole spiritual world upward and on.

In this deeply Christian mood Goethe's life-poem comes to a close. Our next lecture will take up the thread of today's reflections, which were meant to be of an aphoristic nature.

10
The Realm of the Mothers: The Mater Gloriosa

Dornach, August 16, 1915

LET us look back to an earlier scene in the second part of Goethe's *Faust* that I have often mentioned in various contexts. This is the scene that is to make it possible for Faust to unite with Helen. How is this possibility presented within the context of the work as a whole?

We know that for Faust's union with Helen to come about, he has first to go to a region that Mephistopheles himself is not able to enter. This is the so-called "realm of the Mothers." We have often emphasized that the only thing Mephistopheles-Ahriman can do for Faust is hand him the key to this realm, which is "unexplored and not to be trodden" (6222-23). We have also mentioned that what is eternal about Helen is what can be found in this realm of the Mothers, and we have also mentioned how Goethe tried to solve the mystery of Helen's return to the earthly world. We found that Goethe expressed this mystery by having Homunculus come into being and go through the course of earthly evolution, making up, as it were, for what he himself has missed out in the course of earthly evolution. By dissolving himself in the elements, Homunculus then passes over into the elementary spiritual world so that, in uniting with the archetypal image of Helen that Faust has retrieved from the Mothers, he becomes, so to speak, the vehicle for Helen's re-embodiment, with which Faust is now able to connect. Faust's search for Helen has raised him, as it were, onto the great stage of world history. What does he need in order to continue his search for this archetype of Greek beauty?— to find Helen, the woman who brought so much misfortune into the world of the Greeks but whom Goethe portrays in such a way that in the Greek sense she also seems to be innocently guilty. I put it this way as a clear reference to Gretchen. For this is how Helen is when she appears at the beginning of the third act: innocently guilty. By her deed she has incurred much guilt. But Goethe looks for the eternal in the nature of every human being and cannot be taking guilt into account when in a higher sense what he wants to portray is the evolution of humanity. He can only reckon with necessity.

If we now ask what enables Faust to descend into those spiritual realms where he can find Helen, we hear, resounding toward us:

> It is the *Mothers*!
> Mothers! (6216)

And Mephistopheles hands him the key to the Mothers, with his characteristic explanation that Faust should go down to the Mothers, although one could just as well say go up, for in this realm it is not a matter of distinguishing between up and down in any physical sense.

> The Mothers! Mothers! – It sounds so oddly strange! (6217)

We hear this word resounding to us out of *Faust*. And when we remember the way this realm of the Mothers is described, with the Mothers sitting around the golden tripod, and visualize the scenery of the realm of the Mothers as a whole, we wonder how Faust's entry into this realm could ever be expressed. What are these Mothers, these beings that wield unending power but, portrayed as women, represent the forces from which Faust has brought forth Helen's eternal, immortal nature? If we wanted to state how things are at the point when Faust is sent to Helen, we would have to say that Faust can only express his urge to go to Helen and the Mothers by saying: The Ever-Feminine draws us upward or downward—at the moment it makes no difference. We could just as well think of this phrase, which we find at the end of *Faust*, as applying to his going down to the Mothers. But as Faust goes to the Mothers and to Helen, we stand with him on the ground of the ancient pagan, pre-Christian world, the world that preceded the Mystery of Golgotha. What about the closing scene of *Faust*? Here we meet Faust on a similar journey, but this is now the loving Faust, wanting to draw near to the soul of Gretchen. This time, however, we stand with him on the ground of the evolution that has taken place since the Mystery of Golgotha. And what is he striving for now? Is it still the Mothers? Yes, it is, but no longer the Mothers as a trinity. Now he is striving for the one Mother, the Mater Gloriosa, whose role it is to pave his way into "the unexplored, not to be trodden," where Gretchen's soul is waiting. The Mothers, who are also an "Ever-Feminine," are three in number; the Mother, the Mater Gloriosa, is singular. Now these two kinds of striving—to the Mothers on the one hand, which places us in the period of evolution before the Mystery of Golgotha, and to the Mother on the other, the Mater Gloriosa, which places us in the period of evolution after the Mystery of Golgotha—don't they show us with their overwhelming poetic splendor what the Mystery of Golgotha has brought us? Out of the trinity of thinking, feeling, and willing, which is still astral, the humanity portrayed in *Faust* is striving upward toward the threefoldness of the Ever-Feminine. We have often characterized how the unity of the human inner self within the "I" came over humanity through the Mystery of Golgotha. The three Mothers become the one Mother, the Mater Gloriosa, in that the human being has progressed to the point of being inwardly permeated by the "I," in the manner with which we are familiar.

Goethe's *Faust* embodies the whole mystery of humanity's transition in the period before the Mystery of Golgotha. And this transition from the Ever-Feminine as a trinity to the Ever-Feminine as a unity is one of the greatest, most wonderful, most beautiful of all the artistic enhancements in the second part of *Faust*. But no matter how deeply we look into *Faust*'s mysteries, everywhere we find what I have spoken of, without meaning to be pedantic, by saying: In terms of its technical accuracy it all rings true.

I told you earlier that for a full comprehension of the human context we need to realize that the human being is connected with the macrocosm first of all as a total human being; in other words, in the human being the macrocosm finds itself again in image-form as microcosm. We just have to remember that we fail to understand our own earthly evolution as long as we do not know that we bear within our inner nature, as something transitory in terms of earthly evolution but long-lasting in terms of human evolution, that which has developed into human nature in its passage through the Saturn-Sun-Moon evolutions. We know that the first rudiment of the human physical body formed during the ancient Saturn evolution; it developed further and further in the course of the Sun and Moon evolutions until it passed over into our Earth period. I have also shown you that what united with the human being in the three pre-earthly states of evolution has now become an integral part of the human being's external earthly formation in various ways.

Earlier I was able to deal with what needed to be said about this only in a very cursory way, and my remarks today will have to remain at the level of this brief indication. As I said then, when we speak about this we are only just touching upon a significant secret, and the fact that these things can only be hinted at is very natural. If you want to pursue them further, you will have to take what has been hinted at and undertake a meditation on it. Then you will find what you would still like to know, although it may take some time.

We, however, must be very clear that at the end of the Moon evolution the human being began to take part in the Earth evolution; that is to say, it went through the transition from the Moon evolution to the Earth evolution by a sort of dissolving or spiritualizing process, through a cosmic night, and only then re-formed itself into material substance. Of course, the rudimentary predispositions that it had formed for itself during the Saturn, Sun, and Moon evolutions remained, including the potentials that would eventually form the physical body. But it took them with it up into the spiritual and re-formed them again out of the spiritual, so that we have to imagine a time during the Earth evolution in which the human being was not yet physical.

If we disregard everything about human evolution except the fact that the human being in its physical Earth-existence takes on both a male and a female form, we can then make the following general statement: In entering Earth-existence at all, the human being did so at first in etheric form. To be sure, in this etheric human being the first beginnings of human physicality that had evolved during the Saturn, Sun, and Moon periods were already present, but they were still in etheric form. I have already indicated this in greater detail in my *Outline of Esoteric Science*. At this time, the physical, in its turn, has yet to develop out of the etheric. But Lucifer and Ahriman also have their parts to play in this whole evolutionary process. For although their influence shows up again during Earth evolution, they both already intervene earlier in the whole evolution of humanity during Moon evolution, and even during the evolution leading up to the Moon.

Now I have something to say that is hard to understand—less hard for human reason than for the whole human heart and mind, I think—but at some point it really needs to be understood. Imagine the time when in the course of our earthly development we were still etheric, before we gradually took on physical form since the Lemurian and the Atlantean periods. I will now indicate in outline form how we gradually shaped our physical aspect out of this etheric state: So, once we were etheric. As we know, the etheric has a fourfold aspect.† We are acquainted with the ether as a fourfold being, so to speak. Enumerating these from below upward, we have, first of all, warmth ether; then light ether; then the ether with a substantial [*stofflich* : "material"] nature, the chemical ether. This ether, however, has its substantial nature through the fact that substance still fills the tone—the cosmic harmony, the harmony of the spheres—inwardly; for substances are substances by virtue of the fact that they are expressions of cosmic harmony. At first we have to imagine the world in terms of harmony. By resounding through the world, one tone determines, let us say, gold; another tone determines silver; a third one, copper, and so on. Every substance is the expression of a certain tone, so that we can of course also call this the tone or sound ether. Only we must not portray this ether as being perceptible in any earthly sense, but rather as tone which is still resounding in the etheric-spirit sphere. The last ether is the life ether. So when we think of the human being as still being etheric, we see that its etheric is due to the interpenetration and interweaving of these four types of ether. We can therefore say: At the point where Earth evolution is preparing to gradually bring the physical human being forth out of the etheric human being, the human being still appears as an etheric organism before it actually becomes physical, and in this organism warmth ether, light ether, substantial or tone ether, and life ether are all mixed together in an organized way.

Now Lucifer and Ahriman take part in this whole process of human physical becoming. They are always part of it, exerting their influence throughout the whole of evolution. Of course, there are times when their influence is particularly strong, but these special points of time are always present, as you will find stressed in *An Outline of Esoteric Science.* Just as the entire energy of the plant is always in the plant, manifesting sometimes as the green leaves and at other times as the blossom, so have Lucifer and Ahriman always been present in the human being's development throughout the different epochs of Earth evolution; in a certain way they are always around.

If you now disregard everything else, since we can't always mention everything, you will be able to imagine this physical aspect of the human fairly well as it arises out of the etheric organization—including, of course, everything else I have described in *An Outline of Esoteric Science* and elsewhere. Now imagine it in such a way that you see both the male and the female forms coming into being. We are now disregarding what else is at work to help bring this about, but the male and the female forms come into being. If Lucifer and Ahriman had not worked together in this, the male and the female forms would not have arisen, but rather something else that I once described in Munich† as "something in between." So we really have to say: It is due to Lucifer and Ahriman that on earth the human form was differentiated into a male and a female form. And this is how it happened. If we imagine the situation of the human being drawing near to the earth, which is gradually solidifying through the mineral kingdom, and if we imagine further that the earth planet is forming, becoming physically firmer, and that the ether permeating the earth is also all around the earth, then we can imagine that the human being is formed out of the ether of the entire earth and therewith, in its character as a human being, also draws near to the earth, and that within it the etheric-mineral-physical aspect meets the mineral-physical aspect of the earth. But Lucifer and Ahriman are right there, doing their work. They have many means of asserting their influence on the evolution of humanity, and they make use of all these different means in order to involve themselves in the various processes they themselves call forth.

Lucifer has the tendency, above all, to develop the spirit of lightness; he would prefer that the human being not become really earthly. In fact, he would like to keep us from completely coming down to earth at all. After all, Lucifer stayed behind during the Moon evolution and would therefore like to win us over for himself and not allow us into Earth evolution. Above all else, he strives to accomplish this by getting control of the forces of the warmth ether and the light ether. Then he uses these forces in his own way in the processes that now occur as the human being becomes physical. Lucifer has power mainly over the warmth ether and the light ether, which he chiefly dominates. During the Moon evolution he prepared himself well for this task, and he now organizes these ethers in his own way. Thereby he is able to send human development in a different direction. In causing the human being to become physical out of the ether, he is able to bring about the human form by pouncing precisely on the warmth and light ethers and asserting his power within them in a different way than what would have happened without this power. As he now works and weaves in the warmth-light ether, what arises in this working and weaving is not the "in-between" human being, who would otherwise come into being, but its female form. Without Lucifer there would be no female human form. It is the expression of what came forth out of the ether as a result of Lucifer's having gotten control precisely of the warmth-light ether.

Ahriman especially has power over the tone and life ether. At the same time he is the spirit of heaviness, continually striving to work against Lucifer. In essence, a kind of balance is brought about by the fact that the Luciferic power that wants to lift human beings up above the earthly is opposed by the Ahrimanic power through the wise working of the progressive gods. Ahriman's main intention now is to drag the human being down into the physical. He wants to make us more physical than we would otherwise become as "in-between" human beings. Ahriman is prepared to do this by virtue of having special power over the tone and life ether, and it is in tone and life ether where Ahriman works and weaves. And now, the human physical form, coming out of the ether and going into the physical, where it becomes physical in a different way than it would have under the guidance of the progressive gods alone, becomes male. The male form would not have been conceivable, or even possible, without the influence of Ahriman. We can therefore say: The female form is woven out of the warmth and light ether by Lucifer, who works etherically, causing a certain upward striving to flow into this form. The male form is shaped by Ahriman by having a certain striving toward the earth implanted in it.

This has been willed out of the macrocosmic dimension of world evolution, and we can really observe it in the human being in a spiritual-scientific way. If we take the female form, for example, as in this schematic drawing, we therefore have to say that warmth and light have been woven into it etherically by Lucifer, in accordance with his own particular nature. In other words, the female physical form has been woven in such a way that within the light and warmth ether not only the regularly progressing gods have developed their forces, but that, in addition, Luciferic forces have been woven into this female ether body. Now let us assume that in this female ether body the earth's special contribution, the "I"-consciousness, the consciousness that holds everything together, is dampened down so that we have a kind of reduced consciousness that some people call "clairvoyance," a kind of dreamlike, trancelike spiritual vision. In such a case, what Lucifer has woven in the light and warmth ethers emerges in a sort of aura, so that female visionaries, when in their visionary states, are surrounded by an aura with Luciferic forces in it, namely those of the warmth and light ethers. The problem is that this aura which now surrounds the female body when visionary conditions of a mediumistic nature are present is not perceived to be the aura as such. Obviously, if the female body is in the middle of this aura [here he draws], the female organism looks into this aura and projects what it sees in this aura in all directions around it. It sees what is in its own aura. An objective observer would describe the process this way: This person is radiating imaginations; she has an aura around her that consists of imaginations. That is an objective process of no special significance to the observer. It simply means that if this image-filled aura is observed from outside, by someone else, then an aura is simply being seen objectively just like anything else. But if the aura is being looked through by the female visionary herself,[†] all she sees is what Lucifer himself is spreading out within it. There is a big difference whether one sees something oneself or whether it is seen by others. A huge difference!

Associated with this is the fact that with the appearance of visionary clairvoyance in the case of a woman, a great danger is present when this visionary clairvoyance appears in the form of imaginations. At such a time the woman must exercise great caution. And it must always be presupposed that she take her further development firmly in hand so that it is healthy. She must not simply remain at the level of what she sees, for that can simply be the aura that is actually Luciferic, looked at from within, which was necessary for the formation of the female body. And many things that female visionaries describe are interesting for quite a different reason than the one the female visionaries think is so interesting. Whenever they look and describe what they see as though it were an interesting, objective world, they are completely mistaken, totally wrong. But if this same aura is seen from the outside, then it is what made the female form possible out of the ether in Earth evolution. So that we can say that the woman has to exercise special caution whenever she begins to manifest a visionary, imaginative clairvoyance, for on such an occasion there can very easily be lurking the danger of falling into error.

The male organism is different. When we look at the male organism, we see that Ahriman has woven his power into its aura, but now it is in the tone and life ether. In the case of the woman, the warmth ether predominates, and in the case of the man the life ether predominates. With the woman it is mainly the warmth ether that Lucifer is working in; with the man, Ahriman works mainly in the life ether. Now when the man comes out of his consciousness, when the cohesiveness that expresses itself in him as I-consciousness is dampened down, when a sort of passive state occurs, one can again see how the aura around him asserts itself, the aura in which Ahriman wields his power.

But now this is an aura that contains predominantly life ether and tone ether. What is there within it is vibrating tone, so that we actually do not see the aura of the man so directly through imaginative perception. What surrounds the man is not an aura consisting of images but rather something consisting of vibrating spiritual tone. Of course, this all has to do with the form, not with the soul; it has to do with the man insofar as he is physical. So that whoever regards this form from outside can see—and now say—that this person is raying out Intuitions. Those are the same Intuitions out of which his form has actually been modeled, by means of which he is present in the world as a man. All around him living, vibrating tone is sounding. For this reason there is a different danger present in the case of the man when his consciousness has been dampened down to a state of passivity: the danger of only hearing his own aura, hearing it inwardly. The man must be especially attentive not to let himself go when he hears this aura of his in a spiritual way, for what he is hearing is Ahriman wielding his power within him. For Ahriman must be there.

Now you see that neither the male nor the female aspect of the human being would exist on the earth if it had not been for Lucifer and Ahriman doing their work. I would like to know how the woman could flee from Lucifer and the man from Ahriman! I have often emphasized how foolish the sermon is that we should escape from these powers, for they belong to what lives in evolution, now that this evolution is the way it is.

But now we can say: Here on the earth we have a man going through his life in a male incarnation. What he is as a man, what he can experience as a man, what constitutes the male experience, so to speak, is the result of this resounding life ether that is always within him, "choirs of life" (12081), albeit with a strongly Ahrimanic tinge, that actually build up his male form. However, these choirs of life in and around him only become visible and audible around him if he becomes mediumistic.

Now Let's say we have a group of souls who died at birth and want to express the fact that they did not become a "man" during their incarnation here. What would they say? They would say that they had had all the prerequisites they needed to become men in this incarnation but that what makes a man a man had not done its work at their birth. Instead, they had immediately been taken away from what would have made them men in their physical incarnation. They would say:

> Too early were we taken
> From choirs of life. (12080-81)

The Blessed Boys say this.

> Too early were we taken
> From choirs of life;
> But this man has learned, (12080-82)

in other words, this man Faust has experience. He has passed through the long life of earth. He can tell us something about this earthly life.

He will inform us. (12083)

This is how we need to look into the most profound depths of esoteric cognition if we want to understand why some particular word occurs in just this work. Once it is there, the average commentator will come and say: Well, the poet chose a word like "Lebenschöre" (choirs of life), and so on. Anything is fine with him as long as he doesn't have to submit to the inconvenience of learning something. I like to mention such things to show you how technically accurate, in the sense of a spiritual world conception, this work of Goethe's is and what it actually contains.

I have said that this work has something in it that is hard for the human heart and mind to understand. Perhaps by saying this I have burdened your hearts in one direction or another by indicating characteristic points where Ahriman and Lucifer are working in such a way that we can't escape their influence. No matter how we look at it, as we prepare for a new incarnation—and we have to incarnate either as a man or as a woman—if Lucifer isn't in it, then Ahriman is. There's no point in making the extreme statement that we have to escape them both. I can see that I have weighed your hearts down even more by showing you that there is a certain danger inherent in looking into and observing your own aura. But the infinite wisdom of the world consists precisely in the fact that life is not a resting pendulum, but a moving one. And just as the pendulum swings out to one side and then the other, so does life itself swing out to the Ahrimanic and the Luciferic side, not only for humanity but for the entire world. And only because life swings back and forth between Ahrimanic and Luciferic influences, balancing them out and maintaining the energy of this balance, is this life possible at all. For this reason, what I have portrayed to you as something dangerous is always confronted by its opposite: the Luciferic by the Ahrimanic, and the Ahrimanic by the Luciferic.

Let us take another look at the female organism. It radiates a Luciferic aura, as it were. But by raying it out, it pushes away the life or tone ether. As a result, a kind of Ahrimanic aura forms around the female organism, so that the female organism then has the Luciferic aura in the middle and the Ahrimanic one further out. But now, if this female organism is not so inactive as to get stuck within its own aura in the process of spiritual seeing, it can develop further. And this is just the important point: not to remain at the level of the imaginations formed first, which is an unhealthy thing to do, but rather to exert all the will forces you can muster so as to penetrate through these imaginations. You must get to the point where it is not your own aura that appears to you, but where it appears to you as reflected from a mirror, which is now an Ahrimanic aura. You mustn't look into your own aura, but see what is in your own aura reflected back from the outer aura. You see from this that the female organism receives the Luciferic reflected back from the Ahrimanic and is thereby neutralized, brought into balance. By this means it is now neither Ahrimanic nor Luciferic but "de-feminized": It has become generally human. It really has become generally human.

I only ask you to feel how, when we ascend into the spiritual, avoiding both the Luciferic and the Ahrimanic power of our own aura, we are really not looking into either the Luciferic or the Ahrimanic but allowing the one to be reflected so that we receive it back, asexually, without its being either male or female. The female aspect is neutralized in the direction of the male by the Ahrimanic, and the male aspect is neutralized in the direction of the female by the Luciferic. For just as the female-Luciferic aura is surrounded by the Ahrimanic aura, the male-Ahrimanic aura is surrounded by the Luciferic aura, and what one has within oneself is reflected back in the same way as in the case of the female one. We see it as a mirrored image.

Now assume someone wanted to portray this process. When would such a person become able to do this? Well, what occurs in the case of clairvoyance also occurs after death. The person is in the same position. In the case of clairvoyance, the female aspect has to be neutralized into the male and the male into the female. This is also the case after death. What sorts of ideas have to come into play then? Let us take a soul, for example, that has been in a female organism, passed through death, and then had to go through a number of after-death experiences intended to balance out its earthly guilt. Such a soul will then gradually strive for neutralization by working its way out of what it was bound to on the earth. The female aspect will strive for neutralization through the male aspect, as it were. For this process of neutralization, salvation will consist in striving for the most exalted kind of maleness. If, after death, we run across female penitents, it will have to be characteristic of them that their longing in the spiritual world is filled with a striving for the male principle that will balance them out. The three penitent women—the Magna Peccatrix, the Mulier Samaritana and the Maria Aegyptiaca†—are all, to be sure, within the entourage of the Mater Gloriosa, but their task is to strive for neutralization or balance. This is, of course, the reason why the Mater Gloriosa is working in the aura; it is made very clear to us that the Mater Gloriosa can work in her aura, because she has her own aura. Let us hear how this is described:

> Winding around her,
> Cloudlets so gentle,
> Penitents are they,
> Delicate women,
> Her knees surrounding,
> Sipping the ether,
> Needful of grace.
>
> You, the Unapproachable,
> Cannot fail to notice
> How these, led astray with ease,
> Come to you in trust. (12013-23)

But they only barely become aware of this as a kind of consciousness. It does not approach them as something resounding toward them like the fullness of life itself. What resounds toward them is what they are to experience through Christ in connection with the Mater Gloriosa. For this reason we see that everywhere the speeches of the three penitent women are directed toward the male principle, the Christ:

> By the love that let the tears flow,
> Soothing with their healing balm
> The feet of your transfigured Son ... (12037-39)

And in the case of the Samaritan Maria, we have:

By the well to which of old
Father Abram led his herds ... (12045-46)

And here we have it spiritualized:

By the pure, abundant fountain
Pouring now from out that source ... (12049-50)

Indeed, in speaking with the Samaritan woman, Christ calls Himself the true water.

And in the case of the Maria Aegyptiaca we already have to do with the interment:

By the place most sanctified,
Where the Lord was taken down, (12053-54)

We see that in all three something is living that wants to leave its own aura and pass over to what neutralizes itself.

And if we then ask what the man finds that will neutralize him, lifting him out of maleness, we find it as the longing for the female principle that surges through the world.

From here the view is free,
The spirit lifted.
Women are passing by,
Upward are wafting;
Among them the Glorious One
In starry halo,
High Queen of Heaven, as
Her radiance shows me. (11989-96)

He is not immediately attracted by Christ's maleness, as the women are; what attracts him first is what belongs to Christ as the female aspect. And this leads him in turn to what he is karmically connected with in Gretchen's soul, in other words, to the woman. There you see how this profound mystery of the human being's relationship to the spiritual world has been delicately woven into this poetic work. For how could we fail to be moved to our very core when confronted with the esoteric fact of a disembodied soul still containing the elements within itself—remnants of Nature that first must be separated off—and still in need of the female principle for its neutralization? Moreover, we see how the female principle, in striving upward for neutralization, has to assert itself as the "attractor" because in this instance we have to do with the male principle, Faust. Something quite wondrous has been portrayed in this poetic work, and a clear indication is given that it is meant to be there. Faust will continue his striving toward the female through the words of Doctor Marianus, that is, toward the spiritual Ever-Feminine, which is the secret, the mystery. Becoming spiritually aware of the Mater Gloriosa, he says:

> Highest ruler of the world!
> Reveal to me your secret
> Woven in the outstretched blue
> Canopy of heaven. (11997-12000)

Now Let us imagine Faust striving toward the spiritual world, yearning to see the secret of the feminine in the Mater Gloriosa. How will that be possible? Well, it will be possible if the light is neutralized by the light raying in from the opposite direction; in other words, the female light-and-warmth aura will appear, but from the opposite direction, not as it flows out directly. That light has to be neutralized by being connected with the light raying toward it from the opposite direction. The secret is beheld in the outstretched canopy of heaven: the woman with the aura, with the sun. When the light is reflected back from the moon, we see the woman standing on the moon. You know this picture, or at least you should be familiar with it. This is how we see Faust, yearning to behold at last the mystery in the outstretched canopy of heaven: Maria, the woman, clothed in the sun, with the moon at her feet raying back its light. This secret, this mystery in the outstretched canopy of heaven, taken together with what else Faust knows about the Mater Gloriosa, constitutes the feeling-content of the Chorus Mysticus. For what the Mater Gloriosa still has in the way of human form is a simile, for her human form is what is transitory about her, and all of that is a simile. The inadequate—inadequate, that is, in human longing—only here is it attained (12106-07). Here we behold the radiance of the aura as though coming from the sun,† its light working back, glowing back to us from the moon: the indescribable, here it is done (12108-09). What cannot be understood in physical life—that something is sought that rays out from the self but is reflected back in selfless radiance—here it is done. Finally, we have the whole thing expressed through the mouth of a man or for a man's ears in accordance with his feeling:

> The Ever-Feminine
> Draws us upward and on. (12110-11)

We have to say that for many parts of *Faust*, allowing it to work on us really means going directly into an atmosphere of esotericism. And if I should wish to tell you everything that can be said about *Faust* from an esoteric point of view, we would have to spend a lot more time together. You would have to listen to a lot of lectures on this subject. But that is not necessary, first of all, for it is not so much a matter of acquiring as many concepts and ideas as possible. What is of utmost importance is that we deepen our feelings. And when we succeed in deepening our sensations and feelings for this work of world literature in such a way that we have acquired a profound reverence for the earthly sway of the Great Spirit† in whose creative activity the esoteric is truly present, then we are doing something good for ourselves and for the world. If we can stand in the presence of what is spiritually great and experience it with proper reverence, then, that will be a significant pathway toward the portal of spiritual science.

Let us say it once again: It is less a matter of making up far-fetched commentaries than of deepening our feelings. And I wouldn't think it worth very much if all I had been able to do was to tell you, for example, that the speech by the Blessed Boys about having been torn away from choirs of life leads into such esoteric depths. As I said, telling you this one idea would be worth something only if I could be sure that as you hear such a truth being expressed, your hearts and minds and inner sensing are so gripped by this that you feel something of the deeply sacred forces that live in the world pouring themselves into human creative activity, when this activity is really carried out in connection with the secrets of the world. If our spine can tingle in the presence of the fact that something of such depth can be contained in a poetic work of art, then this spine-tingling experience that our soul, our feeling life, our heart has had, is worth far more than merely knowing that the Blessed Boys say they're not united with choirs of life. What grips us should not be our pleasure in the cleverness of some idea. We should rejoice in the fact that the world is woven out of the spiritual, thereby enabling the spirit to so work in human hearts that such creative activity can live on in the spiritual development of humanity.

11
Goethe and the Worldview of German Idealism

Berlin, December 2, 1915

Who is this Faust, as he stands there before us? The noblest representative of all human striving. But the striving he represents—he is, after all, a university professor—is the striving for a certain kind of knowledge! And what is it that, right at the beginning of *Faust*, becomes a great enigma, a great question? Cognition itself, the striving for knowledge! Two elements run freely throughout this literary work, and we have to take note of how they play themselves out if we want to understand, on the one hand, the fundamental character of Goethe's *Faust* and, on the other, the latter's connection with the most profound aspects of German intellectual history.

To be sure, the word "magic" and all it connotes are not especially in vogue today. But Goethe felt it was necessary that once human knowledge had become a question and an enigma for his Faust, the latter should be confronted by magic....

... Why must Goethe's Faust, who had explored all the realms of human knowledge, turn to magic? Why did this man, who had sought to gain clarity about the deep springs from which all existence flows, try to find a relationship to Nature so completely different from that of conventional science? Why? It is because Faust had experienced and felt so keenly the pangs of human striving; he had felt such a profound longing to know the depths of existence and had experienced first-hand the limitations of science as usually practiced. Conventional science casts the laws of Nature into the form of concepts, of ideas. But do such concepts really allow me to stand within reality? Or do these concepts only enjoy a kind of ghostly existence within my own mind? They may be clear in themselves, in terms of the picture of Nature they provide, but do they provide clarity regarding real life and a direct connection with the sources of existence? This question that assails the soul can be felt in a variety of forms. One can feel it weakly, but one can also feel its pangs keenly—so strongly, in fact, that its enigma becomes a kind of nightmare from which the soul longs to awaken. For the soul can say to itself: All this seeming knowledge is just a superstructure I have erected upon the real ground of existence. All this seeming knowledge is a complete abstraction. But I must somehow use what I experience within myself as a way to descend into the depths of existence.

Faust is unable to accept what Schelling,† for example, had the audacity to believe, namely, that living *inside* concepts is the same thing as creating inside Nature. Instead, he wants to descend into Nature itself. He wants to experience Nature as living, creative activity. He wants to develop an activity within his own soul such that, when this activity is going on within his soul and the soul itself is carrying it out, the creativity of the human soul nevertheless coincides with the creativity of Nature itself. Because Faust is unable to accomplish this in any other way, he tries to enliven within himself the path the ancient Magi attempted to follow. Faust tries to harbor something in his soul that not only reflects Nature within him in the form of concepts, but appears to him in what lives behind the phenomena and creates behind the phenomena of Nature. The spiritual element active in Nature's creating, that flows and weaves through the world,† that "wells up and down in floods of life, in storm of deeds" (501-502): this is what he seeks; not just to cognize it, but to unite himself with it in a living way. He wants to commune with it in such a way that this spiritual creativity of Nature will stand next to him, just as one human soul stands next to another, incarnated here in physical life, so that one not only *knows about* existence but actually *experiences* it.

In order to understand Faust's stance toward Nature, one needs only to recall the approach of a thinker such as Jakob Böhme, or the philosophical striving of German Idealism.† There we see Faust, yearning with eager anticipation for revelations from certain deeds that he aspires to perform, finding a relationship to Nature that is entirely consonant with the inmost spirit of German culture: calling forth Nature within the soul and allowing it to become living science, living knowledge. That is why Goethe must lead Faust to magic....

... Just imagine what a challenge it was to create a work of literature such as Goethe's *Faust*. Goethe had to represent the inner life, traditionally the province of the lyric, in dramatic form. Goethe sought to dramatize Faust's relationship to the world by making what lives and lights up within the soul so vivid that it becomes an external event.... Faust's striving was to be depicted as that of a man who has been moved by the enigmas of existence and then goes forth into the world, becomes a warrior in the world. However, the struggles that arise from the enigmas of existence are inward battles. As a rule, one faces them alone; as a rule, there is nothing dramatic about them. Dramas cannot be made simply by allowing the characters' inner lives to unfold. How is it that Goethe became able to turn something that is fundamentally a matter of the inner life of the soul into living, dramatic image? In the same way that he used magic to carry the inner life out into Nature, he then takes hold of another aspect of the inner life and carries it out into the macrocosm.

Goethe wants to show that if one seeks evil and wants to experience its reality, one cannot conceive of it as a merely inner principle that can be explained in entirely inward terms. Rather, one must go forth into life, because it is within the fullness of life that one encounters evil. Thus Goethe cannot look upon evil with a merely philosophical eye; rather, he must look for something that has the nature of a being, one that opposes Faust and is an actual incarnation of evil, one that, as the principle of evil, is as vital as the human being living in a physical body is. And he must sense, he must be able to show, that the struggle against evil is not just an abstract, inner battle, but rather one that is fought every minute of every hour that the human being lives. In everything we do, we encounter the substance of evil. This is how the challenge was met. Thus it was that Goethe was able to fashion as an immediate, substantive presence what would otherwise have remained merely a philosophical abstraction. Something about which one usually *speaks* was made to walk about, to act, to fight....

... Thus it was that in this poetic work our understanding of evil had to be deepened with recourse to that marvelous strain in the history of German intellectual striving that runs through all those deeper thinkers from Jakob Böhme onwards. These thinkers were not content to seek evil merely within philosophical concepts, but wanted rather to go forth into the world. And in going forth into the world, they confront evil, just as one encounters another human being bodily in the physical world. In order to open up the inner life spiritually, their striving had to connect with such a view of evil. That is to say: in the same way that magic made it possible for one to feel one's way right into the very sources of Nature, by displaying evil itself as a spiritually potent being it became possible to experience the reality of spiritual life by inserting it directly into human life. Thus it is that Goethe the poet leads us to the theater of the Ideal, but the Ideal experienced as real life rather than as abstraction.

But Goethe—the great artist of whom Schiller said that he was able to give birth to Ancient Greece again within his soul—faced yet another challenge, the full meaning of which we have barely begun to appreciate. What we have before us in Faust is the striving human being. Many interpreters of *Faust* have emphasized that Goethe accomplished something grand in allowing Faust to be saved instead of somehow perishing, as in earlier treatments of the theme. Goethe allows him to be saved, they say, because in accordance with the more modern worldview we have to assume that the human soul harbors the forces that can gain the victory over evil. But what this viewpoint actually means for the work as a whole is something that is not often considered.... They imagine a grand drama, unfolding through time—with an utterly predictable outcome. And, indeed, they are right: given their presuppositions, that is actually how it would have to turn out. For one has to bring one's own convictions along in confronting the profoundest enigmas of life—or so they say. But the real meaning of such claims is that, from a purely external point of view, *Faust* has to be the most boring work ever written. For every pedant knows today—or at least thinks he or she knows—that if human beings really strive, in the end they must be redeemed. And now we are told that one of the greatest poets who ever lived supposedly wrote a monumental epic in which he employed every possible artistic form in order to demonstrate this self-evident truth!

What Goethe really accomplished, however, was not just to embody the aforementioned thought in some kind of abstract way, but to place life itself before us in a long, long series of vibrant images. Why was this? Because he wanted to show how something grasped inwardly in the form of abstract thoughts would only be a self-evident triviality that would become part of life in a completely different way. Because he wanted to expand life in two directions: toward magic on the one hand, and toward the spiritual world on the other. Because for him striving toward the pole of Nature is not a striving for knowledge, but rather a magical striving. Because striving to know evil is not merely a philosophical affair, but rather a matter of life. How can something become a matter of life that otherwise would remain only an abstract striving within the soul?...

... Knowledge, the very thing by means of which the human personality seeks to save itself from the passions of life, now becomes a huge question. Faust is able to immerse himself in the passions of life; but as he plunges down with the creative forces of his soul, he fails to take up those very forces with which he has just lifted himself up. Instead, he plunges down, seeking to unite the "underworld" of his soul with the "underworld" of Nature. And this plunging down into sensuality, the life of the senses, even into the banalities of life—all this is the source of his errors in Part One. Now he has to confront it in his own personality, because his task is to unite what lives within the depths of his soul with what dwells within the depths of the cosmos. To depict as vividly as possible the error that can try the human soul—*that* is the task of Part One of *Faust*, and a good deal of Part Two as well.

Faust shows how any attempt to take hold of the world by knowing it runs the danger of being dragged down into the depths of one's own personality, and then being pushed along by the currents of life. This is a matter of Faust's own will, his own character, and not of any abstract doctrine. That is what makes it literature. On the other hand, if we are not satisfied with a merely conceptual understanding of evil, then we must break through the limitations of normal consciousness, where we find only concepts, ideas and sensations. We have to transcend this normal consciousness; we must break through to a higher consciousness in which we perceive spiritual substance and activity solely with the eyes of the soul and of the spirit, without using the physical senses. This is the task that confronts anyone seeking to know evil through direct experience of its reality. This becomes Faust's task vis-à-vis Mephistopheles. But human beings cannot confront the reality of evil with an untransformed consciousness. It is a sheer impossibility to approach the reality of evil with the faculties we initially bring to bear. The world stands outside us; we must gain knowledge of it. But knowledge necessarily unfolds within the soul, in the process of forming concepts. What can be experienced only by the soul must be in the soul. As modern philosophers have stressed, so rightly and at the same time so wrongly, we cannot exceed the limits of consciousness. But if we remain within consciousness, then evil remains only an abstract concept; it does not step forth in a substantial form.

So it is that Faust stands before a monumental—we might even say an impossible—task. But, as is clearly stated in the drama itself, greatness lies in "desiring the impossible" (7488). Faust is confronted by the downright impossible task of transcending the sole source of his consciousness, of rising up out of ordinary consciousness. From now on, this becomes his path, the path leading beyond the soul's normal consciousness. Tomorrow we shall speak about this path of knowledge, leading from everyday consciousness to those realms where the spirit is grasped immediately as spirit. Faust is confronted by this task. He is unable to experience the reality of evil in the realm toward which his consciousness is initially directed. He must therefore find a way—and not in some general, abstract, trivial manner—to reconcile himself with existence again; but he must do so in a way that preserves his individual self. The drama must show Faust finding his way from ordinary consciousness to a comprehension of life that arises from profounder faculties of the soul.

Thus we see Faust making his way over the surface of the world, grasping it, touching it outwardly and inwardly in search of the portal that will lead him past the outer shell into its interior. We see him rising to such lofty realms that by transforming his soul more and more he really does experience the depths Jakob Böhme had sought to plumb. These depths are then alluded to in Part Two of *Faust*, in that Faust finds the ultimate, the grandest, the highest and at the same time profoundest experience—which he has already striven for earlier in his descent to the Mothers—at the moment his senses dim, he goes blind and bright, inner light breaks forth within him. Faust must be led from ordinary consciousness to consciousness of a different kind. This other consciousness sleeps in the depths of the human soul, just as the wellsprings of Nature slumber, hidden beneath the veil of Nature we see with our external senses. Faust must be led to a deeper consciousness that constantly accompanies human beings between birth and death, but is not present within the field of normal, everyday awareness. Faust must be led via a strengthening of his inner faculties away from abstract ideas toward the life of spiritual existence itself, where he reaches two different portals. As a Magus, Faust knocks at the door of real existence, which leads from mere reflection upon Nature to the co-creation of Nature. And in his encounters with Mephistopheles, in his living, dramatic encounter with Mephistopheles and everything associated with that, Faust knocks on the other door, which leads from ordinary human consciousness to a supra-consciousness. This supersensible consciousness opens up a spiritual world that is also the real origin of evil. Moreover, the spiritual world it opens up lies behind the normal world of soul, just as the form in which Nature appears to our senses is only the revelation and expression of what lives and weaves entirely within Nature....

... It is itself a significant drama on the stage of world history that a mind such as Goethe's, through its inner deliberations, was able to enter so deeply into popular folklore [i.e., the *Faust* puppet play] that out of these most primitive materials it could create an artistic work of such exalted value that it would also be connected, as we have shown, with the most significant philosophical currents in the greatest era of German intellectual history, namely, those of German Idealism. If we read the drama imaginatively rather than literally, we can see in Faust the striving of Fichte. How so? Unlike Descartes, Fichte does not seek to grasp existence and the self by bringing abstract thought to conscious awareness. Rather, Fichte seeks to understand existence and the self† by placing himself against the background of the cosmic forces of Creation that shine into the depths of the human soul, so that at every moment the self calls itself into being. We see the same dynamic light up again in *Faust*, but transposed into the register of dramatic will and life itself. Faust is not satisfied with the self that has been handed down to him by the inherently human striving for knowledge and can thus be experienced with normal consciousness: he wants to experience his real self within the spiritual world. The whole plot of *Faust* is about the self refashioning itself through its encounter with the world, constantly elevating itself. Fichte lives in Goethe's *Faust*.

Schelling lives there as well, in that Faust strives, on the one hand, to unite his soul with the truths of magic, and on the other to plumb the depths of his own unconscious. He is Schelling when, through his encounter with the representative of evil in its immediate guise as a spirit being, he seeks to find what cannot be found in the ordinary soul activities of thinking, feeling and willing. Faust's search for Nature truly leads him to where Nature is alive with creative activity. Schelling had gone so far as to claim† that to understand Nature is to create Nature! Fichte's stance is healthier when he says: To understand Nature is to enter with one's own creative activity into the creative life of Nature herself. Nevertheless we see what a powerful striving for higher knowledge and for the very sources of existence is also alive in Fichte.

Hegel strove for sober thoughts, and no one is more sober than Hegel. In Hegel's philosophy, the spirit of the cosmos with whom the soul seeks to unite itself becomes a mere logician. Imagine the divine spirit of the cosmos as a soul that is a kind of great logician, building up the world out of nothing but a set of logical propositions! We must not take this literally, but even in this most austere logic we have to see the expression of a striving that remains mystical, seeking to unite the depths of the soul with the pinnacle of the cosmos itself in Nature and in history. Hegel must also be understood as saying that one's own self cannot be found in what the senses convey, but rather only in that which the human soul attains when it rises up out of the world of the senses. That is what Hegel's philosophy strove to achieve.

Faust, too, experiences a bright light within, after the light of his eyes has been extinguished. What Hegel had sought in the right way, without, however, perceiving it to be the correct goal, is what Faust was also seeking: to allow his own lower self to merge with the Self of the cosmos, uniting with it in order to experience the Self of the cosmos within his own, individual self.

12
Faust's Journey through the World and His Rebirth in German Intellectual History

Berlin, February 13, 1916

... I would like to point out first of all that it is very easy for a misunderstanding to arise with regard to Faust's opening monologue. One might be led to think that the moment in which Faust gives himself over to magic coincides with his speaking of the monologue, and that Faust had not given himself over to magic before the feelings that live in this monologue arise in his soul. That would be a misunderstanding, and it would make it extraordinarily difficult to understand the state of Faust's soul in general. Rather, one must assume that when Faust expresses his feelings in that monologue, he is already living deeply inside what he addresses as magic and that he has already made a deep study of magic. We can show this from the text of *Faust* itself. When later on in the drama the poodle that has accompanied him home from his Easter walk assumes various forms and Faust wants to know what is lurking inside the poodle, he reaches for a book of occult magic, and he knows—or at least thinks he knows—exactly how to solve the mystery of this poodle by conjuring with all the formulas in his books; he knows just how to behave in his confrontation with this spiritual phenomenon. Thus one has to assume that Faust has already become acquainted with such things to some degree....

... What kind of a worldview was this?

One needs only to take up something like the works of Agrippa von Nettesheim or some other such medieval philosopher in order to gain insight into what Goethe's Faust actually means by conjuring up the spirit of the macrocosm. Concepts and ideas such as those that surrounded Faust in the philosophy of the Enlightenment—I mean Goethe's Faust, not the Faust of the sixteenth century—were not available at the time when Agrippa von Nettesheim was writing. In the Middle Ages, one did not construct an image of the world using concepts as abstract as those of the Enlightenment; rather, one constructed philosophical worldviews in images, as it were, in the form of imaginations. And one also cherished the belief that one could call forth something that allowed Nature and the spiritual world to express intimately what they actually are. And the worldview that resulted was intimately bound up with the feelings and the sensations of the soul; in a way, it was just like the soul's experience of itself.[†] Today one would say it was very anthropomorphic. And indeed it was. When one abstracted knowledge from the world, one felt the influence of forces that were related to the forces of one's own soul. In experiencing Nature, one spoke of sympathies and antipathies like those within the individual soul. Moreover, at the time when Agrippa von Nettesheim wrote, people put little stock in what they could achieve on their own by shaping their faculties of soul or developing their powers of cognition, in order to give these a form higher than what they have by nature. One did not believe that the human soul was capable of conducting research. Rather, it was believed that one could create an occasion for the spirit that courses through Nature to manifest itself by means of all kinds of external arrangements, this or that experiment. These were of course not experiments in our modern sense. All kinds of procedures were undertaken that people believed would reveal the secrets of Nature. Nobody believed that consciousness was able to penetrate the veil of Nature by means of faculties that it had developed out of itself. Rather, it was felt that one had to make this or that arrangement, to undertake this or that procedure. By employing such magic, as it were, Nature would be made to speak, to express the spirit underlying it. But they sought this apart from human consciousness. They wanted to do something in the outer world whereby Nature would reveal its secrets. Nature, they hoped, would at last reveal the disposition of forces within it that the individual human being uses to build itself up out of Nature and the world of the spirit. What they sought was exactly what Faust was yearning for: communion with the weaving life of Nature itself. And they believed they could attain it.

What stood before them in this way as Nature and the world of the mind was suffused with spirit. And the cosmic necessity underlying evolution required that this all be replaced by an external view of Nature, the worldview one sees in Copernicus, Kepler, and Galileo.† What arose was an image of Nature that removed everything that the medieval philosophers had sought in Nature. In this worldview of Copernicus, Kepler, and Galileo, and everything that followed from it, the ideas that prevailed and were felt to be justified and determinative were precisely those that Goethe's Faust had found so threadbare, so empty of content. Such ideas did not equip one to experience the world fully in one's own soul.

So it is at the moment of Faust's opening monologue; this is why Faust feels the urge to experience cosmic mysteries through the old magic, why he wants to join his own soul to the essence and the lawfulness of the universe. And he thought he could accomplish that by giving himself over to the formulas and the images representing the macrocosm in the book he is holding.

But Faust—let me be very clear: I mean Goethe's Faust, not the Faust of the sixteenth century—is every inch a man of his time. Humanity's inner nature evolves, even if this is not apparent to cursory inspection. At this time, it was no longer possible to penetrate the mysteries of existence in the same way that Agrippa von Nettesheim had done. It was no longer possible to believe that through imagination, through some kind of outer occasion like experimenting with magic, one was dealing with what actually "moves the world in its inmost core." [cf. "What holds the world / Together in its inmost core" (382-383)] And so it is that Faust is forced to recognize: Yes, like the Ancients, I too am trying to unite with the spiritual forces underlying Nature—but what do I gain thereby? Is this really leading me to an experience of the inner life and being of Nature and of the spirit? No, all it gives me is a show! "What a show! But just a show, that's all!" (454).

And in this sense Goethe's Faust is truly the representative of his time. By now it is no longer possible to reach the sources of existence along this older path, to grasp the infinity of Nature—to really experience it, not just penetrate it with mere ideas or natural laws. He can't do it, because the time is past when one might believe that a real knowledge of Nature and the spiritual world can be attained in this way. Just a show! And so he turns away from what contemplation of the Sign of the macrocosm can give him. He turns to the microcosm, to the Earth Spirit....

... It may not be immediately obvious that Goethe wanted Faust to appear to be somewhat mediumistic from the moment the Earth Spirit appears until the end of Part One, but the course of the action really does lead us into this realm. And so it is that one can characterize Mephistopheles as that spirit who calls forth within Faust's inner life just this worldview. Some believe that this mediumistic mode of consciousness reveals the mysteries of existence; such people have no real trust in full human consciousness, so they have come to believe that one must first diminish consciousness, cloud it, in order to penetrate the mysteries of existence. There is a book by Kiesewetter[†]—one-sided to be sure, but not entirely without merit—in which Mephistopheles is depicted as a kind of alter ego of Faust. Not Faust's higher self, but rather the self one finds by turning away from the higher intellectual powers of normal consciousness, and instead descending into the realms of the soul where drives and instincts play themselves out. Not a supersensible world—far from it! Rather, something one might call the *sub*-sensible.... But something else is brought to life for us, something of extraordinary importance in understanding both Goethe's *Faust* and the nature of the human soul in general. By entering into realms that can indeed be known by employing profound, but sub-sensible faculties arising only out of instinctive drives, the realms expressed in scenes such as "Witches' Kitchen" and "Walpurgis Night," Faust succumbs at the same time to tragic moral transgressions. He falls victim to his own impetuous drives. To be sure, the "Gretchen Tragedy" that ends Part One is one of the high points of world literature. But the reason why it represents such a high point is that the poet has succeeded in representing the tragedy that flows from human instincts which have not been sublimated by what can rightly be called our higher human nature. And Mephisto whips up a kind of knowledge of the world for Faust, something that will satisfy his desire for knowledge, with this rise of blind instinct from the depths of Faust's soul, the very depths in which the human individuality abandons itself to its intrinsic nature with no thought of providing its life there with any kind of moral guide. Goethe's *Faust* is a monumental expression of this tragedy. But it also speaks volumes about what is really happening in a certain kind of clairvoyant experience.... This outcome, which many experience as something horrible, arises in the way that Goethe depicts here: this kind of clairvoyance, this somnambulism, arises when one transforms into cognitive forces what lives within human instincts or drives that have not yet been sublimated into normal human cognitive faculties. These blind, unconscious drives are motivated by real impulses, but they are impulses that have not been suffused by moral judgments. What Goethe wants to show is that the worldview expressed in scenes such as "Witches' Kitchen" and the "Classical Walpurgis Night" is merely a reflection of these blind instincts that have been loosed by a pathological state of soul....

... Has Faust in his wanderings through the world made any progress beyond the stage at which he contemplated the sign of the Macrocosm, and called the world "just a show"? Yes, Faust has made progress, very considerable progress! Goethe wants to show that Faust's healthy constitution has withstood the attacks that Mephisto has launched against him, by pushing him down into the sub-sensible realm, a realm one experiences when instinctive drives rather than heightened faculties of cognition are the basis of one's worldview. At the beginning of Part One, Faust is shown having opened up a book by Nostradamus. The Sign of the Macrocosm arises before his soul. He tries to enter into what could be represented in the words and images of the Sign of the Macrocosm. "What a show! But just a show, that's all!" One might say that in this moment, Faust's striving leads him into a kind of pathological state of soul, in which he then remains—keeping in mind that the word "pathological" should not be taken in any prosaic, philistine sense.

After Faust has found his way to a healthy experience of Nature and the spirit, and the spirit has had a chance to work on his normal consciousness, he speaks different words—a parallel, one might say, to the words, "What a show! But just a show, that's all!" Faust finds himself facing the splendors of Nature given birth to by the light of the sun. But then he recoils and turns toward the waterfall, which reflects the power of the sun in colors, as he says, "So let the sun remain behind my back!" (4715) He wants to contemplate the reflection of what the sun calls forth. "In this reflected splendor we have life" (4727)—a wonderful intensification vis-à-vis his earlier words, "What a show! But just a show, that's all!" Now Faust is able to comprehend how spirit truly lives within what confronts him as Nature, because he has developed the right relationship to the spiritual in Nature. He has internalized the wisdom expressed in the final lines of Part Two: "All that must pass away is but a simile" (12104)—grasping in a simile what lives spiritually in Nature. And so it is that we see at the beginning of the second part of *Faust* how it is that, by means of influence exerted upon his normal consciousness by the spiritual world, Faust has been brought into a healthy relationship to the world....

13
Wisdom – Beauty – Goodness
Michael – Gabriel – Raphael

Dornach, August 19, 1916

After dramatic performances of the "Dedication" and the "Prologue in Heaven," with eurythmy

In recent weeks† we have spoken about the three great, highest ideals of humanity, using the names for them by which they have always been known since ancient times: the ideals of Wisdom, Beauty, and Goodness.

In more recent times these three highest ideals of humanity have always been linked with the three forces of the human soul that we know so well, having looked at them from many different aspects. The ideal of Wisdom has been connected with thinking as such, as well as with the act of forming mental pictures or concepts† [*Vorstellen*]; the ideal of Beauty with feeling; and the ideal of Goodness with willing.

We can only acquire Wisdom in the form of clear concepts [*Vorstellungen*], in clear thinking. The Beautiful, which is the object of art, cannot be grasped this way. Psychologists, the investigators of the soul, have been saying for a long time that feeling is the soul force having to do chiefly with Beauty. And what becomes a reality in the world as a manifestation of the Good does so through its connection with willing. What these authorities tell us about the relationships between the three great ideals of humanity and the different forces of our soul seems quite plausible. We can supplement these remarks by referring to the three *Critiques* of Kant.† One of these, the *Critique of Pure Reason*, intends to serve the cause of Wisdom by being a critical analysis of our ability to form concepts. Kant called another one of his critiques the *Critique of Judgment*. This critique has two parts, the *Critique of Esthetic Judgment* and the *Critique of Teleological Judgment*.

In speaking here of the power of judgment, Kant basically has in mind everything included in the knowledge we acquire through feelings, by means of which we affirm that something is beautiful or ugly, useful or harmful. And so we could also say that the power of judgment is related to the concept of the Beautiful, insofar as we're not thinking here only of conceptual judgment, but also of the kind of judgment that comes from the heart—as a sub-category in the particularly Kantian sense; other people have retained this way of designating it. A third critique of Kant's is the *Critique of Practical Reason,* which refers to willing, or striving for the Good.

Now, what I have just said can be found in the works of every psychologist, except for one who came on the scene in the second half of the nineteenth century, having discovered that this whole way of dividing up the forces of the human soul is simply not true because it fails to harmonize with the results of an unprejudiced observation of the human soul. He further maintains that it is just as wrong to assign the great ideals of humanity to the different soul forces of conceptualization [*Vorstellen*], feeling, and willing, with Wisdom as the highest ideal being assigned to conceptualization, Beauty to feeling, and Goodness to willing. The psychologist I am referring to, Franz Brentano,[†] felt duty-bound to overthrow the whole system I have just outlined for you and establish in its place a completely different way of analyzing human soul life. Let us start with conceptualization [*Vorstellen*], which he assigns to Beauty. You see that whereas everyone else assigns feeling, in other words, esthetic judgment, or the power of judgment in general, to Beauty, Brentano assigns conceptualization to Beauty. He goes on to assign the power of judgment to Wisdom, insofar as this is something we acquire. He doesn't call it feeling, however; he calls it the power of judgment. Then, in an odd way, he even dulls willing down by disregarding the actual unfolding of the will, the will impulse itself, directing his attention instead to what underlies the will impulse, namely, sympathy and antipathy. Much can be said in favor of looking at things this way. Language itself can sometimes lead us to connect sympathy and antipathy with the impulse of will, as when we say, for example, that we have an aversion [*Widerwillen*: "something against our will"] to something. We're not "willing" anything here, but we do have an antipathy to something. In a way, we could say, Brentano dulls the will down to sympathy and antipathy by assigning to willing this sympathy or antipathy toward saying yes or no to something. He doesn't get as far as the actual will impulse but only as far as what underlies the will: saying yes or no to something, affirming or denying it.

In Brentano's opinion, the act of conceptualizing in itself can never lead to a true, or Wisdom-filled, view of something, but only to a superficial one. He says, for example, that there's nothing wrong with conceptualizing a winged horse, but that doing so—and we must remember that Brentano is living in the age of materialism— is not a Wisdom-filled activity because there is no such thing as a winged horse. Something must be added to the conceptualization, and that, he says, is the acknowledgement or non-acknowledgement of the conceptualization by our power of judgment. Only then can we speak of Wisdom.

We can now ask what the underlying reason is for such a complete reversal of the soul forces. What moved Brentano to align the soul forces with Beauty, Goodness, and Wisdom in such a completely different way than that of the other psychologists? If we try to find out why he came to this different picture of how human soul life is organized, the only way we can arrive at an answer is by taking his own personal development into account. For the most part, the other psychologists of the modern age are the products of the developmental stream of modern philosophy. One characteristic of the modern philosophers, indeed of all philosophers, is that they know their Greek philosophy relatively well—in their own way, of course—and then philosophy basically starts all over again with Kant. But the modern philosophers don't know much about the period between Greek philosophy and Kant. Kant himself hardly knew much more about what had happened between Greek philosophy and his own work than what he had read in Hume and Berkeley[†]; he was completely unfamiliar with the entire development of medieval philosophy. Kant was totally ignorant of what we call the scholasticism of the Middle Ages. Now certain people enjoy taking things to extremes, and when they see that Kant himself didn't know anything about scholasticism, they use this as an excuse to regard scholasticism in general as so much pedantic foolishness and give up all further study of it. The fact that Kant didn't know anything about scholasticism didn't keep him from not knowing anything about Greek philosophy either.† Other people certainly knew more about this latter area than he did.

Brentano, on the other hand, was a real authority on scholasticism. He had a solid foundation in both medieval philosophy and Aristotle. On the other hand, those who see the world of philosophy through the eyes of Kant are not real experts on the subject of Aristotle, for the great Greek was treated worst of all as modern intellectual life continued to develop. Brentano, therefore, had a thorough knowledge of Aristotle and of scholasticism, but not the kind of knowledge that one would call purely historical. He was not just someone who knew what Aristotle wrote and what the scholastics wrote; anyone can pick up that sort of knowledge just by reading through the history of philosophy! Brentano had made himself fully at home in both the philosophy of Aristotle and the philosophy of scholasticism, this lonely thinking that had been carried on for centuries in the cells of cloisters and that worked with such painstaking technique in the world of concepts [*Begriffe*], that thoroughgoing technique long since completely lost to modern thinking. This is why those who attended Brentano's lectures on psychology in the seventies and eighties† were essentially hearing a completely different tone of human thinking than could, and still can, be heard from other philosophers of our modern era. There really lived in Brentano something like an undertone of what spoke out of the soul of the scholastics. And that is significant because this different way of thinking was the basis of his different way of analyzing the soul. We can therefore say: The peculiar fact is that all our more recent thinkers, for whom scholasticism was, and still is, nothing but a web of concepts, represent the human soul and its relationships to Wisdom, Beauty, and Goodness like this:

Wisdom:	Conceptualization
Beauty:	Feeling
Goodness:	Willing

All the feeling and inner impulses of a scholastic's heart were alive in Brentano, to the extent that such a thing is possible in our time. He *had* to think as differently as he did in analyzing the forces of the human soul and relating them to the great ideals of humanity. Where does that come from?

If you could have decided to ask the angels up there on the stage today, especially the three archangels, how they would analyze the soul and relate its forces to these great ideals, they would have given you an answer similar to the one Brentano was able to give, although in a much more comprehensive form. For their part, Raphael, Gabriel, and Michael wouldn't understand Brentano's analysis of the soul at all, but they would easily find their way into it, only they would transform it more comprehensively. Here we are touching a significant fact in the spiritual evolution of humanity. No matter how far removed from medieval scholastic thinking we may seem to be today, that way of thinking was nevertheless based on something that can be characterized more or less as follows: When speaking of the highest things, scholastic philosophers did not seek to remain at the level of what takes place directly on the physical plane but sought rather to prepare their soul in such a way that the spiritual beings of the higher world could speak out of it. In many respects this speaking will only be a stammering of the human soul because the human soul will of course always be able to express only incompletely what the spirits higher than human beings speak. But to a certain degree the scholastics wanted to speak about the spiritual concerns of the human being in the way a soul has to speak that gives itself over to what supersensible spirits have to say.

Ever since the actual era of humanity has been the era of materialism, we on the physical plane have grown accustomed to forming judgments about what a valid, Wisdom-filled concept is, or is not, in terms of the external physical world. We say that a winged horse is not a valid concept because we have never seen a winged horse. Materialism considers a concept to be filled with Wisdom only when it agrees with the dictates of the external world.

But imagine yourself in the sphere of the angels. They don't have this physical outer world, because this is a world essentially determined by living in a physical body and possessing physical sense organs, which the angels don't have. How do the angels acquire the possibility of speaking about their concepts as though they were true and valid? By establishing relationships with other spiritual beings. For, the moment we cross the threshold into the spiritual world, this world of the senses ceases to spread itself out the way it does before our senses. I have often described how we come into a world of nothing but beings as soon as we cross the threshold into the spiritual world. And it all depends on how these beings meet us whether a concept that we form has any validity or not. This is why Brentano is not speaking quite correctly when he speaks merely of the power of judgment. He would have to speak of the "revelation of [a] being." Then one would come to Wisdom. Once one has crossed the threshold into the spiritual world, the only way to arrive at Wisdom is to establish a right relationship to the spiritual beings that one finds on the other side of this threshold. If we are not able to develop a right relationship to the elemental beings and to the beings of the various hierarchies, we can only develop confused concepts, not correct ones borne on the wings of Wisdom. Correct conceptualization on the other side of the threshold and Wisdom with reference to the spiritual worlds to which the human soul also belongs—these depend entirely on having a correct view of the beings on the other side of the threshold. Because—and you will find this explained already in the final chapter of my book *Theosophy*—there is no external physical reality to cling to there, we have to depend for our Wisdom on the communications of the elemental beings, the beings of the higher hierarchies, and so on. We enter a world that is entirely alive, not the world in which we become mere photographers of reality.

In a certain way, Brentano has given us a last, abstract copy of the speech or language of angels. Angels would say that something is filled with Wisdom if it is in accordance with the whole complex of communications from the beings on the other side of the threshold of the spiritual worlds.

Forming a concept is not enough; this concept must be in harmony with what the spiritual beings beyond the threshold reveal. Therefore, beyond the threshold, conceptualization [*Vorstellen*] by itself is not permitted to be of service to Wisdom. But to what, then, is it permitted to be of service? To Appearance [*Schein*], in which Beauty [*Schönheit*] lives. If, on the other side of the threshold, we apply our conceptualizing directly to the reality beyond the threshold, this does not lead to a correct process of conceptualization. But we may very well apply it to Appearance, in which Beauty works and lives. Brentano was even quite right to say that conceptualization belongs with Beauty. For when the angels want to imagine or conceptualize, they will always say: What kind of concepts are we allowed to form for ourselves? Certainly not ugly ones; they must always be beautiful. But these concepts, which they form in accordance with the ideal of Beauty, will not correspond to reality unless they correspond to the revelations of other beings that meet them in the spiritual world. In that world, conceptualizing can really only be assigned to Beauty. For angels, it is an ideal to do their conceptualizing in such a way that their entire world of concepts is permeated and inwardly illuminated by the ideal of Beauty. You need only read the chapter of my *Theosophy* that deals with the soul world and study there the two forces of sympathy and antipathy in the form in which we find them beyond the threshold of the spiritual world; then you will see how in that world the relationship of sympathy and antipathy underlies the impulses of willing. Therefore that again agrees in a certain respect, only one must relate it to the life of the soul, as this life still originates in the human soul of today, welling up from the subconscious realm, out of the soul world. Here you see how a modern philosopher tries to speak in the terminology of the angels, albeit in the imperfect language of modern materialism, because in a kind of atavistic way he has kept medieval scholasticism alive in his heart. This is an extraordinarily interesting fact. Other than this there is absolutely no way to understand how Brentano could go against the whole of modern psychology by analyzing the soul forces and distributing them among the highest ideals of humanity in a way so totally different from that of all other psychologists.

Now consider all the consequences of what has just been said. I said that when we cross the threshold into the spiritual world, to the extent that we're speaking about what is real we live in a world of beings. Under those circumstances it is therefore impossible for us to form abstract concepts [*Begriffe*] in the same sense as the ones we form here in the physical world when speaking about what is real. We must have beings! Therefore, when we speak about what is real we have to say: It is impossible for Wisdom, Beauty, and Goodness to have the same meaning in the spiritual world as they do here in the physical world. If they did, they would again be abstract concepts [*Begriffe*] of the sort we are able to apply here in the physical world. In the spiritual world, there must be beings.

And so, the moment we speak in terms of Wisdom itself, in other words, the moment we look for something real, we find that beings have to exist there, not just something we abstractly label Wisdom, Beauty, and Goodness. If we speak of Beauty in the spiritual world, we can't say: Beauty is there in the spiritual world as maya, as mere sensory appearance. When, for example, in a drama or in other works of art, we represent Wisdom-filled Beauty or Goodness in the form of Beauty, then the physical world has Beauty and Wisdom imprinted upon it, through the way all of this is joined together. In the same way, Wisdom, Beauty, and Goodness work together in the realm of Beauty over there beyond the threshold. But then we must not speak of them as concepts or apply them in the same way as we would here. Let us suppose that someone from over there wanted to speak to us and wanted to do so from there with the soul-power corresponding to our power to form concepts. That person would not say "Wisdom" or "Beauty" or "Strength," because these are abstract ideas. He or she would have to refer to beings. Wisdom would have to appear there as a being.

What I am explaining now was well known in the language of the old mysteries, and for this reason names were introduced that could express this that do not point to mere abstract ideas but rather to something of the nature of a being. What is Wisdom on this side of the threshold would have to be a being on the other side. If you think about this a little you will easily be able to agree that a being we call, say, a God-beholder [*Gottschauer*], the One-Who-Beholds-God, could be a being that over there corresponds to Wisdom: the God-beholder.

A being corresponding to our physical plane's abstract idea of Beauty would have to manifest. Beauty reveals itself; it is Appearance, that which manifests, that which "shines." The moment we cross the threshold something appears that is much more living than it is here on the physical plane. When we speak of the Beautiful, the intrinsically Beautiful, we are not speaking of something as mute as it is here on the physical plane, or which is merely living in abstractions of human physical hearing or speech. Everything is manifestation, living manifestation. And if you take what I am saying now together with what I said earlier, you will understand that the ancient mysteries coined a word for what corresponds to Beauty over there on the other side of the threshold. This can be designated as God-proclamation [*Gottverkündigung*], God's Word, the God-announcer, say, or the God-proclaimer. We could also call it: Word of God.

In the same way a being must also exist for willing: the One Who Wills God [*der Gottwollende*]. Not the abstraction such as we have it in our soul as "willing," but rather an actual being must exist for the will on the other side of the threshold. A "God-willer"—if we may be allowed to coin the word. Why should we form common, everyday words only when we are getting into realms here for which no words have yet been coined? God-willer, then. If we use the word "God" as a collective name for all the spiritual beings of the higher hierarchies, we can say that this God has within itself not only an activity of willing, as we have in our own souls, but also a "willer" who is a real being. What for us are only the three soul forces of conceptualizing, feeling, and willing, are actual beings for God: the God-beholder, the God-proclaimer, the God-willer. You know that on other occasions I have often mentioned what has happened with translations in the course of time. If we look at the ancient Hebrew expressions, we find that they correspond completely with the words I have tried to coin here. Of course, you will not find them translated quite this way in any Hebrew dictionary,[†] but if we really live into what was intended, this is how we would have to translate the ancient Hebrew words today, so that in our language "God-beholder" is the same thing as Michael; "God-proclaimer," the same as Gabriel; and "God-willer," the same as Raphael. Whereas we work in the physical world through our three soul forces, the essences of the higher hierarchies work through beings themselves. We work through conceptualizing, feeling, and willing; a god works through Michael, Gabriel, and Raphael. And when a god says, "I work through Michael, Gabriel, and Raphael," that means the same thing as "I work through thinking, feeling, and willing" does for our soul. This translation of "I work through thinking, feeling, and willing" into "I work through Michael, Gabriel, and Raphael" is simply the translation from the language of human beings into the language that should be spoken beyond the threshold into the spiritual world if one is really speaking the language of that world. If you look more deeply into many things said in the Bible, you will be able to feel everywhere—if you feel them in a really appropriate way and not as the current interpretation of the Bible leads us to feel, which is really a misinterpretation in many respects—you will be able to feel that these are the sorts of things we must really think about Michael, Gabriel, and Raphael:

Wisdom:	Power of judgment—God-beholder: Michael Revelation or manifestation of a being
Beauty:	Conceptualization—God-proclaimer: Gabriel Power of judgment
Goodness:	Sympathy, affirming / Antipathy, denying— God-willer: Raphael

Now, using this as a basis, think back to how Gabriel, Michael, and Raphael speak in Goethe's "Prologue in Heaven." We can only say that we are shaken to our very core by the instinctive certainty with which Goethe indicates in this "Prologue in Heaven" how the willing being of the Godhead manifests through Raphael, the beholding being of the Godhead through Michael, and the self-revealing, self-proclaiming being of the Godhead through Gabriel, manifesting its full beauty. The willing of the Godhead lies in the harmony of the spheres, in what speaks in the great movements of the heavenly bodies and in what happens while the heavenly bodies are moving:

> The sun intones its ancient tune
> In rival song of brother spheres,
> Traveling with thunderous rush
> Along its pre-established route.
> The sight of it gives strength to angels, (243-47)

—we could also say: Goodness, the strength of the supra-moral life beyond the threshold. For this reason, the three soul forces of Wisdom, Beauty, and Goodness are called by some people "Wisdom, Beauty, and Strength."

> When none may even fathom it; (248)

We have a hard time trying to pin the Faust commentators down on this line: "When none may even fathom it." Most of them say: Oh well, Goethe just meant "even if," or "even though," or "although no one may even fathom it." But a truly great poet never speaks this way—I have often mentioned this, especially in connection with Goethe. A great poet never speaks this way. The activity of fathoming belongs to Wisdom, as this Wisdom lives within the human physical world. Beyond the threshold everything is a matter of getting to know spiritual beings that we encounter there, just as we encounter people here that we can't completely fathom because they must also retain an inner nature. Now this fathoming, as we understand the process here on earth, is something that doesn't exist for the angels at all. They have the reality of the spiritual world in front of them; they don't "fathom" it; they just look at it because each of them has also been given something of Michael's visionary power. Each of them has something of the power of the others, just as each soul force has something of the others: conceptualization, for example, has something of willing in it, for if we could not will while conceptualizing we would always just be dreaming, and so forth. So of course Raphael has something of Michael and Gabriel in him as well.

> The lofty works, uncomprehended,
> Are glorious, as when first begun. (249-50)

Now try to feel these two lines with all the feelings you can have from spiritual science!

> The lofty works, uncomprehended,

(the ones described here)

> Are glorious, as when first begun. (249-50)

What in the world does this mean? Not that these works are glorious, as they are on this day, but as they were on the first day. In other words, as glorious as they were on that first day ["as when first begun"], appearing and showing themselves to the angels, so are they still today—but Luciferic. For whatever has remained behind is Luciferic. Here we really must apply the feelings we acquire from spiritual science. The stars are emitting their light as luciferically as they did the first day. They have not evolved a single step, but retain their original character—another reason why the angels just look at them without fathoming them. For angels, the Luciferic is something they can look at. And the angels are no worse off for this. I have often called the Luciferic a necessary component of world evolution. Here it is presented to us as something the angels have in front of them to look at: Lucifer, not as he operates in the world of human beings, but as he maintains the original glory of the indescribably lofty works as they were on the first day. And in lofty language we are led to the point of being shown how the Luciferic lives its life fully in the cosmos and how the angels are permitted to look at it there, just as they were allowed to on the first day. There it is justified. It must just not sink down to us human beings in the physical world in the way it normally lives up above in the world on the other side of the threshold. Moreover, the world permeated by the thundering cosmic will is only heralded on the earth. Up above, it needs to remain unfathomable; it is not supposed to be fathomed there. The earth is here, with the forces allotted to the human being, and this earth exists so that what is unfathomable for angels may be fathomed by human wisdom. But Gabriel, the God-proclaimer, the Word of God, can only indicate how this appears to him as he sees it from outside the earth. Remember the profound words from the Bible: "They hid their faces before the mystery of human incarnation."[†] This profound biblical passage contains the entirety of what, for angels, is unfathomable about the worlds accessible to the human being through the Wisdom developed on earth. And, since here in the "Prologue in Heaven" the language being spoken is angel-language, Gabriel, the God-proclaimer, characterizes from outside what reveals itself on earth as Wisdom.

> And faster than the mind can grasp it
> The splendor of the earth turns round,
> Paradise's brightness changes
> Into deep, foreboding night. (251-54)

What we live in here, trying to unravel its secrets as it works on us in the surrounding world of the senses: this is how it all looks from outside. Out there it is a marvelous alternation of day and night.

> The surging, foaming ocean sprays (255)

Our human weal and woe depend on this; but out there it only reveals itself as what composes the spherical earth within the foaming waters.

> In rivers broad up anchored rocks,
> And cliff and sea are torn away
> In swift, unending course of spheres. (256-58)

Our whole earthly destiny, tied as it is to the life of our senses, is bound up in this. The God-proclaimer draws a picture of it from outside the earth.

Now what about the meaning of the earth itself? How does it reveal itself? Through the fact that we look not only at what holds true for the surrounding world of the human senses, but also at what sends its effects out into the cosmos. Gabriel portrays the earth as it looks from outside, of course, but he portrays what has meaning for the human being within the surrounding world of the senses as well. Michael, the God-beholder, portrays what rays out into the cosmos but at the same time has its meaning for the environs of the earth, the whole sphere of the heavens. That's why he starts at the outer circle, not down at the bottom where the ocean is streaming and the rivers are streaming, but at the outer circle. He is looking at the outer circle.

> And storms now roar for all they're worth, (259)

A profound statement!

> From sea to land, from land to sea,
> And raging wildly, form a chain
> Of deepest working all around. (260-62)

Imagine the trade winds, for example, as seen from outside, holding sway out there in regular currents. Our limited natural science gives us a picture of everything that goes on in these atmospheric events, but this science nevertheless still has its limitations. If we investigate the regularities in the atmospheric phenomena, we come across a profound interconnection between these regular atmospheric phenomena and the phases or phenomena of the moon. The reason for this, however, is not that the moon is the cause of what goes on in the atmosphere, but rather that the laws of the Old Moon, acting uniformly and in parallel, still govern the moon today and that the atmospheric phenomena are also something still remaining from the laws of Old Moon. It is not that the moon governs the atmospheric phenomena and the ebb and flow of tides, but rather that both of these are governed equally and in parallel by causes that lie far back in the past. For this reason, what goes on in the atmosphere has meaning not only for what affects people in the surrounding world of the senses, but also for what goes on in outer space. We look up to the lightning; we hear the thunder. But the gods see the lightning and hear the thunder too, only they do so from the other side. And for them this means something very different than it does for us, for lightning and thunder are precisely what we don't understand. We can speak about this some other time. But what Michael, the God-beholder, understands about the earth is precisely what lives its life out fully in another direction in lightning and thunder. Remember the first lecture I gave here again this past summer,[†] in which I spoke about this as the sub-earthly aspect of the human soul: the "thunderstorms" of the human soul that I explained to you in connection with the character of Weininger, the young man who died at an early age. What corresponds to these thunderstorms in both the human soul and in the atmosphere works its way outward. And just as these "soul storms" of ours are mitigated and harmonized when we pour our higher soul forces out over them, what storms and thunders in its irregular way here in the meteorology of our atmosphere then becomes regular and harmonious as it works its way out into the cosmos. In the same way, when we develop ourselves, we don't stay at the thunderstorm level either, but advance toward a harmonious state of soul life. Down below, thunder and lightning are the order of the day.

> But, Lord, your messengers

(the angels)

> revere
> The gentle changing of your day. (265-66)

Now everything comes together to form a gentle harmony, as seen outside from the sphere of the angels.

> The sight of it gives strength to angels, (267)

(in other words, it strengthens their willing)

> Since none of them may fathom you, (268)

(it's not a matter of fathoming, but of looking on!)

> And all your elevated works
> Are glorious, as when first begun. (269-70)

That means these works are Luciferic. They are there for angels; they're just not supposed to work their way into our sphere and affect the human being in the same way. Lucifer's presence in the human world is unjustified, insofar as he transfers his field of activity, which is justified for the spiritual world out there, into the human world and applies the same laws here that he should apply only outside in the spiritual world.

Remember that in other lectures on Goethe's *Faust* I dealt with the lack of clarity that Goethe still possessed while he was writing *Faust.* At that time I told you that Goethe hadn't yet made a clear distinction between Lucifer and Ahriman. Mephistopheles is really Ahriman, who has remained behind, only in a different way than Lucifer has. But this distinction has been given only through our more recent spiritual science. Goethe continually confuses Lucifer and Ahriman, throwing them together in such a way that his Mephistopheles is a very confused creation in this respect, possessing both Luciferic and Ahrimanic features. If Goethe had already had spiritual science, this incurable confusion would not be such an integral part of Mephisto's character. I already asked you at that time not to accuse me of failing to honor Goethe sufficiently or of criticizing him in a petty, philistine manner by saying this. Truly, one does a genius no less honor by telling the truth than by gushing with praise. I believe that in the light of everything I have written and said about Goethe, no one can accuse me of giving Goethe only a slight amount of admiration. But the fact that Mephistopheles is a confused spiritual character is something I must always emphasize when I speak out of the impulse of spiritual science. If Goethe had known what was exactly right, he would have had Lucifer appear first, after the lines:

> And all your elevated works
> Are glorious, as when first begun. (269-70)

Lucifer would be the one standing there, the one who works through the sensory appearance of the world of the spheres, through what is beautiful about this world. And because Lucifer has Ahriman as his companion—or Mephistopheles, who is the same as Ahriman—Mephisto would appear next, or else Lucifer would leave and then Mephisto would appear. That is what Goethe would have done if he had known of spiritual science in its modern form. Today we would have seen[†] a red Lucifer first, and only after that the gray-black Ahriman or Mephistopheles. But Goethe never got that far. Therefore he has only Mephistopheles appear, who in his way unites within himself the retarded characteristics that should be at work only up above in the spiritual world and should not work into human life in a human way. Goethe had a correct feeling for this, which is why not everything about this Mephistopheles is quite right, and yet it is right after all. Goethe's feeling for this was working with much more certainty than his understanding was. Much of what we see approaching Faust in the form of temptation really comes from Mephistopheles, but other things do not seem to be related to him at all. For example, the fact that Faust should be tempted by his lower passions cannot be due to Ahriman's influence;

it can only come from Lucifer. And when Ahriman-Mephistopheles says this, Goethe's subconscious memory tells him things don't work that way. At this moment Mephistopheles would actually have to have Lucifer at his side. And so Mephisto also says: "Dust he must eat"—in other words, he must live in his lower passions—"like my aunt, the celebrated snake" (334-35). That's Lucifer. He is remembering his aunt, his good aunt Lucifer! There you have this reminiscence of Lucifer, who should really be there as well.

You see from this that cosmic secrets of tremendous depth are to be found in this "Prologue in Heaven," by which I don't mean to imply that Goethe intended to portray these secrets in the way we feel about them in spiritual science today. But instinctive wisdom is often much more profound than the manifest kind. In ancient times, there *was* only instinctive wisdom, and it was truly a higher kind of wisdom than the kind that gives rise to the science of today, with all its limitations.

And so it is that Mephistopheles-Ahriman has come into our physical world where he doesn't belong. What he has to say also does not harmonize well with the physical world itself or with the intentions the Godhead has in it. He wants to rule in this world, but he finds everything in it "rotten to the core" [*herzlich schlecht*] (296). He has to be different from the others, the true "sons of gods;" for his task is to be here in the physical world where the works are to be fathomed. The fact that Mephisto has come into the physical world at all means that he has to fathom it. The idea that he should not is not true for him. On the earth, however, he is only a sort of half-nature; as a spirit-being he doesn't really belong here. He ought to be able to fathom things, but he cannot, which is why he finds everything "rotten to the core." The question of the extent to which he is here in order to accomplish something is one we'll leave for tomorrow's discussion, in connection with some other teachings of spiritual science. Today we will add only the following.

As we have said, Ahriman-Mephistopheles is here in the physical world in a different way than the true "sons of gods" are, and his presence here must really be put to a different use. His task is to work on what is real in the physical world in a different way than the true "sons of gods" do. The latter do not need to have the "real" aspect of what is earthly in their mental pictures. Their task is to rejoice in "Beauty, rich in life" (345), the Beauty they have in their mental pictures. There is a discrepancy between the angels, the true "sons of gods," and Ahriman, Mephistopheles. What is true for them is that as angels they can't do things the way Mephistopheles can; they rejoice in Beauty, rich in life.

> May what's becoming, ever working, living,
> Embrace you with the holy bounds of Love. (344-45)

This may well be the most profound points of the whole Prologue. Remember what we said about the Cosmos of Wisdom and the Cosmos of Love. And recall once again the statement, "They hid their faces before the mystery of human incarnation." Love does not live for the "divine sons of Wisdom" in the same way as it does for human beings: they are beings within Wisdom, and for these true "sons of gods" there are certain limitations. Furthermore, by living in the great maya,[†] in the glory of the Luciferic world, they weave into it the "enduring thoughts," which in their turn are beings and forces, not abstract ideas or mere thoughts.

It is really quite striking that when this Prologue was composed in 1797, it was not written, so to speak, in human language, but in the language of the gods; and humanity will need much time yet to measure out all its depths. I think it is possible for us to place ourselves a little into the feelings alive in Goethe in 1797 when, under Schiller's fiery inspiration, he again went at the task of continuing the *Faust* he had begun years earlier. At that time it began with the words: "So, now I have studied philosophy, / Legal codes and medicine" (354-57), etc. Still missing were the three parts entitled: "Dedication," "Prologue in the Theater," and "Prologue in Heaven," as well as the entire Easter morning stroll. Some scenes were then written during the Italian Journey of 1787, when Goethe went at it at Schiller's urging. At that time he may well have thought back to the time when he hadn't yet taken *Faust* so deeply; when he had taken him, although already somewhat deeply, only as someone striving out of the world of physical reality and over the threshold into the spiritual world, to the Earth Spirit, and so on. But in those days the twenty-year-old Goethe couldn't take him as he took him now in 1797, when he himself had the feeling that in an abstract way he didn't really understand very much of what he had the urge to say in the "Prologue in Heaven." For there the prevailing language is that of the angels. Those who heard the first strains of *Faust* would have had to develop along the same lines as Goethe did if they had wished to understand what had become of the whole abundant world of *Faust* in Goethe's soul by the year 1797. It had become something different. What he had created as a young man now appeared to him in a higher sphere. Part of something he now had to sense was how it feels to be looked down upon from the sphere of spirits on the other side of the threshold into the earthly world in which that Faust was moving around who said, "So, now I have studied philosophy, / Legal codes and medicine, / And—even worse—theology! / I gave them my all, the best I could" (354-57). At that time Goethe could already say that in those former times he had shared and enjoyed something with his comrades that was different from his current lot. And he may well have felt something of just how little he would be understood. For from the end of the 1790's on, Goethe certainly felt that something like a spiritual science would have to come into existence if people were to fully understand what he sensed and felt instinctively as Cosmic Wisdom, Cosmic Beauty, and Cosmic Strength.

> They do not hear the following refrains,
> Those souls to whom I sang my verses first;
> Dispersed is now that amiable throng,
> The echo—oh!—of those first songs long gone. (17-20)

An echo from the souls to whom he had read aloud the first scenes of the *Faust* he had composed as a twenty-year-old: the very first echo. Nevertheless, there was already some understanding—for this time too has long since passed away in the age of materialism—some understanding for the way a character such as Faust was crossing the threshold, some understanding for his appeal to the Earth Spirit, who "lives and weaves in floods of life, in storm of deeds" (501). But at the same time a remaining at this level of understanding, an inability to rise to the level that Goethe himself had had to struggle so hard to reach. Hence, now, when an angelic language is the main one speaking and the whole matter is being looked at from a different point of view, the old echo is no longer there. Long gone, oh!—this ancient echo! Dispersed the souls, for whom he sang the first refrains. Goethe knew the sorrow endured by everyone who really yearns to see the spiritual world, and he also knew that with this sorrow he stood as a lonely, isolated figure of his age.

> My pain† resounds out to the unknown masses. (21)

Things have not changed all that much as yet in our own day, when the applause lavished on *Faust* could actually frighten us. For how much do people still hear today of the profound wisdom that pervades this work, how much more than mere superficialities!?

Goethe, however, sensing now that he had to lift his song, the song of his sorrow, into the sphere of the spirit realm, was of a mind to say: What formerly was reality for me is now wafting away into far distances, whereas what formerly disappeared is becoming realities: the realities of the still, solemn spirit realm that we approach with the same slight shudder and holy awe we feel when we sense something of the totally different forms of the worlds on opposite sides of the threshold. Hence this "Dedication" also came into being within Goethe out of a profound sense of future possibilities. If, in such cases as well, spiritual science could deepen human hearts in such a way that they would really be able to take deeply what must be taken deeply, it would then be accomplishing one of its tasks. For the words I cited here not long ago† are true, deeply true: "The world is deep, and deeper than the day has thought";† the day, that is, that shows us only the surrounding world as given to us by our physical senses. The world is deep, as revealed to us by the night that of course is night and darkness in comparison to the physical day, but into which we carry the light we ignite as a torch within our own soul and then have to illumine by ourselves. The world is deep, and it must be fathomed by a light that does not glow until we ignite it for ourselves by means of our spiritual striving, so that it can shine in the spiritual world. Then it will shine like the light in what is forever becoming, which works and lives and in which the beings of the higher world have to indulge themselves so that they may clearly see what they will need in order to "consolidate with enduring thoughts" what otherwise "hovers in fluctuating form" (348-49).

We will begin with this point tomorrow as we continue our observations. I should just like to add the request that our friends from Basel not bring children with them tomorrow. Since the presence of the personality from hell who was presented to you today makes this scene particularly inappropriate for the fantasies and dreams of children, we must make an exception this time in requesting that no one under the age of fifteen or sixteen be present.

14
The Historical Significance of *Faust*

Dornach, August 20, 1916

After dramatic performances with eurythmy:
"Dedication," "Prologue at the Theater," "Prologue in Heaven"

I spoke to you again yesterday, as I have often done, about how Goethe's Mephistopheles is actually a figure full of contradictions. By now we know why this is. We could express it by saying that he is a colorful mixture of Mephistophelian (or Ahrimanic) and Luciferic character traits. We could also say that as yet Goethe did not know how to keep these different character traits apart. Now on the one hand, when one regards a work of art such as *Faust* as highly as you know I do, one certainly has a right to call attention to facts like these. Nevertheless, it is peculiar that people hardly ever notice these contradictions solely on the basis of the work itself, although in some instances this has occurred. But it is also a sign of how people come to these things with so little inner participation these days that they do not even notice what is going on at a deeper level. For if people were more active in this respect they would soon be forced to notice such things as, for example, the inner contradictions in this figure of Mephistopheles.

Let us start with a contradiction that is perhaps not quite complete, but still very strong, and could strike us the moment we hear Mephistopheles speaking in the scene we've just been privileged to witness:

> I only see how people plague themselves.
> The world's little god forever stays the same
> And is as singular as when he first was made.
> A little better would he live
> Had you not given him the shining, heavenly light;
> He calls it reason and uses it alone
> To be more bestial than any beast. (280-86)

How does it make us feel when we see Mephistopheles reproaching human beings for the way they act? Certainly none of us will believe that Mephistopheles has very high and selfless goals. In fact, he can't; we can see this already from this first scene of the "Prologue in Heaven." For what does Mephistopheles want anyway? Isn't it to possess Faust completely, to have him all to himself? Which is why he will basically have to consider everything Faust does as good—good in the Mephistophelian sense, of course—so that he can come together with him and "grasp" him, get hold of him. "Grasp" here means "get hold of," not "comprehend"; it is not meant in any abstract, conceptual sense. When the Lord says, "If you can grasp him" (325), he means: "If you can get hold of him." Mephistopheles will be willing to do everything he can to achieve this goal. And so it could work out really well for him if Faust had all the qualities that would drive him straight into Mephisto's claws!

Now let us look at a later passage, in which Mephistopheles is standing in front of Faust himself, in the study, and Faust is speaking about what he thinks of reason and science. Faust goes out, leaving Mephistopheles there by himself in his long gown. We can well imagine that at this moment he will probably be very honest with himself, this Mephistopheles. He says:

> Despise your rationality and science,
> The highest power of the human mind,
> Let strengthen you the Spirit of Deceit
> With works of magic and delusion,
> Then will I have you absolutely. (1851-55)

That is, it would suit him just fine if the human being were not to apply reason and science in the right way, but use them instead to be more bestial than any beast. And the Lord is precisely the one he will try to convince of this:

> Had you not given him the shining, heavenly light;
>
> He calls it reason and uses it alone
> To be more bestial than any beast. (284-86)

As I say, it is not a complete contradiction, but for our feelings it is a strong one.

In the scene I have just cited, in which Mephisto and Faust are standing face to face in the study, it is clear that he is already speaking quite honestly as Ahriman-Mephistopheles. But in the place you heard today:

> He calls it reason and uses it alone
> To be more bestial than any beast, (285-86)

a Luciferic feature enters. It cannot be all right with Lucifer for Faust to use reason to really stir up his bestial passions. But it would have to be just fine with Ahriman for Faust to behave the way Mephisto is reproaching him for here. So at any rate what we have here is not a half-contradiction but at least a three-quarters one!

But now we can ask what we should do with another passage:

> As long as he lives on the earth,
> To you will nothing be forbidden.
> Man errs as long as he does strive.
>
> I thank you, Sire; for with the dead
> It never was my joy to deal.
> What I love most of all are fresh, full cheeks.
> Bring me a corpse: You won't find me at home;
> I'm like the cat that's happy with her mouse. (315-22)

Comparing this with the scene in Part Two, which we may perhaps be able to stage someday, in which Mephisto goes to so much trouble in the end to get the soul as the corpse is just lying there, how are we supposed to bring the two together? The Devil goes after souls after all, but what he says here is just the opposite! There are many such contradictions in this work. I only wanted to point out these two examples: the first one is a three-quarters contradiction that can be found in the poetic text itself. Such contradictions can absolutely be traced back to the fact that the two character traits—the Luciferic and the Ahrimanic-Mephistophelian—are mixed together.

Now the question can arise for us: How does it happen that Goethe puts Ahriman-Mephistopheles beside Faust as the latter's life's companion, concentrating our entire attention on Ahriman-Mephistopheles and more or less completely suppressing Lucifer? This must, after all, be a question. For precisely because Goethe was misled by the general thrust of his era into placing Mephistopheles at Faust's side, he also transferred Luciferic features to him, thereby attaching everything to Mephistopheles-Ahriman that should really be divided up between the two. There must therefore be reasons in that era for him to direct more attention to Mephistopheles than to Lucifer. In treating the Faust-saga, Goethe goes back to the time when the medieval period collides with the modern age, and as he does this he essentially internalizes the new impulses that resulted from the collision of these two ages.

If we look at poetic works from periods lying somewhat further back in time and therefore influenced by the impulses from those earlier periods, we find just the opposite mistake. I can also speak about this some time; today I only want to point it out. In Milton's *Paradise Lost*† you find the opposite error. There, everything that should be ascribed to Ahriman-Mephistopheles has been unloaded onto Lucifer, although not in as crude a way as happened in the case of *Faust*. As I said, I will speak about this some other time. This was the mistake more apt to be made in the Middle Ages: directing attention more to Lucifer. The mistake our modern age makes is to direct our attention more to Ahriman-Mephistopheles. Now we are living in an age in which the correct relationship between the two world powers of Mephistopheles and Lucifer must be recognized by people more and more. This is the reason for our sculpture, the "Group,"† which is meant to stand here in our building in order to show in pictorial form the Ahrimanic and the Luciferic—Mephistopheles and Lucifer—in their correct relationship to each other.

If you want to understand what this is really all about, you have to look at something that still seems totally paradoxical to us today but will one day be understood in all its depths when people no longer exclude spiritual science from belonging to earthly existence. In our modern age we live, and have to live, under quite special impulses. It is right for us to be living under these impulses. Only, we have to recognize them. We must not, so to speak, fail to recognize them. I myself have often explained how the Copernican worldview had to arise at the beginning of the modern age, how fully justified this was. We, of course, come to this Copernican worldview with quite different feelings than the exoteric world does. For when we examine the way the exoteric world feels about the Copernican worldview, there is hardly any other view we can come to than that people say: "Well, antiquity and the Middle Ages didn't know much, but we are more enlightened. In their ignorance, they thought it was the sun that moved, so they constructed all sorts of cycles and epicycle† and came up with the Ptolemaic worldview. And they believed it all because they took it for granted that the heavenly bodies move across the sky the way the eye sees them move."

In a certain sense it is even right to say this about the Middle Ages, in particular the later Middle Ages, for by that time certain confusions had already entered into what had arisen as the Ptolemaic worldview. But the original Ptolemaic worldview was not like that. It was part of the original, ancient, primeval revelation. It had come into human souls by way of the ancient mysteries and not in any way through mere external observation. It was therefore based on revelation. The modern age broke with this revelation, asking itself instead: "How do we have to view the sky now in order to get to know it and its movements?"

Copernicus began by calculating, attempting to show by a simple calculation of the movements of the heavenly bodies how the calculated locations really do harmonize with the actual positions of the heavenly bodies. In this way he invented his Copernican system by way of calculation, setting up three axioms that concern the movements of the heavenly bodies in relation to our earth and can be found in Copernicus's works themselves. In the meantime, however, one of these three axioms has been left out, and this is the origin of today's confused Copernican worldview, which is not the one of Copernicus himself. The third axiom was inconvenient,† so it was simply left out! For this reason someone whose only knowledge of the Copernican worldview comes from conventional books has no idea what Copernicus's view really was. But this is how it had to happen. First, Copernicus had to establish a system that with its three axioms was far more accurate; then our version had to come, based on only two of these axioms. Only when the whole matter has finally been permeated by spiritual science will we see how things really stand.

Then those came who sought to understand the movements of the heavenly bodies and their laws in a more external way, not by means of calculating. The telescope appeared. People learned to investigate outer space in the same way they investigate things on earth. And in this way modern astronomy came into existence, modern astrophysics, a science that originates entirely by casting what has been observed into the form of laws; that is, people want to explain the heavens by observing the heavens. What could be more natural than this? The way modern people think, someone would have to be completely crazy to actually want to get to know the heavens in any other way than by observing them. That's pretty obvious, isn't it? And yet it is not correct! It is one of our great illusions: something that in the future will become very different. In the future we will still be questioning the heavens, even more than we are now; we will want to find out what lives and weaves as movements in the heavenly bodies; we will keep on reading and studying the heavens exactly. But then we will know one thing we don't yet know today, something that looks like a total paradox when we actually express it. This is: that we don't learn anything at all about the heavens when we observe them. The most mistaken way to get to know the heavens and their movements is to observe them the way we do today.

Now I am saying something really crazy, am I not? But we have to look at these crazy things differently than our good Christian von Ehrenfels[†] did, about whom I spoke to you a week ago. People will observe the sky in ever more detail, and let it tell them its secrets. But what will these secrets reveal to people in the future? They will reveal what is happening here on the earth. That's what they will reveal. People will of course observe the sky, but from what they learn by watching the sky they will explain how plants grow on the earth, how animals arise on the earth and how everything that takes shape on the earth lives and weaves on the earth. What the heavens reveal will enlighten us about all of this. No one will even think of asking the heavens about the heavens anymore; instead they will ask the heavens to enlighten them about the earth. And they will apply the most significant of the laws they discover from observing the heavens to the revelation of the secrets of earthly existence. Ancient astrology, the original meaning of which is hardly even recognized today and which for the most part has degenerated into dilettantism, indeed even into charlatanism, will come alive again in a completely new form. Not only will people look for the origin of earthly destinies in the movements of the stars and the laws of the heavenly spaces; they will explain the laws of what lives and weaves as earthly life out of the laws of the heavenly bodies. People will not know why salt crystallizes in the form of a cube, or a diamond in the form of an octahedron, and so forth, until they can explain the forms of things here on earth out of the positions of the heavenly bodies. Nor will they know the secret of the life of animals, plants or human beings as a secret of life *per se* until they explain what lives and weaves here on the earth out of the movements of the heavenly bodies, the effect of which is life itself. The earth explains itself out of the heavens. Of course, what people will know about the heavens will assume a somewhat different form than what they claim to know today. They will still investigate the laws of the positions and movements of the heavenly bodies. But then they will allow what they discover to stimulate them to meditate in order, as it were, to enter into a relationship with the beings that live in the stars. They will allow themselves to be told by the beings that live there what they'll need to know for life on earth.

This is a perspective for the future.† Now it was the case that older ways of thinking were still flowing into the minds of Copernicus, Galilei and Kepler as they tried to glean the laws of the movements of heavenly bodies by observing the heavens. As you know, their way of working continued on down into more modern times, so that Darwin, Lamarck and Haeckel† could work in a similar way as they attempted to discover the laws of earthly life. After all, what could be more natural than getting to know the earth by means of the earth itself! You travel around, as Darwin did; you look through a microscope, as Haeckel did; you think rationally, as Lamarck did, about the nature of the earth and try to recognize the laws by which life on earth is governed. Again, people will think you're crazy if you don't see that this is the normal way of doing things. But the future will not see this as the normal way at all! If you look at the straight, even path of development that modern biology has followed from Darwin to Haeckel and on down to Haeckel's students, you will see that it has led in particular to the formulation of certain laws concerning embryonic life. What is called the "fundamental biogenetic law"† plays a great role in assuring that the developmental stages of the human embryo recapitulate the individual species of animals. As you know, I have often called attention to the "fundamental biogenetic law." In order to discover it, certain observations were made by means of which people hoped to find out something precisely about the life of living beings. It can be said that in our own day people are hard at work trying to unravel these views again, but as yet this is hardly evident outside scientific circles. Copernican astronomy is already under heavy attack on the part of certain individuals who have greater insight.† And one of Haeckel's students, Oscar Hertwig,† has said some things in his most recent publications in particular that are well-suited to cast serious doubt on everything the Darwin-Haeckel theory has brought to light. If we get our information from what is going on in current professional literature, our picture is very different than if our only sources are popular lectures offered to the public by the usual—I don't dare call them "Mauthner-like"†; what should I say?—well, just the usual lecturers. A great deal of what is going on in the scientific literature proper is already setting the stage for what has been offered here as a perspective for the future. It is just that people will have to come to spiritual science if what is happening in this way is to be kept from becoming confusing but will really turn out to be in accordance with the facts.

Now I have to say something else that is a paradox. We learn nothing at all about the earth by observing what happens on the earth. People will know and understand this once they read out of the stars what is happening on the earth. But what is actually going on out in space can be known by making observations in a field such as embryology, for example. Again, as I indicated earlier, one way of dealing with these observations is to make concurrent observations of the heavenly movements and thereby enter into a relationship with the elemental beings† that regulate these movements within the realm of earthly events. Just as people will look to the heavens in order to explain the earth, they will look to the earth in order to explain the heavens. As I said, it is still paradoxical today, but somehow, someday it will happen that this correct way of looking at things will spread over this earth of ours. The astronomers[†] will provide the basis for biology with the resources of their science, and the biologists will provide the basis for astronomy with the resources of their science. And a biology based on a genuine astrology will be spiritual science, while an astrology based on the resources of a genuine embryology will be spiritual astronomy. If you think about this you will have to see that the evolution of humanity doesn't proceed in a straight line but in a forward-moving wavy line, as it were, up and down. And so, for the correct spiritual way of looking at things to be prepared for in the right way, the error needed to arise that people in the more modern age would want to explain the heavens by means of the heavens and the earth by means of the earth. This is the impression people were living under.

Goethe, however, was not living fully under this impression—not quite. He, you see, had anticipated Darwinism in a certain way, but his Darwinism was of a much more spiritual nature. He didn't limit himself to the external sensory appearance of the series of phenomena he was investigating, but went on to the archetypal plant and the archetypal animal as well. I have often referred to the well-known conversation between Goethe and Schiller[†] in which, after the two of them had seen from a lecture by the botanist Batsch in Jena how plants are studied side by side and Schiller had found this very unsatisfying, Goethe had sketched the so-called archetypal plant for him with a few strokes. Unfortunately, Goethe's drawing no longer exists. In the introduction to Goethe's morphological writings in Kürschner's *National-Literatur*[†] that I wrote in the eighties I tried to re-draw this sketch of the Goethean archetypal plant. You can find my drawing in that edition. But Schiller said: That's not a reality; it is only an idea. Goethe said: Then I see my idea with my eyes. He had absolutely no doubt that this had been an actual visual experience for him, not something he had merely thought out, arrived at by a process of rational thinking. And if we get to know Goethe really intimately, by means of his poetic efforts in connection with his scientific ones, or the other way around: through his scientific works in connection with his poetic ones—as I have striven to do in my own interpretation of Goethe—we see that Goethe just doesn't feel comfortable explaining the heavens by means of the heavens and the earth by means of the earth and that with his ideas he is forever poking holes in this principle of our more modern age. This is why it is still so hard for us today to understand Goethe's color theory,[†] for what Goethe has in mind is actually an astronomical explanation of the secret of color. And if you read Goethe's morphological studies very attentively, you will see certain things play into them that stem from the very beginnings of an astronomy. We feel this especially strongly when we look at his essays on the spiral tendency of plants.[†] But that would lead us off into details that I can only call your attention to today; I wish only to refer to it.

Now let us raise the question: How has the more modern age, which we now calculate as having begun with the collision of the Middle Ages and the modern age—with the rise of Copernicanism, Galileiism and Keplerism—and then trace on down to Darwinism, Haeckelism and Lamarckism; how has this age come to fix its gaze on explaining the heavens by means of the heavens and the earth by means of the earth, instead of the earth by means of the heavens and the heavens by means of the earth? This is the result of a double seduction of human beings: we've been seduced by both Ahriman and Lucifer. During the preparation for these things in the Middle Ages, which were heading in the direction of Copernicanism and Darwinism, the activity was more Luciferic; Luciferic impulses were doing the preparing. After the rise of Copernicanism the enticement was more Ahrimanic. Ahriman is the one who lives essentially in human beings by causing them to turn around and go the other way, as I have described. For, in the final analysis, modern science is completely under the influence of Ahriman. Goethe was right in his feeling that Ahriman, or Mephistopheles, is close to human beings in the more modern age. He felt it was less important to focus on Lucifer's relationship to the human being than to focus on Ahriman's. His quite special powers of attention had to be directed to this. Lucifer's influence was of less concern to him, for Faust, after all, has been presented to us by history itself from the very beginning as the prime example of the human being of our modern age. The various theological aberrations of the waning Middle Ages owe their origins to Lucifer. The moment Faust appears, however, he lays the Bible aside under his bench and is ready to become a doctor and a man of the world. That is, he wants to explain the earth by means of the earth and the heavens by means of the heavens, and not do as the old theologians of the waning Middle Ages did who were still making final, atavistic-like attempts to use the revelations of theology—the heavens, in other words—to explain the wonders of the earth. Ahriman took his place at the human being's side in the modern age. People who felt this but had no deep sense of how necessary this was were filled with a fear of the Devil. This was why they would curse Faust and say horrible things about him, while he himself was only following the inexorable impulse of the modern age. This, then, was the background of the *Faust*-book of the sixteenth century, which ended by having Faust burn in hell because he had fallen prey to Ahriman. Those who were still under the influence of medieval atavism gave this work its final form, so to speak. The Middle Ages no longer had such power over Goethe, and for this reason he could no longer let his Faust burn in hell. But now he had to confront the urgent question that arose for him: What in the world should I do?

Let us state the problem in very concrete terms. What are we really doing when we try to explain the earth by means of the earth? Let us try to get hold of this with an example that may be closer to us just because it is a little farther away from the usual scientific approach. Let us take a myth or some poetic work and then think of a commentator or an interpreter of the sort I have often criticized—you will remember my doing this! Let us assume this commentator or interpreter is standing in front of us, explaining the myth or the saga or the poetic work, as he says, out of the work itself; he is looking for the laws of the poetry in the poem or the myth. Now this person may be very ingenious. Certainly there are people who can interpret myths and poetic works with great ingenuity. But they are all sinners, because a myth or a piece of poetry can never be explained by applying intellectual reasoning to it. Oh, how much have interpreters of *Hamlet* not written in order to explain *Hamlet*! How much have even the *Faust* scholars not written in order to interpret *Faust*! What great efforts have theosophists not made to interpret all sorts of myths! The only way to get to the bottom of a myth or of poetic works is to understand how to turn one's gaze outward to where these things originate: from heaven itself.[†] This brings us back to what we spoke of earlier as a perspective for the future. It is also more obvious than if we were using science as a point of reference. We call on myths when we need them to illustrate something, such as when we have discovered the grandiose connections between things in the cosmos of the heavens; then, at least, we can allow the myths to reflect these things. And when we have some insight into the cosmic laws that operate in those worlds, we also will not be calling on the intellectual skills of literary commentators; for what crops up when we cull out of the myth or the poem what these intellectual interpreters usually come up with? Well, we can always have a certain image in front of us when a myth interpreter or a poetry commentator of the sort we have today goes to work. At that point something makes its appearance that looks like the fellow who came forth in his grayish, bat-like form† to confront the living life inherent in poetry and myth. This is the moment in which we make our acquaintance with Ahriman-Mephistopheles.

We could extend this to cover everything that is going on in modern science. In saying this I am not criticizing this science in any way. My purpose is to show you just how necessary it is for things to be this way. Ahriman had to intervene for a certain length of time. Otherwise, the medieval way of life would have turned into one that would all too easily have allowed people to grow listless and apathetic. People love a life of ease. So, the world gives them a devil that then has to work like the devil, teasing and luring and toiling away (341-343). Ahriman's intervention is an absolute necessity. And it makes no sense at all for someone who has heard something about Ahriman and Lucifer to then ask questions like: "Could that be an Ahrimanic influence? Is this a Luciferic influence?" We have to keep from doing this!

Goethe understood what role Ahriman is playing! But why did Ahriman have to play a role of this sort in our modern age? In fact, why did Ahriman-Mephistopheles have to enter the human sphere at all? Well, as we know, evolution† runs its course in such a way that we first have the so-called Lemurian period, then the Atlantean period and finally our own post-Atlantean period. We also know that in the Lemurian period the human "I", or consciousness, was hardly active at all as yet; it only really begins to be active here, in the post-Atlantean period.

But it still takes human beings a long, long time to clearly realize what is living and weaving in them as an "I"-impulse. Only gradually do they come to see how they stand in relation to Lucifer and Ahriman by virtue of having an "I" living within their souls. Human beings can

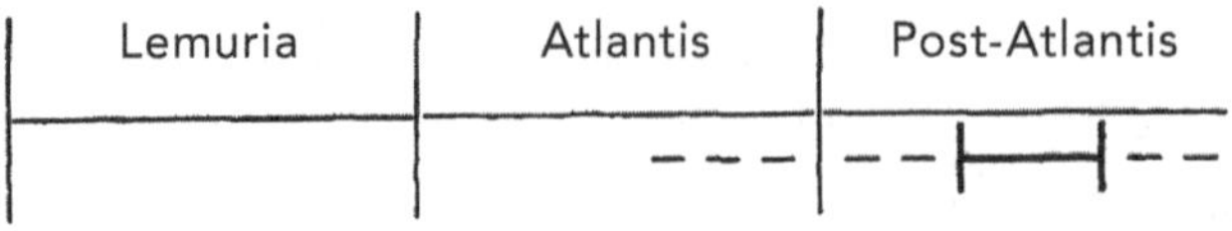

achieve this clarity only over time. If we focus on what must become a guiding principle in future times, stated schematically† it looks like this: pointing to the earth to discover the secrets of heaven; pointing to heaven to discover the secrets of the earth. If we do this the other way around, which is the only way our time knows how to do it, we don't find the secrets of the earth. Instead, what emerges out of the earth in place of heavenly laws and heavenly secrets that should emerge is the Ahrimanic, which then approaches human beings in its attempt to get to them. This must be rejected, because we don't need to seek intellectually in the earth for what the earth gives but rather for what it reveals about heaven. Lucifer comes in from cosmic space, but he has to step aside. If he would actually get to the human being, it would then be so that people would look for something out in cosmic space that can't be found there, namely, the secrets of heaven itself. This connection will eventually have to be realized.

There was once a time when people had to realize how close Lucifer was to them. Something made it possible for them to realize this, namely, a symbol, but one that is much more than a symbol: a symbol that points into the depths of the secrets of the spiritual world. If we want to characterize what Lucifer is for the human being as a whole, there is no more intimate way of doing this than to picture how Lucifer approaches the forces of the woman, working his way into the world with the help of these specifically female forces, and then how the man is led astray by the woman with Lucifer's help. This symbolic picture had to be put before humanity so that it could be there during the fourth post-Atlantean period, when people first had the task of grasping the relationship of Lucifer to the human being, in order to sense and feel this relationship and bring it to conscious awareness. There was no better way to do this than to study the beginning of the Bible and see how the serpent approaches the woman, taking hold of her forces and thereby bringing about the temptation and the seduction of the world. This significant symbol had a tremendous effect on the fourth post-Atlantean cultural period, although it had already been in existence even earlier. The secret of Lucifer can be found in this symbol.

The fifth post-Atlantean period had to make the human race consciously aware of the Ahrimanic-Mephistophelean secret. A second symbol had to be added to the first. The symbol of the Luciferic tempter of the woman stands at the very beginning of the religious book that refers to the spiritual world, showing us how the man is co-seduced by Lucifer's scheming, carried out with the help of the woman. A counter-image of this had to arise in the fifth post-Atlantean period: Ahriman, who approaches the man and seduces him first, then goes on to seduce the woman with the help of the man. Even if the attempt to do this in the first part of *Faust* was perhaps not a grandiose success, Gretchen's deeply moving tragedy is largely based on the fact that just as Adam is seduced by Lucifer in a roundabout way through Eve, Gretchen was seduced by Ahriman-Mephistopheles in a roundabout way through Faust. The inner necessity of the matter compelled a world-book [*Weltbuch*] to be placed over against the theology-book [*Theologiebuch*]: the seduced man and the seducing woman; the seduced woman and the seducing man; Lucifer, Ahriman. Lucifer's relation to the woman on one hand, Ahriman's to the man on the other. This is a profoundly significant spiritual connection.

For this reason, the world-book of *Faust* came into being as a contrast to the theology-book out of a genuine inner spiritual impulse. And the clarion call of the more modern age is to find the pathways between Ahriman and Lucifer, for all the forces through which Lucifer works into the world are similar to the forces by which Lucifer successfully seduced the woman, although they're not exactly the same. All the forces through which Ahriman works his way into the world are similar to the forces with which Ahriman seduces the man. Now, just as we rightly imagine that the Luciferic seduction presented in the Bible took place in the Lemurian period, we have to look for Ahriman at a place in the Bible that never quite became clear because the Ahrimanic secret isn't yet revealed in the Bible in the same way as the Luciferic one is. While, as I've often explained, we assign the Luciferic secret to the Lemurian age, we have to assign the Ahrimanic secret to the Atlantean period. The Bible contains only a hint of this,† and it is by no means as clear and far-shining a picture as the one of the temptation in Paradise. All we have in the Bible is the remark that through the impulses that entered earthly existence, the sons of the gods took pleasure in the daughters of men [Gen. 6:2]. This remark is only a hint of what's coming into the world as an Ahrimanic impulse.

Goethe's *Faust* already has a certain historic significance. And this historic significance lies in what I tried to sketch for you today. If we want to call attention to what spiritual science wants to become and is intended to become for humanity, we will have to say many paradoxical things today that will seem curious to many people. But they are true, nevertheless. When people will one day have changed in such a way that their science will again remind them of that primeval revelation, so that they will explain earthly life out of the secret of heaven; when earthly science will be of such a nature that the deepest secrets of heaven, for example, will be recognized on the basis of the shaping of the embryo during its development, then will humanity have found its right relationship to Ahriman and Lucifer. Then, in a certain way, there will have been realized in human life what the "Group" statue in our building is supposed to represent, in which the Representative of Humanity is placed between Ahriman and Lucifer with the correct gesture.

What lies buried in Goethe's *Faust* will be grasped in greater and greater depth as time goes on. But it will need to be grasped in freedom rather than imposed by some outside authority. As a lady in our Society once said, people who only want to understand things by "making a long face" to express their inner mood of soul will not attain their goal. This lady was not used to speaking German, which is why she made a grammatical mistake when she said this. But that doesn't matter; she found the right term for it. She was referring to people who lack the possibility of including humor in their understanding of the world. Sometimes things can get pretty bad if you don't have a sense of humor. Things must therefore get to the point where people will need to find their way in the world in the manner I have characterized. Whoever merely wishes to approach the things of the world in a mood of sentimentality will of course prefer to also understand a work of art such as Goethe's *Faust* by "making a long face" with every line of it. On the other hand, whoever truly wants to understand *Faust* will have to grasp it without the aid of any authority whatsoever. Then they will have to work their way through the contradictions, but the very act of doing so will at least offer them the possibility of understanding. After all, something like the "Prologue in Heaven" is not child's play! If we shy away too much from a certain irony and a certain humor in our everyday encounters with the world, we will all too easily fall prey to the greatest humorist of all, who, as a companion of the one who appears before us in Goethe's Mephistopheles, is more of a burden to the Lord than the jester is, as well as a somewhat more dangerous spirit of the sort who are in a position to deny (338-39).

My wish is to encourage a deeper understanding of things that already occupy an exceptional position in the spiritual evolution of humanity. For these things are also a way of entering into the secrets on the other side of the threshold, where everything is very different from what is on this side, where we must become familiar with the fact that many things sound paradoxical when spoken of out of a true knowledge of the facts that lie on the other side. The present age doesn't want to know much about those secrets. Of course, most minds of our present age have always been firmly convinced of how gloriously far we have brought things. Well, I don't know how much of this conviction people will preserve in the time directly ahead of us, a time that has brought these things so gloriously far and yet is only living in the consequences of what it has believed for centuries. But even though many people today still find paradoxical what is proclaimed from realms beyond the threshold, they will have to develop more and more understanding for these secrets of existence. A wholesome evolution of humanity into the future will largely depend on our developing an understanding for what sounds paradoxical today in so many respects.

The world may still find it foolish to be told that the earth has to be explained by means of the heavens and the heavens by means of the earth. Whoever looks into everything that reveals itself from beyond the threshold with its compelling influence on human destiny knows that what people find so foolish and so paradoxical is nevertheless wisdom in both the eyes of the spirit and the eyes of the world. We may say this today without becoming presumptuous because when we say it out of an awareness of the spiritual world we are already summoning up the necessary humility that permits us to say it, since this humility is already living in our hearts. Though we may have to expend a great deal of energy saying something forcefully enough that we would prefer to say with a gesture of humility, the more forceful gesture could give the impression of arrogance. But only an Ahrimanic interpretation could see it this way if in this case it would manage to mistake humility for arrogance. We will talk about this on another occasion.

15
The "Burial": The Nature of the Lemures, the Fat Devils, and the Skinny Devils

Dornach, September 4, 1916

We will shortly be performing the scene in the second part of Goethe's *Faust* that comes right before the closing scene, which, as you know, we have already staged. That scene, beginning with the words of the holy anchorites:

> Woodlands come swaying up,
> Cliff sides weigh heavily, (11844-45)

is called "Faust's Ascension" by Goethe, and the preceding one is usually the "Burial." Today we want to begin with the scene even before this latter one to get a broader sense of how this Burial is represented.

As we go from one section of Goethe's *Faust* to another, we find ourselves amazed again and again at their infinite depth, especially in the second part of the work. The source of this depth is the objectivity of the way in which the spiritual world is represented in them, which spiritual science can fully confirm. And the remarkable thing is that Goethe represented the spiritual world with such objectivity at a time when spiritual science as such did not yet even exist. We can make short work of a question I was once asked after I had given a lecture many years ago[†] on Goethe's *Fairy Tale of the Green Snake and the Beautiful Lily*. An old-school theosophical authority asked me whether I thought Goethe had been aware of everything that had just been said in justification of the deeper secrets of the *Fairy Tale* on the basis of spiritual science. I could only reply by asking him whether he thought a plant has to know everything a botanist can say about it in order to be able to grow precisely according to the laws of plant growth. When you hear a question like this, it usually makes you aware of how clever the questioner prides him- or herself on being. But when you keep in mind the whole context of such a question, you begin to see how terribly foolish people often are when they think they are being so clever. So we don't need to worry about whether Goethe had studied spiritual science somewhere as we can today, even though a point of view that thinks about this question can easily come up with such objections. So Let's go straight to the matter at hand.

We are immediately shown three kinds of figures, in addition to the ones we already know from the other parts of *Faust*. These three kinds of figures have to do with the period of time that elapses between Faust's death and the ascension of his soul into the regions of spirit. The first kind we are shown are the Lemures.[†] The others are devils: the Fat Devils with a short, straight horn and the Skinny Devils with a long, crooked horn. Both kinds of devils are "old-school devils through and through" (11638).

Now we can ask: What spiritual instinct, or we could just as well say, what deeper wisdom is Goethe following in presenting us with these three kinds of figures at Faust's "Burial" just before his ascension? As this "Burial" is introduced, we see that Faust has grown old in his evolution; Goethe himself has told us that he is a hundred years old. And so, at the beginning of this scene we have to do with a Faust who is a hundred years old and still chained to Mephistopheles, but in such a way that he can now believe that Mephistopheles has become his servant.

Faust has resolved to wrest a piece of land away from the sea, cultivate this piece of land and thereby create the foundation for a region of prosperity where a portion of humanity will be able to grow and develop in peace and freedom. Since this land has been wrested from the sea by Faust's work, the land itself is Faust's creation, so to speak. But the work has yet to be finished: a swamp that is still on the property needs to be drained off through a ditch so as to purify the air and keep the swamp's poisonous vapors from endangering the health of the people who are to grow and develop there in peace and freedom. By now Faust is of the opinion that Mephistopheles has become his foreman in this beneficial work and is managing the crew of workers who are to carry out this one last task. Faust himself, as the previous scene shows us, has already gone blind, so he doesn't see what Mephistopheles is up to on the outer physical plane, and we can understand from this why he later confuses the words "graben" and "Grab." While Faust believes a ditch [*Graben*] is being laid out to drain the contents of the swamp out to sea in order to purify the air, Mephistopheles is having his Lemures dig Faust's grave [*Grab*]. And so, the hundred-year-old Faust experiences yet another deception, entangled in the web of lies woven by Mephistopheles, who is having the grave dug [*graben*] while using the similarity of the words to make Faust think what's being dug is a ditch.

There are very many secrets in all this already, but I'd rather not get into them today. Perhaps we can speak about this on some other occasion. What I would prefer to do is to make clear what is the nature of these three kinds of beings. Right at the beginning of this scene, which is set in the forecourt of the palace that Faust has built for himself, Mephistopheles enters as the aforementioned foreman of the group of workers that Faust thinks *he* has gotten together, whereas Mephistopheles has actually called in his Lemures. Mephistopheles characterizes these Lemures, not in a special stage direction but in the scene itself:

> Come here, come here! Come in, come in!
> You Lemures with your quaking,
> Stitched up from ligaments and tendons
> And bones, half-beings, shaking! (11511-14)

This is how they're described to us: as beings composed of nothing but ligaments that hold the limbs of the human body together, anatomical tendons and bones. In other words, what is holding these patchwork figures together is something in the human organism that hasn't even developed as far as muscles yet. They aren't fully whole human beings; they're only half-beings, since what they do have is not blood or muscles or nerves, but only tendons and ligaments and bones, stitched together. We then learn more about them from the chorus in which they characterize themselves, and what they say shows us two things. The first is how they have actually come to the point of carrying out a piece of work under Mephisto's direction; but this in turn tells us something right away about their nature. The Lemures express themselves in such a way that we can hear in their trembling tones:

> We're right here at your beck and call,
> And, as we've half perceived,
> It's all about some wide, fair land
> We'll get as our reward. (11515-18)

So the Lemures are also laboring under a delusion at first: they have half perceived that they are supposed to get a wide piece of land. As far as Mephistopheles is concerned, they are supposed to dig the grave. But they have heard, although they have only half heard it, that they are supposed to get a wide piece of land, and for this they have brought along some pointed stakes:

> Pointed stakes we've brought along;
> We'll measure with this chain.
> But why to do this we were called
> We've now long since forgotten. (11519-22)

Something like a call is still reverberating and clattering through their half-present natures, patched together as these are out of tendons and ligaments and bones. But they have forgotten the content of that call: what they are actually supposed to be doing. This is a perfect picture of their character. We can say that they exist, but with no idea of why they exist. They half know why they exist; they have heard something, but they don't know what they have heard. They have heard a call, but they have forgotten it again. So there they are in front of us, these Lemures, and right away Mephisto takes them to task for it. He tells them there is nothing to this idea of theirs about wanting to have a piece of land and that they should get moving in accordance with their own measurements, as is appropriate for beings that consist only of bones and tendons:

> Lie down full-length, the tallest one of you. (11525)

The one Lemur has to lie down full-length; then Mephistopheles gives them all instructions about how they're to dig the grave.

In the Lemures' next chorus we hear that they still have in them a sort of half-memory of once being something like human beings, of coming from something sort of human:

> How young I was and lived and loved,
> It all seems, oh, so sweet;
> To happy tones and merry speech
> I moved my nimble feet. (11531-34)

(that is all behind them now; they are only half aware of it.)

> Now sly Old Age has caught me up
> And hit me with its crutch;
> I stumbled through the grave's wide gate,
> Why was it just then open! (11535-38)

In other words, they half remember that they stem from dead people. These are the ones Mephisto tried to make do with at first, the kind he first needs.

Now I ask you to remember that I have often spoken of our physical body as not being something we just carry around on ourselves as though it had no meaning and then finally slough off like some empty garment. As I have often said, it is not just our garment; it is our tool. It contains the forces through which we are connected with the mineral earth. Now I ask you to note the following as well: We, as we stand here with our physical body between birth and death, have been formed during Saturn, Sun, Moon and Earth.[†] Let's imagine that everything implanted in us during Saturn, Sun, Moon and Earth evolution is summed up in what I am drawing for you here. Let us also imagine what becomes part of our nature during Earth evolution through the fact that in this Earth evolution we receive an "I" as a tool, that this "I" is integrated into us as a physical tool. Then, imagine this in there, too.

During the Earth period our physical body once again receives what was originally implanted in it during Old Saturn, and then developed further during the Old Sun and Old Moon periods. But now, through the working of the "I" in this physical body, something is integrated

into us that has not come to us from Saturn, Sun and Moon evolutions, but only from Earth evolution; this something is an external physical expression of the "I" itself. In death the "I" goes out of this physical body. What remains in us from Saturn, Sun and Moon evolutions has no continuing existence in the life of the Earth; it has nothing to do with the forces of Earth evolution. The physical forces of Earth evolution would never produce our muscles, for example; these had to have been produced already through the physical forces of the Moon evolution; the earthly forces would also never produce our nerves, and so on. But what *have* come about during Earth evolution, through the impulses of the "I," are our bones. In fact, the bones even waited until the Atlantean evolution to appear; the ligaments and tendons originated through the salt deposits in the Atlantic Sea. Only through the forces of the earth did all this become part of us. Here is where we bear the earth in ourselves: in our bones, our tendons and our ligaments. In these the Earth Spirit is living. We find the same forces living in them that are present in all mineral nature or are at work in all earthly technology. In the composition of our bones, our tendons and our ligaments, everything is living that can proceed from the mineral-physical effects of an earthly nature, as well as from the effects of technology. When we now pass through the portal of death, we leave our Saturn, Sun and Moon parts behind. These are destroyed because they cannot continue to exist in the earth. Bones, tendons, and ligaments must be destroyed by the forces of the earth itself. Whether the human body decays or is cremated makes no difference; the special forces of the earth have to destroy them.

Through Faust's death, therefore, that in which the special forces of the earth hold sway is given over to the earth—the same earth to which all deceased human beings are given over, insofar as they are made up of bones, tendons and ligaments. A deeply spiritual insight into Nature shows through the way Goethe has shaped this scene, an infinitely profound knowledge of Nature! For we should not believe we've told the whole story about what remains of us when we say: "Well, the physical body falls away from us and our soul aspect—however we describe it—goes on into the spiritual worlds."

This is not the case at all. Hidden spiritual forces fill the entire physical body, and these remain with the earth. The only thing is, the earth can't hold what it itself has not produced; all it retains are the forces from the bones, tendons and ligaments. Bury the body and let it rot, or cremate it: whether it decays or is cremated, what works as forces in bones, tendons and ligaments will remain in the body of the earth itself for all time to come! We give what we can call our "bony man" [*Knochenmann* is also a German figurative name for Death] over to the earth, and it will stay there until the earth itself has arrived at the goal of its evolution. Our "bony man" is taken up by the "bony men" of all the human beings who have previously died, thereby joining the community of those who have preceded it in death. It would be a superficial view to say that "everything there must pass away." Only the form must pass away. The forces working within it are contained in the activity of the earth. And if you take the physical forces working in the earth today, if you look right into the earth, you will see the forces in it that have come into it through the fact that human beings have been buried in the earth or that their bodies have somehow undergone a process of destruction. The forces that have formed the human being are now within the earth, are working in the earth's interior and are preserved there.

Thus we can say that Mephisto is first of all faced with the task of dealing with the pathway, or pathways, the physical body wants to take. To do this, he needs the Lemures, which, I'd like to say, are not ghostly beings but sub-ghostly ones, phantom-beings that are always united with the earth-body as the remains of deceased human beings. These are what he needs.

Do you know what would happen if what has typically belonged to our bones, tendons and ligaments ever since the Atlantean period were to pass away? The earth would already be close to this today, and it would soon be even closer to everyone's being born with so-called "angelic limbs,"† limbs without any marrow or strength in them. People would then be born with rickets, for the earth only has a certain amount of the energy needed for the movements of our bones and the development of our tendons. And what we give back again in death passes over into future human bodies along a mysterious pathway. Otherwise, people would be born rachitic. And if they are born rachitic, it is a sign that within their total karmic picture they haven't established a right relationship to the forces the earth provides again and again, and receives back again and again from the bones, tendons and ligaments of all humanity.

An immensely deep and spiritual thought of Nature is expressed in the fact that Mephisto has called these sub-ghostly, purely phantom beings to his aid and that Faust's own phantom joins their ranks. Of course, we have to understand this scene in a purely spiritual sense. Scholars of *Faust* have always believed that what are walking around here are skeletons. But they are really only the supersensible forces within the bones, tendons and ligaments. The scene must be grasped in an entirely spiritual way, by means of, and in the manner of, spiritual vision only. What these Lemures have about themselves is thus what we human beings also carry around with us because we have an "I." But the "I" [of the Lemures] is outside. As a result, any attributes that would be due to the presence of an "I" are also gone, or rather are only half-present, as mere echoes. This is why they are both there and not there. We human beings don't fully exist, aren't fully present, until we send our I into our bones, tendons and ligaments. This "I" the Lemures no longer have. We don't understand something we have heard until we send our "I" through our bones, tendons and ligaments. All the Lemures have is the echo. They hear, but don't know what they are hearing. They have heard a call, but they have only half heard it—they have forgotten it because their memory is in their system of bones, tendons and ligaments. Therefore, since Mephistopheles has to deal first of all with the pathways that Faust's physical body takes, but also wants to assert his rights on the earth even though he is a spiritual being, he of course finds it necessary to busy himself with the Lemures, as we understand them here, because they are the ones from whom he would be able to snatch the spiritual aspect of Faust's physical body away. After all, the physical body also has a spiritual foundation, and this spiritual component is what he would be able to get hold of.

Now let me remind you of something we need in order to understand this picture in all its aspects. We can find it in the chapter of my book *How to Know Higher Worlds* that deals with the Guardian of the Threshold. There you will find a discussion of the fact that when we undergo higher spiritual development the individual forces otherwise united in our normal, everyday human consciousness separate. I've characterized these forces there as the capacities of willing, feeling and thinking, each of which becomes something quite individual as they go their separate ways. Mephisto, having lagged behind at the Moon stage in his own development, was still familiar with the Old Moon evolution. This is how you have to understand him: Mephisto's understanding of practical life is informed by what he knows from the Old Moon evolution. But it was also part of the atavistic, Old Moon way of looking at things that the different members of the human being were still separate, in the sense that they had not yet been united through the activity of an "I." And so, when Mephisto wants to get hold of Faust's spiritual nature in the only way he can, he really has to go after it from the standpoint of its having three separate parts. First of all he has to take hold of it as the spiritual aspect of the physical body, at which point he has to deal with the Lemures. Then he has to try to catch its second member, the etheric body, which separates off very soon after death. And he knows that that is where he has to try to get it. Finally, he has to try to get hold of it in what has freed itself from the etheric body and passes over into the spiritual world. But the fact that these three aspects could be held together by an "I" is not yet part of his world; it is an idea he is not at home with yet, which is why he can still only deal with them as separate entities. For this reason he is instinctively driven to attach great importance to getting his hands on the spiritual aspect of the physical body. At this point he has to put the Lemures to work. Now, since he knows the soul only as something made up of separate parts, he has to try to get hold of one of these separate parts—he just doesn't know which one—namely, the etheric body, which exits through the human being's lower limbs. This is where he stations the Fat Devils, whose job it is to grab the etheric body for him. After that he has no idea how things will go. Maybe he can get hold of Faust's spiritual aspect with the third member of his being, the one that wants to go up into the spiritual world? So he puts the Skinny Devils there, in his attempt to get hold of Faust's spirit this way. But he has to use his devil's instinct, so to speak, to bring the three parts together that can hand the physical body over to him directly in its spiritual form—etheric body and soul-spiritual aspect.

Etheric body—well, you see, the ether in the world around us is something that physics has a hard time coming to grips with because this ether has a peculiar property that distinguishes it from normal materiality. It is not heavy; it has no weight. Normal earthly gravity cannot hold on to the ether. But Mephisto wants to hold on to it, and he wants to do this with the help of spiritual beings. Since the ether has already become spiritual, it has to be held onto by spiritual beings. Mephisto needs the Fat Devils for this, since as spiritual beings they have a certain heaviness.

This is why they have to be poor, potbellied devils with enormously fat bodies—short ones, of course, for if these were too tall they would reach up too far into the upper regions. And so they have to be short and fat, and what is spiritual about them has to be related to the earth in such a way that they can keep what wants to fly upward toward the spirit down on the earth. So they have to be short and cunning, and everything that contributes to their physical appearance as human beings has to be ungainly. They also have to have powerful forces in their rather stocky bodies. For this reason, those of their limbs that are more spiritualized are small; they should really have small hands—stumps—stumps of arms. This is hard to portray; in fact, it can only be portrayed successfully if the actors try as far as possible to move only the lower part of their arms. Naturally, they will really have to practice this and learn to do it.[†] The nose tends to be thick as well. In the Devils' case the nose has become a horn with a tendency toward heaviness; along with the forehead, it has been shaped into a thick organ that doesn't connect the human being with the air but operates through its own heaviness.

We know what pathway the etheric body takes, since it is not subject to earthly gravity. Mephisto needs beings like these to hold the etheric body back for him within the general realm of the earth. He has to position them where they will be able to grab the etheric body when it emerges from the lower regions of Faust's body. So he assigns positions to them:

> On the double now! Let's show some spark,
> You gentlemen with straight and crooked horns,
> Straight from the old-school devils' haunt
> You bring the gaping maw of hell along.
> Of course, the maws of hell are many! many!
> And everyone she gulps down goes by rank;
> But in the final stages of this game
> She'll pay a lot less heed to those she takes.
>
> *(The hideous maw of hell opens on stage left.)*
>
> Eyeteeth gape; the gullet's vaulted ceiling
> Spews forth a raging stream of fire,
> And in the seething vapor of the background
> I see the flaming city's endless glow. (11636-47)

This is of course the same flaming city we find in Dante![†]

> The red breakers . . . and so on. (*Inferno* VIII: 74)

Here they come, the Fat Devils first with their short, straight horn! Now he describes them:

> You paunchy rascals with the fiery cheeks! (11656)

We see them in the same constitution in which the Old Moon beings still breathed fire. They're "paunchy rascals with fiery cheeks" that "hell's brimstone" has made "good and greasy."

> Short, stumpy necks that never moved! (11658)

Nothing moves; their mobility is already half spiritual. Everything about them is so stiff and awkward that they have to force the spirit into gravity because they are supposed to hold on to the ether, which is light. And so he assigns them their posts:

> Watch out down here for some phosphoric glow: (11659)

(to see whether the etheric body they're supposed to catch is coming out there)

> That is the soul, or Psyche with her wings,[†] (11660)

(he sees it as the soul!)

> Once they're plucked off, she's just a nasty worm; (11661)

So he seems to want to have the etheric body in the form of a dragon.

> I'll set my seal upon her with my stamp,
> Then whirl away with her in fiery storm! (11662-63)

Now, as he positions the Fat Devils there, he makes the apt remark:

> Stay with his body's lower regions,
> You clumsy fatsos, that's your job;
> Whether that's where she's at home
> No one really knows for sure. (11664-67)

And how should he know? All he knows about are the three separate members of the soul; he has no idea what he should go after!

> The navel's where she likes to live, (11668)

This is the region where the etheric body has to start leaving the human body.

> Be on your guard, that's where she'll slip right past. (11669)

So there we have the Fat Devils with their short, thick horn that want to try to shape the spiritual in such a way that it develops earthly weight.

As for the third part, Mephisto wants to get control over it by means of the Skinny Devils. These characters have to be really skinny, and again this is not easy to portray! Very skinny; and everything about them is already so spiritualized that in their case the nose and brow have merged into a single horn to overcome matter as much as possible, but in a devilish way, by being long and crooked, because the real reason they want to achieve a high degree of spirituality is to overcome earthly gravity completely. This is why Goethe calls these beings, with their rapid, whirling, top-like movements, "silly clowns" [*Firlefanze*] (11670). They now have to be so placed that they can catch the third element as it goes out into the spiritual world. In other words, they're supposed to rush after the forces just working their way out from under the influence of gravity. What they are not supposed to insert into earthly gravity is something they *are* supposed to develop like a top—opposed to gravity—through their long, mobile limbs, which would really have to be growing out of them. This is the way they should develop. Mephisto positions them as follows:

> You giant, silly clowns, like men with wings!
> Reach in the air, till you're about to drop,
> With arms straight out, (11670-72)

(straight out means long in this case, that they become thin and long)

> With arms straight out, and show us your sharp claws, (11672)

(so they have long claws instead of fingers)

> To catch her as she flutters in her flight. (11673)

(this is the soul on its way into the spiritual world)

> She doesn't feel right in her former house;
> The genius (11674-75)

(this is the "genius," which is always soul-spiritual, in contrast to the etheric body)

> The genius wants to go right out the top. (11675)

There you see how clearly Goethe has delineated the function of the Lemures with respect to the physical body, of the Fat Devils with respect to the etheric body, and of the Skinny Devils with respect to the soul-spiritual aspect, in complete accordance with the constitution of the human being!

At this point we see the heavenly host approaching: the legion of beings belonging to the worlds of spirit. And the affair is portrayed in such a way that none of the beings who can be of any service to Mephisto—the Lemures and the Fat and Skinny Devils—get anywhere at all. The heavenly host approaches:

> Follow, you sent ones,
> Related to Heaven,
> In moderate flight;
> Sinners forgiving,
> Dust re-enlivening;
> Grant to all natures
> Welcoming traces
> As you float down in
> Your lingering course. (11676-84)

These, to be sure, are beings with no experience of the Earth sphere proper, but they are also not intent on working into this sphere; their only desire is to work on the soul-spiritual nature of the human being. Mephisto is decidedly out of place; he has remained a spirit who *does* work into the earthly sphere, but as a spirit of the Old Moon. The other spirits have remained in their proper sphere. For this reason they must seem to Mephisto like human beings who never actually became human, but are still pre-human, immature, even less than children.

> Discordant tones I hear, a nasty tinkling,
> Come from above and with this day unwelcome;

It's like the plunking of little boys and girls,
Which sanctimonious taste would love to hear. (11685-88)

And so on. Of course, Mephisto knows very well how closely related he himself is to these angels as spiritual beings, since both he and they have remained spiritual beings. This is why he calls them devils of his own kind, but devils in disguise.

They're devils, too, but in disguise. (11696)

Now the struggle begins between this host of angels and what's working down below in the Fat and Skinny Devils to get hold of Faust's soul. Mephisto has to take part in this struggle, so there he stands, sensing something is about to happen and giving his devils instructions. What does he think might happen? Well, he knows about the three-ness of the soul, but this knowledge is incapable of grasping the oneness of the "I." He doesn't believe the oneness of Faust's "I" is strong enough to hold the soul's three-ness together. This is his big mistake. He goes on and on about the three-ness of the soul, but at this moment the oneness, or unity, of the soul aspect is asserted from out of the spiritual world, which holds everything together. Were it not for this oneness, the unity of the "I," the Lemures would be able to draw the physical body's spiritual aspect to themselves, which would then lose any connection it ever had with the cosmos as a whole, and the Skinny Devils would be able to get hold of the soul, the "genius." Each of the soul's three parts does go its own way, of course: the body goes to the earth, the etheric body goes into the region of the ether, and the soul goes into the region of the spirit. But because in the earthly human being they are held together by the "I" between birth and death, all three are destined to remain attuned to each other. A connection remains. And as soon as the connection called forth by the character of the "I" is present, the Devil himself can do no more. Nevertheless, he puts himself in exactly the right places and behaves exactly as he should.

Why do you duck and twitch? Is that hell's custom? (11710)

(the Fat and the Skinny Devils feel a different element approaching)

Stand your ground and let them strew. (11711)

They're strewing roses as a symbol of descending spiritual love.

Every fool to his own place!
They seem to think that with such little flowers
Hot devils will end up snowed in;
They'll melt away before your breath. (11712-15)

Now they begin as he orders them to:

Now puff, you puffers! (11716)

They puff and blow away what is surrounding them as pangs of love, which they feel as a searing heat they cannot endure. Then they puff some more, but they puff too hard because they cannot find just the right amount to blow. They have not learned how to handle anything formed in the process of Earth evolution.

—That's enough, enough! ...
Amazing, how you never know the right amount! (11716-17)

He doesn't know it out of his own nature either. He only knows it insofar as he has observed it on the earth. But since he was around Faust for so long and saw what his needs were, he realizes what the right proportions are for human beings, at least for a while.

—That's enough, enough!
The whole swarm pales from your foul breath.—
Not so much power! Close your mouth and noses!
Indeed, your breath's now much too strong.
Amazing, how you never know the right amount!
It's not just shrunk, it's brown and dry and burning.
Here it floats with clear and poisonous flames.
Press close together, brace yourselves against it!—
Their strength is going out! All courage gone!
The devils sense strange glow of flattery. (11716-25)

Love is only flattery for him; he transforms everything into something purely egotistical. And so we see how, through the struggle that ensues here within Mephisto's imagination—for this whole scene really does take place within Mephisto's imagination, since for a time he lets himself fall back into his life during ancient Moon†—how the possibility arises for Mephisto's imagination that he could possess this soul in its three-ness, whereas in actuality it is torn away from him through the oneness of its unified nature.

The interesting thing is that this scene is precisely where we also find an awareness of the inner spiritual evolution of humanity. Think of what I've often told you: how only a certain narrow-mindedness can believe that if we go back to the earliest times of human existence, people always looked the same; that is, people imagine that the soul life of the Romans, the Greeks and the Egyptians in particular was already more or less the same as that of modern-day people, whereas major developments have taken place since this time. People who are constantly thinking only of the most recent centuries have no idea what human beings have gone through in their evolution in the course of many centuries. But the spiritual beings notice this, because they look at the matter spiritually. This is why it is so beautiful that from Mephisto's words to Faust here, we see what he, Mephisto, who is quite an old fellow, of course, has been through in the whole course of Earth evolution. You know he says at one place (6864) that he once found "crystallized human folk†"! Indeed, Mephisto sees how things are different now:

> There's the body, and if the spirit wants to flee
> I'll quickly show the contract writ in blood; (11612-13)

What does he want, anyway? Faust's dead. The soul is what he wants, but the only thing he knows about it is its three-ness. We recall that Faust made a contract with Mephisto and even signed it in blood—a contract. So what does Mephisto really want now, this Mephisto-Ahriman? What does he want? He wants to refer to his contract. He believes that if he produces the contract the moment the soul comes out, the soul will not be able to slip away from him. Now, I would rather not say anything more from this perspective in view of the many vile words that have been spoken in these turbulent times of ours.† Now that our friends have been accused of not thinking correctly about contracts and treaties, I don't intend to develop a theory of contracts that could somehow be taken advantage of. If precisely in this scene I were not to side with Mephisto, but were to do so with Faust, it could perhaps even be said that Faust was a real pan-German in view of his concept of a treaty! I don't want to say any more about the trouble one could get into, for one would either have to take sides with Mephisto-Ahriman, or else, because Faust doesn't go along with the document signed in blood, one would expose oneself to the danger of having that chalked up to us as a pan-Germanic attitude. Therefore, we prefer to keep silent about the deeper insights we would have to unfold if we were to speak about this contract between Faust and Mephisto. Let us leave it at that!

But the inner meaning of evolution approaches us in Mephisto's words when he draws our attention to the fact that as times change, so do the impulses inherent in the evolution of humanity. Earlier, in ancient times, which as we know were times of relative clairvoyance—although people today call it superstition—he still had a fairly good understanding of how to capture souls. Back then the souls were readily available in their three-ness, and he really was still able to capture these souls when the affair was well prepared. And in the final analysis he did prepare it very well in Faust's case. But now, as the fifth post-Atlantean period is approaching and the soul's unity is being established by the activity of the "I," he has not managed to complete his own schooling yet.

> Too bad so many ways exist today
> To cheat the Devil of his souls.
> We, on the old path, cause offense,
> And on the new, we're poorly recommended. (11614-17)

Attention must really be called to Mephistopheles-Ahriman's nature in the fifth post-Atlantean period, in which he finds himself especially "poorly recommended." The Devil is also not very well recommended because he is not acknowledged when he is introduced somewhere as Mephistopheles-Ahriman; on such occasions people regard him as being outside their rank or class.

The little people never feel the Devil's there,
Even when he has them by the collar. (2181-82)

He is there, but he is not recommended. And so he goes and gets some assistants who he thinks will be able to help him attain what he is after: the soul in its three-ness. But the fact that the soul is no longer there in the form of its original three-ness is what allows it to slip away from him.

Now there is a curious thing about this Mephisto-Ahriman. These beings that belong to the spiritual world come down into his spheres, and he, well, he actually falls in love with them. Goethe portrays quite accurately a love scene that takes place between Mephisto and the angels. The Devil has an intellect, and a love affair between Mephisto and the angels is truly an "absurd infatuation" (11838). That's what Mephisto himself calls it, and it is an absurd infatuation. But what makes it possible for this absurd infatuation to come over him, anyway? In fact, for feelings of love to arise in him at all? If he had not spent so much time at Faust's side, trying to beguile him by arousing in him such tempting feelings of a similar nature, these feelings would not have passed over into him. So here again you have a marvelous and profound piece of wisdom. The Devil actually has no capacity to love in the earthly sense, erotically or otherwise. He simply has none. Infatuation is naturally absurd for him, for, as we know, the earth is the Cosmos of Love. He comes from the Cosmos of Wisdom. But he is out of place, wandering around on the earth and forever trying to incorporate the earth into his own kingdom. By this means he goes from one situation to another in which he incorporates into himself characteristic features that develop on the earth but now no longer fit with his nature. In order to build up his hopes of capturing a soul, he has to prepare this soul for the Devil, that is, make it suitable for taking hold of the characteristics implanted by Lucifer in the beginning. But in the process he himself becomes infected by this characteristic and, in turn, makes himself incapable of holding Faust's soul. Here you see happening on a large scale, in the case of the Devil, something that also happens on a small scale. Just imagine how it is that we human beings also have a natural tendency to arouse passions, but if we allow these to develop to a certain point, they will destroy our organism. We can therefore only allow this to go so far. The Devil has to suck in human characteristics, like a vampire, so to speak, so that he can arouse certain passions in Faust. But in so doing he destroys the devilish nature within himself that is perfectly right for him. This makes it possible for his "absurd infatuation" with the angels to arise, diverting his attention so that he fails to notice that the angels are snatching the soul away from him. This darkening of his awareness, this shift of consciousness into the subconscious, had to happen to him.

Since we have yet to see today's performance, I cannot say anything more. But I think enough has been said by way of introduction to give you some understanding, especially of the three-ness that permeates this scene. I also think that when we devote ourselves to considerations such as these, we can readily perceive the infinite depth of what Goethe himself said he had secretly inserted into the second part of *Faust.*

People who were able to summon up within themselves a picture of how spiritual wisdom passes through the evolution of humanity, of how only in our own age this has receded somewhat, and how this spiritual wisdom can often be found only in shadow form in all kinds of justified or not-so-justified esoteric societies—such people always knew, as individuals, what profound, real, concrete wisdom of the world can be found in Goethe's *Faust.* This is why they have spoken as they did along these lines. Such a person dedicated a short poem to Goethe's *Manes* at a Saint John's festival[†] in 1880, a poem in which he wished to express how much he felt at one with Goethe in spiritual wisdom. In earlier times, when people spoke to the immortal parts of a human being, they always called them *Manes,* because the same spirit lives in them that lives in the Manas.[†] As a result of the erudition of his materialistic age, this man actually had very little of Goethe in him any longer, very little that was concrete. And since spiritual science hadn't yet been born at the time he was writing, he had only a dull feeling that this spiritual science was living in Goethe as an instinct. As it happened, the *Faust* commentary that this man Oswald Marbach wrote[†] didn't turn out to be particularly significant. But the poem he dedicated to Goethe's *Manes* at a big Masonic festival of wisdom shows that a connection with the greatness living in Goethe's poetic work was always present, even if only in a sort of half-conscious form and in a few lonely souls. For all these reasons, this man, who felt so closely connected with Goethe's *Manes*, with Goethe's individuality, was able to say on the occasion of this Masonic festival of Saint John in 1880:

> To you, our Brother, Father, illustrious Master!
> To whom today, as in this century past,
> We lift our hands, firmly entwined, as token
> Of the most faithful love of our free spirits;
> Of all the spirits, greatest and most free!
> To whom on high we strive, to be like him;
> To you we dedicate ourselves, our sons,
> So that perfection one day crown our frame!
>
> Both you and we have striven; yet your striving
> For self-knowledge which guides all to Wisdom
> Was ever filled with matchless, healthy life,
> With creator-strength that strides toward deeds,
> Toward works that raise themselves to Light.
> Around these, glow of beauty ever spreads.
> You strove with God, as Israel strove with God,
> Until as victor you had mastered Self!
>
> What us with you mysteriously allies
> No word shall ever say to the unworthy;
> Yet may it be proclaimed before all people
> Through never-tiring deeds of purest love,
> Through light igniting spirit in the spirit,
> Through ever-greening seeds of life eternal.
> Lead on, O master! Whither you have gone,
> Most fervent longing draws us in your train.

May a time come once again in which such words both may and can be truth!

16
Goethe's Insights into the Secrets of Human Existence

Dornach, September 9, 1916

After a performance of the "Midnight" and "Burial" scenes with eurythmy

Once again we have had a portion of Goethe's *Faust* pass before our souls. In my last address here, on the nature of the Lemures and the Fat and Skinny Devils, I attempted to develop some insights that would lead to an introductory understanding of these scenes on the basis of spiritual science. On occasions like this we always try not only to find something that will help us understand this particular poetic work, but also to derive something of general significance for spiritual science from the work itself, to broaden our horizons by looking directly into the same true realities Goethe himself was seeking to attain in writing his *Faust*.

Today I would like to make a few observations about what has just passed before our souls. The more we think about it, the more significant it can appear to us that the scene that has just come to an end is not the final scene of Goethe's *Faust*, but is followed, as we know, by that other scene we saw performed here not so long ago. You remember that scene: gorges, woods, cliffs, a mountain wilderness, holy anchorites, a chorus, an echo, woodlands that come swaying up, and so on; we are led through the chorus of Blessed Boys by the rapt meditations of Pater Ecstaticus, Pater Profundus, and Pater Seraphicus; we again encounter the angels that in today's scene bear Faust's immortal part up into the higher regions where we go on to encounter the trinity of the Penitent Women, Doctor Marianus, the Mater Gloriosa as Gretchen's guide; and finally the closing chorus, the Chorus Mysticus itself:

> All that must pass away
> Is but a simile ... (12104-05)

All of this comes after the scene we saw today, which portrays the struggle of the Spirits of Light with the Spirits of Darkness for the soul of Faust.

When people attempt to explain *Faust*, they often go from scene to scene, and indeed often from sentence to sentence, without asking any of the questions that not only could be asked but would actually spread some light over this great and powerful poetic work. Today we saw what happened at Faust's Burial, how Mephistopheles-Ahriman lost the game and how the soul was carried up into the regions of the spirit. From a certain point of view we could ask: Couldn't *Faust* actually end with this? Don't we basically know by now what this is all about? Don't we know that Mephistopheles has lost his wager, that all the efforts he made accompanying Faust his whole life long have come to naught, that Faust's soul has been taken up into the region of light, and that therefore the words addressed to the Spirits of Darkness in Lessing's Faust[†]: "You shall not be the victors!" have likewise been fulfilled? Couldn't we believe it was all over now and that *Faust*, as a poetic work, had come to an end?

The question arises: Why in the world does the ending we know so well still come after what we've seen today? By raising this question and then devoting ourselves to its answer we touch upon significant secrets of human life in its connection with the entire universe. The very fact that Goethe shaped the conclusion of his *Faust* the way he did shows what profound insights into the mysteries of human existence he carried in the subterranean realms of his own life at a time when spiritual science did not yet exist. Many, many things are buried in the scene we saw performed today, and even more in the fact that this scene is followed by other closing scenes. Much of this proves that Goethe knew the deepest secrets of existence, but also that he felt obliged to present these secrets of existence in such a way that they are only accessible to someone willing to enter more deeply into the life of the spirit, into the depths of his or her own nature. Goethe fully intended to express many things in a veiled way, inserting many secrets into his *Faust*, as he himself said. He only gave veiled hints of much that would arouse the hatred and opposition of dull, thick-headed people who, out of fear and indolence, have no desire to draw near to knowledge of the spiritual world. As a result, for the last eighty-four years people have more or less failed to understand Goethe's *Faust*, but little by little it will reveal its depths to humanity if we can manage to live on into the future. In fact, we can really maintain that only spiritual-scientific knowledge will be able to set those artistic feelings free that will make an understanding of this poetic work possible.

First of all, Let us look back to that shatteringly impressive scene in which Faust first sets eyes on the four Gray Women: Lack, Guilt, Need, and Care. We have to realize that by the time Faust experiences the four Gray Women he has passed through many, many spiritual life-experiences, that is, life-experiences that have brought him to a certain spiritual understanding. Goethe imagines his Faust as being a hundred years old at the time portrayed in this closing scene; in fact, Goethe has told us this himself. When we first saw Faust today, he was standing on the balcony of his home with all these spiritualized experiences in his soul. He had built this home at a work site from which he desired to achieve something for the future of humanity. In these feelings within his soul we see a kind of summation of the satisfaction he feels, a summation of what he has been allowed to achieve for humanity by wresting a free piece of land away from the sea for the benefit of free human beings.

> The stars now harbor gleam and glow,
> The fire sinks and blazes small,
> Fanned by a showery shudder-wind
> That brings both smoke and mist to me.
> Commanded quickly, done too fast! (11378-82)

Now before his gaze it seems, but in reality before his inner vision, something happens that shapes the appearance of the four Gray Women:

> What floats so shadowlike toward me? (11383)

We have to imagine that the deepening which Faust's soul has undergone has made this soul capable of having the vision of these four figures—Lack, Need, Care and Guilt—out of its own deep inner source. This "Scene at Midnight," an inner experience in the truest sense of the word, is called forth in Faust by the fact that his soul is beginning to separate from his body. For this is the remarkably mysterious feature that Goethe has quite evidently intended, namely, that from the moment the three Gray Women speak the words:

> The clouds drift away with the stars' disappearing!
> Back there, way back there! From far away distance
> He comes now, he comes; it's our Brother, it's—Death. (11395-97)

—from this moment Death is already spreading itself out over Faust's life. We understand this scene in the right way only if we imagine Faust from this moment on as a dying man whose soul is slowly detaching itself from the body. And it would be wrong to think that what comes next is meant to be realistic only in an externally sense-perceptible way. This it is not! As we see Faust in the room of his palace where Care has come in, we can tell from the way he is sitting that his soul has already loosened itself from his body to a certain extent and that the experiences of physical life are flowing together with the experiences the soul has when it has already loosened itself from the body. And we understand how remarkably deeply these sentences are interwoven only when we pay attention to the interplay of the two worlds: the spiritual world Faust has already begun to enter by means of his loosening soul, and the world of the physical senses, which he is still in, because his soul hasn't managed to completely detach itself yet. Lack, Guilt and Need have been powerless to act. Their only role has been to proclaim the approach of Death. But the gnawing figure of Care remains, as the vision changes to become the vision of the soul that has already become separate from the body:

> Four I saw come, three only go;
> The meaning of their speech I could not grasp,
> Its after-echo was like—Need,
> Then came a somber rhyme-word—Death.
> It sounded hollow, muffled like a ghost. (11398-402)

If we know what Goethe felt when he used the expression: "like a ghost,"—and Goethe was a man in whom words aroused feelings of much greater concreteness than they do in today's dull, unresponsive materialists—we will not take a line such as this one lightly:

> It sounded hollow, muffled like a ghost. (11402)

Instead, we will sense how weighty and full of being it is, and seek out the feeling he had as he was putting these words into Faust's mouth. Among other things in Goethe's writings, you will find an especially beautiful passage[†] in which he says the following: "Sometimes life seems to me as though events from a far distant past were entering my present consciousness, and then, everything long past seems like a ghost transposing itself into the present day." Goethe had a very concrete conception of what he called ghostly. Epochs of his own life from thousands of years earlier stood there in visionary form before his soul, and he often believed he could see them making their way into his present-day life like ghosts. These are not arbitrary statements; everything I am saying can be verified exactly on the basis of what Goethe himself said when he was speaking intimately about the experiences of his inner life.

So now the views and thoughts are flowing together that Faust, half standing in the spiritual world and half still living on the physical plane, is having. Imagine the interplay of these two worlds and you have what Faust is going through. What he is experiencing can really only be experienced in this interplay of the two worlds and would not even be developing as it is if he were farther away from his physical body than he is. He still feels the events from the other side of the threshold as bound to the events of physical life:

> To freedom have I still not fought my way. (11403)

And now, we have the peculiar passage that will come across to some as a mere contradiction but will be understood the moment the experience is regarded as taking place between physical and spiritual life. Faust has spent his whole life trying to reach the spiritual world, but of course in those days there was no such thing as spiritual science in the true sense of the word. To come to know the spiritual world he has tried to use the magic he took over from the Middle Ages, that magic which has connected him with Ahriman-Mephistopheles in the way we have often discussed, such as in the previous lecture. This magic, which enabled him to make his way into the spiritual world, is not to be separated from Mephistopheles. If you look back at all that went on around Faust, you will see that Mephistopheles was the one staging all the magical events. For this reason we cannot hope that Faust wants to cling to this magic, now that he is already standing halfway in the spiritual world:

> Could I but distance magic from my path,
> Forgetting all the charms once and for all. (11404-05)

He means the magic charms he has garnered from ancient books, charms that have become Luciferic or Ahrimanic because they have come down to him from ancient times. This leads him to see, now that he is really entering the spiritual world, that what he attained was not what he was looking for after all. And now he begins to look back, as one does the moment the soul begins to loosen, into this life of his, which is just ebbing away. A certain moment stands there in living fullness before him: the moment before he first reached for the medieval books, before he uttered the word so fraught with consequences:

> And so I've given myself to magic. (377)

The grace of the good powers that have guided him in the sense of the "Prologue in Heaven" has protected him from the fruits of that magic, which he would have had to harvest if the grace-filled working of these special Powers had not been with him throughout his life. Now, as he looks into the spiritual world, he sees everything in a different light. All this plays into it. Knowing this, he would do things differently now:

> Stood I before you, Nature! one man alone,
> To be a human would be worth the effort. (11406-07)

Earlier, before his soul had loosened from his body, he was not able to say this in this way. At that time he still had to go through life, making all his mistakes. Now he looks back and sees that his pathway had to lead through Mephistophelian darkness. First he looks back to the time of his life when Mephistopheles had not yet crossed his path:

> That's what I was,

(one man alone)

> before I searched in darkness,
> Blasphemed and cursed the world and myself.
> And now with such a spook the air's so filled
> That no way to avoid it has been found. (11408-11)

The whole weight of past events lies heavily on his soul.

> And though our day be clear, with sense and laughter,
> The night entangles us in web of dreams;
> From fresh young meadow happy, we return; (11412-14)

This, after all, is how he has lived his life: half only in the physical world, but already—even though in the physical body—half in the spiritual world, having been placed there by Mephisto. From the physical he looks over into the spiritual world but has to go back into the physical world again and again because Mephistopheles cannot find, and so cannot show him, the way into the spiritual world, since he is unable to connect the two in a proper way himself.

> That raucous bird, what does he caw? Misfortune. (11415)

The only thing to be found on this pathway is superstition.

> Ensnared by superstition, soon and late:
> It comes to pass, makes itself known, and warns.
> Intimidated in this way, we stand alone. (11416-18)

The path of superstition has always been mingled with Faust's path, a strong one, to be sure, since Faust's own strong nature enabled him to take it. And now he has the vision that has been able to stay with him since his soul is loosening more and more—the vision of Care. Try to feel here how in his very language Goethe allows his words to be reminiscent of that which is the very highest. When we feel the weight of these words, we could say that the whole history of the world lies heavily on our souls. Care steals in and Faust asks whether anyone is there:

> Is someone here? (11420)

The answer resounds:

> The question calls for Yes! (11420)

Not just a simple "Yes!" but a whole sentence: "The question calls for Yes!" I have said that the whole history of the world is already pressing into our souls in the very way these words are put together. For how, when we hear these words, could we fail to think of the magnificent scene in which Christ Jesus is asked before the court, "Is it you, the Son of God?" His answer is also not a simple "Yes," but rather, "You say so!"[†]

Here again, no abstract word is being used to express who it is that Faust is now experiencing:

> I'm simply here. (11421)

But she is in him. This conversation is really a monologue, a profound conversation within Faust himself. Only gradually and through inner experiences will humanity come to know the full gravity of this inner conversation. Along with what is to be imparted as spiritual science, humanity will also receive knowledge associated with deep, deep feelings and sensations about life that a dull, obtuse materialism never dreams of, not to mention the easily acquired worldview that believes that everything has been gained by means of statements that simply characterize what is physical or what is spiritually real. We know about such statements that people have struggled through difficult inner experiences in order to achieve them. Such people harbor them in their hearts and carry them about through life. But they are not what they really can and must be for the human soul unless they are accompanied by moods of every possible kind. These moods often make it seem as though the life of the soul were vegetating over an abyss. But once we have attained spiritual knowledge, Care can never leave us—that Care which comes over us concerning the connection of our spiritual knowledge to the whole reality of life. At the very moment we enter the spiritual world, we human beings must feel how shallow it is to speak with a false asceticism about how this earthly life is only something base that we would prefer to simply strip away. Spiritual knowledge is precisely what gives us a feeling for the immense depth of what this earthly life means for eternity: that this earthly life must be lived through so that what is out there can be incorporated into the impulses we carry through death into the sphere of Eternity. But how could things be otherwise than that at the end of an especially arduous life, at the moment the soul has loosened somewhat, we realize in a mood of Care-laden solemnity what the fruits can be of a life such as the one we have just lived through, now that we have to go through the spiritual world with this soul of ours. Faust has fought his way through many, many things. Yet he is great. Why is this? Because—having just entered the spiritual world, half in it and half still feeling his way back to physical earthly existence—in the profoundly significant comparison resulting from such a life-and-death situation between the physical and the spiritual, he knows:

> I've only rushed my way through life;
> Ev'ry desire, I grabbed it by the hair,
> What failed to satisfy got dropped,
> What got away, I let it go.
> I've only lived to crave and to achieve
> And then to wish for more, and so with might
> I've stormed my way through life, first great and mighty,
> But now things go more thoughtfully and wisely. (11433-40)

Feel the harmony of everything now arising in his soul: how he has gone through both the small and the great worlds, as these are called in *Faust*, and also how, with the all-encompassing view just opening up for him in this significant panorama of his life—only now, since starting to feel a spiritual light shining into his vision from above, he is able to survey in a wise and thoughtful manner all he has experienced in his mad rush through the floods of life. And now: What does he see? What is he beginning to see into more deeply? He is beginning to see more deeply what he has experienced in the realm of earthly existence. Think of all we have discussed concerning the panoramic review that comes over the soul at the beginning of life after death and is now slowly coming over Faust. Think of this review. He sees his earthly life in such a way that he has to say to himself:

> The whole earth's realm, I know it well enough. (11441)

What he sees now is what he had experienced in his earthly surroundings. He is already half in the spiritual world. Feel the words coming out of this mood:

> Our view into the other world is blocked. (11442)

We can say this at the very moment we are looking back at our life on earth. This is no philosophical profession of materialism; it is an immediate experience of what happens after death has already half seized our soul. Incompetents who have become *Faust* commentators have explained this passage as though in his old age Faust were reverting to a materialistic profession of faith. Now, however, in this situation Faust would truly be a fool if he were wanting, already now, to bypass the life review and look with squinting eyes at the spiritual world often painted in such glowing colors by those fools who simply build up this spiritual world out of poetic, pie-in-the-sky imaginations of their own inner natures, such as is done in many professions of faith. Faust wants to stand firmly on the end results of his own life. And now we hear deeply significant words in the face of which every appearance of materialism must entirely disappear. Those dreadful, fuzzy-headed mystics that are always talking about merging into the All and wanting to take hold of eternity in the chaotic All-darkness that they call All-light, want to wander off into eternity. But whoever wants to take hold of the spiritual life in a concrete way takes hold of it where it *can* be taken hold of in all its concreteness. Such people do not become fools, swimming away into some indefinite distance where there really *is* nothing for the soul to dream its way into but emptiness and empty space. They are not misled into wandering off into such eternities but come to grasp knowledge in a concrete way. What such a person comes to know can then be grasped:

> So may he roam along through earthly day. (11449)

Think how wonderful this sentence becomes when we realize that the review of his life on earth is beginning: seeing, itself, is making its way along through the days of his earthly life. Faust has now reached the point where he can find the right relationship to those haunting spirits to which he has here been misled by Mephistopheles.

> When spirits haunt him,

(now, in the life review)

> let him go his way;
> May he in striding on find weal and woe,
> He! in no moment ever satisfied. (11450-52)

We have to imagine the panoramic review as not yet quite complete but breaking in on him now, still fully permeated by the weight of Care through which fruits can be carried into the spiritual world out of the earthly day he has just experienced. And so it goes, back and forth from one world to the other: experiencing in the spiritual, but also in the physical, because he is still clinging to his body. This is the state Faust is in when we find him. Care still holds him to his physical body. But his task is to enter the spiritual world consciously, made conscious by the very Care that weighs him down. This is also why he grows into the spiritual world in such a way that while he already carries it in his soul he nevertheless still believes he can command the physical world. People who share the banal view of our present age—that human beings have basically always been the way they are now—do not know that many Greeks died the way Faust is dying, or rather, the way Goethe has

Faust die. We can prove from Greek literature that the Greeks found this kind of death especially desirable, as though still experiencing something of physical existence even though their souls were already somewhat detached. You can find passages in Sophocles† that indicate how the Greek saw something special in this way of dying, one that was not sudden but took its time, so that even though the dying person's awareness of the physical world had already dimmed down to half its former power, what was entering physical consciousness as twilight was gradually being illumined so that it could gaze fully into the spiritual world. Goethe did indeed try to carry many elements of Greek culture over into the second part of his *Faust*. We may well imagine that he had wanted to portray Faust as something like a dying Greek. This is why the feeling-content Faust puts into his words is already flowing out of the spiritual world, even though he is still giving orders here. We can pursue this further, showing how fully aware Goethe is of portraying everything of which I've been speaking to you.

You saw Faust come to the place where his grave is already being dug. Once again we may say: Certain Goethe commentators must not be very tasteful people if they think Goethe capable of the tastelessness of having the grave dug while Faust is still alive. That would, of course, be merely an act of bad taste! What we see is Faust dying. From this viewpoint it is not an act of bad taste; it is a marvelous imagination to also see, next to the dying Faust, the grave being dug by the Lemures, those half-spiritual beings whose nature I recently spoke about. But how does Faust speak? Well, first of all I want to skip over the words he speaks as he gropes for the door-jamb in stepping out of his palace. I want to call your attention to the words Faust speaks as he gives orders to dig the ditch for draining off the waters of the polluting swamp. At first all this can seem to be meant in a purely physical sense. But Goethe was well aware that Faust is speaking half out of a spiritual awareness, and this is how he wants these words to be understood. And what is then revealed out of this physical-spiritual, spiritual-physical awareness? First of all, a marvelous feeling of well-being in Faust. Think what he says:

> A swamp extends along the hills,
> Polluting everything we've done:

To drain this rotten pool would be
The last and greatest deed of all.
I open spaces up for many millions,
Not safe, of course, but active, free to live. (11559-64)

All well and good, but now come other words:

Green the fields, and fertile; men and herds
In ready comfort on the newest earth,
Immediately settled on the strength
Of hill rolled up by bold and busy people.
In here, a land of heavenly delight, (11565-69)

These words are chosen in full consciousness, out of the physical-spiritual, spiritual-physical interplay. The paradisiacal "land of heavenly delight" is the spiritual, playing into physical awareness and back again:

Out there, let flood tide rage up to the brim. (11570)

Of course, this also refers to the external situation, but the careful selection of these words was a fully conscious happening on Goethe's part.

A common impulse hies to close the gap. (11572)

And now these peculiar words:

To this view, yes! I'm fully given over,
The end to which all wisdom leads:
No one but he deserves both life and freedom
Who daily both must take by storm.
Thus here will spend, with danger all around,
Each old man, man and child his active year.
A throng like this I'd like to see,
With free folk standing firmly on free ground.
To such a moment I might utter:

Stay but a while, you are so fair!
The traces of my earthly days can never
In future eons pass away. (11573-84)

We're forced to hear these words repeated again and again these days as though Faust were saying something particularly nice because he feels: "You've done something for the common good; you've had an effect on the world." But as he speaks them he is overcome by the tremendous feeling of how he has established the foundation of his fame through his deeds, as it were, and of how this will work on for eons, and so he gives himself over to this feeling of well-being. As I said, we often hear people quote these words. I have even heard them cited by some people who did so because they wanted to say something especially nice to other people. After all, you can also say: "The traces of my earthly days—that is, of *your* earthly days—*will* never in future eons pass away." Nevertheless, no matter how fine we think these words are, we still must be clear that both they and this feeling of basking in fame are purely Luciferic. Once again we feel Faust's soul being completely seduced as if by Lucifer, as the unchecked egotism of his spirit not only looks back at the deeds he has done but feels his fame enduring on through the eons as well. This egotism expands to gigantic proportions, and in the end he rewards its boundlessness with his seal of approval:

Forefeeling happiness of such high degree,
This moment is the highest one for me. (11585-86)

Truly, the Devil is no slouch. After this Luciferic outburst we might already think the Devil has him, since his blissful feeling is once again of an entirely Luciferic nature, a lusting for Eternity of the highest degree. And we mustn't be thinking of some dumb devil here but rather of the clever Mephistopheles-Ahriman, as he now says something right on the mark:

No happiness or pleasure is enough
As on he strives for ever-changing forms;

The final, worthless, empty moment is
The one to which the poor man wants to cling. (11587-90)

His soul has completely separated from the body now, but it has something of the Luciferic in it. This connects very nicely with the no less inwardly blissful words that Faust uttered as he stepped out of the palace and made his way past the door-jamb:

What joy the scraping of the shovels gives!
The masses toil on my behalf. (11539-40)

We should not think that it is not a temptation to imagine at this final moment that the masses are toiling for us! The Luciferic temptation is present once again, and in all its clarity. And Mephistopheles is not so stupid to believe that the moment has arrived that can connect with the conversation in which Faust signed his soul over to him. We recall now their conversation with each other in the first part, when Faust was not yet speaking out of a half-attained spiritual awareness but only out of an awareness of the physical when he said the following words:

Once you have smashed this world to pieces,
Then let the next one come to be.
This earth is now the source of all my pleasures
And this bright sun shines down on all my sorrows;
If I can ever part from them,
Then let, what will and can, occur.
If people still will love and hate,
Of this I wish to know no more,
Or whether also in those spheres
There's such a thing as Up or Down. (1661-70)

We could think that in looking back to that time, Faust could very well say:

I've only rushed my way through life. (11433)

Then Mephistopheles says:

With this conviction you can chance it.
Commit yourself; and in the coming days
You'll like to see the tricks I have,
I'll give you what no one has ever seen.

Faust: And what, poor devil, would you give?
Was ever any human spirit, nobly striving,
Understood by such as you?
Yet, if you've food that never satisfies,
Or have red gold like mercury
That never rests, but melts within your hand,
A game no one can ever win,
A girl who leaning on my breast
Commits to someone else with sideways glances,
Or honor, that pleasure of the gods,
That like a meteor will vanish?
Show me the fruit that rots before it's picked
And trees that every day put on new green!

A task like that won't scare me off,

(answers Mephistopheles)

Such treasures I can serve you with,
But, my dear friend, there soon will come a time
For us to feast on something good at leisure.

And now come Faust's momentous words:

If ever, pacified, on bed of ease I'm lying,
Then let that be the whole thing's end!
If you can flatter me with lying
So that I come to love myself,
With pleasure ever you delude me;

That then will be my final day!
That's my wager! (1671-1698)

How could anyone say this was not fulfilled? In the mere anticipation of eternal fame, Faust already experiences his highest pleasure.

Mephistopheles: Perfect!

Faust: Hand on hand!
If to that moment I will say:
Stay but a while, you are so fair!

(Doesn't he say it?!)

Then you may put me in your chains,
Then I'll be glad to meet my end!
Then may the death knell sound for me,
Then from your service you'll be free,
The clock may stop, its hand may fall,
Let time for me be past and done!

Mephistopheles:
Keep that well in mind, we won't forget it. (1698-1707)

And he doesn't forget it. He recalls it now, after Faust has enjoyed his "highest moment":

No happiness or pleasure is enough
As on he strives for ever-changing forms;
The final, worthless, empty moment is
The one the poor man longs to cling to.
Now old, resisting me so long,
As time takes o'er, he lies here in the sand.
The clock has stopped— (11587-93)

The complete fulfillment of the situation, for Faust had said:

The clock may stop; its hand may fall. (1705)

Mephisto: The clock has stopped—
Chorus of Lemures: Has stopped! No sound, as if at midnight.
The clock hand falls. (11593-94)

What was ordered in advance at the moment of the wager has now arrived. Mephistopheles can assume that his work is done:

It falls, now it is finished. (11594)

Out of the mouth of Mephistopheles we hear the Word of the Cross: "It is finished." But the Chorus of Lemures immediately counters this with the voice of the Earth:

Now it's all done. (11595)

Mephistopheles' soul is terribly unsettled by this remark. He had said: "It is finished." But the Chorus of Lemures answers: "Now it's all done." The difference is vast. "All done"—he doesn't like this word:

All done! A stupid word.
Why then: "All done"?
All done and nothing left, complete monotony! (11595-97)

We have to look closely at these words to see what is going on here. At first we see Mephistopheles in conversation with his Lemures; he is thinking the whole affair "is finished," but it is really only "all done." Then he remembers himself and wants to understand the contradiction between "finished" and "all done."

All done and nothing left, complete monotony!
Why bother then with our non-stop creating!
Just snatch our work and turn it back to naught!
"There, it's all done!" What's that supposed to mean?
It might as well have never been at all,

And yet it's circling round as if it were.
Eternal Emptiness I would prefer. (11597-603)

As I said, these words contain the essence of what we have to look for. The fact that Goethe chose such words, building the scene as he did out of Faust's enjoyment of his highest moment and having Mephistopheles converse the way he does with his Lemures, proves that Goethe was able to say something of infinite depth. Today we can only touch on this, because in it lies the reason for why the final scene must then follow.

If the matter were the way many *Faust* commentators have thought it is, namely, that Mephisto has simply misunderstood everything, has been taken in by it, then there really would have been no need for this final scene. In that case the matter would be simple enough; it would be such that Faust never had the thought that such a high pleasure could exist as the one expressed in the words:

The traces of my earthly days can never
In future eons pass away ... (11583-84)

Mephisto had also not thought of this; neither one of them thought of it. It never occurred to either of them that Faust would ever say to any moment: "Stay but a while, you are so fair." But because it is something higher to feel the moment in such way, the stupid Devil is done out of his wager: this is more or less the way it is explained by all the *Faust* commentators put together. Well, in that case the Devil would have lost the soul, the angels would have carried it off, and everything would have been in order. We wouldn't need the final scene. And Goethe would certainly not have written it, since he was a man of poetic economy. But we will never understand *Faust* if we read it in such a superficial manner. We will understand it only by fully realizing that what Goethe wants here is to have Faust experience one more temptation of a genuinely Luciferic nature, even if it is at the very moment of his death. And Lucifer is really present again the moment Faust speaks the words:

Forefeeling happiness of such high degree,
This moment is the highest one for me. (11585-86)

What follows now is the actual Burial, as Mephisto prepares to make off with Faust's soul with the help of the spirits of hell. The angels come and win their victory over the Devil. Apparently the soul has been saved and is carried away, but the drama is not over yet. What is going on here? Well, Goethe himself was not able to answer this question without further ado. But there are many words here by means of which he expressed his meaning clearly enough for anyone who has the will to understand. It is just that the concept we so easily form of the chorus of angels that arrives to fetch the soul is wrong. It is not all that incorrect to say that the angels who show up here are all too haughty and pride themselves on being the "fullest spirits of light," despising both the fat and the thin devils and taking themselves to be so fine and pious. But Goethe already indicated he didn't want them to be thought of in this way by having Mephisto, whom he did not by any means put there as a stupid devil, speak words that are just sort of woven into the text at one point:

> This priestly look does not suit you at all, (11795)

and especially the very significant line:

> They're devils too, just in disguise. (11696)

They are part of Lucifer's family too. This observation is not in the text just for the fun of it! I want to speak more about this tomorrow, to the extent that words can even say how seriously this is intended.

17
Perspectives on the Realities Goethe Was Seeking

Dornach, September 10, 1916

Today and tomorrow, using Goethe's *Faust* as a starting point, I will try to say some things about certain relationships the human being has with the spiritual worlds. Anyone who delves into this poetic work fully equipped with the tools of spiritual science may assume that it was precisely in these final scenes that Goethe intended to express some of the deepest aspects of the worldview he had achieved through inner experience in the course of his long life on earth. "Worldview" here also means that Goethe added these scenes instinctively, as a matter of course, as it were, composing them in such a way that in them one can really feel his attitude toward the evolution of humanity as well, toward the impulses of human evolution, to the extent that knowledge of these was accessible to him. If we bring spiritual-scientific ideas to the figures Goethe created in his *Faust*, this of course must be understood in a very specific way. It would be completely wrong for you to believe that Goethe took the ideas we are speaking of here as a basis and then draped the speeches and characteristics of the different figures over them like hanging clothes on a coat rack. This is not the case! If we speak about these figures in Goethe's *Faust* the way we wish to here, we have to understand as we do so that Goethe knew them face to face, as it were, and characterized them as well as he could, whereas spiritual science can go into the matter even more deeply and is fully justified in doing so. Now you will surely agree that if you meet someone for the very first time, you will not see everything there is to see in this person's soul right away. Nevertheless, it is all there. If now, after this first meeting, you go on to describe this person, you will probably describe only certain aspects, something purely external perhaps. And yet this is someone that either you or someone else who can see more deeply into this person's soul would have to characterize with much deeper ideas after seeing him or her more often. So, in order for me to be able to say everything of significance today and tomorrow that can be said in connection with *Faust*, and I begin by asking, "Who is this Mephistopheles of Goethe's anyway?" you should not imagine that Goethe had in mind any of the ideas I will develop for you in speaking about Mephistopheles. Goethe simply characterized Mephistopheles as he knew him; but this is just why Mephistopheles, as he really is, remains a definite figure that can also be characterized using spiritual-scientific ideas. The significant thing is that with this spiritual-scientific characterization we can look more deeply into the individuality of Mephistopheles or of other figures that appear in *Faust*.

In any case, from the point of view of spiritual science we have to imagine a figure such as Mephistopheles as one who, in a certain sense, has lagged behind during the Old Moon evolution. In this case the underlying premise, the spiritual-scientific premise, is that Mephistopheles is a being that in passing from the Old Moon, or already from the Old Sun, let us say, to the Earth, or through the Old Moon to the Earth, didn't take part in the evolution it *could* have taken part in if it had done so in an appropriate form. But even though he comes before us in the shape of an earthly human being—albeit as a visible spirit—we would fail to understand his nature if we said something to the effect that he had fallen behind during Old Moon as compared to human evolution. Mephistopheles is at a decidedly higher level on Earth than human beings are, referring to his evolution, of course, not to his talent for evil. You can also say, if you want to, that Mephisto's genius for evil ranks him lower. But whatever you say, in the end his rank as a hierarchical being is obviously higher than that of human beings. Therefore, if we went back to the Old Moon evolution we would find that human beings are clearly at a lower level of development in their Old Moon evolution than this being of Mephistopheles is, which in the meantime has become Mephistopheles on Earth. In Mephistopheles we must therefore look for a higher being that has simply lagged behind during the Old Moon evolution with higher faculties than the human being ever had. How could we use an analogy to make the actual constitution of such a being even clearer?

Suppose we were looking at the evolution of our present earth. Even during our present Earth evolution we find that some people have developed further than others. Some, in fact, have made such decided progress in their development that during Earth evolution we speak of them as having gone through initiation. Such people already see into the world beyond the threshold, whereas for the great majority of people in our present earthly cycle this is not yet the case. Naturally, such advanced people can also follow a path of evolution that allows them to progress at their own rate. But these people can also fall behind in a certain way at different stages of their Earth evolution and live on into the Jupiter evolution in such a way that at some critical point in the Jupiter evolution they say, as it were: "If everything were going the way it should in the regular course of cosmic evolution, we'd be experiencing this or that on Jupiter right now. But we don't want this. We are stopping at the point we reached during Earth evolution." Perhaps this standpoint is a higher one than any that human beings have been able to attain in the course of Earth evolution; its nature is such that during Earth evolution the Jupiter evolution may already have been anticipated. But these beings, who are human beings in this case, do nevertheless remain behind at the point they were at on Earth, after which they place themselves into the Jupiter evolution with a Jupiter evolution they already went through during the Earth period. As a result they've fallen behind with respect to their own personal standard of development, but not in terms of the evolutionary scheme in general. They are just not evolving the way human beings in general will on Jupiter; they remain Earth beings, Earth human beings, but they bear within them the Jupiter evolution they're bringing with them from the Earth.

You must be absolutely clear that the various evolutionary processes are really quite complex and that processes such as the ones I've just characterized do actually exist. And if you now transfer what I said about "Jupiter-Earth" back to "Earth-Moon," you will begin to get an idea of who this Mephistopheles is that appears in Goethe's *Faust*. He has to be included in the Ahrimanic hierarchies because he already anticipated the Earth evolution of the human being during the Old Moon period but now places himself into the Earth period in such a way that he does not bring Earth reason, Earth intellect, Earth individuality into Earth evolution as they're given by the Earth, but rather as he acquired them ahead of time on Old Moon. This is why, in the "Prologue in Heaven," he feels so immensely superior to the human being, Faust. And he *is* superior to him, for Goethe intends this human being, Faust, to be a real human being of the Earth who has not remained behind in a region of dullards but relies entirely on earthly forces and earthly impulses to develop what he has to within his soul. Faust is a human being of the Earth, an Earthly fighter. Mephistopheles, as a "human being" of the Old Moon, naturally feels vastly superior to Faust when he comes face to face with him because he himself, while he was still in the spiritual regions of the Old Moon, took on the kind of reason and knowledge that earthly human beings otherwise only have on Earth. This, of course, is why Mephistopheles can only be a spiritual being. If he were to assume a human form like any other human being, he would have to accommodate himself to Earth evolution as well. But he doesn't do that. And so we see in Mephistopheles a being that can feel extraordinarily superior to an earthly human being. However, since the first possibility of having moral impulses only appears during Earth evolution—remember some of the lectures given here in just the past few weeks[†]—since human moral impulses, in particular everything arising from the impulse of love, only make their debut during the Earth period, Mephistopheles, who has kept a firm grip on his Old Moon evolution, doesn't just have these impulses of love as a matter of course. He does not have them as a matter of course. He thus belongs to a hierarchy of spiritual beings that was able to achieve a certain loftiness out of its whole collective nature because it held itself back and also rose to a very high level in former evolutionary epochs.

Let's compare this Mephistopheles with the higher angels. Imagine a present-day angel, in other words, a being that's now an angel, standing next to Mephistopheles. What kind of being is this one that's now an angel? It is a being that will have to descend during the Jupiter evolution in order to perform certain services for Jupiter's humanity that other beings—Let us say archangelic beings, for example—are performing for earthly humanity today. This angel is therefore a being that by its very nature, because it is spiritual, as it simply stands there next to Mephistopheles, is not as far along in its evolution as Mephistopheles himself is, or more specifically, as the hierarchy he belongs to is.† Only during the Jupiter evolution will the angelic beings be able to achieve the degree of intellectuality that Mephistopheles already achieved through his hierarchy during Old Moon—even if he did not do this through his own power, if we regard him as a "human being" of the Moon, as a Moon-initiate. One could even say that, despite having lagged behind in its evolution, the immediate superior of Mephistopheles is nevertheless an extraordinarily high-ranking being, so high, in fact, that a being such as one of the rank of the archangel Michael feels himself to be below the rank of Mephistopheles's immediate superior. These evolutionary processes complicate the ranking of the spiritual beings. A being such as Mephistopheles has developed very far during the Old Moon evolution. As a result, it is ahead of the normal development of the angels. But a being such as Mephistopheles has remained a spirit. Because it is a spirit, something in it is related to the normal evolution of the angels. Angels, after all, are spirits, too. So we can say: From the Mephistophelean point of view Mephistopheles is perfectly correct when he calls these angels an "infantile lot." Compared to him they really *are* an infantile lot, since they haven't advanced as far as he himself has along the lines he values so highly.

Now, of course, within the hierarchy of the angels there are all possible stages of evolution as well. There too, speaking in a somewhat pedantic, philistine manner, we can posit a "normal" stage of angelic evolution. But, we must also assume—and this is indeed a fact—that certain angels have lagged behind by "luciferizing" themselves, if I may coin such an expression. Certain angels lag behind in their normal development and become Luciferic. They don't go along with their fellow angels but remain behind at earlier stages. The angels that became Luciferic in this way, having actually already done so in the pre-Lemurian age of the Earth, continue to occupy a very special position today. For how did they manage to acquire the ability to "Luciferize" themselves at that time? If I were to express myself in everyday language, even though this can perhaps only be an approximation, because it can't be anything else, I'd have to say that at that time the group of beings who were human were just about to go through the [recapitulation of their Old] Moon-evolution. What now took place is what we call the Luciferic temptation, brought about by spiritual beings that had Luciferized themselves. This luciferization led certain beings to bring about for human beings during the Lemurian evolution what you know about from my *Outline of Esoteric Science*. After this the Ahrimanic evolution set in and brought about the developments during the Atlantean period that you are also familiar with from *Esoteric Science* and from recent lectures. We thus have to say that during the ancient Lemurian period a certain impulse went out from Luciferic quarters in which all the beings that had previously Luciferized themselves took part on behalf of humanity. The nature of this impulse[†] was such that it caused the human being to descend more deeply into the material world during Earth evolution than this being should have in its normal course of development; its longings, drives and passions thereby became, as we could say, deeply entangled in this material evolution. Some kind of counterweight had to be provided, and this came in the form of the Ahrimanic evolution. As a result the human being now sways in the balance between the Luciferic and the Ahrimanic evolutionary streams. In a certain higher sense, however, or "style," this delicate balance is part of the whole scheme of progressive evolution.

Now that I have recapitulated all this for you, you can say to yourselves that Faust, a real Earth being, will face both Luciferic and Ahrimanic powers. And Goethe shows you the Ahrimanic powers Faust is facing, especially in the figure of Mephistopheles, whom he places at Faust's side as the representative of Ahrimanic power. We have already spoken about why Goethe refrained from giving us a detailed picture of how Faust is approached by the Luciferic impulses. Nevertheless, as I have pointed out, it shimmers through everywhere that Goethe really did place Faust right in the middle between the Mephistophelean and the Luciferic powers. I have repeatedly and expressly emphasized the fact that because spiritual science as we have it today didn't exist in Goethe's time he was not yet able to get an absolutely clear picture of how Faust relates as a human being to Ahriman-Mephistopheles and to Lucifer. And yet he did have a certain instinctive awareness that Faust faces these two kinds of impulses.

Now we wonder: What did Mephistopheles himself, or his relatives, as the case may be, actually have in mind for human beings? What he had in mind for human beings is actually nothing less than what would have made the very existence of human beings on Earth impossible. For only on Earth did human reproduction by means of the sexes, the male-female principle, become possible for the very first time. Mephistopheles, a real Moon-initiate who has only lagged behind, absolutely can't stand this; to rid the world of the possibility of having a human race on Earth by means of sexual reproduction is what he regards as his most important task. This must not be. Let's state this very precisely. Normal human evolution on Earth consists of the human race reproducing itself *on the Earth* by means of the sexes. But Mephistopheles wanted to remain behind at the stage of the Old Moon evolution. For this reason he did not want love to lead to love between the sexes on Earth. Mephistopheles is the enemy of love between the sexes on Earth. In fact, he is its archenemy. He therefore feels especially called to reduce to absurdity anything that in any way leads to love between the sexes. Goethe characterizes this absolutely correctly. What Mephistopheles wants to have happen in the relationship between Faust and Gretchen—well, just read the Gretchen scenes with close attention and you will sense everywhere that he wants all kinds of things that are within the purview of Ahriman-Mephistopheles. But a love between Faust and Gretchen, a genuine, human, earthly love, is the one thing he does not want to come about, and he will not tolerate it, either from Faust or from Gretchen. On the other hand, he is completely in his element in the laboratory where Homunculus is being produced. You know from other presentations I have made on *Faust* that the reason Homunculus is produced at all is so that he himself can become a producer of something human—Helen—directly out of Nature, without the intervention of any love between the sexes. Mephistopheles sets himself the task of producing a certain type of humanity: not one with a progressive evolution that runs its course on Earth through sexual love, but one produced along a different path. It will come from forces that have been allotted to Ahriman and will be of a very different sort than the human race that was intended for the Earth. Think of more than just Homunculus: Euphorion, for example, or the whole way in which Helen comes up again: everywhere you see Mephistopheles at work. But nowhere in all this should there be the slightest trace of any regular love between the sexes. Mephistopheles could therefore not have been assigned a better role, and this role can be fully justified from the standpoint of spiritual science. There is immense depth in this.

And now take this peculiar passage, spoken by Mephistopheles just as the heavenly host begins to make its appearance:

> Discordant tones I hear, a nasty tinkling,
> Come from above and with this day unwelcome;
> It's like the plunking of little girls and boys,
> Which sanctimonious taste would love to hear.
> You know how we in deeply loathsome hours
> Planned out annihilation for the human race. (11685-90)

Mephistopheles credits the angels with knowing that they themselves were looking on as he and his cohorts were planning out the annihilation of the human race. Now he takes on the speech of an earthly human being as he goes on to say:

> The thing most shameful we invented, (11691)

The most shameful thing is this very annihilation of the human race. One calls it "the thing most shameful."

It is of course extremely difficult to approach these things, for in them Goethe wanted to express the deepest human feelings, sensations and knowledge that he himself was able to have as a spiritual being. In order to move forward in understanding these things we will need to make something like the following observation. You know that—for us, at least—there exists a spiritual science, even though today it is only at the beginning of its development. You also know that there always was such a thing, even though in earlier ages it was attained in a different way: a true knowledge of the world that goes beyond mere surface appearance and finds its way to reality. Now you are also aware that this spiritual treasure, which was preserved in the mysteries and aimed at true knowledge of the world, was watched over in an especially careful way, particularly in more ancient times. Furthermore, this spiritual treasure was communicated only to those who showed that they were mature enough to receive it. If we now ask what the nature of this special way of knowing actually was, in other words, what kind of spiritual treasure was being communicated in those mysteries, the best way to go about answering this is to compare our fifth post-Atlantean period with the ages preceding it: the Greco-Roman, the Egypto-Chaldean, and so on.† We might also ask, in making this comparison, how the entire way in which human beings have conceived the world has changed in passing from those earlier periods of time down to our present cultural epoch. It is really true that important and significant things have occurred in the course of human evolution, and that it is only a *fable convenue*† to believe that all we need to know about human evolution is what our trivial history, or what people nowadays call history, tells us. The earlier cultural eras were completely different from the way they were imagined to be according to the *fable convenue* of customary history. Remember the depth of a verse such as the one I cited once before†:

> O Sun, of this world a king,
> By Luna is your race preserv'd;
> By Mercury you two are wed.
> In vain is all if you lack Venus' favor
> Who Mars has chosen as your man.
> Jove's grace is your support and stay
> That thereby Saturn, old and gray,
> Himself in many colors may display.

An immense depth lies behind the clumsy wording of such a verse, but this depth was really there once. There was a time when people saw into the realities a verse like this was pointing to, even if they could only do so with the results of an atavistic clairvoyance. The fifth post-Atlantean period has come forth out of this knowledge of the foundations of all existence, but it has strayed from its proper path in two directions. I characterized one of these directions for you in a certain way by calling it the initiation of the fifth post-Atlantean period, which

I illustrated with the work of Lord Bacon, Bacon of Verulam.† Here we have the longing to treat everything outside the realm of the sense-perceptible as mere idols. As you know, Bacon postulated four types of idols, which we've already mentioned: *idola tribus, idola specus, idola fori* and *idola theatri.*† At the beginning of the fifth post-Atlantean period, the one tendency expressed itself through these through Bacon's mind, namely, the tendency to base everything, absolutely everything, only on knowledge obtained through sensory observation and through concepts that are themselves the results of sensory observation. Everything that goes beyond sensory observation is an "idol" whose content amounts to nothing more than words. This is the one stream, as it were, and we have already characterized it.

Now Let's take the other stream that expresses itself in such words as: "O Sun, of this world a king," words that still penetrate deeply into the foundations of existence. Let's express this stream in the form of a diagram to see how it continues on into the future. We can say that if it wanted to develop purely on its own from the fourth post-Atlantean period over into the fifth, it would go this way (white line in drawing). The stream that evolves in the direction of the idols goes down underneath this evolutionary stream (blue line). It refuses to acknowledge that a spiritual reality can be perceived just as directly as a sensory reality can; it disposes of everything spiritual by regarding it as nothing more than what is contained in the word-idols. This, then, is the evolutionary stream inaugurated by Bacon.

Now, what would be the opposite of this? Its counter-image would be an evolutionary stream that would recognize the presence of a spiri-

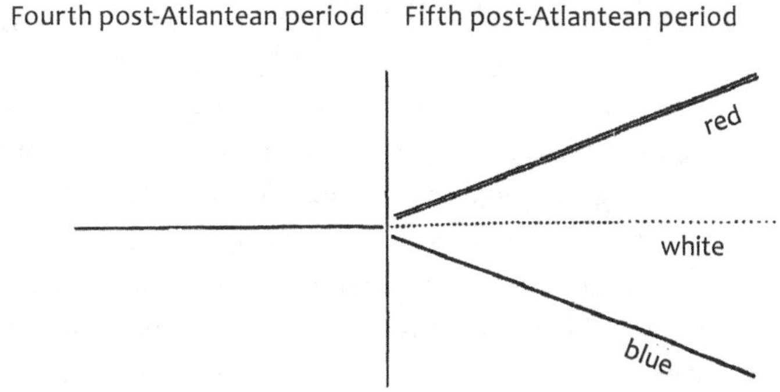

tual or soul-spiritual element but nothing of a physical-material nature at all. That would be the contrasting image. We could therefore ask: Is this stream present as well? Just as Bacon says that the only reality is a sensory reality and that anything else is nothing but word-idols, is there also an expression for the idea that the only reality there is, is spiritual and that there is nothing material-physical that enters our senses? Indeed, there is. Somewhat later than Bacon there lived a man by the name of George Berkeley,† and he represents this other line of evolution (red line). Let me make clear in a few words what the essential feature of Berkeley's worldview is.

Berkeley's view essentially grew out of his theological background as an [Anglican] bishop. For him, everything that is outside the human being and perceived by the senses is only present as long as it is being perceived by the senses. We can perhaps best characterize this view by means of a contrast. Imagine the following, starting from a point of view that is naive compared to Berkeleianism itself: Let's say you come into the room and see Mr. Bauer sitting here,† but when you see him you assume he had already been sitting there beforehand and you are now seeing him later on. As we said, there is not the least bit of evidence that what you see sitting on this chair was there before you saw it. And when you go out again, you think the gentleman keeps on sitting here and does so the whole time you're turning your back to him and going out. In Berkeley's view, there's no proof that what you saw here, Let us say, is still sitting here. It sits here as long as you look at it, for the picture-forming activity in your eye is something living, and how, after all, could this formative activity be going on in your eye if you weren't looking somewhere? Bacon's worldview can be completely proved by logic, and so can Berkeley's; for Berkeleianism contains no logical contradictions. It can be totally substantiated by logic, even though it is at odds with naïve consciousness. Berkeley is namely not of the opinion that you conjure up Mr. Bauer when you come into the room and make him disappear again when you go out. This is not his view. But it is his view that what you see *does* first come and then go away again with your act of looking. *Esse est percipi*: To be is to be perceived. And there is no other kind of being than to be perceived in the surrounding world. This is why for Berkeley, as you can now imagine, everything that makes up the world of the senses is only in a process of becoming. You look, and there it is; you look away, and it is gone again, no longer there. It is all only there in what you see as you are looking. As was said: *Esse est percipi*, nothing exists outside perception itself, outside the process of perceiving. But behind this process of perceiving, which is therefore nothing at all but this process of perceiving, stands divine-spiritual Being itself. It is not just your own perception that is concerned with Mr. Bauer; so is God, who places him wherever He will. And when you come in, this God creates the image of Mr. Bauer in you out of what is only in Him. Then, when you go away, He causes this image to disappear again. Therefore, this world of the senses does not exist; the soul-spiritual is all there is. All of you standing before me here are only the creations of my eyes. Over and above what my eyes create there is only the divine-spiritual, soul-spiritual world, which, however, maintains and carries you in quite a different way than you exist as the creation of my eyes.

I've only characterized this view, which is really capable of the most rigorous philosophical proof. But it is what provides the other half of the world given us by Baconism, so to speak. The worldview of the fifth post-Atlantean period as a whole vacillates between these two poles, in the red or in the blue direction. Either this worldview entangles itself in acknowledging only what is a reality for the senses and declares itself powerless to behold anything genuinely spiritual within this sensory reality; or else it exhausts itself in acknowledging only the soul-spiritual, seeing everywhere only God and divine thoughts and declaring itself powerless to come down into a sensory reality from its life in God and in divine thoughts. These two aberrations are absolute realities in the fifth post-Atlantean period. Whoever observes the life of the spirit as it evolves outside of esotericism will always find it developing in the one or the other of these two directions, the red line or the blue one. The external, exoteric aspect is not to be found along the line I've drawn here in white.

We can say that the human being of the fifth post-Atlantean period experiences a certain tension between these two ways of viewing the world. Goethe had a strong sense of this tension. What I've presented to you here could be called the theoretical, more philosophical impulses, but the matter did not stop with these, by any means. All life, as it progresses, weaves back and forth between the purely soul-spiritual aspect on the one hand and the purely material and sense-perceptible aspect on the other. Goethe was eminently aware of this tension. You will not find it surprising that he felt everything living in the external world as being under the influence of the stream of the blue line, for this is essentially the general direction of our evolution in the fifth post-Atlantean period: going as far as it can in the direction of the material and acknowledging nothing but the material.

But Goethe could already feel the other line as well. He felt it deeply; it was just that in his day it was really less problematic, shall we say, than it is today to call materialism materialistic and to point out the aberration that this blue line expresses. Today, spiritual science has to make the aberration of the blue line clear, and as a result it will have to bear the brunt of all sorts of fearful attacks. These must come, because what wants to enter the world as knowledge is always met at first by prejudice and hatred. More and more, materialism will come to be canonized, although in a worldly way. But we can say that materialism will be canonized, nevertheless. Materialistic medicine, just as many other endeavors today, is very close to declaring itself sacrosanct in the sense of materialism and of the aberration the blue line represents, the aberration away from the soul-spiritual. We must remember, however, that the soul-spiritual bears the sensory-material within it as its revelation. What is sense-perceptible and material belongs to the soul-spiritual, is one with it, and the unity of the two must be affirmed by what we call spiritual science. The so-called inquisitorial persecutions of earlier ages and within other realms have yet to come about in the realm of materialism. These, in fact, are only just now beginning to assert themselves, even though the forms are changing. The rebellion against the materialistic coloring of knowledge will fall prey to a future inquisition that will take somewhat different forms. This will happen just as surely as earlier aspirations fell prey to the inquisitions of their day. Make no mistake: everything that goes astray in the direction of the blue line will become just as intolerant as aspirations in other areas have.

The red line was less evident in former times. It did not separate off, as it were, until the fifth post-Atlantean period, and even then it did so somewhat later than the blue line did, but it was already a part of earlier endeavors. It actually appeared first in a special form, with Berkeley as its greatest and most significant philosophical representative, although it had a sufficient number of other representatives as well. It emerged in the fifth post-Atlantean age, but certain things remained from its earlier forms, and this was why in Goethe's day it was already problematic to speak seriously about the red line, whereas Goethe had no problem speaking about the blue line at all. What is actually striving along this red line that makes speaking about it so problematic? All those worldviews that refuse to extend their gaze out over the world, over the whole breadth of the world. These worldviews would like to revel in a universal soul-spiritual element that prefers to be powerless in the face of what our senses reveal. It is a way of looking at the world that wants to talk about the supersensible, but doesn't really want to *know* anything about it. We have a broad area here, and almost all the religious confessions and all the sects have gradually turned to it in the course of time, for the peculiar thing is that these worldviews scrupulously avoid any real comprehension of the world. All they want to do is speak about something or other of a supersensible nature in the most general terms while reveling in their speaking. What they *don't* want is to acquire the positive, concrete power of knowing which would enable them to take what they arrive at and talk about and really dive down with it into the world of reality.

Maybe you will understand better what I am getting at if I try to say it this way. Imagine what an average person's life looks like today. Let's say this person is a man who spends six days a week in a factory or an office or wherever, working with nothing but what he observes with his physical senses. There is nothing spiritual in any of this today and there is less and less as time goes by. In fact, it is just the opposite. Anyone who attempts to bring something spiritual into it comes across as a real nut case. However, all the forces modern science is willing to recognize in this area are functioning, every human connection and relationship that the modern worldview wants to pounce on and make its own. In short, everything has been fully worked out in the way of thoughts and concepts that indulge themselves in a running commentary on the reality spread out before our eyes. Now suppose that our friend, who has spent his whole week in a factory or an office dealing with what can be known in a purely material way—or has even been teaching it, since nothing is taught in typical schools today but what can be known in a purely material way—suppose, to his credit, that he is a very decent, sincere person who goes to church on Sunday. There he hears people speaking as people do in churches today about things as they have evolved over the past few centuries. Now please try, if you can—and by that I mean if you've gone to church often enough to be able to do this and have listened to sermons with open ears and have seen what goes on there with open eyes—try and ask yourselves: Was there anything in what you heard there that was really capable of shedding light on the world we see outspread around us? The claim is, of course, that the God spoken of there is the foundation of the world, but nowhere is anything ever said about how this divinity uses its forces and impulses to reach into world processes and act in them. There is one worldview for six days of the week—the blue line—and another one for Sunday—the red line. If we look really closely, we see that we never, ever, have any connection between the two. Just ask yourselves: What does what is taught from the pulpit have to do with chemistry, physics or biology? No connection is sought at all; in fact, people are horrified that there might even be such a connection.

If you now take spiritual science, you can see right away what the difference is. Spiritual science does not speak about the sense-perceptible, material world as ordinary physics or chemistry do, but does so in such a way that all the details of what it says about the spiritual world can flow into what it says about the physical-sensory world. It doesn't have one view for weekdays and one for Sunday, but rather a view that pours itself out over the spiritual world and then flows down, as it were, into the details of the physical, sense-perceptible world. It does not declare itself powerless to grasp the world of the senses from the standpoint of the spiritual, as Berkleianism does. It also doesn't declare itself powerless to find the spirit in the world of the senses, as Baconism does, which only finds idols there instead. Where does all this come from, anyway? Well, we've already seen where. It is inherent in the very nature of the fifth post-Atlantean period that the evolution indicated schematically by the blue line should have come about. We were able to name Bacon as its inaugurator. At some time or other the human being had to plunge down fully into matter. I've dealt with this topic many times, as well as with the fact that spiritual science is by no means opposed to materialism but understands why the material stage of evolution is noticed and recognized as such in the fifth post-Atlantean period. But it can't be recognized as such unless one allows oneself to be inspired by a spirit such as Ahriman. And no matter how long you allow this materialism of the fifth post-Atlantean period to continue developing in its Ahrimanic sense—and you can be sure of this, but what will assure you of it is not the fact that I say it but rather that you will understand it out of the whole spirit of spiritual science—this materialistic-Ahrimanic way of thinking will have to hold fast to what Ahriman-Mephistopheles swore "in deeply loathsome hours" (11689), namely, to want to have nothing to do with the regular progression of the human race on Earth. For this reason, this science, which has grown out of this materialism, will never fully penetrate the mystery of human incarnation, the riddle of embryology, and so on—never! It would be able to arrive at an understanding of the origin of such beings that can form themselves the way Homunculus does. But this science will never come to this point [i.e., to the point of understanding the aforementioned riddles.] Now this is only one stream of evolution. But many, many things are connected with this Ahrimanism. Knowledge is only one part of it. Nevertheless, this Ahrimanism runs through the whole of modern culture.

Goethe felt the other stream, indicated schematically by the red line, equally deeply; it just was not possible for him, we might say, to put forms for it on stage that were as clear as the ones he was able to put there for the blue line. For the blue line he came up with the figures of Mephistopheles and his Fat and Skinny Devils and the Lemures. There they are, standing right in front of us. This much he dared to do. I say "dared" because from our own age onward people who speak about the Lemures and the Fat and Skinny Devils the way we do in spiritual science are going to be slandered more and more. In Goethe's time this was not yet as problematic as it is today. But something else was problematic, and Goethe saw this quite clearly. This was the fact that he well knew that if this red line inserts itself into our present age, if a view is really present that declares itself powerless and will declare itself ever more powerless to move forward from the acknowledgement of the soul-spiritual to a thorough penetration of the real world, then this view is based on the fact that certain Luciferic spirits are keeping streams that were justified in earlier times from progressing further in their development. Groups of Luciferic beings are keeping certain currents, religious and sectarian currents, from making further progress. These streams are therefore unable to penetrate the world and have gotten bogged down in merely acknowledging that the soul-spiritual exists. Berkeleianism is only one special expression of this, based as it is on a kind of Luciferic retardation. How does it express itself for Goethe, for example? Mephistopheles remembers himself and his siblings, those who once "in deeply loathsome hours"—which means something different in the language of Mephistopheles—swore annihilation for the human race, meaning that they wished to know nothing about the way the human race populates the earth. Mephistopheles remembers it to be an essential part of his nature that in the Age of Ahriman, pictorially speaking, he had been present at a significant meeting of his spirits who determined at that time that no human being should ever be born on earth in a natural way; instead, the forces existing on earth as sexual ones should be used for something completely different. In that ancient time, these Ahrimanic beings decided not to allow love between the sexes to even come into being. But now—without identifying himself, of course, but imagining himself in Mephistopheles's place—Goethe says: There are others, not inspired by Mephistopheles, but inspired nevertheless. These, to be sure, don't say anything about how the human race on earth is not supposed to reproduce in a normal human way. But they begin to pray, and then they find that people who don't do anything in the sense of normal human reproduction are the first ones to lead the truly holy life, who disregard it and don't want to know anything about it. These are the ascetics, the saints, who go around with those well-known long faces we have often spoken about when it comes to anything having to do with the love between the sexes. Mephistopheles, on the other hand, assumes there are such beings in the host of angels, and he finally sees them there. There he sees the inspirers of these other ones, who are basically worshiping what Mephistopheles and his siblings have decided on:

> . . . how we in deeply loathsome hours
> Planned out annihilation for the human race;
> The thing most shameful we invented,
> Is just the thing their worship needs. (11689-92)

This is what their worship is fixed on. The Luciferized inspirers of less-progressive church communities, communities of monks, and various sectarian tendencies, the Luciferized inspirers, are really standing there among the other hosts. Not for nothing does Mephistopheles say to the one tall fellow that he finds especially pleasing:

> The priestly look is not for you at all. (11795)

At this point Goethe secretly inserted much of what was weighing heavily on his soul concerning the worldview that goes around with a priestly look, the Sunday worldview he considered Luciferic in comparison to the Ahrimanic one. Mephistopheles feels related to those who have taken up into their worship what he himself has taken up into his science and into his will.

How we have to think about all these things in a purely spiritual-scientific way is something we can speak about later. Now, however, we want to speak about them in the Goethean sense. What I have just been speaking of is an "archetypal" Goethean feeling, if I may put it that way. At first the Ahrimanic world—Lemures, Fat Devils, Skinny Devils—stands opposite something that bears a faint tinge of the Luciferic. Goethe expresses this quite clearly. As I said, something with a Luciferic tinge stands opposite the Mephistophelian element but does so in such a veiled way that this can only be expressed by the one personality who has, well, been granted permission to do such things, namely, the Devil. He can speak about the "priestly look," the "most beloved boys," and so on. These things are actually standing there, face to face: on one side Mephistopheles, who, as we might say, has mortgaged Faust's soul. How has he mortgaged it? By driving Faust through everything of an earthly nature that reaches down into the sub-earthly realm, beneath the sphere that has come about in the process of Earth evolution and beneath human incarnation, which takes place through sexual love. He can lay claim to Faust's soul because he has led him into the whole Ahrimanic realm. However, even though Mephistopheles really can't do anything about what came into Gretchen's love through Faust, he has done a pretty good job of turning it into its opposite. Afterwards everything takes a completely Ahrimanic turn. Only Ahrimanic devices come into play in order to conjure up certain external features of the world of ancient Greece. What Ahrimanic wiles are capable of achieving is first of all achieved within the context of the State—let's say this very quietly. Then it is sought in the realm of human becoming, in connection with evolution, but with sub-human and sub-animal evolution, in connection with the mechanized Homunculus, the historically mechanized Homunculus. Helen is brought up from the Underworld in a manner totally at variance with earthly human existence. Then some earthly activities are engineered, but in the final analysis the beings that help do this, in the form of Eilebeute ("Speedy Booty") and Habebald ("Get-it-Quick"), are, well, not Earth beings at all. Under the influence of Ahrimanic devices, all of this is already very much in hock, and is so by virtue of the only thing Ahriman can have from the actual blessing of the Earth, which is the human being—by virtue of the fact, in other words, that he leads the human being through shallow insignificance. And as far as Earth existence is concerned, it is only shallow insignificance, although for all that it is not something that doesn't have an enormous amount of reason and science in it. This is why the soul is in hock to him. But it is also in hock through the other thing he has from the actual blessing of the Earth. What is this other thing? Only now, on Earth, has the human being received its "I," and therefore, only now, its blood as well. Mephisto can have bones, tendons and ligaments, whatever constitutes the patched-together half-beings of the Lemures. Of course he would like to have the actual blessing of the Earth as well: the blood itself, which is the representative, the physical-material representative, of the human being of Earth. But that's the very thing he cannot have. Since his evolution came to a stop on Old Moon, all he can have from that is the title signed in blood, only what can be put into the form of an abstract contract, as it were, something in no way connected with the impulses that exist in reality but remaining in the abstract realm of the contractual. That is all Mephistopheles can extract from the blood. He cannot extract the living impulse itself.

The soul is in hock to him. Well, in his language, it seems the host of angels has simply smuggled it away from him, snuck off with it. But that's not quite the way things are. As we showed yesterday, Mephisto already has Faust pretty much in his claws right up to the moment of his death. But if you view his death as we did yesterday, not as waiting until Faust falls over for it to occur but as setting in gradually, then you see that what Faust experiences after his soul has loosened itself from his body, and especially the blissful feeling I described in closing yesterday, is an experience he has when he is already in the spiritual world. At that point Faust's soul—or as Goethe first wrote, Faust's "entelechy,"[†] which we'll talk about tomorrow —slips over into the Luciferic sphere, where it would dissolve away. If this were to happen, Faust would profit from it just as little as if he were to fall prey to Mephistopheles. Just think what a threat this is to him!

> Turn now to clarity,
> Flames, with your loving!
> May all the self-condemned
> Be healed by truth;
> That from the Evil One,
> Joyful, self-saved,
> In intimate union
> They may know bliss. (11801-08)

But this bliss would lead to dissolution in the Universal All and thereby to a transition into the Eighth Sphere![†] The result of all this for Faust would be his dissolution in the universe, which would be the same thing as annihilation. Now look at the last scene. I've already spoken of its necessary connection with the previous one: of how it belongs to it and must be there. We see the action continuing on in it, but now in an entirely different realm. Again the angels come, bringing Faust's entelechy or immortal part with them. But as they bring this entelechy, this immortal part, they tell us what has enabled them to bring it here. As the Younger Angels say in the final scene:

Roses from the lovely hands
Of loving, holy penitents
Helped us gain the victory
And carry out the noble deed
Of capturing this treasured soul. (11942-46)

And so it is that the angels—not through their own nature, but through the fact that they have the roses of the loving, holy Penitent Women—the angels lift Faust's soul, or entelechy, out of the human sphere, out of that element into which human beings have grown who have experienced what it is like to live as earthly humans on Earth and have really developed further as a result of their earthly lives. Goethe shifts the whole evolution away from Mephisto and the angels and onto human evolution by having the angels rescue the entelechy, not through their own power only, but by virtue of the fact that they've received the roses from the hands of the loving, holy penitents. This is a thought of infinite profundity. Here Goethe reveals his conviction of the importance of the ongoing evolution of humanity and of the Earth. And this is why he has to find something in the nature of the *human* being that overcomes the merely Ahrimanic-Mephistophelian. We see Mephistopheles standing there, giving orders to the Lemures—those half-natures that are just patched together out of bones, ligaments and tendons—as well as to the Fat and Skinny Devils. I have explained what this means: that the only thing there is in all this, is sub-human Nature, which could never give rise to a human being, Nature as a kind of bedrock out of which no human being can ever grow. Now everything in *this* is something that the worldview running along the blue line can comprehend, but the world around us must not be understood this way. Ever since his time during Old Moon Mephistopheles has had only those forces at his disposal that can give orders to the Lemures and the Fat and Skinny Devils. But what these beings draw out of Nature—out of Earth Nature, that is—is only its Mephistophelian aspect, whereas something else can be drawn out of it as well which Mephistopheles cannot know because, in his way, he did not take part in Earth evolution. What draws it out is the search for the relationship with the earthly forces and elements, carried out under the inspiration of the—now real—sanctification and ennoblement of physical Nature.

> Infinite fire of bliss,
> Luminous bond of love,
> Turbulent pain in my breast,
> Feverish joy in God,
> Arrows, tear through my flesh,
> Lances, restrain my flesh,
> Cudgels, now batter me,
> Lightning bolts, shatter me; (11854-61)

And so on. Here you have the storming-through of Nature, which is so much a part of the human being and yet rises up to a higher level, in spite of its also being bound up with what is Luciferic and devilish. Here you have this Nature. And on the Earth, or for the Earth, the angels have been assigned the task of taking along with them the care and nurturing of the human race. The angels that do not lag behind but advance to the point where they can nurture and care for the human race, as should be the case on Earth, are the ones Goethe regards as the actual saviors. Remember what mission the Lord gives the genuine angels:

> But you, who are true sons of gods,
> Are to rejoice in Beauty, rich in life!
> May what's becoming, ever working, living,
> Embrace you with the holy bounds of Love (344-47)

Their task is to help and intervene, and this they do. The angels that concern themselves with the loving, holy penitents and receive the roses from them are the ones who really advance among the angelic hosts. Just as each individual human being takes up the task allotted to it in Earth evolution, so do these angels, who don't lag behind during the Old Moon evolution but go along with Earth evolution, accept the forces offered them by beings such as those portrayed in the last act in the form of the loving, holy penitents. This brings them forward. Goethe's conviction is that the angels will evolve on beyond the Luciferic. As I said, my intention with all this has been to give some indication of what Goethe's idea is and how he was connected with all the great ideas of evolution in his own way.

We will speak more tomorrow. I hope you have seen from what was presented today how Goethe plumbs the depths of evolution and its cosmic secrets in order to create his *Faust*, as well as how he wanted to pass his judgment on the main currents of thought that were then developing. Very, very much indeed is contained in this *Faust*! And we must admit that humanity would derive infinite benefit from trying to orient itself along the lines of everything that Goethe, to use his own expression, "secretly inserted" in it. But we want to speak further about all this tomorrow, as well as about some connections of these *Faust*-ideas with the ideas of spiritual science.

18
Goethe Plumbs the Depths of Evolution and its Cosmic Secrets in his *Faust*: The Luciferic and the Ahrimanic Temptation

Dornach, September 11, 1916

After a performance of the "Midnight" and "Burial" scenes with eurythmy

There would of course be very much to say if we were to take every topic that flows out of the thoughts contained in these closing scenes of Goethe's *Faust* and deal with it from all the perspectives in which it presents itself quite naturally to spiritual science. Today, however, I would like to select a few more things from what could still be said without giving the impression that this could at all exhaust the subject.

I have already pointed out the two important facts of Earth evolution that we have to start with in particular in order to understand these closing scenes. The first of these is in the Lemurian period, and the second one is in the Atlantean period. I will only characterize them as far as we need to for today. The fact having to do with the Lemurian period, as seen from one perspective, is that as a result of all the events you can read about in *An Outline of Esoteric Science* or in the lecture cycles, human beings entered more deeply into matter than was originally intended. This came about through the Luciferic impulse. As a result, one of the intentions was fulfilled, as it were, that Mephistopheles is referring to when he speaks of what he and the others undertook in those deeply loathsome hours when annihilation was being planned out for the human race (11689-90). With this fact—that humanity entered more deeply into matter than had actually been intended—human consciousness connected itself in a different way than it should have with everything the human being's existence in Earth evolution signifies. We have often pointed out that as a result of this Luciferic impulse the human being now connects a completely different type of awareness with procreation, with sexual reproduction. At that time, sexual reproduction was drawn into the domain of conscious awareness, so to speak, and we can say that in a certain sense what had originally been a supersensible fact had thereby been made into a sense-perceptible fact. That's the first thing.

The other fact, which we then find in the Atlantean period, is that by that time the human being was already more deeply entrenched in sensory experience than it was originally intended to be, and this led to its shaping its entire organism in such a way that what we could call the "ahrimanization" of the human being could take place, in that it connected its spiritual forces with the sensory-physical forces and facts of Nature, as we have often described. You know that in the Bible the first of these two facts is expressed in the image of the Luciferic seduction. This image can be characterized chiefly by the words Lucifer speaks in referring to the human race: "Your eyes will be opened and you will know the difference between good and evil."[†] Your eyes will be opened: this absorption of sensuality into conscious awareness through the opening of the eyes is precisely what constitutes the fall of humanity into matter. So that, now, humanity had fallen more deeply into matter than it had been predestined to do. The original intention had been for humanity to look upon the material world from outside the material world. Through the Luciferic seduction humanity sank down into the material world, and through the Ahrimanic aspect of the Atlantean period a relationship of the human being to what is material came about *within* the material which should have come about *above* it, so to speak, in its spiritual counterimage. What should have taken place up above, hovering, as it were, above the material, took place within the material itself.

The first fact is expressed by the words spoken over the human being: "Your eyes will be opened and you will know the difference between good and evil"—externally, by means of sense perception. The second fact is expressed in the Bible, as you know, in the words: "And the sons of the gods found that the daughters of men were beautiful, and they joined with them in matter." This biblical passage expresses a far-reaching fact, as I'd like to say basing my remarks on the human being and what lives in the human being. For everything that has to do with the way Ahriman works in the human race is included in this far-reaching fact. Through the same power with which heavenly love sank down, drew into matter and became earthly love—through the power underlying the fact of the transformation of heavenly love into earthly love—through these impulses, and this fact, it was at the same time brought about that the human intellect connected with matter in an earthly way and created the materialistic form of science. Ahrimanic impulses find their expression in the most human of all facts,[†] as it were, namely: "And the sons of the gods found that the daughters of men were beautiful, and they joined with them in the flesh." If these Ahrimanic impulses had not gained a foothold in the human being and thereby entered the human race, those other impulses would not have entered also which make use of the human intellect to produce all kinds of instruments that are only combinations of material forces and that consist in the fact that every possible thing is produced by machinery for any purpose whatsoever, even though this purpose is the annihilation of the human race. If this Ahrimanic seduction had not taken place, it would not have become possible on Earth to think up such things as instruments of murder. For if human beings had kept the relationship between the intellect and creative activity up above and not down below in matter, they would not now also be pouring the intellect into matter in order to create structures like the ones being created in our purely demonic mechanisms that are playing an ever increasing role in the materialization of human culture. Just as all the confusions and aberrations of human emotional life are expressed through the fact: "And your eyes will be opened, and you will know"—externally, through your senses—"the difference between good and evil," so are all the facts that both the pride of human beings and the Ahrimanic nature of human beings stare at in amazement, as it were, as being great steps in the progress of humanity: this purely mechanical culture, which originated in the same principle as what is hinted at in the Bible: "And the sons of the gods found that the daughters of men were beautiful and they joined with them in the flesh." The documents express these things in their own unique way. Within a certain area they shine their light on where these impulses are at home. But the impulses themselves are at work as far as the eye can see. In the present age, it must be fully recognized that the task of humanity is to overcome the Luciferic and the Ahrimanic. A clear insight must spread out more and more in our time over what has come about through the opening of our eyes and through the joining of the sons of gods with the "daughters of men"—through the descent, in other words, of heavenly love to earthly love. This must be fully illuminated by the light of clear understanding.

With his instinctive feeling-knowledge, Goethe reached out and felt the need for this clarity of understanding just as he was composing the final scenes of *Faust.* This is of such enormous significance. What is this all about, anyway? As you know, we don't accomplish anything by saying: "Oh, I'm going to run away from Lucifer; I'm going to run away from Ahriman." That's just foolish talk, because we can't do either. All we can do is strike a balance between the two. So what we have to do in the course of future human evolution is paralyze the Luciferic with the Ahrimanic and the Ahrimanic with the Luciferic. Goethe sensed this and inserted it secretly into the final scenes of his *Faust.*

Let us once more recall the profoundly unnerving scene with Care. Remember how it was said in an earlier lecture cycle that the rightful kingdom of Ahriman-Mephistopheles is the kingdom of death.[†] In a certain way therefore, annihilation—dying—already belongs to the kingdom of Ahriman; he just must not be allowed to apply his impulses in the wrong place. If he applies them to situations where they don't belong, the result will be something very bad. Goethe has Lack, Need, and Guilt leave the scene the moment the physical body begins to loosen itself from the soul-spiritual. By doing this Goethe shows he knows the connections that exist, precisely for life spent in the physical body on Earth, between the human being on the one hand and Lack, Need and Guilt on the other. But once the soul is somewhat loose and the three have already said that death is drawing near, Care, who is after all the sister of the other three, remains. She stays on, we could say, during the time when death is already at work. The figure of Care has been sent in from Ahriman's rightful realm. Ahriman could not do anything worse for Faust than to keep Care from remaining with him during the whole onset of his death, for quite mysterious forces play into this. Here we touch upon a deep mystery. What does Care do, this figure of Care who has been brought here by Mephistopheles-Ahriman, just as all the gray women have been, since Mephisto's magic keeps on working all the way up to this point? What does Care do? She destroys everything in Faust that Lucifer has managed to achieve: she closes Faust's eyes again. Think of the depth in this way of looking at the world! What has come to the human being through Lucifer's impulse now becomes paralyzed by an impulse of Ahriman's, working in an indirect way through the figure of Care. It was through Lucifer that the human being became a seeing being in the realm of the physical. Now this human being is made blind again—that is, in such a way that he acquires an inner way of seeing—by the figure brought in here, sent in here, from the Ahrimanic realm.

> And yet within my self there shines bright light. (11500)

The depth of this is immense. What Goethe is really seeking here in the dying Faust is not to undo the effects of the Luciferic on a human being, but to shape the Luciferic in such a way that it enters life in balance with the Ahrimanic. And now Care utters a profound word, as it were, in order to interpret what she's doing. Lucifer had once said: You humans shall become seeing because your eyes shall be opened. What does Care say? Care confronts the Luciferic with the Ahrimanic. It is true that humans have become able to see in an externally physical way, but they're blind to anything spiritual and remain this way their whole life long. How can this blindness be overcome? By consciously diving down into it, grasping it, recognizing it; this is how spiritual sight, spiritual vision, can be regained. Now Care speaks words of which we could well say at first that they're just as full of mystery for clever people as they are for fools:

> Human beings all their lives are blind,
> Now, Faust, become so in the end as well! (11497-98)

This is what Care seems to be saying:

> Human beings all their lives are blind,
> Now, Faust, become so in the end as well! (11497-98)

At first we cannot make head nor tail of these two sentences. We wonder what in the world they mean. From the physical point of view, people can see their whole life long, but Care calls this being "blind."

> Now, Faust, become so in the end as well! (11498)

Now he really does become blind. But she's using this word in a completely different way; what she really means is that he receives a power of inner vision. It is all a matter of learning to read these sentences in the right way, which is, that

> Human beings all their lives *are blind*,
> Now, Faust, *become so* in the end as well! (11497-98)

Experiencing means *becoming*. For human beings, *being* blind is simply a given. But Faust isn't supposed to *be* blind; he is supposed to experience what it is like to enter into blindness. *Become* blind; experience the connection between being able to see and being blind as the one is changing into the other. Now take this passage and connect it with a different one:

> But you, who truly are the sons of gods,
> Rejoice in Beauty, rich in life!
> May what's becoming (344-46)

(he points right to it!)

> May what's becoming, ever working, living,
> Embrace you with the holy bounds of Love. (346-47)

That which "becomes" as it lives and works on into eternity is referred to in the "Prologue in Heaven" as "the spiritual," as the reflection of the spiritual; and this "becoming" is now poured out over Faust by Care:

> Human beings all their lives are blind,
> Now, Faust, become so in the end as well! (11497-98)

Experiencing the connection between seeing and being blind as a process of "becoming" is a very different thing from not experiencing it by simply being in a state of "seeing blindness."

If we know Goethe well, we can easily relate to his peculiar feelings about "being" and "becoming." And then, precisely by looking at this passage in this particular way, we come to something very, very deep about Goethe. It shows us how Goethe presses forward to the most profound mysteries of the human being. Faust's blinding by Care is really the counterpart of the human being's receiving the power of sight through Lucifer in Paradise.

Now to go on. Let us take a look at Mephistopheles as he stands there in front of the sons of the gods, who have received the roses from the hands of the loving, holy penitents so that they can really have this soul-treasure. What has happened here? These penitent women were once on the Earth; they experienced earthly love, which had been brought into being by the Ahrimanic seduction during the Atlantean period. But what was achieved by the experiences of human beings such as the ones these penitent women had to go through? Earthly love became heavenly again! Gretchen herself, as we see at the end, bore the earthly love she had experienced up into the regions of the spirit. What took place here on Earth was transformed into something spiritual and heavenly. Gretchen is up among the Penitent Women who are strewing the roses. Love that became earthly comes to meet us again in heavenly form, having been led back into the heavenly realm through the human process: the process of passing through what human beings are able to experience. At the place where the Bible speaks of the heavenly seduction, it is expressing the idea that heavenly love has become earthly love; Goethe is pointing to the human process, in which earthly love again becomes heavenly. Mephistopheles, meanwhile, stands down below as someone who is also a son of the gods himself but now joins with the "daughters of men," who have become spiritual again, through the roses they have strewn. The process is the opposite of the one hinted at by the Bible: And the sons of the gods joined with the daughters of men. The Mephistopheles who once went astray with the "daughters of men" connects himself again with the "daughters of men" who have been taken up by the gods. It is the same process, but this time in reverse. Each process is turned into its opposite: the Paradise process of the Luciferic seduction and the later one as well, hinted at by the words: The sons of the gods joined with the daughters of men in the flesh. Ahriman-Mephistopheles, himself a son of the gods, joins with the daughters of humans, who have in turn been taken up into the nature of the gods, but now in heavenly love, not in earthly love, and in the spirit and the soul, not in the flesh. The reverse process: again a wonderful mystery, by means of which the events of *Faust* are directly linked to the highest traditions of humanity.

And now, looking at things this way, we understand for the first time what Goethe actually means, for only now are we in a position to understand what's happening here as an absolutely real process. It is highly interesting to follow how Goethe was led, so to speak, by the necessity of the matter at hand to shape the conclusion of his *Faust* precisely the way he did. He did not let himself be guided by some merely inner whim, but really by the matter itself. Consider the fact that once, when the thing was not finished yet but had ripened within him to the point where he was able to work on it, he made a kind of outline for himself about how he wanted to shape this scene. This is what he wrote:

> "Four gray women"—Well, he carried this out.
> "Faust and Care"—carried out.
> "Mephistopheles and Lemures"—carried out.
> "Faust satisfaction"—carried out.
> "All done. Corpse. Lemures burying. Taken away. Satans and maw of hell"—good.
> "Expecting decomposition"—he did that.
> "Because the soul flees later than otherwise"—also carried out.
> "Satanic positionings to catch it"—well, that's what we tried to perform today!
> "Angels, heavenly halo come floating up. Mephistopheles' Resistance. Angels strew roses. These wilt under the breath of the Satans. Transformed into flames of love. Satans flee. Mephistopheles' love-pangs. Angels float away. Mephistopheles to the [court of] appeal." (Paralipomena, 111: to Act V)

It was Goethe's original intention to link on to this scene in which, as it were, Mephistopheles appeals to Heaven for Faust's soul. This, then, is the note he made for himself: Mephistopheles off to the appeal. Then he adds to this: "Heaven, Christ, Mother"—in other words, the Mater Dolorosa—"Evangelists and all the saints. Judgment [passed] on Faust" (Paralipomena, 112: to Act V). So we see that shortly before Goethe finished writing his *Faust* he had wanted to complete it by having Mephistopheles appeal to Heaven for Faust's soul; he had in mind to have a sort of trial take place with a sort of heavenly scene in which Christ, the Mother of God, the evangelists and all the saints would be gathered together. In other words, Goethe had thought of arranging the scene more or less the way we find the upper part of the well-known painting by Raphael, where the sacrament is in the center.† We know this picture. Faust should have had a judgment pronounced on him. But Goethe did not carry it out this way because during the time when he wrote that down he was more of a mind to follow his inner whim. He was driven to carry it out differently by the subject itself.

The first way could have been quite nice, but one might say it could have been written that way in earlier times as well. It no longer fit the Age of Goethe. Only people who don't understand anything about the history of human evolution believe that you can write anything at any time, and that at any given time you can write about everything in the same way. People involved in the process of human evolution in a living way do not do this, which is why Goethe did not carry it out. On the other hand, what he did carry out is what we now know and what was performed here some time ago: the scene with its upward movement through the holy anchorites, from which we are then led into the region where the angels come, and then into the region of the Blessed Boys where the Penitent Women and Gretchen herself appear. What this means is that Goethe humanized the final scene entirely in harmony with what the age in which he lived required of him, bringing in what has to do with humanity as a whole with all that this signifies for spiritual reality. He himself once stated that, in a sense, the central element of the solution to his Faust-problem lies in the words contained in the closing scene:

> *"Who ever striving self exerts,*
> *By us can be redeemed;"*†
> And if, from on high, love has shed
> Its rays on him at all,
> The blissful host will meet him then
> And welcome him with warmth. (11936-41)

One must not take such a statement by Goethe lightly. *Faust* commentators have taken it very lightly. By pointing this out, Goethe wanted to show how profoundly he was able to grasp the mystery of the grace-filled working of the divine-spiritual principle in the human being. And he worked in accordance with this in a deeply significant, but always living way. During her time on earth, Gretchen had certain experiences at Faust's side and was then raised up into the spiritual worlds herself. All this created a bond between Faust and Gretchen, and Goethe wants to show that things of this sort are a reality for him and remain a reality, even when death has passed over them. The human being is placed into the connections that form during its physical existence, but once death has passed over them, these connections take on a spiritual form.

> And if, from on high, love has shed
> Its rays on him at all, (11938-39)

—that is, he has entered into an elective affinity† with what has become spiritual out of the sense-perceptible. What has become soul then welcomes him with warmth, and now he is not only a free human being, but one woven into the workings of Grace. Goethe is pointing here to how profoundly significant everything in the nature of an elective affinity becomes for the human being who enters into it, as well as to how real what has been taken up out of the physical into the spiritual is for whoever is woven into it in any way at all. And he is also pointing to the fact that what human beings do in the realm of the moral and the spiritual are realities too—not just something transitory, as materialism believes, but something that works on into the future and has meaning for a humanity that is busy developing itself. Goethe shows this in the final scene, and this is what makes the closing scene so magnificent.

What else can materialism say besides: Well, there's Pater Ecstaticus. He is just fooling himself; when he is dead, it will all be over and done with. The same goes for Pater Profundus and Pater Seraphicus, and so on. For Goethe, however, what these anchorites experience are processes that are just as real as the rising and the setting of the sun. And just as something is brought about here for the human being of the physical world by the rising and the setting of the sun, for Goethe a real process is brought about in Faust's soul by what streams through the world out of the ecstasies and prayers and mystical transports of the anchorites. What Goethe puts before us is the reality of the spiritual world, to the extent that this spiritual world has its roots in human feeling and in human inner experiencing. And the pictorial ideas he puts there are not merely the supra-earthly ones that to a certain extent have been detached from the human being, but the supra-earthly ones that have a deep inner connection with the human being. This is what makes his *Faust* THE poetic work of the beginning, or first part, of the fifth post-Atlantean period.

But there is one thing we cannot fail to notice if we study the different notes Goethe made for himself before he wrote the individual scenes. I have already spoken of some of his notes in another context. When Goethe was getting ready to work on his *Faust* again in the closing years of the eighteenth century, he wrote down a few sentences to sketch out how he might lead what he had already written over into what was yet to come. He writes:

> Ideal striving to work one's way and to feel one's way into Nature as a whole. Appearance of the Spirit as genius of the world and deeds.

All this is in Goethe's notes.

> Battle between Form and formlessness.
> Preference for formless content
> Over empty form.
> Content brings form with it.

> Form is never without content.
> Make these contradictions more disparate instead of uniting them.
> Brilliant, cold scientific striving. Wagner.
> Dull, warm scientific striving. Student.
> Enjoyment of life by the Person, seen from outside. Part I.
> In dullness, passion.
> Enjoyment of deeds toward the outside, Part II, and enjoyment with conscious awareness.
> Beauty.
> Enjoyment of creation from within. (Paralipomena 5)

Here he is already pointing in the direction he wants to take toward the end of *Faust.* And then he writes down something that he never carried out: "Epilogue in Chaos on the way to hell."

I have already mentioned the misunderstanding people had that there was to be this epilogue held in Chaos on the way to hell. People have wracked their brains about how *Faust* was supposed to have closed with an epilogue in Chaos, on the way to hell. In other words, it seemed that at a relatively late stage in his work on *Faust,* Goethe didn't want to have Faust be redeemed but wanted him to go to hell. People never thought of Mephistopheles as being the one to speak this epilogue instead of Faust, going off to hell himself and delivering it there after losing the wager. But Goethe was never able to write this epilogue, and so it really doesn't exist. Why not? Because at that time it could not be written out of the deep mystery, and, at the same time, out of the mystery of the time in which he lived. For what would have been the content of this epilogue in Chaos on the way to hell? Let us imagine what it would have contained. What has happened up to now? The various interactions between the Ahrimanic and the Luciferic forces, which we have observed as they are portrayed at the close of Goethe's *Faust,* have not led to Faust's soul being carried off by Ahriman-Mephistopheles after all; instead, his soul has entered the spiritual world in the proper way in order to join with the forces coming from the blissful host, as I have explained. As a result, the Luciferic element has gained a slight predominance at first. A kind of spiritualization has taken place for Faust, instead of the materialization that should have come about through Ahriman by means of which Faust's soul would have remained united with matter through earthly gravity, as it were, and Faust would have sunk down into an abyss—Ahriman-Mephistopheles is, after all, the lord of matter! But that did not happen. The scale pan swung down more on the Luciferic side, so to speak, and this enabled Faust's soul to enter the region it then enters, where the human effects of the Penitent Women and of Gretchen herself are in the spiritual sphere, now that the Ahrimanic has been overcome in the appropriate way.

Now, there stands Mephistopheles, all by himself. His whole desire has been to carry off this soul, and now he has lost it. He didn't manage to connect it with earthly gravity; if he had, it would have remained with the corpse or else been snatched up in the circle of Lemures or grabbed by the Fat or Skinny Devils. But none of that has gone as planned. Such a state of balance has been established between the Ahrimanic and the Luciferic that Faust has begun to move heavenward. But Mephistopheles has come to a standstill. The soul has escaped. But now he could say to himself: Well, here I am; this soul has gotten away from me, but it will come under my influence when it comes back to Earth again. Then I'll recognize it and be able to get close to it again, for it will have to undergo new Ahrimanic testing. If Goethe had managed to carry out something like this, the result would have been the "Epilogue in Chaos on the way to hell." For the peculiar thing about Mephistopheles-Ahriman is that he always thinks he will win out in every incarnation. Yet in every incarnation, if the proper state of balance is established with respect to Lucifer, he can lose the victory again. That's the peculiar thing. But the human being must swing back and forth between the two poles of Ahriman and Lucifer; otherwise the human personality could not develop itself. The human personality only evolves by means of resistance. Just think: If we didn't have two eyes that we could direct toward things in such a way that their axes of sight intersect, or two hands that touch each other and wash each other, our awareness of being a personality in a bodily sense could never be developed. Ahriman-Mephistopheles is also the Lord of All Resistances and the Lord of All Hindrances. This is why Ahriman had to acquire such enormous influence in the fifth post-Atlantean period, because this fifth post-Atlantean period is the very one in which the forming of the personality is to be perfected. In earlier eras the human being had far less personality, in the Egypto-Chaldean age almost none at all; at that time the human being was still almost completely enclosed within a community consciousness, as I have often explained. The personality really only begins to become conscious in the Greco-Roman period, but even then it is a slow process because a great deal of the community consciousness is still present. Then, in our fifth post-Atlantean era, the time comes when the personality has to become fully aware of itself so that it can create what it has to attain for this fifth post-Atlantean era entirely out of itself. The characteristic feature of the fifth post-Atlantean period is that it makes the strongest possible demands on the life and creativity of the personality's impulses.

In this fifth post-Atlantean period, spiritual science must enter into human evolution. But to be understood, comprehended and taken hold of, this spiritual science will call for a stronger engagement of the forces of the intellect, of feeling and of will—in fact, a stronger engagement of all the forces of personality—than was ever there before. Goethe had a deeply felt recognition of the impulses of his time, and the fact that he placed Ahriman-Mephistopheles at the side of Faust, whose task it is to develop this personality-based consciousness in the midst of all his trials, flowed directly out of this recognition. This Faust is someone who has to develop himself by resisting various Mephistophelean influences; he has to recognize what lives in the one-sided training in reasoning and science that he has received from Ahriman-Mephistopheles, but he also has to maintain himself within it. For a personality who had explored the whole of science—"So, now I've studied philosophy, legal codes and medicine, and—even worse—theology!" (354-57)—and had also turned to magic and the magical practices that had come down from earlier times, the only possibility was to fall into mystical rapture in his encounter with the Earth Spirit:

> In floods of life, in storm of deeds
> Up and down I well,
> Back and forth I weave!
> Birth and grave
> An eternal sea ... (501-05)

And weave along with it! But this is an absorption, a becoming nebulous yourself in the weaving life of this storm of deeds ... let fuzzy-headed mystics yearn for this if they want to lose the personality! Engagement of the strongest forces of personality is just what the fifth post-Atlantean period demands, and this should give rise to knowledge and will in the human being in the fifth post-Atlantean period. For this reason, however, humanity in this fifth post-Atlantean period has been given the task of fully engaging the personality. It will become an ever greater demand of the fifth post-Atlantean period to build up the strength and the forces of the personality through its full engagement. Also, with respect to a moral attitude toward life, people who do not wish to lag behind in their development will need to engage the personality more and more strongly. This strengthening of the personality will be a demand of the age. And this strengthening of the personality is fully in accord with the spirit of normal, good, proper evolution. The weakening and "sulphurization"† of the personality is not in accord with the impulses of the rest of the fifth post-Atlantean period. This absorption of the personality into the nebulous is an atavistic regression back into ancient times. If, however, the Luciferic and Ahrimanic forces hostile to human beings are left to themselves, they work against the human being and undermine its tasks. Because the human being must fully engage the personality by means of spiritual science, which for the fifth post-Atlantean period is to arise out of the strongest forces of the personality, it is precisely Ahrimanic counter-forces which are working against the personality. One has only to understand this and then consider our own age from this point of view.

If we look back to earlier times, we will really find many more encounters of an objective nature, in spite of everything personal that is already at work. In our time, the Ahrimanic forces work in such a way that they want to draw the objective struggle gradually but entirely into the sphere of personality in the case of those individuals who can be found for this purpose. Think of how everything is gradually being diverted away from what is objective and onto the personality. This is no mere accident; it belongs to the character of our age. Let us say that someone is working to advance evolution in a proper way. Instead of going after the matter in question, the battle will be aimed more and more at that person's personality; personal slanders and distortions will take the place of everything objective. And we already see today how far things have come in our time, how people no longer know how to distinguish what is a purely personal suspicion from what is being attacked in an objective way. And the strongest and most grotesque expression of this can be found just where the attempt to pursue spiritual science is being made in an improper and disrespectful way.

Just remember our own struggles and how objectively everything had to be presented against that movement linked in more recent times with the name of Mrs. Besant.† In the response from the other side, was there a single objective argument in any of the objections made? Not one! Nothing but personal suspicions of the strongest sort. It was all personal suspicions! This is only a grotesque prefiguration of a characteristic of our time that will become more and more prevalent and must be understood with complete consciousness. Because personality will have to come to our aid—since personality is the only thing through which something will be able to manifest more and more in the future that in the past was provided more by a "public" or "common" mentality—the battle against personality is now also beginning. And because strength of personality is the new requirement and indolence has no desire to derive this strength from the matter being striven for, personality itself, so weak and incapable of anything, is being guided into, or is drilling into itself, a kind of artificial strength by its own authoritarian command. Nowadays people do one thing or another purely out of the arbitrariness of personality without learning anything, without having seriously occupied themselves with anything or gone into anything in some depth. And no one has any idea how to come to grips with these things.

We can make some fine studies of this in our own area as well. How often was it necessary to reject the self-important foolishness and vanity that developed in our movement over the years? The trouble is, vanity doesn't see that it needs to be rejected. For example: Once when I was in Frankfurt I was called to the phone by someone who told me he had to speak with me right away. And when he came, with hair down below his shoulders and a patriarch's beard to match, he declared that he'd been traveling around after me for some time and wanted to come to a kind of compromise between what he had to give the world and what I was representing. Well, sometimes you can't help offending against a principle of mutual respect that regards amateurish stupidity as just as worthwhile as what's being striven for in an honest way. You have to be presumptuous enough to make a distinction in such cases and tell people like this to get lost; there is no need to bother with them any longer. You don't need to get abrupt with them, but you do have to show them that you think they are what they are and that you have no intention of honoring any lukewarm principle of equality that would consider any puffed-up idiocy to be as significant as anything else. Well, some time later the man in question showed up here in Switzerland and even announced that he was going to give lectures against me in various cities. Some of you sitting here know that he caused other kinds of mischief as well. This is the way enmities form: personality, which has to come to our aid on all sides today, has to permeate itself with something; but if it can't do this, it just wants to be strong without first working to make itself strong by using the forces that permeate it. We have to see clearly what brings these conflicts about. That is what is necessary. We really have to understand our time and not just do all sorts of things out of arbitrary impulses. Again, our time demands the fullest possible engagement of personality; this is why our time is now waging the Ahrimanic battle against personality.

The second thing our time urgently demands is that we develop a deep sense for what is truly factual. Humanity will become more and more dependent on understanding the spiritual world. In this spiritual world, things are not such that we can sense a process of being corrected. I have shown in the last chapter of my *Theosophy* that we don't get corrected if we have done something wrong. Read that part again. What we need is a sense for facts, real facts. But in our time the strongest possible Luciferic battle is unfolding against this sense for facts. At no time, in spite of all that has happened, have facts ever been as falsified as they are in our time! The Luciferic instincts call up Ahrimanic forces that represent facts in the form of lies. This tendency to represent facts in the form of lies is only in its first stages and will get more and more out of control. Again, it is important to see this clearly.

Getting used to a sense for facts and also to the fact that we will really need to engage our personality more and more in whatever cause needs to be fought for: this is what belongs to the fifth post-Atlantean period.

Try to understand how the Ahrimanic and the Luciferic battles are particularly evident in our own area and how we find the lack of a sense for facts being used against us right up to the most recent events. Things are already being written and said today that no longer have any truth in them whatsoever.

Goethe felt all this very, very deeply. If you go through his *Faust*, you will see that he brings the Luciferic and Ahrimanic forces to Faust's nature, combining them the way we have to view them as human beings if we want to place ourselves correctly and consciously into the impulses of the fifth post-Atlantean period. The Ahrimanic and the Luciferic forces work against the human being both in individual instances and within the larger picture. If we did not recognize Ahriman or Lucifer, we would not be able to go on living in the right way. All of this is what must be brought about by spiritual science. This cannot be stressed enough today, when there is still so little comprehension of the gravity of what we must gain from spiritual science. Things are taken too lightly and forgotten just as readily. We could say that the external events of world history themselves are what work against a deepening, or strengthening, of personality and a sense for facts—true facts—which are the two great demands of our time. Two things are working against what is necessary for the progress of humanity. The first of these is a principle of nationalities that is nonsensical because it has now become atavistic. This absurd principle of nationalities, especially as brought into the world by the Napoleons of the nineteenth century, in the name of which an appeal is made to many impulses today that go *against* the true intention of human evolution; a befogging principle of nationalities that surrounds concepts with a confusing mist and sends them off into the wrong spheres of activity. Let me make myself clear in the following way.

We are justified, in a certain way, in talking about a green meadow as long as we understand the matter rightly. But we only understand it rightly if we know that what is green about the meadow is the greenness of its individual plants. If I wanted to have the concrete greenness of the meadow without the concrete greenness of the individual plants, I would have to paint the meadow green, but then it would not actually be a green meadow. I can only talk about the greenness of a meadow when I know that in a concrete sense I can only mean the greenness of the individual plants. I have to know that in this case the concept of greenness can only be applied to the individual plants and not ascribed to a greenness of the meadow as a whole. This is a confused way of thinking that I must strictly avoid. If I use the term "greenness of the meadow" in an abstract way, I have to be clear that I am only forming an abstraction that embraces the concrete instances, the individual green plants. Such concepts have to be formed with absolute clarity. People must learn, for example, that the words "freedom" and "rights"† can only be applied to individual, concrete human beings, just as "greenness" can only be applied concretely to individual plants, and that if I talk about the rights and freedom of peoples or nations, I can only mean something abstract, like the greenness of a meadow.

Today, however, the most deceitful campaign slogan there can possibly be is being spread over nearly half the world by declarations of what one wants to fight to achieve in the name of the rights and freedom of peoples; this is the same foolish nonsense as the ridiculous thought that you can paint all the plants of a meadow green instead of the meadow's being green because of its individual plants. Nevertheless, because people have had the wool pulled over their eyes by the untrue principle of nationality, there is much talk of this ridiculous slogan about the rights and freedom of nations. And someone will be considered very foolish, if not downright insane, for saying something that must be said because it has a direct connection with *Faust*, where Faust himself says: "To stand with people free upon free ground"—not with a free nation, of which there could be no talk at all. And yet this idea of a "free nation" has been thought out in such an inexact, sloppy and ill-intentioned way because it brings in something atavistic that does not belong in our time because it teaches the individual to have a consciousness that arises out of weakness and not out of the strength of personality. Anyone, however, who rebels against something so beautiful, so great, so ideal and well-meant today, will be absolutely pilloried as an ill-intentioned fool.

The other thing that works against the progressive principles in our time is the politicization of the life of thought. It is important to understand these two things, the politicization of the life of thought as well as the nonsensical principle of nationalities. In a different context I've already called your attention to the meaning of "policy," where people are always talking about policy, about putting certain thoughts into action in order to achieve certain ends. Think how widespread this is in the world today! The absolute worst aspect of our fifth post-Atlantean period is the result of this politicization of the life of thought. An earlier age, which could still believe, in a certain way, that it was inspired in its forming of thoughts, was able to adopt some dogma or other at its councils, which was then used to accomplish something or other in the world. Our age, however, is totally uninspired in its materialistic makeup; if it fails to take a thought and connect it with something out of a feeling of responsibility for impersonal Truth, it will only grasp that thought out of an arbitrary aspiration that is either purely personal or based on some club or association or some other kind of communal interest or experience. If any of these is the case, the thought is not placed into the world because someone understands its correctness but because someone wants to use it to gain some political advantage. This politicization of the life of thought goes on and on. What people are taught by this is not to arrive at the correct thought, the true thought, but rather at a thought that can be used for political ends, such as the thought of not practicing vivisection on animals. Such a thought is then not grasped in terms of its truth content, but in terms of its potential for political agitation. People agitate with this thought, politicking with it in temperance unions, anti-vivisection associations, etc. A person may fail to grasp a thought in its reality—such as "abstinence" or "vivisection"—and yet go on to politicize in terms of it. The thoughts are submerged into the political activities that go on everywhere. A false principle of nationalities and false politicizing with thoughts, especially as the latter lives today in the way we exaggerate the importance of clubs and organizations—all this is what runs counter to the correct and progressive kinds of evolution taking place in present-day humanity. Associations are not formed to represent truth but to attain some end or other. Through them, even a correct idea can be turned into a fanatic, one-sided one, whereas the fifth post-Atlantean period in its fundamental character has the obligation to work by means of truth.

Herman Grimm, who had immersed himself in Goethe's life, was fully justified in saying that Goethe's *Faust* is a work of poetic art truly conceived out of the organization of the human personality. Its central figure is a university professor of modest rank who goes astray in his scientific striving and has all sorts of experiences as a result. But what he undergoes is representative of all human striving in the highest sense. If we look into it deeply enough, we see that it truly contains everything in the way of philosophical questions that can emerge for the human being of our present age, but also everything in the way of questions of the heart and of political forces. We could add to these remarks, out of the depths of spiritual science, that what is contained in this *Faust* is precisely what is purely human, the content of "humanity" itself, in the sense of what it means to be good and noble in the highest sense. What nation does *Faust* belong to, anyway? To none, of course. Furthermore, it is a most fervent protest against the false principle of nationalities current today, which Grillparzer[†] characterized so fundamentally with his harsh-sounding but deeply truthful words: From humanity to nationality to bestiality. That's the way, all right! If nationality is emphasized so much that it becomes the source of all aspirations, it leads away from humanity and, very soon, straight into bestiality. Of course, politics is necessary in the world, but the politicization of thoughts is not. Look at how thoughts are "de-politicized" by Goethe. Try to understand the second part of Goethe's *Faust* from this point of view; it was written out of immeasurable depths. It is a most marvelous document, not only of our time but of all ages of humanity, for it touches on questions that have their place directly beside the great biblical questions, as we have seen. The scene with Care stands next to the scene in Paradise; the scene in which Mephistopheles faces the spirits of heaven stands next to the picture the Bible gives: that the sons of the gods found favor with the "daughters of men" and joined with them in the flesh.

One would like to have much, much better words to indicate what should be very deeply inscribed in the human spirit and in human hearts, what should not be forgotten, but unfortunately is always forgotten much too quickly once it has been heard. For the healing of the great evils of our time can only come from an understanding of those things that have been touched upon here.

If I have tried today to cite some specific features of the fifth post-Atlantean period's impulses in connection with Goethe's *Faust* and to show how these are in accordance with the spirit, I would like above all for some understanding to come about for how the sins against these impulses show themselves everywhere in the world and a lack of understanding becomes evident for the very things that must be understood. Oh, how I would like to have the words with which I would gladly speak about these things! But maybe, in times to come, other people will find better words to discuss the things that are so little understood today because there are so many people that would be quite willing to allow their personality to sink down into a comfortable dependence on one thing or another. They would like to become something by finding their place in some movement or other, where they would never again have to leave their imprisonment in the false principle of common interests or nationalities or the politicization of thoughts. And yet—anyone on this wrong track will fall prey to Lucifer and Ahriman. Only those will continue to thrive who know that nothing can be achieved by following this path! No matter how comfortable people may feel with all the agitations and organizational activity of our day, the path that must be found will be found only in the service of the kind of human activity that seeks wisdom in truth and is convinced that the goal of humanity in our epoch can be attained only through the incorporation of truth in human beings. This activity will also know that all politicizing of thought, all agitating with thoughts as though with dogmas, must stop, and that these must be grasped with a full feeling of responsibility for the truth, not for their value as material for agitation or for however much we may happen to like them. These thoughts must not be allowed to enter our sphere because we find them pleasing, but because we really have a full feeling of responsibility for truth and for the value of truth.

With what has been said here as a supplement to Goethe's *Faust*, I would like to have said much more than can be contained in the words themselves. I would like for this to go on working in your hearts and souls, for I know how much there is in these words which must be soul-spiritual medicine for our whole epoch and for the humanity of our epoch who are making their way along such false paths. If people are unable to admit to themselves that these false paths exist and keep on going the way they're going now, they will also not be able to advance in the right way with the goal which is right and necessary for humanity to pursue.

NOTES AND COMMENTARY

The entries in italics below are translations of the useful endnotes provided by Edwin Froböse and Hans Erhard Lauer, who edited the third German edition (1967) of GA 272 (i.e., volume 272 of the standard German edition of Rudolf Steiner's Gesamtausgabe, or Complete Works). (The fourth edition of 1981 is a "photomechanical reproduction" of the third.) Italicized notes referring to excerpts from other texts not included in GA 272 are likewise translations of notes provided by the various editors of the other volumes of the GA. The rest were provided by Frederick Amrine, with kind help from Burley Channer as noted.

In these texts on *Faust*, Rudolf Steiner often alludes to other of his own lectures and publications. Froböse and Lauer have done an excellent job of tracking down the references to the appropriate volumes of the Gesamtausgabe. In 2006, SteinerBooks began the immense project of publishing Steiner's Collected Works systematically in an English-language edition, corresponding volume for volume to the GA, a project that will require decades to complete. Of course, many of Steiner's books and lecture cycles have long since been translated into English, with widely varying degrees of success, but the titles and contents do not match up consistently with the GA, which makes the job of referencing English translations rather difficult. In the following notes, I refer to Steiner's works by their volume number in the GA, and I try as best I can to indicate the most recent English translation available, even if it has not yet appeared in the new Collected Works by SteinerBooks.

In the preparation of [the third German edition], all the extant stenographic manuscripts were again consulted. A transcription of the second lecture (Berlin, December 17, 1911) was found only recently among the papers of Clara Michels, who recorded numerous lectures stenographically. The lecture of May 30, 1915 is offered here for the first time in its entirety, but the excerpts from lectures of May 29, 1915, and August 28, 1915, have not been included in this edition, since these will now be included in other volumes of the Collected Works (GA 161 and 163).

EXTRACTS

On the Idea of Faust

1 **Schiller** Friedrich Schiller (1759-1805), the dramatist who became one of Goethe's closest friends and collaborators. Schiller was also a lyric poet and a historian, but Rudolf Steiner, like several of Schiller's contemporaries, considered him a great philosopher above all. Steiner was influenced deeply by Schiller's essay *On the Aesthetic Education of Man in a Series of Letters* (1794). A magnificent English translation by Elizabeth M. Wilkinson and L. A. Willoughby, with facing German and extensive commentary, was published by Oxford UP in 1967 (rpt. in paperback since), and it has helped bring this neglected masterpiece some measure of the attention it deserves.

1 **Schelling ... Hegel** Friedrich Wilhelm Joseph Schelling (1775-1854), the youngest of the four main philosophers in the movement conventionally known as German Idealism, the others being Immanuel Kant (1724-1804), Johann Gottlieb Fichte (1762-1814), and Georg Wilhelm Friedrich Hegel (1770-1831). Like Hegel, Steiner was often critical of Schelling, and for the same reasons, chiefly his desire to investigate Nature by employing abstract metaphysical principles apart from, or even prior to, empirical experience.

2 **Heine** Heinrich Heine (1797-1856). This late Romantic poet was popular in the 19th century, and he is known for his mordant satires and bitter ironies.

3 **I would like initially to [?] the thought...** This fragmentary text breaks off in the middle of a sentence with a direct object but no verb; at the end, the editors have written, "The continuation of this essay, which was probably undertaken in the middle of the 1880s, could not be found in the Archive."

Faust *Explained According to Goethe's Own Method*

4 **Karl Julius Schröer** Schröer (1825-1900) was born in Preßburg (now Bratislava), which was then part of the Austro-Hungarian empire. After long stints as a schoolteacher in various locations, he moved to Vienna in 1860, where he was appointed professor of literature at the Technical University. Schröer was a folklorist, a philologist, and an important interpreter of Goethe's *Faust*, principally in the edition with commentary under review here.

Steiner attended Schröer's courses at the Technical University, and eventually became his protégé: it was Schröer who saw Steiner's extraordinary talents and recommended him for the prestigious task of editing Goethe's scientific writings for the critical edition of Goethe's complete works, which is referred to as the *Weimarer Ausgabe*. Steiner owed a great debt to Schröer, and this review is predictably laudatory, but there is no reason to doubt its sincerity. Steiner considered Schröer a great man, and he continued to speak warmly of him long after Schröer had died. In many places, Steiner's interpretation follows Schröer's closely. Steiner's relationship to Schröer will be covered extensively in the introduction to the second volume (GA 273), in which the lectures and essays are much less vehicles for teaching anthroposophy, and *Faust* is interpreted more in its own right.

5 **"I do not rest until I find a pregnant point..."** This quote is from Goethe's essay "Significant Help Given by an Ingenious Turn of Phrase," collected in his *Scientific Studies* (New York: Suhrkamp, 1988), p. 41. See the notes to p. 266 **the well-known conversation** below for bibliographic information regarding English translations of Goethe's scientific works.

5 **In its original sixteenth-century form** Steiner means the *Faustbuch* of 1587, which was quickly translated into numerous languages, and became one of Europe's earliest "bestsellers." This chapbook remained in print continuously through Goethe's day. The edition of choice for English speakers is *The English Faust Book: A Critical Edition Based on the Text of 1592*, ed. John Henry Jones (Cambridge: Cambridge UP, 1994). See also the notes to pp. 97 ***Dr. Georg Faustus*** and 99 below.

5 **"ever striving"** a reference to the all-important lines spoken by the angels near the end of Goethe's *Faust*: "'Whoever strives in ceaseless toil, / Him we may grant redemption'" (ll. 11,935-6, tr. Walter Arndt). Note that the angels' words are set within quotation marks in Goethe's text, implying that they are repeating some higher power's words or principle.

6 ***The Fellow Culprits*** *Die Mitschuldigen*, a comedy. This is a minor work, seldom read; the only point here is that it contains a reference to Dr. Faustus.

6 **Theophrastus Paracelsus** Phillipus von Hohenheim (1493-1541), better known by his pen-name Paracelsus, the Swiss physician, botanist, and esotericist. Paracelsus is one of the most important and influential thinkers of the early modern period. Goethe knew his writings intimately. We were tempted to include in this volume Steiner's long lecture "From Paracelsus to Goethe" of November 16, 1911 (collected in GA 61), but we decided that the main ideas regarding Goethe's *Faust* were already represented here. Steiner's appreciation of Paracelsus in this rather biographical lecture is sensitive and insightful; unfortunately, it seems not to have been translated into English.

6 **the "Golden Chain of Homer"** *Aurea catena Homeri* is the title of the Latin original. Anton Kirchweger (d. 1746) wrote or edited and published this short alchemical text in 1723. BiblioBazaar issued a reproduction of an earlier English translation in 2007. It is also available as a Kindle Edition from Amazon.

7 **Friederike Oeser** Friederike Elisabeth Oeser (1748-1829), daughter of the eminent artist Adam Friedrich Oeser (1717-1799), whose students included the founder of modern art history, Winckelmann, and the young Goethe (1765-1768). Goethe struck up a friendship with Friederike, and continued to correspond with her for several years after the end of his lessons. On Winckelmann, see the note to p. 49 below.

7 **Hans Sachs** (1494-1576), the cobbler-poet to whom more than 6,000 works have been attributed. He is most famous now for having been portrayed as a leading character in Wagner's opera *Die Meistersinger von Nürnberg* (1868).

7 **the painter, Friedrich Müller** Better known as "Maler" (the painter) Müller, this sentimental poet and artist was an exact contemporary of Goethe (1749-1825). Both in this commentary and in an earlier publication, Schröer had pointed to this letter as evidence that Goethe had in mind when imagining the death of Faust the apocryphal account of the Archangel Michael fighting with the Devil over Moses' corpse.

A New Book on Goethe's Faust

9 **the genetic approach** a reference to the positivism that dominated literary studies at the end of the 19th century. The unnamed villain here is Wilhelm Scherer (1841-1886), under whom Goethe had worked at the Archive in Weimar while editing Goethe's scientific writings. This important topic will be covered fully in the introduction to the second volume of commentaries (GA 273), which will focus on Steiner as a scholar of Goethe and an interpreter of *Faust.*

10 **Herman Grimm** Herman F. Grimm (1828-1901), the son of the famous linguist and folklorist Wilhelm Grimm, wrote extensively on literature and the history of art. He was widely read in the later 19th century. See also the notes on p. 97 ***Dr. Georg Faustus*** and p. 170 below.

10 ***Urfaust*** This previously unknown version was discovered by the literary scholar Erich Schmidt in 1887, when he was going through the papers of Luise von Göchhausen, a highly cultivated lady who had served Princess Anna Amalia of Weimar during the years after Goethe's first arrival there in 1775. She would have borrowed Goethe's unpublished ms. and made a copy for herself after having heard him read it aloud in his capacity as Court Poet. We are uncertain of the exact date, but it almost certainly falls between 1775 and 1786. The prefix "Ur-" is common in German: it means "original" or "primal" or "archetypal" (recalling the city from which Abraham first set out on his journey, which marks the beginning of the three Abrahamic religions). Cf. Goethe's *Urpflanze,* the "archetypal plant."

11 **Raphael** Raffaello Sanzio da Urbino (1483-1520), part of the great triumvirate of Renaissance art famous enough to be known by their first names only: Leonardo, Michelangelo, Raphael. Steiner's analogy here fits with his earlier reference to Herman Grimm, who wrote extensively on Raphael. See also the note to p. 347 below.

11 **Homunculus** The symbolic child born to the alchemical King and Queen, literally the diminutive of the Latin word *homo,* human being. As an important figure in Part Two of Goethe's *Faust,* Homunculus is discussed extensively in many of the following texts, and especially in the second volume of lectures.

Faust: ***A Tragedy by J. W. Goethe***

13 **Du Bois-Reymond** Emil du Bois-Reymond (1818-1896), an important German scientist who is credited with having founded the discipline of electrophysiology.

Du Bois-Reymond is notorious among Goethe scholars for the inaugural address he gave in 1882 at the beginning of his tenure as the Rektor (roughly, President) of the University of Berlin, "Goethe and More Goethe" [*Goethe und kein Ende*]. There he expresses puzzlement at Goethe's Faust, and wishes aloud that he had just married Gretchen, legitimized his child, and gotten on with the serious business of inventing vacuum pumps and such. This is tantamount to the President of Harvard declaring in public that Hamlet should have just married Ophelia and taken up animal husbandry or some other useful pursuit.

13 **"On the Boundaries of Natural Science"** du Bois-Reymond gave the famous and influential address, "Über die Grenzen des Naturerkennens," before the German Association of Doctors and Scientists on August 14, 1872, in Leipzig. See also lecture 1 (September 27, 1920) in GA 322, *The Boundaries of Natural Science*, tr. Frederick Amrine and Konrad Oberhuber, intro. Saul Bellow (New York: Anthroposophic Press, 1983), where Steiner refers to this address as a symptom of the failure of late 19th-century skeptical positivism. Indeed, the title of this lecture cycle seems to be an ironic reference to the physiologist's speech.

13 **Fr. A. Lange's *History of Materialism*** Friedrich Albert Lange, *Geschichte des Materialismus und Kritik seiner Bedeutung in der Gegenwart* (1866); many English-language editions, including one with an introduction by Bertrand Russell: *The History of Materialism and Criticism of Its Present Importance*, 3rd edn. (London: Routledge, 1957). This book was widely read, and it exerted a great influence on Nietzsche.

13 **certain "riddles of the universe"** a reference to yet another famous and influential address, "The Seven World Riddles," given by du Bois-Reymond before the Berlin Academy of Sciences in 1880. Regarding such issues as "simple sensation," "the ultimate nature of matter and force," and "the origin of motion," he declared "ignoramus et ignorabimus": "we do not know and we shall not ever know."

14 **Delivery alone assures the orator his success** Here Steiner echoes a line spoken by the pedant Wagner in Goethe's *Faust* (546).

15 **who constantly desires evil** a reference to the famous lines in which Mephistopheles describes himself to Faust as "Part of that force which would / Do ever evil, and does ever good" (1335-1336, tr. Walter Arndt).

Goethe's Faust *as a Picture of His Esoteric View of Life*

17 **the "Ever-Feminine"... becomes a "simile"** This is an allusion to the enigmatic "Chorus Mysticus," which concludes Part Two of *Faust*. It begins, "Alles Vergängliche / Ist nur ein Gleichnis," which might be rendered: "Everything mortal / Is but a simile."

17 **Goethe expresses this in his *West-östlicher Divan*** Here Steiner is quoting the final lines from one of Goethe's most famous lyrics, "Blessed Yearning" ["Selige Sehnsucht"], which is part of Goethe's collection *The West-Eastern Divan*

[*Der West-Östliche Divan*] (1814). Goethe was inspired by the Divan of the great medieval Sufi poet Hafiz (or Hafez or Hafis), which was translated into German by Joseph von Hammer-Purgstall and published in 1812-13. Alas, there is no adequate English translation of Hafiz. Goethe's *Divan* is one of the pinnacles of the German lyric, as widely admired as Shakespeare's sonnets or Keats's odes are in the English-speaking world. A sensitive English translation of Goethe's text has been published by Martin Bidney: *West-East Divan: Poems, with "Notes and Essays": Goethe's Intercultural Dialogues*. My own feeble attempt to translate the full text of "Selige Sehnsucht" follows:

BLESSED YEARNING

Tell it to no one, wise ones only
Since the mob will only mock you,
I would praise the thing that's living
That for flaming death is longing.

In the cooling of the love-nights
That engendered you, engendering,
Alien feeling overcomes you
When the silent candle glistens.

No confinement any longer,
In the shadows of the darkness,
And a new desiring pulls you
Upward to a higher creation.

No remoteness makes you heavy;
Flying and enchanted, drawn,
Til', at last, the light desiring,
Butterfly, you end up burnt.

And so long as you are lacking
This: First die and then become!
You remain a gloomy guest
Upon the darkened earth.

17 ***Sayings in Prose*** Goethe published these in 1819. A good English-language edition of this and other similar material was edited by D. J. Enright under the title *The Sayings of Goethe* (London: Duckworth, 1996).

17 **the mystic, Heraclitus** the darkly obscure pre-Socratic philosopher who was a native of Ephesus (ca. 535-ca. 475 BCE). The fragment to which Steiner refers, No. 127, is powerful indeed. Brooks Haxton has translated it thus in verse:

Dionysus is their name for death.
And if they did not claim
the statue of the drunk
they worshipped was a god,

or call their incoherent song
about his cock their hymn,
everyone would know
what filth their shamelessness
has made of them
and of the name of god.

[*Fragments: The Collected Wisdom of Heraclitus* (New York: Viking, 2001), p. 89.]

17 **the "higher meaning will not be lost on the initiated"** Johann Peter Eckermann, *Conversations with Goethe, 1836-1848* (multiple editions available in English), conversation of January 25, 1827. Eckermann (1792-1854) was Goethe's personal secretary during the last decade of Goethe's life; he is Boswell to Goethe's Dr. Johnson, as it were. His records of their conversations are a treasure-trove of insight into Goethe's thinking at the end of his life, and Eckermann's own style is very fine. Nietzsche declared it his favorite book, and the sculptor Henry Moore claimed to have read it at least once a year. See also the note to p. 61 below.

18 **the eternal in the womb of the Mothers** The reference is to the scene "Dark Gallery" in Part Two. See Harold Jantz, *The Mothers in* Faust*: The Myth of Time and Creativity* (Baltimore: Johns Hopkins UP, 1969). Jantz is excellent on Faust generally: his erudite study *Faust as a Renaissance Man: Parallels and Prototypes* (Princeton: Princeton UP, 1951) is also highly recommended.

18 **a series of previous incarnations** This thought was very much alive in the Age of Goethe. Not only did Goethe himself clearly believe in reincarnation: Herder and even the arch-rationalist Gotthold Ephraim Lessing published essays arguing for the idea. See the notes to p. 19 **Lessing**, p. 46, and p. 297.

18 **daemons** Not Christian devils, but rather pagan *daemons*, benevolent "middle spirits" such as the tutelary *daimonion* Socrates describes in Plato's *Apology*, or Ariel in Shakespeare's *Tempest*. For a fuller treatment of this topic, esp. in light of more recent thought, see Angus Nicholls, *Goethe's Concept of the Daemonic: After the Ancients* (Rochester, NY: Camden House, 2006).

Goethe's Gospel

19 **imported from the East ... theosophy** Theosophy had brought ancient Hindu and Buddhist teachings from India to the West. The word *theosophia* was coined by the early Christian Fathers, who use it as a synonym for "theology." Various movements have claimed the name or been so labeled throughout history, but Steiner refers here specifically to the Theosophical Society that was founded in New York City by Helena Blavatsky and others in 1875. After many failed attempts to find a receptive audience elsewhere, Steiner accepted their invitation to lead the German Section of the Theosophical Society in 1902. It was an uncomfortable alliance on both sides, and by 1913, Steiner had resigned and founded his own, independent organization, which became the Anthroposophical Society.

19 **Lessing** Gotthold Ephraim Lessing (1729-1781), a major dramatist, philosopher, and theologian of the generation preceding Goethe. Lessing was a fascinating figure, who hardly fits the stereotype of "Enlightenment rationalist" so often foisted upon him. A posthumous report that he had been a closet Spinozist (tantamount to an atheist in the minds of many) started a huge controversy that involved many of the major writers of the day, Goethe included.

Anthroposophists will be intrigued to learn that late in life (ca. 1780) Lessing argued that humans must necessarily have more than five senses, and that we seem to be restricted to five only because the other, higher senses have not yet evolved. Lessing also published a later treatise, *The Education of the Human Race* (1777-1780), in which he attempts to reconcile the tensions between the religion of the Old Testament, the New Testament, and "the Christianity of reason" (as he termed it) by invoking the idea of reincarnation. A good English translation of these and other essays, edited by H. B. Nisbet, was published recently: Lessing, *Philosophical and Theological Writings* (Cambridge: Cambridge UP, 2005).

19 **in Herder's writings** Johann Gottfried Herder (1744-1803), one of the most seminal thinkers of the 18th century. Goethe was still a student when he met Herder by chance in Straßburg; the older man would become his most important mentor. How appropriate that the name of the inn where they met was "Zum Geist" – "At the Sign of the Spirit"! Isaiah Berlin's study *Vico and Herder: Two Studies in the History of Ideas* (New York: Viking, 1976) is deservedly considered a classic work of intellectual history. See also the outstanding first chapter, "The Aims of a New Epoch," in Charles Taylor, *Hegel* (Cambridge: Cambridge UP, 1975). It is hard to overestimate Herder's influence on Goethe.

19 **Schiller** Friedrich Schiller (see note to p. 1), *Philosophical Letters* (Boston: IndyPublish.com, 2007), also available from Amazon as a Kindle e-book.

19 **Novalis** the pen-name of Friedrich von Hardenberg (1772-1801), a Romantic poet and philosopher of infinite talent and promise who, tragically, died young.

20 **his autobiography *Poetry and Truth*** *From My Life: Poetry and Truth*, 2 vols. (New York: Suhrkamp, 1987; rpt. Princeton: Princeton UP, 1994). We are extraordinarily fortunate in that Goethe's other major autobiographical writing, the *Italian Journey*, has been translated by the great English poet W. H. Auden, and is now available as an inexpensive paperback (Penguin, 1970).

20 ***The Green Snake and the Beautiful Lily*** Goethe published this cryptic tale in 1795 in Schiller's journal *The Horae.* Much as Wordsworth's *Prelude* of 1805 is a literary counterpart to Coleridge's more philosophical reflections in his *Biographia Literaria*, Goethe's *Fairy Tale* can be taken as a poetic reflection of Schiller's essay *On the Aesthetic Education of Man in a Series of Letters* (see note to p. 1 above). A translation of Goethe's "Fairy Tale" issued in 2009 by BLTC Press as a Kindle eBook contains two of Rudolf Steiner's essays on the work, by way of introduction.

21 **Devachan** theosophical term for a high region of the spiritual world.

21 **Pythagorean harmony of the spheres** Pythagoras of Samos (ca. 570-ca. 495 BCE), the greatest of the pre-Socratic philosophers, who held that the cosmos was ordered in the same mathematical proportions as the ratios underlying the musical intervals (e.g. the octave=1:2).

21 **astral** This is Steiner's early, theosophical term that corresponds generally to "soul" or "psyche." Like Freud and Jung, he sees it as internally differentiated and transformed by the activity of the higher faculty of the "ego." The *locus classicus* among Steiner's introductory works is the uncharacteristically schematic and static description in his early book *Theosophy* (1904; many English editions are available, including now a very inexpensive Kindle Edition from Amazon). A much more dynamic (but also much more difficult) account is to be found in the middle four lectures of Rudolf Steiner, *A Psychology of Body, Soul, & Spirit* (New York: SteinerBooks, 1999), which includes a valuable introduction by Robert Sardello.

22 **Jakob Böhme's first work** Jacob Böhme (1575-1624) was a great and prolific mystic and theologian. Böhme began writing *Aurora* twelve years after a powerful spiritual experience that befell him in 1600; although it was his first work, it remained unfinished at his death. Multiple translations are available, some in the public domain on the internet.

22 **his fragment, *The Mysteries*** Goethe began this epic poem in 1784, but by 1789 he had already given up on completing it, so he published it as a fragment. As best we can reconstruct his intentions, Goethe seems to have imagined a kind of secret society led by a sage named Humanus, who had gathered around him twelve "knights," each of whom practiced and represented one of the world's great religions. The works of Johann Valentin Andreae (1586-1654), who is thought to be the author of *The Alchemical Wedding* and other Rosicrucian texts, exerted a strong influence on Goethe here. Many of Goethe's esoteric ideas regarding religion were realized in Goethe's late novel *Wilhelm Meister's Journeymanship* of 1829. See also the note to p. 220.

24 **Montserrat** a mountain in Catalonia, Spain, northwest of Barcelona; the site of a famous Benedictine abbey; long thought to be the home of the Grail. For centuries it has been inhabited by hermits, and it was this aspect that inspired Goethe in writing the final scene of *Faust*.

24 **Parsifal** Wolfram von Eschenbach's *Parzival* (early 13th c.), the great medieval epic that was rediscovered during Goethe's lifetime.

24 **the Wanderer in the Vale** A cryptic reference. Does Steiner mean perhaps the famous, archetypally Romantic painting by Caspar David Friedrich, "Der Wanderer über dem Nebelmeer" [The Wanderer Above the Sea of Mist] (1818)?

24 **Buddhi** See the following note.

The Esoteric Foundation of Goethe's Creative Work

26 **Atma-Buddhi-Manas** These are theosophical terms referring to very high levels of spiritual consciousness that are currently exceptional, but will have

become normal human consciousness in the very distant future. These concepts are introduced in Steiner's books *Theosophy* and *An Outline of Esoteric Science*, on which see the note to p. 70 ***the fourth post-Atlantean cultural epoch.***

26 **And so long as this you lack** the final lines of Goethe's lyric "Blessed Yearning." See note to p. 17.

Goethe's Secret Revelation – Esoteric

28 **the *Fairy Tale*** See the note to p. 67 **a little monograph**.

The Riddles in Goethe's Faust *– Exoteric*

31 **Trithemius of Sponheim, Agrippa of Nettesheim** the controversial scholar and occultist Johannes Trithemius (1462-1516), so named because he was elected Abbott of the Benedictine abbey of Sponheim at age 21; and Agrippa of Nettesheim (1486-1535), author of the highly influential collection of magical and occult texts, *De occulta philosophi libri tres [Three Books of Occult Philosophy]*.

31 **Giordano Bruno, Galilei, Copernicus** The Italian Dominican philosopher, scientist, and theologian Bruno (b. 1548) was burned at the stake by the Catholic Church on February 17, 1600. See the classic study by Frances Yates, *Giordano Bruno and the Hermetic Tradition* (Chicago: U of Chicago P, 1964). Galileo Galilei (1564-1642), the Italian physicist, astronomer, and philosopher, is of course better known by his first name in the English-speaking world. Nicolaus Copernicus (1473-1543) was the first astronomer to publish a comprehensive and persuasive heliocentric account of the universe, *On the Revolutions of the Heavenly Spheres* (1543).

32 **the Luciferic Power** See the note to p. 89 **Lucifer and Ahriman**.

32 **maya or illusion** "Maya" is a theosophical term that Steiner uses frequently. It is a contraction of the Sanskrit terms *maha* [great], *a* [not or non-, like "alpha privative" in Ancient Greek; cf. "apolitical"], and *ya* [being]; hence, maya means literally "the great non-being." It is illusory because it seems to exist, but ultimately does not.

32 **Zarathustra** or Zoroaster, reputed to be the author of the *Gathas* and thereby the founder of Zoroastrianism. There are no historical records of his biography, and scholars have suspected that he may be a mythological figure, but Steiner asserts that there was indeed such a historical personage, who was a high initiate and one of humanity's greatest "spiritual guides." Nietzsche's fictional Zarathustra recalls this figure in name only.

32 **Ahriman** See the note to p. 89 **Lucifer and Ahriman**.

33 **The Helen scene** This part of what would become Act III, Part Two of *Faust* had a long and complicated genesis. A version of 300-plus lines was written in 1800, but Goethe was unsatisfied with it, and thus did not include the episode when he published Part One in 1808. The final version of Act III as a whole was published as a free-standing text in Goethe's collected works of 1827, under the

title *Helena, Classical-Romantic Phantasmagoria, an Interlude*, but it was only after Goethe's death that the whole of what we now consider Part Two was published.

34 **spiritual or spiritual-scientific** Wilhelm Dilthey (1833-1911) had used the same term (usually in the plural, *Geisteswissenschaften*) to distinguish the "humanities" (as we call them in English today) from natural science (*Naturwissenschaft*). He argued that the latter seeks to explain in terms of cause and effect, whereas the former explains by relating parts to wholes. (See Wilhelm Dilthey, *Introduction to the Human Sciences*, Selected Works, vol. 1 [Princeton: Princeton UP, 1991]). But a century earlier, Hegel had described a "science of the spirit" (*Wissenschaft des Geistes*), and already during his theosophical phase, Steiner employs the word *Geisteswissenschaft* in a fundamentally different sense that makes it a synonym for "anthroposophy." In such contexts, the term is best translated by the firmly established locution "spiritual science."

The Riddles in Goethe's Faust *– Esoteric*

35 **the physical and etheric bodies** "Etheric body" is Steiner's early, theosophical term for the body of supra-physical forces that sustains life. Later he would also refer to it variously as "the life body," or the "formative forces body," or (echoing Spinoza's distinction between *natura naturans* and *natura naturata*), the realm of "living working" as opposed to the physical realm of "finished work." Theodor Schwenk's *Sensitive Chaos: The Creation of Flowing Forms in Water and Air* (London: Rudolf Steiner Press, 1996) is a scientifically compelling and aesthetically beautiful exploration of these forces.

38 **It smells so green** Steiner is following closely Schröer's commentary on this passage.

LECTURES

1. Goethe's Faust *from the Standpoint of Spiritual Science*

43 **Public lecture** Steiner distinguished rather sharply between his published books and public lectures on the one hand, and his private lectures to members of, first the Theosophical, then later the Anthroposophical Society. The latter were taken down stenographically, and not reviewed or revised by the author before being circulated among the members. Only after Steiner's death did the Society begin to publish the hundreds of volumes of private lectures, always with the same disclaimer that precedes both of these volumes (q.v.). As one might imagine, the public lectures are in general much less esoteric than Steiner's talks before the members.

43 ***in the earlier lectures*** *These lectures began in Winter 1905.*

44 ***Using Goethe's words, we might say: There are such things as spiritual eyes and ears*** Goethe's Scientific Writings. *Ed. Rudolf Steiner. Vol. I, 1883. "Outline for a General Introduction to Comparative Anatomy, Commencing with Osteology. (p. 262) "We learn to see with spiritual eyes, without which, as scientists – as elsewhere – we grope* *about like blind men." Rudolf Steiner's commentary on this passage: "In these words one finds the key to Goethe's view of nature. To see with spiritual eyes means to see the form of the animal not just as it presents itself to the senses, but rather to be able to comprehend it (intuitively) in its underlying Idea in that Idea's proper form. Every empirical form then manifests a variation on that Idea, but the Idea gives us the norm and the criterion for deciding how to explain such a particular form." See also the passage on Kaspar Friedrich Wolf in "Sequel: On the Formation and Transformation of Organisms": "...that the eyes of the spirit must act in an ongoing, living alliance with the eyes of the body, because otherwise one runs the danger of looking without seeing." Rudolf Steiner's comment: "These words demonstrate yet again how profound Goethe's views are compared to those of mere empiricism. Whereas empiricism recognizes only what the senses perceive, Goethe wanted above all for us to see with the eyes of the spirit, i.e., to make the goal of our research the lawfulness that underlies and governs the concrete, sensory presentation, while persisting as a spiritual reality" (p. 107).*

45 ***Francesco Redi*** *1626-1697*, Tuscan physician to the Medici and naturalist, most famous for his experiment of 1688 in which he disproved the prevailing notion of "abiogenesis" or "spontaneous generation," replacing it with the epochal theory that Huxley would later term "biogenesis." See Francesco Redi, *Experiments on the Generation of Insects* (1688), trans. Mab Bigelow (Chicago: Open Court, 1909).

46 ***shown absolutely scientifically*** *In 1903 Rudolf Steiner had already published an essay entitled "Reincarnation and Karma, Two Concepts Necessitated by Modern Science." It has been republished in vol. 34 of the Complete Edition [GA],* Luzifer-Gnosis: Gesammelte Aufsätze [Lucifer-Gnosis: Collected Essays] 1903-1908. This volume seems not to have been translated into English.

48 ***finds expression in his beautiful prose hymn*** *"Nature"* [Johann Wolfgang von Goethe, *Scientific Studies*, ed. and trans. Douglas Miller (New York: Suhrkamp Publishers, 1988), pp. 3-5]: *"Nature! We are surrounded and embraced by her – powerless to leave her, and powerless to enter her more deeply. Unasked and without warning she sweeps us away in the round of her dance and dances on until we fall exhausted from her arms....She thought and she thinks still, not as a man, but as nature. She keeps to herself her own all-embracing thoughts which none may discover from her....She loves herself, she adores herself eternally with countless eyes and hearts....It is not I who has spoken of her. No, what is true and what is false, all this she has spoken."*

Because Goethe included this text in one of his journals, he was long thought to have been the author, although Goethe told his secretary late in life that he could not remember having written it. Scholars are now in agreement that the author was Johann Georg Christoph Tobler (1757-1812), a Swiss theologian whom Goethe knew. Goethe also told Eckermann that in any case the "hymn" captured very well his own thinking at the time. Freud claimed that reading this short piece as a young man persuaded him to become a scientist.

49 **"Antiquity" in his beautiful book on Winckelmann** The German art historian and classical archaeologist Johann Joachim Winckelmann (1717-1768).

Given its brevity, it would be more accurate to describe Goethe's "Winckelmann" (1805) as an essay. Many consider Winckelmann the founder of modern art history, and Goethe was among the first to appreciate his importance. Goethe's essay is a widely admired classic. For more on Winckelmann himself, see the splendid recent study by Alex Potts, *Flesh and the Ideal: Winckelmann and the Origins of Art History* (New Haven: Yale UP, 1994).

50 **Susanne von Klettenberg** 1723-1774; she helped nurse Goethe back to health during his grave illness, and introduced him to many hermetic and alchemical texts that influenced his later work profoundly.

50 **"Confessions of a Beautiful Soul"** This is the title given to Book Six of Goethe's novel *Wilhelm Meister's Apprenticeship*, which has been translated admirably by Eric Blackall (New York: Suhrkamp, 1989; rpt. Princeton: Princeton UP, 1995). This archetypal *Bildungsroman* is arguably the most important and influential novel in all of German literature. The "Confessions of a Beautiful Soul" is a fictional document that needs to be read with care: its many ironic undercurrents make it clear enough that Goethe was both sympathetic to the Pietism it evokes and highly critical of it.

51 ***because no one has any idea what these signs are supposed to mean*** *In the original, one finds the following "Explanation of the figure "Abyssae Duplicatae or, Of the doubled, fleeting, and fixed Abyss" accompanying the "sign":*

One abyss calls forth the other,
Together, they form a hard bouquet:
The fluid shall become entirely fixed,*
Water and vapor return to earth.
Heaven itself must be earthly,
Otherwise no life enters into the earthly realm.
That which is most high shall become lowest,
The lowest shall become the highest and best.
The fixed shall become completely fluid,*
A water and a vapor earth shall become.
Earth must fly up to the highest heaven,
Heaven crawl into the center of the earth.
In this way, heaven and earth must be inverted,
The lowest shall become highest.
The fluid dragon kills the fixed one,*
The fixed dragon compels the death of the fluid one.*
In this way, the quintessence, and all that it can do,
Must be revealed unto the light of day.

The original is rhymed in couplets, which I have not attempted to render in this literal translation. /* Translating the German word "flüchtig," which can also mean "fleeting" or "fugitive."

52 **namely, the cathedral** See Goethe's important essay "On German Archi-tecture [Von deutscher Baukunst]" of 1772 (*Essays on Art and Literature*, ed. John Geary,

vol. 3 of *Goethe: The Collected Works* [Cambridge, Mass.: Suhrkamp, 1986; rpt. Princeton UP], pp. 3-10). This panegyric on the architect of the Straßburg Cathedral, Erwin von Steinbach, is an important document of German proto-Romanticism, which is often referred to as the *Sturm und Drang* or "Storm and Stress" movement. Goethe praises von Steinbach as a prime example of the "genius" who, unlike the neo-classical craftsman who has learned rules, has tapped into the living powers of Nature, and uses them to create entirely new, organic forms. Although few art historians would agree with him today, Goethe saw the Gothic style in architecture as a prime example of organic form, and hence a model for the new art Goethe, Herder, and others of his generation were envisioning.

53 ***Oh, he [Goethe] said*** *Rome, August 18, 1787, letter to Knebel: "After everything that I have seen in Naples, in Sicily, in the way of plants and fish, I would, if I were ten years younger, be tempted to undertake a journey to India,* ***not in order to discover something new, but in order to view that which I have discovered in my own way.****"*

53 ***in one letter*** *Rome, September 6, 1787.*

54 **Nostradamus-aura** Michel de Nostredame (1503-1566), the notorious French apothecary best known for his book of *Prophecies* (1555).

55 **following his Italian journey** Steiner refers here to the scene "Forest and Cave" (3217-3373), which was composed in 1788-1789, at the end of Goethe's two-year stay in Italy, and right after his return to Germany.

56 **in his drama *Pandora*** A fragment, published as such in 1808, and never completed. This dense, symbolic piece elicited head-scratching even among Goethe's closest friends: his secretary Eckermann, for example, told Goethe that, even after reading this "difficult" text so many times he had nearly memorized it, he felt he had only barely begun to understand what it might mean (conversation of October 21, 1823). *Pandora* would be an early example of Goethe's enigmatic "late style," which arrived full-blown the following year in Goethe's third novel, *Elective Affinities.*

57 ***They say Faust's pretty good*** *in* Deutsche Nationalliteratur, *Bd. 3. 1 (Goethes Werke, Dritter Teil, 1).*

58 ***to the Mothers*** In the scene "Dark Gallery," in Part Two (lines 6173-6306).

60 **Anaxagoras and Thales** Anaxagoras of Clazomenae (ca. 500-ca. 428 BCE) and Thales of Miletus (ca. 624-ca. 546 BCE). Both are important pre-Socratic philosophers. Aristotle considered Thales to have been the first Greek philosopher, and Betrand Russell credits him with having founded the whole of Western philosophy. An excellent resource on the pre-Socratics in English is G. S. Kirk and J. E. Raven, *The Presocratic Philosophers: A Critical History with a Selection of Texts* (Cambridge: Cambridge UP, 1971).

60 ***Then Homunculus is told*** *In the final scene of the "Classical Walpurgis Night," "Rocky Inlets of the Aegean Sea"* (as translated by Arndt in the Norton Critical Edition):

HOMUNCULUS
Here a most gentle ether breezes,
It smells so fresh [Es grunelt so], and the aroma pleases!
(8265-8266)

THALES
Espouse the recommended part,
Begin creation from the start.
For swift enchantment gird your will!
You move there by eternal norms,
Through thousand thousand, countless thousand forms,
There's time enough for manship still.
(8321-8326)

61 ***This is why he was able to say to Eckermann*** On Eckermann's *Conversations*, see the note to p. 17. *January 29, 1827*: *"And yet, everything is concrete, and would please everyone's eye if performed on the stage. I sought nothing more than this. As long as the majority of the crowd takes pleasure in the* ***appearance****, the higher meaning will also not be lost on the adept, as is the case with* The Magic Flute *and other things."* (The German word translated "adept" here is "der Eingeweihte," literally: "the initiate.")

63 ***these closing words*** *"Hier wird's Erreichnis"* [lit., "Here it becomes attainment"]. *Here Steiner follows the conjecture put forth by Ad* [albert] *Rudolf* [ca. 1883]. *But in 1928 a manuscript in Goethe's own handwriting was discovered that gave "Ereignis"* [lit. "event," "occurrence"] *in this line.* Schröer's commentary on this passage mentions Adalbert Rudolf's speculation, but for the text of his edition, Schröer also chose "Ereignis." (See the note immediately following.)

64 **What is ... inadequate** "Das Unzulängliche," which means, literally, "the inadequate" (as a noun); "that which falls short." Here, Goethe's use of this word is thus highly unconventional. It seems to refer to human action as viewed from a divine perspective. Yet, Faust has arrived in a realm where the goal of human activity is nevertheless attained, through divine Grace. On this reading, the language is still puzzling, however, the underlying notion turns out to be surprisingly orthodox.

2. The Relationship of Goethe's Faust *to Goethe*

67 ***Frau Wandrey's*** *Camilla Wandrey, 1819-1941, member of the Anthroposophical Society in Berlin; later she lived in Dornach* [, Switzerland].

67 ***a little monograph*** *In 1918, Steiner published "Goethes Geistesart in ihrer Offenbarung durch seinen Faust und durch das Märchen 'von der Schlange und der Lilie'* [*Goethe's Thought as Revealed by Faust and by the Fairy-Tale of 'The [Green] Snake and the [Beautiful] Lily'*]." *This long essay was published as GA 22.* The only available translation of this work seems to be an edition published by the

Anthroposophical Publishing Company, London, in 1925, now long out of print, with the infelicitous title *Goethe's Standard of the Soul as Illustrated in Faust and in the Fairy Story of "The Green Snake and the Beautiful Lily."* Excerpts from this essay will be included in the second volume of commentaries (GA 273), in keeping with the chronology of its publication. See also the note to p. 20.

*69 **They say Faust's pretty good** See the note to p. 57.*

69 **in his *Tasso* and his *Iphigenie* ... *Götz von Berlichingen*** Three of Goethe's early dramas: *Torquato Tasso* (completed 1790), *Iphigenia in Tauris* (completed 1786), and *Götz von Berlichingen with the Iron Hand* (1773). Each had a complicated genesis with multiple versions. *Tasso* and *Iphigenia* are contained in Goethe, *Verse Dramas and Prose Plays*, vol. 8 of *The Collected Works* (New York: Suhrkamp, 1987; rpt. Princeton: Princeton UP, 1995); *Götz* is contained in vol. 7, *Early Verse Dramas and Prose Plays* (New York: Suhrkamp, 1988; rpt. Princeton: Princeton UP, 1995).

70 **the marvelous scene beginning, "Exalted spirit..."** See note to p. 55.

*70 **the fourth post-Atlantean cultural epoch*** Steiner uses this theosophical term to designate a major historical era he saw as having begun ca. 747 BCE, and ended ca. 1413 CE. He also terms it the Greco-Roman Epoch. The name implies that Greece and Rome were the "vanguard" cultures during the period, i.e. the loci of innovation and progress. He sees other cultures such as ancient India, Persia, and Egypt having been the leaders during even earlier periods. Steiner's terminology is idiosyncratic here, but the underlying thoughts are commonplaces of intellectual history.

See Rudolf Steiner, An Outline of Esoteric Science, *trans. Catherine E. Creeger (SteinerBooks, 1997) [GA 13].* An excellent earlier translation by George Adams bore the unfortunate title *Occult Science*. At the time of writing Steiner was the head of the Theosophical Society in Germany, and the word *Geheimwissenschaft* in his title was meant to echo Blavatsky's tome, *The Secret Doctrine*. GA 13 is now considered one of the four "basic books" of anthroposophy.

*70 **he wrote from Italy** Rome, January 28, 1787. Literally: "I surmise that they – those incomparable artists – proceeded according to exactly the same laws as Nature, and it is those laws I am trying to track down."*

70 **Spinoza** Baruch de Spinoza (1632-1677), the great and greatly misunderstood Dutch rationalist. Together with his mentor Herder, Goethe was instrumental in saving Spinoza from obscurity after he had been declared heretical by all sides. Goethe famously included Spinoza on a list of three figures who had influenced him most deeply, and there is an important letter of May 5, 1786, in which Goethe claims to have dedicated his life to Spinoza's project. On Goethe and Spinoza, see Frederick Amrine, "Goethean Intuitions," *The Goethe Yearbook*, 18 (2011), 35-50.

*71 **as he said** Rome, September 6, 1787.* The following quote is contained in that letter.

71 **the fifth post-Atlantean cultural epoch** See the note to p. 70 ***the fourth post-Atlantean cultural epoch*** above. This is Steiner's theosophical term for the current historical epoch, which he sees as having begun ca. 1413 – i.e., with the Renaissance.

71 **the isolated, finished quality and calm perfection** The allusion here is surely to Winckelmann's famous characterization of Greek art as "noble simplicity and quiet grandeur." See the note to p. 49.

71 **the "how" of the work** Here Steiner is echoing a famous line from *Faust*, spoken by Homunculus to the pedant Wagner in Part Two, Act Two: "das Was bedenke, mehr bedenke wie" (6992), which translates literally: "consider the what, more consider how."

71 **Dürer or Holbein** The greatest German painter of the Renaissance, Albrecht Dürer (1471-1528), and probably Hans Holbein the Elder (1460-1524), rather than his son Hans Holbein the Younger (1497-1543), since he was Dürer's contemporary and more of a pioneer.

73 ***the "Guardian of the Threshold"*** *Rudolf Steiner,* Knowledge of the Higher Worlds: How is it Achieved? *(London: Rudolf Steiner Press, 2004). GA 10.* An older translation (originally 1947) is still available under the title *Knowledge of the Higher Worlds and its Attainment.* Also see *How to Know Higher Worlds* (Great Barrington, MA: SteinerBooks, 1994).

74 ***in Blavatsky's works*** *H[elena] P[etrovna] Blavatsky (1831-1891), founder of the Theosophical Society.*

79 **the Old Moon** This term from Steiner's highly esoteric cosmogony refers not to the current satellite of planet Earth, but rather an earlier evolutionary stage or "incarnation" of the entire cosmos. "Old Moon" was preceded by "Old Sun," and that was preceded in turn by "Old Saturn." Future states of the cosmos he terms "Jupiter," "Venus," and "Vulcan." The *locus classicus* is ch. 4 of Steiner's book *Outline of Esoteric Science* (see the note to p. 70 **the fourth post-Atlantean cultural epoch**), but it is one of the most challenging texts in all of Steiner's works – definitely not for beginners.

80 **he speaks of an "*Übermensch*"** This word, conventionally translated "superman," was Goethe's coinage, and it was indeed (as one might suspect) the inspiration for Nietzsche's notorious concept. The word first occurs early in Goethe's *Faust*, where it is hurled at Faust by the Earth Spirit as a sarcastic epithet, intended to mock his lack of spiritual maturity.

82 **in ever-changing water** literally, "in the metamorphosing water," an image of the dynamic, mobile kind of thinking that is needed to interpret texts of such high spirituality.

82 ***All that must pass away*** *The* [now established] *closing verses were not quoted, but rather* [the variation described in the notes to pp. 69 and 70 above].

3. (From GA 139) The Gospel of St. Mark

83 This excerpt is a revision by Burley Channer of Conrad Mainzer's translation, published in Rudolf Steiner, *The Gospel of St. Mark* (New York: Anthroposophic Press, 2000).

84 **the great philosopher Empedocles** The standard English translation is to be found in *Ancilla to the Pre-Socratic Philosophers*, trans. Kathleen Freeman (Cambridge, Mass.: Harvard UP, 1957), pp. 51-69. See also Kirk and Raven (cited in the note to p. 55 above), pp. 320-361.

85 **the Mystery of Golgotha** One of Steiner's terms for all that is more conventionally referred to as the Incarnation, the Passion, the Resurrection. One of Steiner's earliest publications, his book *Christianity as Mystical Fact*, situates Christianity squarely within the context of ancient mystery religions (rather than mysticism, which the title might seem to imply). This important text is now vol. 8 of the Collected Works, and the latest edition (New York: Anthroposophic Press, 1997) was both translated and introduced by Andrew Welburn, who is himself a scholar and an anthroposophist of great stature. In the same spirit, Steiner also refers to the Easter Mystery.

87 **a real historical personage living in the sixteenth century** The standard study of the historical Dr. Faustus remains Philip M. Mason and Robert P. More, *The Sources of the Faust Tradition* (New York: Oxford UP, 1936). See also E. M. Butler, *The Myth of the Magus* (New York: Macmillan, 1948; rpt. Cambridge UP, 1993).

4. Faust's Struggle for the Christ-Permeated Source of Life

89 **Eurythmy** the new art of movement inaugurated by Steiner in 1912. See the introduction to this volume.

89 ***the transformation of the scenery*** *At the words, "Christ has arisen," the black color of the scenery had changed to red.*

89 ***what could be said yesterday*** *Lecture of April 3, 1915,* now included in a volume of the Complete Works [GA 161] entitled *Wege der geistigen Erkenntnis und der Erneuerung künstlerischer Weltanschauung [Paths to Spiritual Knowledge and the Renewal of the Arts]*. This volume seems not to have been translated into English.

89 **Lucifer and Ahriman** Rudolf Steiner spoke often about the dual nature of evil, ascribing its source to supersensible beings he calls Lucifer and Ahriman. For an excellent discussion of Steiner's ideas as applied to Goethe's *Faust*, see Alan P. Cottrell, *Goethe's View of Evil and the Search for a New Image of Man in our Time* (n.p.: Floris Press, 1982).

Lucifer might be termed the "red devil," who tempts humans to sin on the side of *superbia*: pride, anger, egotism, erotic passions, etc. "Ahriman" is a traditional name for a black demon, beginning with the Zoroastrian figure Angra Mainyu, opponent of the Sun God Ahura Mazda. Ahriman's temptations are those of *acedia*: laziness, greed, denial of the Spirit generally.

Lucifer and Ahriman also appear as characters in Steiner's own expressionist *Mystery Dramas* (1910-1913). See GA 14, Rudolf Steiner, *Four Mystery Dramas*, trans. Ruth and Hans Pusch (SteinerBooks, 2007) rpt. SteinerBooks, 2014. Both figures are part of Steiner's statue "The Group," which he discusses extensively in Lecture V (May 22, 1915) below.

In a lecture of 26 August 1916, now published as GA 170, *The Riddle of Humanity: The Spiritual Background of Human History* (London: Rudolf Steiner Press, 1990), Steiner draws a striking parallel between the account of the Fall in Genesis and its "complementary symbol" [*Gegensymbolum*] in Goethe's *Faust*. Just as Adam and Eve must encounter Lucifer in the Garden of Eden, so Faust and Gretchen must grapple with Ahriman. But here the seduction is inverted: Steiner sees Ahriman tempting Gretchen via Faust's lies about theology. See also the lecture of August 28, 1916, in this volume.

92 **the Christ-impulse** "Impulse" is one of Steiner's favorite words. It crops up everywhere, and it is always (but only mildly) metaphorical. Because the term is so resolutely physical, but its referent is invariably spiritual or cultural, the effect can be jarring. As is so easily done in German, Steiner will frequently coin new terms by conjoining it with other words, e.g. "Faust-impulse" (p. 96), "Resurrection-impulse" (p. 104), and "I-impulse." "Christ-impulse" occurs very frequently, and it makes sense in the context of Steiner's view of Christianity as a cosmic event unfolding over eons, of which even the Incarnation is but a single chapter.

93 **the Jupiter existence** See note to p. 79 **the Old Moon** above.

93 **the Easter Mystery** See the note to p. 85 **the Mystery of Golgotha** above.

96 **a "yellowed, time-stained manuscript"** *Italian Journey*, March 1, 1788 (during the "Second Stay in Rome").

96 ***Goethe told him how ... the old monster*** **Faust** *Goethe's letter to Schiller of December 6, 1797: "Surely I shall take up my Faust first of all, partly in order to get rid of this monster*, and partly in order to prepare myself for a higher and purer mood..." See the chronology in vol. 2 of this edition,* [*sub*] 1794. /*The word Goethe uses here is actually *tragelaphos* [*Tragelaph*], an arcane and erudite allusion to a creature from Greek mythology, half-goat and half-stag. According to Giovanna Sillitti (*Tragelaphos: Storia di una metafora e di una problema* [Naples, 1981]), the tragelaphos is often invoked in Classical philosophy as a metaphor implying something fabulous, unreal, or monstrous.

97 **one man who is by no means stupid** The author of the following quote was Friedrich Theodor Vischer (1807-1887), most famous as the author of a ponderous treatise on aesthetics that appeared in four volumes from 1846-1854. He also lampooned the second part of Goethe's *Faust* in his own imagined continuation, *Faust: Part Three* (1886).

97 ***lectures I once gave in The Hague*** *March 20-29, 1913; published as GA 145,* The Effect of Spiritual Development *(Rudolf Steiner Press, 1978).* Steiner obviously considered this cycle of ten lectures important: he refers to it in each of the following two lectures as well. Here, he seems to be referring to lectures 4, 6, and 7 (March 23rd, 25th, and 26th). In lecture 4, he contrasts our spatial experience of the physical world with the etheric world, which is experienced by the initiate as a realm of flowing time-processes. In lectures 6 and 7, Steiner offers extended discussions of Grail myths (especially Wolfram von Eschenbach's *Parsifal*), and then goes on to recount the same "prehistory" of the Faust-theme (St. Augustine, the Manichaean Bishop Faustus, and Fausto Andrelino) that follows immediately here.

97 ***Dr. Georg Faustus*** *This account of the historical Dr. Faustus follows closely Herman Grimm's essay "Die Entstehung des Volksbuches von Dr. Faust [The Origin of the Faust Chapbook]," collected in Herman Grimm,* Fünfzehn Essays [Fifteen Essays], *vol. 3 (Berlin, 1882), pp. 192-219.* For more on Herman Grimm, see the notes to p. 10 and 170. Grimm's essay begins by tracing the Faust chapbook back to three known sources: gossip and anecdotes surrounding a known historical figure, Georg Faust; the Manichean Bishop Faustus who is described in Augustine's autobiographical *Confessions*, and was for a time Augustine's mentor; and an Italian Professor at the University of Paris, Fausto Andrelino (1450-1518), who was a fearless opponent of the Scholastics, and seems to have exhibited the kinds of erotic and other sensual desires we find in the chapbook. Grimm concludes his essay with a lengthy conjecture about a lost dramatic version, perhaps in the form of a Latin school comedy, that he imagines vividly, but had not been able to find. For more on the chapbook, see the note to p. 5.

97 **Master Georg Sabellicus** Steiner is quoting here verbatim from p. 194 of Grimm's essay.

98 **the daemonic world** Not to be confused with "demonic"; see the note to p. 18.

99 **the medieval "Faust Book"** Steiner means the aforementioned chapbook of 1587, which might be more accurately described as "early modern" rather than "medieval."

100 **Erasmus of Rotterdam** Desiderius Erasmus (1466-1536), the "Prince of Humanists," who published a critical edition of the New Testament in Greek, and championed the idea of human free will against the Lutheran and Calvinist notions of predestination. One of the most important texts of the Reformation, Luther's tract *On the Bondage of the Will*, is a polemic against Erasmus.

102 ***even in Marlowe's*** **Faust** *Christopher Marlowe, English dramatist (1564-1593);* Doctor Faustus, *ed. David Scott Kastan (Norton Critical Edition, 2004).*

102 **atavistic clairvoyance** One of Steiner's central ideas is that the structure of human consciousness itself has evolved over time (often referred to as "the evolution of consciousness"). He argues that a dreamlike but direct awareness of the spiritual world even in waking life was ubiquitous in ancient cultures. Remnants of this consciousness survive among aboriginal peoples to this day. Steiner studies this phenomenon chiefly as it manifests in mythology, but there is of course much additional evidence available in other areas such as shamanism, totemism, and the various hermetic sciences that were revived by intellectual elites

during the Middle Ages and the Renaissance. The best single treatment of this idea is Owen Barfield's masterpiece, *Saving the Appearances: A Study in Idolatry* (1957; most recently rpt. Middletown: Wesleyan UP, 1988). On "atavistic clairvoyance," see Ch. VI, "Original Participation," where Barfield connects Steiner's insights with more familiar anthropological notions such as Émile Durkheim's work on totemism and Levy-Brühl's "participation mystique."

104 ***our building, dedicated as it is to spiritual investigation*** *Steiner refers here to the First Goetheanum, which was still under construction in 1915, and was eventually destroyed by an arsonist on the night of December 31, 1922–January 1, 1923.*

5. Faust's Forced Entry into the Spiritual World

108 **my book, *Theosophy*** See the note to p. 21.

109 ***in the Vienna lecture cycle of April, 1914*** *GA 153,* Inner Nature of Man and Our Life Between Death and Rebirth *(London: Rudolf Steiner Press, 1995).*

114 ***at the time he wrote this scene*** *Goethe had composed this colloquy between Faust and the Earth Spirit already in the 1770s.*

114 **to become a super-man** See the note to p. 80 **he speaks of an "*Übermensch.*"**

116 ***read the lectures given in the Hague*** *See note to p. 97* ***lectures I once gave.*** Here Steiner seems to be referring to lectures 4, 5, and 6 (March 23rd, 24th, and 25th), where he describes a "heightened feeling for time" [*gesteigertes Zeitgefühl*] that arises during spiritual development. For the initiate, time itself becomes "independent" and "differentiated," a substantial medium in which one can swim, as it were. This heightened feeling is able to perceive directly that time itself is an integral component of the wisdom that streams toward the perceiver.

117 ***to have a performance of* Faust *sometime*** *In Steiner's staging at the Goetheanum in Dornach, Wagner appears in a costume similar to Faust's, so that the juxtaposition described here is clear.*

120 *Knowledge of the Higher Worlds and Its Attainment;* ***How to Know Higher Worlds*** See the note to p. 73.

125 ***eight months ago*** *The outbreak of World War I.*

6. Pentecost Mood: Faust's Initiation with the Spirits of the Earth

128 ***the Mystery of Golgotha*** See the note to p. 85. *See also Steiner's many cycles of lectures on the Gospels.*

129 **a statue that we intend to erect** Steiner was still working on this monumental sculptural composition in his atelier, so it was spared when the First Goetheanum burned to the ground on New Year's Eve 1922/1923. It remained incomplete at his death in 1925.

131 **Michelangelo's painting of the *Last Judgment*** This immense fresco covers the altar wall of the Sistine Chapel in the Vatican. It took Michelangelo Buonarotti (1475-1564) four years to complete the project (1537-1541).

133 **the non-Christian kind of theosophy** i.e., the main, Anglo-American theosophical movement, as opposed to theosophy as taught by Steiner as Secretary of the German Section.

134 **"tragelaph"** See the note to p. 96 ***Goethe told him how.***

134 ***he called his* Faust** *Goethe's letter to Schiller of June 17, 1797: "Your remarks on Faust pleased me very much. As is only natural, they conform very well to my plans and intentions, only I'm making it more comfortable for myself with this barbaric composition by only touching on the highest demands, rather than fulfilling them."*

135 ***Rieger*** *Maximilian Rieger (1828-1909),* a[n obscure] scholar *of German literature.* Rieger wrote extensively on Goethe's contemporary Friedrich Maximilian Klinger (1752-1831), who also wrote a version of *Faust* which was published in 1791.

136 **his musican friend, Zelter** Carl Friedrich Zelter (1758-1832), a mediocre musician who became a close friend of Goethe's and, unfortunately, the arbiter of Goethe's taste in music. Their correspondence is massive, running to 891 letters over 33 years. The scholarly consensus regarding Zelter's musical judgment and personality has long been negative, but a recent edition of the correspondence in English (Lorraine Byrne Bodley, ed., *Goethe and Zelter: Musical Dialogues* [Ashgate, 2009]) has attempted to place him in a more positive light.

136 ***A significant passage!*** *Goethe's letter to Zelter of February 11, 1830: "One must be mindful that, with every breath, an etheric Lethe* [ein ätherischer Lethestrom] *permeates our entire being, so that we recall joys only vaguely, and sorrows hardly at all. I have always prized this divine gift, which I learned to employ and to intensify at will."*

136 **an etheric Lethe-stream** In Greek mythology, Lethe was a one of the five rivers of the underworld, Hades. The name means "oblivion" because all who drank from it would forget everything. The Ancient Greek word for truth, *aletheia*, means literally "the un-forgotten."

141 ***Read my last cycle of lectures given in the Hague*** *See note to pp. 97 and 116.* The relevant lectures here seem to be the 4th and 5th (March 23rd and 24th), which describe how spiritual development leads to an enhanced sensitivity to the changing seasons, and then eventually to an experience of the macrocosmic etheric realm, where wisdom flows toward the perceiver on streams of time.

7. Faust, *The World's Greatest Poetic Work of Human Striving: The Classical Phantasmagoria*

150 ***the other lectures I gave here a week ago*** *GA 161; see note to p. 89 above.*

151 **between death and a new earthly birth** This is an important and recurrent motif in Steiner's work. An excellent introduction to the topic would be Ch. 3, "Sleep and Death," of his "basic book" *An Outline of Esoteric Science* (GA 13; see note to p. 70 ***the fourth post-Atlantean cultural epoch***). A fuller treatment is available e.g. in GA 153, *The Inner Nature of Man and Our Life Between Birth and Death* (London: Rudolf Steiner P, 1995).

153 **This is how the idea of being destroyed** Steiner's phrasing of this complex idea, that watching one process of destruction (an diesem Anschauen) develops the capacity to watch a different one (für das Anschauen), is exactly parallel to Goethe's phrasing of the idea that the eye has developed "by virtue of" the light "for" the light (am Lichte fürs Licht). J.W. von Goethe, Introduction to *Theory of Color.* (B.C.)

156 **my book, *Riddles of Philosophy*** GA 18; the latest English translation was reprinted by SteinerBooks in 2009. Originally published in 1914, this compendious history of philosophy (627 pp. in the German critical edition) is one of the most important texts in which he worked out the idea that Owen Barfield has termed "the evolution of consciousness." As opposed to conventional intellectual history, in which a succession of different ideas are seen as inhabiting epistemological structures presumed to be constant, Steiner argued forcefully that the structure of human consciousness itself has changed, and that it is the evolution of the structure of consciousness itself that is the main contributor to the succession of different paradigms or mentalities that are the object of intellectual history.

157 **Kant** Immanuel Kant (1724-1804) was surely the most important modern philosopher, a great revolutionary who changed philosophy utterly and irrevocably. Hans-Georg Gadamer went so far as to argue that all subsequent philosophy has been little more than a series of attempts to rewrite Kant. He was the founder and the inspiration of both German Idealism and German philosophical Romanticism, and the German philosophers within those movements who influenced Steiner most directly (Goethe, Fichte, Schiller, and Hegel) were all profoundly indebted to Kant while simultaneously criticizing what they saw as major shortcomings in his philosophy. Fichte and Schiller both described their philosophical work as attempts to rewrite the letter of Kant in the spirit of Kant. As a philosopher, Steiner was also both deeply indebted to Kant and at the same time sharply critical of him, although his most trenchant criticisms are usually directed not at Kant's actual positions, but rather the reductive neo-Kantianism of Steiner's contemporaries. Steiner's relationship to Kant is an important and controversial issue that greatly exceeds the scope of this commentary.

159 **suddenly disappeared in the dead of night** Steiner is referring to Goethe's unannounced departure for Italy, which took even his closest friends by surprise.

163 **working and feeling one's way into the whole of nature** This passage has a distinctly Spinozistic ring to it: cf. the famous passage in his early treatise *On the Improvement of the Understanding*, where Spinoza defines the highest human ideal as "knowledge of the union of the mind with the whole of nature." See the note to p. 70.

163 ***"the old tragelaph, the barbaric composition."*** *See the note to p. 96* ***Goethe told him how.***

166 **Edinger, one of the most significant philosophers of our time** Steiner surely means Ludwig Edinger (1855-1918), in which case "scientist" might be more accurate than "philosopher." Ludwig Edinger has been called "the founder of modern neuroanatomy," and he had been named the first German professor of neurology the previous year (1914). Apparently, he was also an accomplished artist and "a noted hypnotist" (!). See e.g. L. Edinger and A. Wallenberg, *Bericht über die Leistungen auf dem Gebiete der Anatomie des Centralnervensystems* (Bonn, 1912). His daughter, Tilly Edinger (1897-1967), would become one of the leading vertebrate paleontologists of the 20th century. Having fled the Nazis, she came to the United States in 1940, and eventually held an appointment at Harvard's Museum of Comparative Zoology.

170 ***he told Eckermann*** *We quote here the passage in Eckermann's* Conversations with Goethe *(1836-1848) dated 13 February 1831: "...all that can be done with such a composition is to make the individual components meaningful and clear. The work as a whole, on the other hand, always remains incommensurable, but for just that reason, it calls upon us to contemplate it over and over, like an unsolved problem."* On Eckermann's *Conversations*, see the note to p. 17 **the "higher meaning."**

170 ***Herman Grimm*** See the notes to pp. 10 **Herman Grimm** and 97 **Dr. Georg Faustus**. *Steiner refers here to the first of Grimm's* Goethe: gehalten an der Königlichen Universität zu Berlin *[Lectures on Goethe Held at the University of Berlin] (Berlin, 1874/1875): "Goethe's first century is now at an end, but, as far into the future as we are able to peer, no subsequent century will be spared the effort of coming to terms with Goethe. For that to happen, the German people would have to change their very nature. For millennia, there has existed a discipline called 'Homer' that has found admirers with unbroken continuity. For centuries, there has been a whole discipline devoted to Dante, and another to Shakespeare. From now on, there will always exist a discipline called 'Goethe'."* These lectures seem never to have been translated into English, but the German original remains in print to this day; indeed, multiple editions are currently available.

8. Faust's Ascension

172 ***ever since 1884*** *This was the year in which the first volume of Goethe's scientific works, edited by Rudolf Steiner with an introduction by Karl Julius Schröer, appeared in the "Kürschner" edition.* The introductions to the various sections of this edition were later published as vol. 1 of Steiner's Collected Works. The latest English edition is a handsome offering from the Anthroposophic Press, *Nature's Open*

Secret: Rudolf Steiner's Introductions to Goethe's Scientific Works (2000). Earlier translations can still be found: *Goethe the Scientist* (Anthroposophic Press, 1950), and *Goethean Science* (Mercury Press, 1988). *See also the essay "Goethes Recht in der Naturwissenschaft: Eine Rettung [Goethe's Place in Science: An Apology]," in GA 30,* Methodische Grundlagen der Anthroposophie 1884-1901: Gesammelte Aufsätze zur Philosophie, Naturwissenschaft, Ästhetik und Seelenkunde [Methodological Foundations of Anthroposophy 1884-1901: Collected Essays on Philosophy, Science, Aesthetics and Psychology], *pp. 227-231.* [Unfortunately, this essay seems never to have been translated.] *This lecture contains the central thoughts of the various Introductions.*

173 ***Soothsayings of Bakis*** *Die Weissagungen des Bakis* (1799). Available in English as *The Soothsayings of Bakis: Goethe's Tragi-Comic Observations on Life, Time and History* (Baltimore: Johns Hopkins UP, 1966).

175 **Parca** usually plural, *Parcae*; in Roman mythology, the three spinning goddesses of fate: Nona, Decima, and Morta. They correspond to the Greek *Moirai*: Clotho, Lachesis, and Atropos.

175 **"Faust's Ascension"** The last, and the least conventional by far, Mahler's *8th Symphony* is the only satisfying musical setting of Goethe's *Faust*. Like Goethe, Mahler understood the difference between spirituality and religion; only Mahler's "new music" (Adorno) delivers just the right sense of continual discovery, transcendence, and endless transformation that was both Goethe's and Mahler's vision of heaven. See the Introduction to this volume for a fuller discussion.

181 ***Spirits of Form / Spirits of Movement*** *See note to 70* ***the fourth post-Atlantean cultural epoch*** [on Steiner's book *An Outline of Esoteric Science*].

182 **And were it of asbestos, / It's still not clean** perhaps also a reference to the "magical" tablecloths woven of asbestos, which allowed wealthy hosts to astonish their guests by throwing them into the fire at the end of a meal, and then pulling them out perfectly clean, all the food stains having burned away. Charlemagne is reported to have owned such a tablecloth.

9. Mystical Knowledge and Spiritual Revelation of Nature: Perception of Spirits

186 ***at the Feast of the Assumption*** *The premiere of Steiner's first Mystery Drama,* The Portal of Initiation, *took place on August 15, 1910 in Munich.* See GA 14, Rudolf Steiner, *Four Mystery Dramas*, trans. Ruth and Hans Pusch (SteinerBooks, 2007).

189 **Swedenborg** Emmanuel Swedenborg (1688-1772), the Swedish scientist and inventor who had a life-changing spiritual experience in 1744, after which he claimed to be able to experience heaven and hell clairvoyantly. The best known of the 18 books on theology he published after his epiphany was *Heaven and Hell* (1758), which influenced William Blake among many other later thinkers and artists.

190 ***once our building is finished*** Steiner is referring to the so-called First Goetheanum: see the note to p. 104. *The uncut production of Goethe's* Faust *directed by Marie Steiner and performed in the Second Goetheanum* [after Steiner's death] *conformed to the indications given here.*

190 ***Filippo Neri*** *Saint Philip Romolo Neri (1515-1595). See Goethe's autobiographical* Italian Journey, *trans. W. H. Auden (Penguin Classics, 1992), May 26, 1787, p. 313.* Goethe's brief account of his life is delightful.

190 **Meister Eckart, Johannes Tauler, or Suso** The great trinity of "Rhineland" mystics: Eckart or Eckhart of Hochheim (ca. 1260–ca. 1327), and his students Johannes Tauler (ca. 1300–ca. 1361) and Heinrich Suso or Seuse (ca. 1300–1366). Of the three, Meister Eckart was the profoundest by far: his thinking is sophisticated, and his language is intensely poetic. Many consider him an important philosopher as well.

191 ***Goethe made a remark to Eckermann*** *Eckermann,* Conversations with Goethe, *February 12, 1829: "...Moreover, you will admit that the ending, where Faust's soul has been saved and is carried upward, was very difficult to pull off. In dealing with such supersensible, incomprehensible matters, I could very easily have gotten lost in vagueness if I had not made use of sharply outlined figures and concepts from the history of the Christian church to give much-needed form and solidity to my poetic intentions."*

195 **ancient mysteries** Steiner wrote and lectured extensively on the ancient mystery religions and cults, such as the Eleusinian mysteries, Mithras, and the mysteries of Isis. See also the note to p. 85. A comprehensive list of references to this topic in Steiner's works would include hundreds of entries.

195 ***the following words*** *This paralipomenon to Goethe's* Faust *ends with four additional lines not quoted in the lecture:*

> *Ich aber bin nichts nütze mehr an diesem Platz.*
> *Gespenstig spinnt der Dichtung Faden sich immer fort*
> *Und reißt am Ende tragisch! Alle seid gegrüßt,*
> *Wo ihr mich wieder findet, werd' es euch zur Lust.*
> [But I'm of no more use here in this place.
> Spectrally the poem forever spins its thread
> And, tragically, it breaks at last! To one and all, farewell,
> And wherever you find me again, may it please you.]

There are many fascinating paralipomena to Goethe's *Faust*. Steiner would have known about them from his work in the Goethe Archives in Weimar, and he makes much use of them in his many writings on Goethe. In this, as in so many other regards, Steiner was very much ahead of his time: only very recently have important scholars such as Albrecht Schöne begun to argue that the paralipomena are keys to the interpretation of Goethe's epic drama.

196 **an etymological brew** this cryptic aside is probably a reference to Nietzsche, whose arguments from etymology (notably in *The Genealogy of Morals*) are dubious. As we shall see in the lecture of August 19, 1916, below, Steiner

seems not to be adverse to arguments from etymology in principle, and the anthroposophist Owen Barfield made brilliant use of them, notably in his early book *History in English Words* (London: Methuen, 1926; rpt. Lindesfarne Books, 2002). Steiner knew Nietzsche's philosophy as well as any of his contemporaries, and published a sympathetic study of Nietzsche early in his career (GA 5, *Friedrich Nietzsche: Ein Kämpfer gegen seine Zeit* [1895]; *Friedrich Nietzsche: Fighter for Freedom* (Englewood, NJ: Rudolf Steiner Publications, 1960; 2nd rev. edn. Garber Communications, 1985). Steiner saw Nietzsche above all as a telling symptom of the pathologies of his age. The allusion here is typical of Steiner's later stance towards Nietzsche, which runs from mildly to sharply critical.

197 **This last word is difficult to translate** The Hebrew word in question is *tōv*, which does indeed mean both "good" and "beautiful." One sees the same equivalence in ancient Greek culture: cf. e.g. John 10:11, "I am the good shepherd," in which the Greek adjective is *kalos*, literally "beautiful" (but clearly meaning "good").

199 ***the Kassel cycle on the Gospel of St. John*** *GA 112,* The Gospel of St. John and its Relation to the Other Gospels *(Anthroposophic Press, 1982). These lectures were presented in Kassel from June 24-July 7, 1909.*

200 ***the whole architecture of our building*** On Rudolf Steiner as an architect see especially *Architecture as a Synthesis of the Arts: Lectures by Rudolf Steiner* (London: Rudolf Steiner Press, 1999); Rex Raab et al., *Eloquent Concrete* (London: Rudolf Steiner Press, 1979); and Wolfgang Pehnt, *Expressionist Architecture* (London: Praeger, 1973; London: Thames & Hudson, 1980), pp. 137-148. The Second Goetheanum, which stands to this day in Dornach, is but a shadow of the First, yet even so, Pehnt calls it "one of the most magnificent pieces of sculptural architecture of the twentieth century" (p. 148).

200 **the Samaritan woman and the well and finally the Egyptian Mary** The story of the Samaritan woman at the well is told only at the beginning of John 4. Mary of Egypt, also known as Maria Aegiptica, does not appear in the Bible. Like Mary Magdalene, she was a former prostitute who converted and became a saint; indeed, "Mary Gipcy," as she was called in Elizabethan England, became the patron saint of penitent women.

202 ***our earthly evolution*** *See note to p. 79.*

10. The Realm of the Mothers: The Mater Gloriosa

209 ***the etheric has a fourfold aspect*** *See e.g. GA 122,* Genesis: Secrets of Creation *(Anthroposophic Press, 2002). These lectures were originally presented in Munich, August 16-26, 1910.*

210 ***I once described in Munich*** *GA 147,* The Secrets of the Threshold *(Kessinger, 2010), originally given August 24-31, 1913 in conjunction with the premiere of Steiner's fourth Mystery Drama,* The Souls' Awakening.

212 **the female visionary** perhaps a reference to H. P. Blavatsky?

217 **the Magna Peccatrix, the Mulier Samaritana, and the Maria Aegyptiaca** Respectively, the "Great Sinner" or Mary Magdalene, the Samaritan woman, and Mary of Egypt. See the note to p. 200.

200 ***Here we behold the radiance of the aura*** *See Rudolf Steiner's lecture on Goethe's unfinished poem "Die Geheimnisse" [The Mysteries], published in GA 98,* Natur- und Geistwesen – Ihr Wirken in unserer sichtbaren Welt [Nature-Spirits and Spiritual Beings – Their Workings in Our Visible World], *18 individual lectures presented between November 5, 1907 and June 14, 1908.* This volume seems never to have been translated into English. See also the note to p. 22.

220 **the Great Spirit** Steiner almost never uses this theosophical term. This lecture has generally more a theosophical than an anthroposophical cast, and is in that sense rather out of character at this point in Steiner's career.

11. Goethe and the Worldview of German Idealism

223 **Schelling** See the note to p. 1 **Schelling** above.

223 **that flows and weaves through the world** Steiner is echoing the Erdgeist's song in the opening scene of *Faust*, lines 501-509.

223 **German Idealism** the conventional name in intellectual history for the profoundly influential philosophical movement of which the main thinkers are Kant, Fichte, Schelling, and Hegel. Schiller's philosophical essays and Goethe's writings on science certainly belong under this rubric as well. See also the note to p. 157.

229 **Fichte seeks to understand existence and the self** See especially *The Science of Knowledge: With the First and Second Introductions* (Cambridge: Cambridge UP, 1982), which is now the standard English translation of Fichte's *Wissenschaftslehre* of 1794.

229 **Schelling had gone so far as to claim** This notorious sentence from Schelling's *Erster Entwurf eines Systems der Naturphilosophie [First Draft of a Systematic Philosophy of Nature]* (1799) translates literally, "To philosophize about nature is to create nature." The roots of such thinking lie in Spinoza's concepts of *natura naturans* (nature as creating process, rather than finished product), and the faculty he calls *scientia intuitiva* or intuitive (i.e., non-discursive) thinking.

12. Faust's Journey through the World and His Rebirth in German Intellectual History

232 **intimately bound up with** The "evolution of consciousness" Steiner is describing here has been masterfully summarized and interpreted by Owen Barfield in *Saving the Appearances*; see the note to p. 102 **atavistic clairvoyance**. Another brief but outstanding treatment of this topic, however without reference to Steiner, is *The Discarded Image: An Introduction to Medieval and Renaissance Literature* (1964; rpt. Cambridge: Cambridge UP, 1994) by Barfield's closest friend and fellow Inkling C. S. Lewis.

233 **Copernicus, Kepler, and Galileo** Copernicus and Galileo, see the note to p. 31. Kant pronounced German mathematician, astronomer Johannes Kepler (1571-1630) the most rigorous thinker who ever lived. He is most famous for discovering and mathematically modeling the elliptical motions of the planets, and for major contributions toward the theory of gravitation eventually formalized by Newton.

234 **Kiesewetter** Carl Kiesewetter (1854-1895), a prominent theosophist, widely read in his day. The book to which Steiner refers is *Faust in der Geschichte und Tradition: Mit besonderer Berücksichtigung des occulten Phänomenalismus und des mittelalterlichen Zauberwesens [Faust in History and Tradition: With Special Consideration of Occult Phenomenalism and Medieval Magic]* (Leipzig: Spohr, 1893; rpt. Hildesheim: Ohms, 1963), 2 vols.

13. Wisdom – Beauty – Goodness: Michael – Gabriel – Raphael

237 ***In recent weeks . . . ideals of humanity*** *July 29-*September 3*, 1916. These lectures were published as GA 170,* The Riddle of Humanity: The Spiritual Background of Human History *(Rudolf Steiner Press, 1990). See the note to p. 256 below.*

237 **the act of forming mental pictures or concepts** This entire phrase attempts to capture the sense of *vorstellen* (verb), *Vorstellung* (noun), and, in this instance, *Vorstellen* (the gerund). Translators' introductions or notes invariably comment on the difficulty of translating this and a few other German philosophical and psychological terms such as *Geist*, *Anschauung*, and *Gemüt*. Tellingly, in the title of Schopenhauer's *magnum opus*, *Die Welt als Wille und Vorstellung*, the term has been rendered three different ways: initially as "Representation," but then more recently as "Idea" and "Presentation."

Both Michael Wilson's translation of Steiner's *Philosophy of Freedom* and Owen Barfield's *The Case for Anthroposophy* (see the note on ***Franz Brentano*** below) begin their discussions by noting that the standard translation of this Kantian philosophical term is "representation." But then Wilson goes on to argue (rightly) that this is too technical a term for most contexts, and that "representation" has other, distracting meanings outside of philosophy, which led him to translate *Vorstellung* and its variants as "mental picture." Barfield chooses "representation," which is understandable given that the context is Steiner's discussion of Brentano's neo-Kantian treatise. The translator of the text by Brentano to which Steiner is referring (see note to p. 238 ***Franz Brentano*** below), Linda L. McAlister, is inconsistent.

The reasons why this term is so very difficult to translate are (1) that it encompasses many different kinds of mental acts; (2) it refuses any sharp distinction between subjective and objective; (3) it can refer to a faculty, the activity of a faculty, or the result of that activity; (4) it often has a distinctly visual quality, but it can also refer to abstract concepts; and (5) it straddles the conventional divide between philosophy and psychology. [F.A.]

A NOTE ON THE TERM "BEGRIFF": Another, less problematic equivalent of the English word "concept" is *Begriff*, a term Steiner also uses here, and elsewhere, to express the idea of an abstract concept that has not yet been elevated / raised to the level of an image (as a *Vorstellung* has been). [B.C.]

*237 **the three*** **Critiques** ***of Kant*** *Kant's* Critique of Pure Reason *(1781/1787); his* Critique of Practical Reason *(1788), and his* Critique of Judgment *(1790),* conventionally referred to as the First, Second, and Third Critiques respectively. See note to p. 157 above.

238 ***Franz Brentano*** *Philosopher, 1838-1917. See vol. I of his* Psychology from an Empirical Standpoint, *International Library of Philosophy (Routledge, 1973; rpt. 1995), originally published in German in 1874.* Brentano was an important thinker and an even more influential teacher. Many of his students went on to become leading philosophers within Central Europe, and one, Thomas Masaryk, became the founder and the first President of Czechoslovakia.

Brentano died in 1917, and Steiner devoted two chapters to him in a book published later that same year, GA 21, *The Riddles of the Soul* (Mercury Press, 1996). Ch. III of that text is a 44-page obituary of sorts; # 7 of the Addenda, "Brentano's Separation of the Soul Element from What is External to the Soul," is much shorter. Another, earlier translation is invaluable: Owen Barfield, trans. and ed., *The Case for Anthroposophy: Being Extracts from* Von Seelenrätseln *by Rudolf Steiner* (Rudolf Steiner Press, 1970; rpt. The Barfield Press UK, 2010). Barfield's edition contains a brilliant and succinct introduction, but only a partial translation of Steiner's text. Because Brentano is "so little known to English readers," Barfield decided to omit chapter 3 and section 7 of chapter four, but he discusses both in his own introductory essay.

Steiner held Brentano in the "highest possible esteem," while describing at the same time the many ways in which Brentano's excessively narrow and reductive view of science caused him to fall back into mere "anthropology" every time he arrived at the threshold of "anthroposophy." See also the note to p. 240 on Brentano below.

239 ***in Hume and Berkeley*** *David Hume (1711-1776), Scottish historian and philosopher; George Berkeley (1685-1753),* a.k.a. Bishop Berkeley, Anglo-Irish philosopher and theologian. (His name is pronounced "BARK-ley.") Both thinkers are referred to as "British Empiricists," although their philosophical positions were antithetical, and Berkeley's would be more accurately described as "subjective idealism." Berkeley's philosophical motto was *esse est percipi*, "to be is to be perceived." Hume is by far the greater and more influential figure of the two: Kant claims that Hume's radical skepticism was one of three alarms that awakened him from his "dogmatic slumber." The case could be made that German Idealism as a movement grew directly from Kant's attempts to refute Humean skepticism.

239-240 **ignorant of what we call the scholasticism of the Middle Ages . . . not knowing anything about Greek philosophy either** These claims are surely hyperbolic, but they may be true in some relative sense. Part of the problem is that Kant tends to discuss philosophical positions without necessarily associating them with specific historical individuals. Nevertheless, searches in a reliable electronic edition of Kant's major works (Digitale Bibliothek [Berlin: Directmedia

Publishing, 2004], ISBN 3-89853-014-0) yielded no entries for Thomas Aquinas, Albertus Magnus, or Anselm of Canterbury; none for any of the major pre-Socratic philosophers except a single reference to Zeno; a mere 14 mentions each of Plato and Aristotle; and only three references to Socrates.

240 ***This is why those who attended Brentano's lectures on psychology*** Although Steiner laments that he was able to hear only a few of Brentano's lectures while a student in Vienna, in his *Autobiography* (GA 28; Anthroposophic Press, 1999), Steiner reports that Brentano had a strong influence upon him, and that he had followed Brentano's subsequent career closely, reading nearly everything he published.

According to his biographer, Peter Gay (*Freud: A Life for our Time* [New York: Norton, 1988]), Freud "attended no fewer than five courses of lectures and seminars offered by this 'damned clever fellow,' this 'genius,' and sought him out for private interviews"; Brentano's "psychological writings left significant deposits in Freud's mind" (p. 29).

Brentano was also, famously, the teacher of the founder of phenomenology, Edmund Husserl (1859-1938). Hence, Brentano exerted a direct and significant influence on at least four major intellectual movements of the 20th century: anthroposophy, psychoanalysis, phenomenology, and existentialism!

245 **you will not find them translated quite this way in any Hebrew dictionary** Indeed, the conventional etymologies of the names Michael, Gabriel, and Raphael would be "Who is like God?"; "the [strong] man of God"; and "God has healed," respectively.

248 **"They hid their faces from the mystery of human incarnation."** Steiner is probably referring to Isaiah 53:3, long taken as a prophecy of the coming of Christ: "He is despised and rejected of men; a man of sorrows, and acquainted with grief: and we hid as it were our faces from him; he was despised, and we esteemed him not."

250 ***the first lecture I gave here again*** *July 29, 1916. See note to p. 256 below.*

252 ***Today we would have seen*** *In the dramatic performance including* [the new, dance-like art form created by Rudolf Steiner,] *eurythmy.* See the discussion of eurythmy in the introduction.

254 **the great maya** See the note to p. 32.

256 **my pain** Most editions of Goethe's *Faust* published before his death have the word *Leid* ("pain, sorrow") here, considered by some to be a printing error for *Lied* ("song"), which has been adopted in some, but not all later editions. Steiner bases his interpretation of this passage as "the song of his sorrow" on Goethe's interweaving of these two themes in the poem, "Dedication" (1-32), with which *Faust* opens. [B.C.]

256 ***the words I cited here not long ago*** *Lecture in Dornach, Switzerland on August 6, 1916; included in GA 170 (see note to p. 237, above).* In this lecture, which features an extended meditation on the Platonic notion of *dikaiosyne* [justice], Steiner claims that there is a very real sense in which, just as we incarnate into the four elements at birth, we incarnate into the Platonic triad of the Good, the Beautiful, and the True after death.

256 **"The world is deep..."** Here Steiner quotes lines from a poem by Nietzsche entitled "The Drunken Song" [*Das trunkene Lied*], 5-6. (B.C.)

14. The Historical Significance of Faust

261 ***In Milton's* Paradise Lost** *John Milton (1608-1674),* Paradise Lost: A Poem in Ten Books *(1667). Cf. lecture 1(November 21, 1919) of GA 194,* "The Mission of the Archangel Michael: Revelation of Essential Secrets of the Human Being," *in* The Archangel Michael: His Mission and Ours, *ed. Christopher Bamford (SteinerBooks, 1996), pp. 99-111* (on Lucifer and Ahriman).

261 **our sculpture, the "Group"** See note to p. 129.

262 **cycles and epicycles** The issue that vexed Ptolemaic (geocentric) astronomy for many centuries was the seemingly irregular, retrograde motion of the planets. One model frequently explored involved counter-rotating, smaller planetary orbits (epicycles) affixed to larger orbital paths (cycles), which could be made to approximate the motion. Some of these models are fabulous indeed. Cf. Book VIII of Milton's *Paradise Lost*, where the Archangel Raphael describes God's laughter at the "quaint opinions" of astronomers who "contrive / To save appearances, [and] gird the Sphere / With Centric and Eccentric scribbl'd o'er / Cycle and Epicycle, Orb in Orb" [80-84].

262 **setting up three axioms ... the third axiom** *See GA 323,* forthcoming as CW 323, *The Relationship of the Various Scientific Disciplines to Astronomy: Third Scientific Course: Eighteen lectures given in Stuttgart from January 1-18, 1921*, ed. and trans. Frederick Amrine et al. (SteinerBooks). Steiner discusses this issue more fully in the second lecture of this cycle, where he complains that the axial precession of the earth through the signs of the zodiac postulated by Copernicus' third axiom is effectively ignored by modern astronomy, which has distorted our model of the earth's motion relative to the sun. This difficult issue will be discussed more fully in the forthcoming edition of CW 323.

Unfortunately, the only translation of this intensely brilliant and profoundly important cycle of lectures currently available is *The Relation of the Diverse Branches of Natural Science to Astronomy -Third Scientific Course,* likely the work of George Adams. It has circulated for many decades (perhaps even since the 1920s) first as a typescript, then in the form of various internet postings, and now more recently an extremely rare, lightly revised Australian publication in book format. The typescript is (understandably) a very rough draft and often inaccurate, and the internet postings are riddled with so many simple errors of transcription as to be worse than useless.

263 ***our good Christian von Ehrenfels*** *Christian von Ehrenfels* (1859-1932), Kosmogonie [Cosmogony] (1916). This book has not been translated into English.

Ehrenfels was an Austrian philosopher who studied with Brentano and Meinong; among the students drawn to his lectures in Prague were Franz Kafka and Max Brod. The appellation "good" might be meant unironically: he was only two years older than Steiner, who was also a student of Brentano's at the University of Vienna, so they may have known each other or even been friends (even though von Ehrenfels is not mentioned in Steiner's autobiography).

In Steiner's lecture of August 13, 1916, collected in GA 170 (see the note to p. 237), he discusses the first chapter of this work, which is entitled "Reversion: A Paradox of Human Knowledge." Ehrenfels engages in long, meticulous thought experiments about a boulder falling, a hare running leaving tracks in the snow, etc., and ends up concluding that reversing such processes would be so absurd, he would refuse to believe even empirical evidence that it had happened; rather, he would describe such reports to the influence of an evil demon!

On a more positive note, his paper "On Gestalt Qualities," published in 1909, was fundamental to the eventual development of the school of Gestalt psychology, and the most important figure in that movement, Max Wertheimer (1880-1943), was von Ehrenfels' student.

It was von Ehrenfels who coined the now-famous phrase, "the whole is greater than the sum of the parts." An outstanding musician, he often compared the structures of human perceptual systems and the biology of organisms generally to musical compositions: this insight was taken up and worked out systematically by, among others, the great biologist and founder of environmental studies, Jakob von Uexküll (1864-1944).

264 ***This is a perspective for the future*** *GA 219,* Man and the World of Stars *(SteinerBooks, 1980).*

264 **Galilei and Kepler ... Lamarck and Haeckel** Jean-Baptiste Lamarck (1744-1829), a French naturalist and a major early theorist of biological evolution. He is best remembered for his (now discredited) idea that acquired characteristics were passed on through inheritance. Ernst Haeckel (1834-1919) was the chief proponent of Darwinism in Germany, and himself a great biologist who propounded the "ontogenetic law" that "ontogeny recapitulates phylogeny." (On which, see the following two notes.) Haeckel was also an accomplished artist, whose drawings of natural forms are prized to this day, and a major philosopher. Steiner studied Haeckel intensely, and he credits Haeckel's ideas with having contributed greatly to his own spiritual discoveries. On Galilei, see the note to p. 31. On Kepler, see the note to p. 233.

265 **the "fundamental biogenetic law"** or "ontogenetic law" that was given its fullest and most precise expression by Ernst Haeckel. See the previous and following notes.

265 **Copernican astronomy is already under heavy attack** This comment in passing certainly seems to be a reference to Einstein's theory of general relativity, which had only just been published! General relativity renders moot the whole issue of geo- vs. heliocentric models.

265 ***Oskar Hertwig*** *1849-1922,* developmental biologist. Oskar Hertwig studied under Ernst Haeckel at Jena, and then became himself a leading developmental biologist at the University of Berlin. Hertwig's early research was devoted to embryology, in the spirit of Haeckel's "ontogenetic law" that the development of the individual organism recapitulates in small the whole evolutionary history of its species. His zoology textbook of 1906 was widely used and highly influential.

Steiner is referring here to *Das Werden der Organismen: Zur Widerlegung von Darwin's Zufallstheorie durch das Gesetz in der Entwicklung [The Development of Organism: On the Refutation of Darwin's Theory of Chance by the Law in Evolution]* (Jena, 1916), which would have appeared recently, and it is impressive to see that Steiner is abreast of the latest research in biology. This 700-page critique of the role of chance in Darwin's theory of evolution seems never to have been translated into English, but the German edition of 1918 is available on Google Books. Hertwig's attack on the concept of "natural selection" is rigorous and fundamental: his main philosophical point is that selection among qualities that necessarily have already arisen can in no way be imputed as the *cause* of those qualities. Hertwig also criticizes the vagueness of the Darwinians' vocabulary, and the troubling slippage that occurs between social and biological contexts when invoking terms such as "survival of the fittest."

Also, cf. Stephen J. Gould's early book, *Ontogeny and Phylogeny* (Harvard UP, 1977), which became the foundation of developmental evolutionary biology as it is currently practiced by taking seriously Haeckel's long-dismissed notion that ontogeny recapitulates phylogeny. For a good, brief discussion, see: K. J. McNamara and M. L. McKinney, "Heterochrony, disparity and macroevolution," in *Macroevolution: Diversity, Disparity, Contingency: Essays in Honor of Stephen Jay Gould*, ed. E. Vrba and N. Eldredge (The Paleontological Society, 2005), pp. 17-26. Gould seems to view Hertwig as his predecessor in reinterpreting (and thereby saving) Haeckel's ontogenetic law as central to evolutionary biology (p. 147).

265 ***"Mauthner-like"*** *The reference is to Fritz Mauthner (1849-1923),* one of Steiner's *bêtes noires.* Mauthner is most famous today for his three-volume *Kritik der Sprache* [*Critique of Language*] (Stuttgart, 1901-1903), largely because Wittgenstein claimed it had influenced him in the writing of his *Tractatus.* The *Critique* seems not to have been translated into English, but for an extensive recapitulation and discussion of the argument, see Gershon Weiler, *Mauthner's Critique of Language* (Cambridge UP, 1971). Mauthner had studied with Ernst Mach in Prague, so he had philosophical and scientific pretentions, but (apart from Wittgenstein) the academic world rejected his *magnum opus.* Mauthner also wrote fiction, and he wrote journalistic feuilletons and satirical pieces for the *Berliner Tageblatt* [*Berlin* Daily] in the 1890s, when Steiner was also active in Berlin. It is this last side of his work to which Steiner seems to be referring here. Steiner invokes Mauthner frequently, and seems to have viewed him as an archetypal philistine. The neo-Kantian skepticism of Mauthner's *Critique* is exactly the kind of shallow reductionism Steiner's *Philosophy of Freedom* (GA 4, 1894) was meant to counter.

The previous year, in a cycle of lectures that have been published in GA 163 (*Chance, Providence, and Necessity* [Anthroposophic Press, 1988]), Mauthner had come under heavy attack right from the first lecture. In the third (August 28, 1915), Steiner quotes from the entry on "History" in Mauthner's *Philosophical Lexicon* (1910ff.), and then compares Mauthner unfavorably with Goethe's fictional Faust. Mauthner argues that we ascribe necessity only to phenomena that recur (such as the sun rising), and hence, since historical events are all singular, they must be ascribed to chance. Steiner praises Mauthner for carrying his argument to its logical conclusion: Napoleon's decision to invade Russia, and Mauthner's having smoked more cigars during one time period than usual, are equally random events: "He rightly confessed: With the means available that contemporary scholarship views as valid, there is no way to distinguish between the fact that Julius Caesar once lived and 'in this hour I smoked one more cigar than usual'." But then Steiner mocks Mauthner for not having noticed he has performed a perfect *reductio ad absurdum.* How far we now seem from the age of Goethe and Hegel, Steiner laments, in which these questions were taken up with a seriousness that can only be described as "shattering." "There is so very, very much in Goethe's *Faust* that points towards the profoundest enigmas in the human breast....Necessity! Just imagine a personality such as Faust confronting the question of necessity in the historical life of humanity. Why am I here, he would ask, at this particular point in human evolution? What power has inserted me into this world? What necessity coursing through that which we call history has brought me to just this moment in human development? – Out of the very depths of his soul, Faust poses this question." Mauthner is not Faustian enough to understand the full consequences of his own assertions. Only when we achieve this level of Faustian intensity, Steiner argues, will we be ready to understand the concept of historical necessity in its profounder dimensions, as he had sought to reveal them in his own lectures and writings.

265 **the elemental beings** Steiner affirmed the existence of these supersensible creatures, and he refers to them frequently in his lectures.

*265 **The astronomers ... and the biologists** See the note to p. 262 on Copernicus' three axioms.*

266 **the well-known conversation between Goethe and Schiller ... the so-called archetypal plant** took place on July 20, 1794, when the two met while leaving a lecture on botany in Jena. It was apparently the first substantive conversation between two men, who would go on to become friends and collaborators on many fronts, but according to Goethe's report, the exchange was testy. Goethe tried unsuccessfully to convey to Schiller what he meant by the "archetypal plant" [*Urpflanze*], which is the central notion informing his treatise on *The Metamorphosis of Plants* (1790). The English-language edition of choice is now Johann Wolfgang von Goethe, *The Metamorphosis of Plants* (Cambridge, MA: MIT Press, 2009), trans. Douglas Miller, with an introduction and beautiful color photographs of the species Goethe describes by Gordon L. Miller.

*266 **the introduction to Goethe's morphological writings** See note to p. 172.*

267 **Goethe's color theory** set forth principally in Goethe's study *Theory of Color* (1810). The best English translation is Johann Wolfgang von Goethe, *Scientific Studies*, vol. 12 of *The Collected Works*, ed. and trans. Douglas Miller (New York: Suhrkamp, 1988; Princeton: Princeton UP, 1995), pp. 157-298. This volume also contains *The Metamorphosis of Plants* (pp. 76-97), but without illustrations.

267 **his essays on the spiral tendency of plants** An excerpt is included in Goethe's *Scientific Studies* (previous note), pp. 105-107.

268 **where these things originate: from Heaven itself** For a remarkable echo of Steiner's ideas, see Giordio de Santillana and Hertha von Dechend, *Hamlet's Mill: An Essay on Myth and the Frame of Time* (Boston: Gambit, 1969; reprinted since with a different subtitle).

269 ***in his grayish, bat-like form*** *Thus in the staging at the Goetheanum: Mephistopheles rising up out of the abyss.*

269 ***evolution*** *See GA 11,* Cosmic Memory: Atlantis and Lemuria, *Harper Library of Spiritual Wisdom (Harpercollins, 1981).* Various other editions have appeared recently in English, including a Kindle eBook (Amazon, 2010).

270 ***stated schematically*** *A sketch of the motif of* [Rudolf Steiner's] *sculptural "Group" in the Goetheanum.* It was originally intended for the back of the stage in the First Goetheanum, which was destroyed by an arsonist. Fortunately, Steiner was still working on it in an adjacent building, so it has been preserved. Today it can be seen displayed in the Second Goetheanum, but not at the back of the stage, as originally intended.

271 ***The Bible contains only a hint of this*** *"That the sons of God saw the daughters of men that they were fair; and they took them wives of all which they chose" (Genesis 6:2). In the* [apocryphal] *Book of Enoch (6:1-2), one finds the following passage referring to the same verse in* Genesis*: "And it came to pass when the children of men had multiplied that in those days were born unto them beautiful and comely daughters. And the angels, the children of the heaven, saw and lusted after them…"*

15. The "Burial": The Nature of the Lemures, The Fat Devils, and the Skinny Devils

275 ***many years ago*** *See note to p. 67.*

276 **Lemures** as described by the Roman poets Horace and Ovid, these were the restless and hence threatening shades of the dead. Ovid's *Fasti* describes a three-day ritual to feed, appease, and thus exorcise them by having the *paterfamilias* cast black beans behind him with an averted gaze.

279 **Saturn, Sun, Moon, and Earth** Steiner means here the earlier stages of cosmic evolution described in the note to p. 79 **the Old Moon**.

282 **"angelic limbs"** "Englische Glieder" is an uncommon German euphemism for richitis or rickets.

284 ***they will really have to practice this*** *The "fat" and "thin" devils were played by eurythmists.*

285 **the same flaming city we find in Dante!** Dis, the capital of Hell, which Dante first encounters in Canto VIII of the *Inferno.*

286 **Psyche with her wings** The Greeks would sometimes depict this mythological figure with diminutive wings, and they sometimes drew the human soul in the form of a butterfly leaving the body at death. Hence there is a species of butterfly and a genus of moth named "psyche."

291 **for a time he lets himself fall back** A central feature of Steiner's view of evil is that it arises when certain higher beings "fall behind" in their own evolutionary development. He sees evil arise within human culture in much that same way: when atavistic ideas or social forms are retained long after they have lost their validity. Steiner discusses Mephistopheles in this context at the beginning of his lecture on September 10, 1916 below.

291 ***"crystallized human folk"*** *Faust II, Act 2, "Laboratory"; as translated by Walter Arndt:*

> *MEPHISTOPHELES. He who has lived has learned a lot,*
> *To him the world can offer nothing new;*
> *Upon my wanderings from spot to spot*
> *I've come across synthetic people too. [6861-6864]*

In the German original, Mephisto describes them literally as "crystallized people." Stuart Atkins has offered a persuasive gloss on this passage: "The basis of Mephistopheles' claim of having seen *kristallisiertes Menschenvolk [crystallized people]* is folkloristic (story of Lot's wife, Pretorius's 'Stein-Leute' [stone people] and the butt of its irony is mental rigidity, but its raison d'être is to satirize mechanistic materialism: When Wagner declares that what Nature once 'organisieren ließ, / Das lassen wir kristallisieren' [called forth organically, / That we crystallize] (6859f.), he is working from the premise of scientists like Jean-Claude de la Métherie (1743-1817), who claimed it known for a fact that life originated through crystallization" ("Renaissance and Baroque Elements in Goethe's *Faust*: Illustrative Analogues," *Goethe Yearbook*, 11 (2002), 1-26; p. 11). Schröer glosses these lines in the same spirit. The family name of the obscure French naturalist to whom Atkins refers is spelled variously, more often as a single word: Delamétherie.

Johannes Praetorius (1630-1680) published two massive and cryptic tomes entitled *Anthropodemus plutonic* describing fabulous humanoid creatures, including humans made of stone. He also wrote extensively on demonology and witchcraft, notably on the folklore surrounding the *Blocksberg* (scene of the "Classical Walpurgis night" in Part One). Hence Mephisto's reference is an appropriate echo of the earlier scene and a reminder that he is out of place in the Classical world Faust is about to enter. On Pretorius generally, see the recent study by Gerhold Scholz Williams: *Ways of Knowing in Early Modern Germany: Johannes Praetorius as a Witness to His Time* (Ashgate, 2006).

292 ***in these turbulent times*** *The events immediately following the outbreak of World War One in 1914.* Steiner had attracted to the Goetheanum and was trying to keep together a large group of people from all the different nations involved in the conflict. It seems that the members had been arguing among themselves, which would have been a bitter disappointment to Steiner: hence the heavy sarcasm. "Pan-German" was an invidious term 1916, roughly tantamount to calling someone a "fascist" today.

294 **Goethe's *Manes* at a Saint John's festival** *Manes* or *Di Manes,* often found in association with the *Lares* and the *[Di] Penates.* These Roman deities are the ghosts of the dead, to whom magic spells are usually addressed. Roman tombstones often show the letters *D. M.,* an abbreviation for *Dis Manibus,* meaning "for the Manes."

294 **that lives in the Manas** see the note to p. 26.

294 ***the*** **Faust** ***commentary*** *Gotthard Oswald Marbach,* Goethes *Faust,* Erster und Zweiter Theil *(rpt. Nabu Press, 2010).* Marbach's dates are 1810-1890; his commentary on *Faust* was originally published in 1881 in Stuttgart. The full text of this commentary is available on Google Books. The poem Steiner proceeds to quote is found on pp. v-vi, preceding the Preface: clearly it was intended as an epigraph to the entire volume.

16. Goethe's Insights into the Secrets of Human Existence

297 **Lessing's *Faust*** See the note to p. 18 **a series of previous incarnations**. It seems that Lessing planned to write a drama about Faust, but for reasons unknown he never followed through. The only texts that have come down to us are (1) an undated ms. entitled *D. Faust* with a "Prelude" and some lines in which Faust interviews a devil; and (2) a brief passage in the 17th of his *Letters on the Most Recent German Literature* (1759), which also shows us Faust interviewing devils. Both texts together amount to only only three or so printed pages. Steiner quotes *verbatim* not from these surviving texts, but rather from a posthumous report of a conversation with Lessing published by Johann Jakob Engel in 1886. Engel's recollection is confirmed in a similar report by someone named Blankenburg (1784). No doubt Steiner knew of these texts by having read the recently published, brief anthology with commentary by Wilhelm Petsch (*Lessings Faustdichtung* [Winter, 1911]).

300 ***an especially beautiful passage*** *Cf. Goethe's* Italian Journey, *entry for March 1, 1888.* I have not been able to find a passage in Goethe that corresponds exactly to Steiner's quote, but there is paragraph in Pt. III, ch. 14 of Goethe's autobiography *Poetry and Truth [Dichtung und Wahrheit]* that is very close. Steiner may very well have been quoting it from memory, in which case he certainly has remembered the spirit and some of the key concepts, if not the exact wording: "A feeling, however, which grew powerfully within me, with an uncanniness that defied expression, was a sense of the past and present as united – a way of looking at things that brought something spectral [*etwas Gespenstermäßiges*] into the present. It is expressed in many of my longer and shorter works, but it always has a salutary effect in poetry, even though whenever it expressed itself directly in and through life it must have seemed strange, inexplicable, perhaps unpleasant." The editors of the German original, Froböse and Lauer, are reminded here also of the entry for March 1, 1888, in Goethe's autobiographical *Italian Journey*, where he writes about taking up again the long-neglected manuscript of *Faust*, and marvels how little he has changed: "Since long rest and absence have brought me back to the *niveau* of my own existence, it is remarkable to what degree I resemble myself, and how little my inner life has suffered at the hands of time and circumstances." There is much other evidence besides this passage that Goethe believed in reincarnation.

303 **"You say so!"** or, as the Authorized Version translates these words, "Thou sayest" (Matthew 27:11), "Thou sayest it" (Mark 15:2, Luke 23:3), and "Thou sayest that I am a king" (John 18:37).

307 **You can find passages in Sophocles** The death of Oedipus as depicted in *Oedipus at Colonus* seems to fit this description.

17. Perspectives on the True Realities Goethe Was Seeking

319 ***lectures given here in just the past few weeks*** *See note to p. 237.*

320 **the hierarchy he belongs to** Steiner's account of Mephistopheles beginning here qualifies many things asserted in earlier lectures. Up to this point, Steiner seemed to indicate that we should view Mephisto as a confused expression of Lucifer and Ahriman themselves, but here Mephisto has been demoted to an under-devil in their service. During his first interview with Faust, Mephisto twice describes himself as "a part" of a larger evil power (lines 1335 and 1350), the latter after Faust has quizzed him on this issue specifically, so this more nuanced account fits well with Goethe's text.

In the terminology of traditional Christian angelology, Mephistopheles would be a "fallen" Angelos, who should have attained the level of Archangelos during Earth evolution, but chose to remain behind at the earlier level of consciousness (hence, he is a "Moon-man"). Michael is, both for Steiner and explicitly in Goethe's *Faust*, an Archangel during Earth evolution. If Mephisto's "immediate superior" outranks Michael, he must be one of the Archai (two ranks higher than Angels), which fits with Steiner's description of Ahriman elsewhere.

321 **The nature of this impulse was such that** This passage is a very elliptical reference to Steiner's account of what orthodox Christian theology calls "The Fall of Man."

324 **the Greco-Roman, the Egypto-Chaldean** See the note to p. 70 **the fourth post-Atlantean cultural epoch.** "Egypto-Chaldean" is Steiner's name for a long epoch he sees as having ended ca. 747 BCE. The implication of the term is that the Egyptian, Sumerian and Babylonian cultures were in the vanguard of human cultural evolution during that period – quite a conventional notion after all, despite the idiosyncrasy of the label. Because it has become a standard anthroposophical

term, "Chaldean" stands here rather that Sumerian and/or Babylonian, which would be more conventional in English.

324 ***fable convenue* ... our trivial history, or what people nowadays call history** a reference to the famous witticism by the French writer Bernard le Bovier de Fontenelle (1657-1757), who complained that "L'Histoire n 'est qu'une fable convenue [History is nothing but an agreed-upon fable]" – i.e., a convenient myth that historians have conspired to present as fact. Steiner was inordinately fond of this remark, and he quotes it often when attacking what today's historians would call "master narratives."

324 ***the depth of a verse such as the one I cited once*** *See note to p. 237* ***in recent weeks****:* [Rudolf Steiner's] *lecture of September 3, 1916.*

325 ***Lord Bacon, Bacon of Verulam*** *British philosopher and statesman (1561-1626).*

325 ***idola tribus, idola specus, idola fori, and idola theatri*** The reference is to Francis Bacon's *Novum Organum* (1620), Aphorism 39: "There are four classes of Idols which have beset men's minds. To these I have for distinction's sake assigned names – calling the first class *Idols of the Tribe*; the second, *Idols of the Cave*; the third, *Idols of the Market-place*; the fourth, *Idols of the Theatre*." These refer to the distortions of knowledge stemming from, respectively, human nature generally, individual temperament, social conventions, and "the various dogmas of philosophies." The subtitle of Owen Barfield's magisterial treatise, *Saving the Appearances: A Study in Idolatry*, is meant as an ironic inversion of Bacon's world-view: for Barfield (and Steiner), it is the paradigm of "onlooker consciousness" which Bacon did so much to establish that is actually idolatrous. Barfield's book is deeply rooted in passages of Steiner's lectures such as this.

326 **George Berkeley** see note to p. 239 **in Hume and Berkeley**.

326 ***Mr. Bauer sitting here*** *Michael Bauer (1871-1929), the friend of* [the famous German poet] *Christian Morgenstern* (1871-1914). Morgenstern was, by the way, a devoted student of Steiner. His poems, which were inspired by English nonsense verse generally and Lewis Carroll in particular, have become modern classics since Morgenstern's early death. The most famous collection is his *Gallows Songs* [*Galgenlieder*] of 1905. They have been translated by, among others, the Pulitzer Prize-winning poet W. D. Snodgrass (U of Michigan P, 1967), the noted translator of children's books Anthea Bell (North South Books, 1995), and Walter Arndt (Yale UP, 1993), whose masterful English translation of Goethe's *Faust* (2nd edn., Norton, 2000) is the most respected and widely used as of this writing.

335 **"entelechy"** originally an Aristotelian term, closely related to *energeia*: in Aristotle, *entelecheia* refers to the state of realized potential. The great German metaphysician Gottfried Wilhelm Leibniz (1646-1716) appropriated the term, using it to describe the autonomy of "monads" or "simple substances," as in this passage from his *Monadology* (1714): "18. All simple substances or created Monads might be called Entelechies, for they have in them a certain perfection (*echousi to*

enteles); they have a certain self-sufficiency (*autarkeia*) which makes them the sources of their internal activities and, so to speak, incorporeal automata" [trans. Robert Latta]. In the key passage at the end of *Faust* to which Steiner refers, Goethe initially used this unconventional Leibnizian term to describe Faust's immortal spirit, rising heavenward after death.

335 ***the Eighth Sphere*** *See the lecture of October 18, 1915, "The Eighth Sphere," in GA 254:* The Occult Movement in the Nineteenth Century and its Relation to Modern Culture *(Rudolf Steiner Press, 1973), pp. 79-102.* For Steiner, this sphere is a realm of Mephistophelean delusions, composed of "densified Imaginations" that tempt humanity to abandon the autonomous striving that is connected with the materiality of the Earth. *See also the lectures of November 23, 1919 (GA 194:* The Archangel Michael: His Mission and Ours *[SteinerBooks, 1996]) and November 27, 1916 (GA 172:* The Karma of Vocation *[Rudolf Steiner Press, 1984]).*

18. Goethe Plumbs the Depths of Evolution and Its Cosmic Secrets in His Faust: The Luciferic and the Ahrimanic Temptation

340 **Your eyes will be opened** Genesis 3:5, "For God doth know that in the day ye eat thereof, then your eyes shall be opened, and ye shall be as gods, knowing good and evil."

341 **the most human of facts** See note to p. 271.

342 ***in an earlier lecture cycle*** *See note to p. 210.*

347 ***the well-known painting by Raphael*** *The "Disputa."* The "Disputation of the Holy Sacrament" (1508 or 1509) was the first of the three great frescoes Raphael painted to adorn Pope Julius II's library, which is called the *Stanza della Segnatura.* It stands opposite the more famous "School of Athens" (1509), and next to "Parnassus" (1510). On Raphael, see the note to p. 11 above. One of the greatest recent scholars of Raphael was the anthroposophist Konrad Oberhuber, who died in 2007 at the age of 72. He has written on these works in his book *Raphael: The Paintings* (Prestel, 1999). Raphael would later figure prominently in Steiner's writings on reincarnation and karma.

348 ***"Who ever striving self exerts, / By us can be redeemed;"*** These are famous lines, arguably the most important in *Faust.* In Goethe's original manuscript and in most subsequent editions, these words are set off by quotation marks within the text, implying that the Angels are citing a higher authority. The editors of GA 272 have chosen to follow Schröer, who does not include the quotation marks. It is fair to assume that Steiner would have followed Schröer if he had reviewed his text for publication, but Steiner's intentions are not known, and we prefer to follow Goethe's original manuscript here.

348 **elective affinity** The word translated here, "Wahlverwandtschaft," is a term from early nineteenth-century chemistry that was used to explain the propensity for certain chemical species to form compounds. Goethe employed the term ironically in the title of this third novel, *Die Wahlverwandtschaften* [*Elective Affinities* or

Kindred by Choice] (1809), which revolves around illicit sexual attractions. Max Weber then famously employed the term, recalling Goethe, to describe the strange attraction between Protestantism and capitalism.

353 **"sulphurization"** It seems that Steiner's coinage of this term is entirely metaphorical.

354 ***Just remember our own struggles ... Mrs. Besant*** *The controversy with the Theosophical Society, which eventually led to the expulsion of the German Section* [of which Steiner had been the leader]. Annie Besant *née* Wood (1847-1933) was a prominent and longstanding theosophist who became President of the Theosophical Society (and hence, Steiner's "boss") in 1907. They disagreed on almost everything.

357 **the rights and freedom of peoples** a typical attack on Woodrow Wilson – typical of Steiner, and typical of Central European intellectuals generally. Freud, for example, broke all his own rules to join a scurrilous attack on Wilson, pretending to analyze a man he never had met. The episode is described in Peter Gay's otherwise sympathetic biography *Freud: A Life for Our Time* (New York: Norton, 1988), pp. 553-562.

359 **Grillparzer** the reference is to an epigram written in 1849 by the Austrian poet and playwright Franz Grillparzer (1791-1872): "Der Weg der neuern Bildung geht / Von Humanität / Durch Nationalität / Zur Bestialität." A full, literal translation would be: "The path of modern culture runs / From humanity / Through nationality / To bestiality."

RUDOLF STEINER'S COLLECTED WORKS

The German Edition of Rudolf Steiner's Collected Works (the Gesamtausgabe [GA] published by Rudolf Steiner Verlag, Dornach, Switzerland) presently runs to over 354 titles, organized either by type of work (written or spoken), chronology, audience (public or other), or subject (education, art, etc.). For ease of comparison, the Collected Works in English [CW] follows the German organization exactly. A complete listing of the CWs follows with literal translations of the German titles. Other than in the case of the books published in his lifetime, titles were rarely given by Rudolf Steiner himself, and were often provided by the editors of the German editions. The titles in English are not necessarily the same as the German; and, indeed, over the past seventy-five years have frequently been different, with the same book sometimes appearing under different titles.

For ease of identification and to avoid confusion, we suggest that readers looking for a title should do so by CW number. Because the work of creating the Collected Works of Rudolf Steiner is an ongoing process, with new titles being published every year, we have not indicated in this listing which books are presently available. To find out what titles in the Collected Works are currently in print, please check our website at www.steinerbooks.org, or write to SteinerBooks 610 Main Street, Great Barrington, MA 01230.

Written Work

CW 1	Goethe: Natural-Scientific Writings, Introduction, with Footnotes and Explanations in the text by Rudolf Steiner
CW 2	Outlines of an Epistemology of the Goethean World View, with Special Consideration of Schiller
CW 3	Truth and Science
CW 4	The Philosophy of Freedom
CW 4a	Documents to "The Philosophy of Freedom"
CW 5	Friedrich Nietzsche, A Fighter against His Own Time
CW 6	Goethe's Worldview
CW 6a	Now in CW 30
CW 7	Mysticism at the Dawn of Modern Spiritual Life and Its Relationship with Modern Worldviews
CW 8	Christianity as Mystical Fact and the Mysteries of Antiquity
CW 9	Theosophy: An Introduction into Supersensible World Knowledge and Human Purpose
CW 10	How Does One Attain Knowledge of Higher Worlds?
CW 11	From the Akasha-Chronicle
CW 12	Levels of Higher Knowledge
CW 13	Occult Science in Outline
CW 14	Four Mystery Dramas
CW 15	The Spiritual Guidance of the Individual and Humanity

CW 16	A Way to Human Self-Knowledge: Eight Meditations
CW 17	The Threshold of the Spiritual World. Aphoristic Comments
CW 18	The Riddles of Philosophy in Their History, Presented as an Outline
CW 19	Contained in CW 24
CW 20	The Riddles of the Human Being: Articulated and Unarticulated in the Thinking, Views and Opinions of a Series of German and Austrian Personalities
CW 21	The Riddles of the Soul
CW 22	Goethe's Spiritual Nature and Its Revelation in "Faust" and through the "Fairy Tale of the Snake and the Lily"
CW 23	The Central Points of the Social Question in the Necessities of Life in the Present and the Future
CW 24	Essays Concerning the Threefold Division of the Social Organism and the Period 1915-1921
CW 25	Cosmology, Religion and Philosophy
CW 26	Anthroposophical Leading Thoughts
CW 27	Fundamentals for Expansion of the Art of Healing according to Spiritual-Scientific Insights
CW 28	The Course of My Life
CW 29	Collected Essays on Dramaturgy, 1889-1900
CW 30	Methodical Foundations of Anthroposophy: Collected Essays on Philosophy, Natural Science, Aesthetics and Psychology, 1884-1901
CW 31	Collected Essays on Culture and Current Events, 1887-1901
CW 32	Collected Essays on Literature, 1884-1902
CW 33	Biographies and Biographical Sketches, 1894-1905
CW 34	Lucifer-Gnosis: Foundational Essays on Anthroposophy and Reports from the Periodicals "Lucifer" and "Lucifer-Gnosis," 1903-1908
CW 35	Philosophy and Anthroposophy: Collected Essays, 1904-1923
CW 36	The Goetheanum-Idea in the Middle of the Cultural Crisis of the Present: Collected Essays from the Periodical "Das Goetheanum," 1921-1925
CW 37	Now in CWs 260a and 251
CW 38	Letters, Vol. 1: 1881-1890
CW 39	Letters, Vol. 2: 1890-1925
CW 40	Truth-Wrought Words
CW 40a	Sayings, Poems and Mantras; Supplementary Volume
CW 42	Now in CWs 264-266
CW 43	Stage Adaptations
CW 44	On the Four Mystery Dramas. Sketches, Fragments and Paralipomena on the Four Mystery Dramas
CW 45	Anthroposophy: A Fragment from the Year 1910

Public Lectures

CW 51 On Philosophy, History and Literature
CW 52 Spiritual Teachings Concerning the Soul and Observation of the World
CW 53 The Origin and Goal of the Human Being
CW 54 The Riddles of the World and Anthroposophy
CW 55 Knowledge of the Supersensible in Our Times and Its Meaning for Life Today
CW 56 Knowledge of the Soul and of the Spirit
CW 57 Where and How Does One Find the Spirit?
CW 58 The Metamorphoses of the Soul Life. Paths of Soul Experiences: Part One
CW 59 The Metamorphoses of the Soul Life. Paths of Soul Experiences: Part Two
CW 60 The Answers of Spiritual Science to the Biggest Questions of Existence
CW 61 Human History in the Light of Spiritual Research
CW 62 Results of Spiritual Research
CW 63 Spiritual Science as a Treasure for Life
CW 64 Out of Destiny-Burdened Times
CW 65 Out of Central European Spiritual Life
CW 66 Spirit and Matter, Life and Death
CW 67 The Eternal in the Human Soul. Immortality and Freedom
CW 68 Public lectures in various cities, 1906-1918
CW 69 Public lectures in various cities, 1906-1918
CW 70 Public lectures in various cities, 1906-1918
CW 71 Public lectures in various cities, 1906-1918
CW 72 Freedom – Immortality – Social Life
CW 73 The Supplementing of the Modern Sciences through Anthroposophy
CW 73a Specialized Fields of Knowledge and Anthroposophy
CW 74 The Philosophy of Thomas Aquinas
CW 75 Public lectures in various cities, 1906-1918
CW 76 The Fructifying Effect of Anthroposophy on Specialized Fields
CW 77a The Task of Anthroposophy in Relation to Science and Life: The Darmstadt College Course
CW 77b Art and Anthroposophy. The Goetheanum-Impulse
CW 78 Anthroposophy, Its Roots of Knowledge and Fruits for Life
CW 79 The Reality of the Higher Worlds
CW 80 Public lectures in various cities, 1922
CW 81 Renewal-Impulses for Culture and Science–Berlin College Course
CW 82 So that the Human Being Can Become a Complete Human Being
CW 83 Western and Eastern World-Contrast. Paths to Understanding It through Anthroposophy

CW 84 What Did the Goetheanum Intend and What Should Anthroposophy Do?

Lectures to the Members of the Anthroposophical Society

CW 88 Concerning the Astral World and Devachan
CW 89 Consciousness–Life–Form. Fundamental Principles of a Spiritual-Scientific Cosmology
CW 90 Participant Notes from the Lectures during the Years 1903-1905
CW 91 Participant Notes from the Lectures during the Years 1903-1905
CW 92 The Occult Truths of Ancient Myths and Sagas
CW 93 The Temple Legend and the Golden Legend
CW 93a Fundamentals of Esotericism
CW 94 Cosmogony. Popular Occultism. The Gospel of John. The Theosophy in the Gospel of John
CW 95 At the Gates of Theosophy
CW 96 Origin-Impulses of Spiritual Science. Christian Esotericism in the Light of New Spirit-Knowledge
CW 97 The Christian Mystery
CW 98 Nature Beings and Spirit Beings – Their Effects in Our Visible World
CW 99 The Theosophy of the Rosicrucians
CW 100 Human Development and Christ-Knowledge
CW 101 Myths and Legends. Occult Signs and Symbols
CW 102 The Working into Human Beings by Spiritual Beings
CW 103 The Gospel of John
CW 104 The Apocalypse of John
CW 104a From the Picture-Script of the Apocalypse of John
CW 105 Universe, Earth, the Human Being: Their Being and Development, as well as Their Reflection in the Connection between Egyptian Mythology and Modern Culture
CW 106 Egyptian Myths and Mysteries in Relation to the Active Spiritual Forces of the Present
CW 107 Spiritual-Scientific Knowledge of the Human Being
CW 108 Answering the Questions of Life and the World through Anthroposophy
CW 109 The Principle of Spiritual Economy in Connection with the Question of Reincarnation. An Aspect of the Spiritual Guidance of Humanity
CW 110 The Spiritual Hierarchies and Their Reflection in the Physical World. Zodiac, Planets and Cosmos
CW 111 Contained in CW 109
CW 112 The Gospel of John in Relation to the Three Other Gospels, Especially the Gospel of Luke

CW 113 The Orient in the Light of the Occident. The Children of Lucifer and the Brothers of Christ
CW 114 The Gospel of Luke
CW 115 Anthroposophy – Psychosophy – Pneumatosophy
CW 116 The Christ-Impulse and the Development of "I"- Consciousness
CW 117 The Deeper Secrets of the Development of Humanity in Light of the Gospels
CW 118 The Event of the Christ-Appearance in the Etheric World
CW 119 Macrocosm and Microcosm. The Large World and the Small World. Soul-Questions, Life-Questions, Spirit-Questions
CW 120 The Revelation of Karma
CW 121 The Mission of Individual Folk-Souls in Connection with Germanic-Nordic Mythology
CW 122 The Secrets of the Biblical Creation-Story. The Six-Day Work in the First Book of Moses
CW 123 The Gospel of Matthew
CW 124 Excursus in the Area of the Gospel of Mark
CW 125 Paths and Goals of the Spiritual Human Being. Life Questions in the Light of Spiritual Science
CW 126 Occult History. Esoteric Observations of the Karmic Relationships of Personalities and Events of World History
CW 127 The Mission of the New Spiritual Revelation. The Christ-Event as the Middle-Point of Earth Evolution
CW 128 An Occult Physiology
CW 129 Wonders of the World, Trials of the Soul, and Revelations of the Spirit
CW 130 Esoteric Christianity and the Spiritual Guidance of Humanity
CW 131 From Jesus to Christ
CW 132 Evolution from the View Point of the Truth
CW 133 The Earthly and the Cosmic Human Being
CW 134 The World of the Senses and the World of the Spirit
CW 135 Reincarnation and Karma and their Meaning for the Culture of the Present
CW 136 The Spiritual Beings in Celestial Bodies and the Realms of Nature
CW 137 The Human Being in the Light of Occultism, Theosophy and Philosophy
CW 138 On Initiation. On Eternity and the Passing Moment. On the Light of the Spirit and the Darkness of Life
CW 139 The Gospel of Mark
CW 140 Occult Investigation into the Life between Death and New Birth. The Living Interaction between Life and Death
CW 141 Life between Death and New Birth in Relationship to Cosmic Facts
CW 142 The Bhagavad Gita and the Letters of Paul

CW 143	Experiences of the Supersensible. Three Paths of the Soul to Christ
CW 144	The Mysteries of the East and of Christianity
CW 145	What Significance Does Occult Development of the Human Being Have for the Sheaths – Physical Body, Etheric Body, Astral Body, and Self?
CW 146	The Occult Foundations of the Bhagavad Gita
CW 147	The Secrets of the Threshold
CW 148	Out of Research in the Akasha: The Fifth Gospel
CW 149	Christ and the Spiritual World. Concerning the Search for the Holy Grail
CW 150	The World of the Spirit and Its Extension into Physical Existence; The Influence of the Dead in the World of the Living
CW 151	Human Thought and Cosmic Thought
CW 152	Preliminary Stages to the Mystery of Golgotha
CW 153	The Inner Being of the Human Being and Life Between Death and New Birth
CW 154	How does One Gain an Understanding of the Spiritual World? The Flowing in of Spiritual Impulses from out of the World of the Deceased
CW 155	Christ and the Human Soul. Concerning the Meaning of Life. Theosophical Morality. Anthroposophy and Christianity
CW 156	Occult Reading and Occult Hearing
CW 157	Human Destinies and the Destiny of Peoples
CW 157a	The Formation of Destiny and the Life after Death
CW 158	The Connection Between the Human Being and the Elemental World. Kalevala – Olaf Asteson – The Russian People – The World as the Result of the Influences of Equilibrium
CW 159	The Mystery of Death. The Nature and Significance of Middle Europe and the European Folk Spirits
CW 160	In CW 159
CW 161	Paths of Spiritual Knowledge and the Renewal of the Artistic Worldview
CW 162	Questions of Art and Life in Light of Spiritual Science
CW 163	Coincidence, Necessity and Providence. Imaginative Knowledge and the Processes after Death
CW 164	The Value of Thinking for a Knowledge That Satisfies the Human Being. The Relationship of Spiritual Science to Natural Science
CW 165	The Spiritual Unification of Humanity through the Christ-Impulse
CW 166	Necessity and Freedom in the Events of the World and in Human Action
CW 167	The Present and the Past in the Human Spirit
CW 168	The Connection between the Living and the Dead
CW 169	World-being and Selfhood

CW 170 The Riddle of the Human Being. The Spiritual Background of Human History. Cosmic and Human History, Vol. 1
CW 171 Inner Development-Impulses of Humanity. Goethe and the Crisis of the 19th Century. Cosmic and Human History, Vol. 2
CW 172 The Karma of the Vocation of the Human Being in Connection with Goethe's Life. Cosmic and Human History, Vol. 3
CW 173 Contemporary-Historical Considerations: The Karma of Untruthfulness, Part One. Cosmic and Human History, Vol. 4
CW 174 Contemporary-Historical Considerations: The Karma of Untruthfulness, Part Two. Cosmic and Human History, Vol. 5
CW 174a Middle Europe between East and West. Cosmic and Human History, Vol. 6
CW 174b The Spiritual Background of the First World War. Cosmic and Human History, Vol. 7
CW 175 Building Stones for an Understanding of the Mystery of Golgotha. Cosmic and Human Metamorphoses
CW 176 Truths of Evolution of the Individual and Humanity. The Karma of Materialism
CW 177 The Spiritual Background of the Outer World. The Fall of the Spirits of Darkness. Spiritual Beings and Their Effects, Vol. 1
CW 178 Individual Spiritual Beings and their Influence in the Soul of the Human Being. Spiritual Beings and their Effects, Vol. 2
CW 179 Spiritual Beings and Their Effects. Historical Necessity and Freedom. The Influences on Destiny from out of the World of the Dead. Spiritual Beings and Their Effects, Vol. 3
CW 180 Mystery Truths and Christmas Impulses. Ancient Myths and their Meaning. Spiritual Beings and Their Effects, Vol. 4
CW 181 Earthly Death and Cosmic Life. Anthroposophical Gifts for Life. Necessities of Consciousness for the Present and the Future.
CW 182 Death as Transformation of Life
CW 183 The Science of the Development of the Human Being
CW 184 The Polarity of Duration and Development in Human Life. The Cosmic Pre-History of Humanity
CW 185 Historical Symptomology
CW 185a Historical-Developmental Foundations for Forming a Social Judgment
CW 186 The Fundamental Social Demands of Our Time–In Changed Situations
CW 187 How Can Humanity Find the Christ Again? The Threefold Shadow-Existence of our Time and the New Christ-Light
CW 188 Goetheanism, a Transformation-Impulse and Resurrection-Thought. Science of the Human Being and Science of Sociology
CW 189 The Social Question as a Question of Consciousness. The Spiritual Background of the Social Question, Vol. 1

CW 190 Impulses of the Past and the Future in Social Occurrences. The Spiritual Background of the Social Question, Vol. 2

CW 191 Social Understanding from Spiritual-Scientific Cognition. The Spiritual Background of the Social Question, Vol. 3

CW 192 Spiritual-Scientific Treatment of Social and Pedagogical Questions

CW 193 The Inner Aspect of the Social Riddle. Luciferic Past and Ahrimanic Future

CW 194 The Mission of Michael. The Revelation of the Actual Mysteries of the Human Being

CW 195 Cosmic New Year and the New Year Idea

CW 196 Spiritual and Social Transformations in the Development of Humanity

CW 197 Polarities in the Development of Humanity: West and East Materialism and Mysticism Knowledge and Belief

CW 198 Healing Factors for the Social Organism

CW 199 Spiritual Science as Knowledge of the Foundational Impulses of Social Formation

CW 200 The New Spirituality and the Christ-Experience of the 20th Century

CW 201 The Correspondences Between Microcosm and Macrocosm. The Human Being – A Hieroglyph of the Universe. The Human Being in Relationship with the Cosmos: 1

CW 202 The Bridge between the World-Spirituality and the Physical Aspect of the Human Being. The Search for the New Isis, the Divine Sophia. The Human Being in Relationship with the Cosmos: 2

CW 203 The Responsibility of Human Beings for the Development of the World through their Spiritual Connection with the Planet Earth and the World of the Stars. The Human Being in Relationship with the Cosmos: 3

CW 204 Perspectives of the Development of Humanity. The Materialistic Knowledge-Impulse and the Task of Anthroposophy. The Human Being in Relationship with the Cosmos: 4

CW 205 Human Development, World-Soul, and World-Spirit. Part One: The Human Being as a Being of Body and Soul in Relationship to the World. The Human Being in Relationship with the Cosmos: 5

CW 206 Human Development, World-Soul, and World-Spirit. Part Two: The Human Being as a Spiritual Being in the Process of Historical Development. The Human Being in Relationship with the Cosmos: 6

CW 207 Anthroposophy as Cosmosophy. Part One: Characteristic Features of the Human Being in the Earthly and the Cosmic Realms. The Human Being in Relationship with the Cosmos: 7

CW 208 Anthroposophy as Cosmosophy. Part Two: The Forming of the Human Being as the Result of Cosmic Influence. The Human Being in Relationship with the Cosmos: 8

CW 209 Nordic and Central European Spiritual Impulses. The Festival of the Appearance of Christ. The Human Being in Relationship with the Cosmos: 9
CW 210 Old and New Methods of Initiation. Drama and Poetry in the Change of Consciousness in the Modern Age
CW 211 The Sun Mystery and the Mystery of Death and Resurrection. Exoteric and Esoteric Christianity
CW 212 Human Soul Life and Spiritual Striving in Connection with World and Earth Development
CW 213 Human Questions and World Answers
CW 214 The Mystery of the Trinity: The Human Being in Relationship with the Spiritual World in the Course of Time
CW 215 Philosophy, Cosmology, and Religion in Anthroposophy
CW 216 The Fundamental Impulses of the World-Historical Development of Humanity
CW 217 Spiritually Active Forces in the Coexistence of the Older and Younger Generations. Pedagogical Course for Youth
CW 217a Youth's Cognitive Task
CW 218 Spiritual Connections in the Forming of the Human Organism
CW 219 The Relationship of the World of the Stars to the Human Being, and of the Human Being to the World of the Stars. The Spiritual Communion of Humanity
CW 220 Living Knowledge of Nature. Intellectual Fall and Spiritual Redemption
CW 221 Earth-Knowing and Heaven-Insight
CW 222 The Imparting of Impulses to World-Historical Events through Spiritual Powers
CW 223 The Cycle of the Year as Breathing Process of the Earth and the Four Great Festival-Seasons. Anthroposophy and the Human Heart (Gemüt)
CW 224 The Human Soul and its Connection with Divine-Spiritual Individualities. The Internalization of the Festivals of the Year
CW 225 Three Perspectives of Anthroposophy. Cultural Phenomena observed from a Spiritual-Scientific Perspective
CW 226 Human Being, Human Destiny, and World Development
CW 227 Initiation-Knowledge
CW 228 Science of Initiation and Knowledge of the Stars. The Human Being in the Past, the Present, and the Future from the Viewpoint of the Development of Consciousness
CW 229 The Experiencing of the Course of the Year in Four Cosmic Imaginations
CW 230 The Human Being as Harmony of the Creative, Building, and Formative World-Word

CW 231 The Supersensible Human Being, Understood Anthroposophically
CW 232 The Forming of the Mysteries
CW 233 World History Illuminated by Anthroposophy and as the Foundation for Knowledge of the Human Spirit
CW 233a Mystery Sites of the Middle Ages: Rosicrucianism and the Modern Initiation-Principle. The Festival of Easter as Part of the History of the Mysteries of Humanity
CW 234 Anthroposophy. A Summary after 21 Years
CW 235 Esoteric Observations of Karmic Relationships in 6 Volumes, Vol. 1
CW 236 Esoteric Observations of Karmic Relationships in 6 Volumes, Vol. 2
CW 237 Esoteric Observations of Karmic Relationships in 6 Volumes, Vol. 3: The Karmic Relationships of the Anthroposophical Movement
CW 238 Esoteric Observations of Karmic Relationships in 6 Volumes, Vol. 4: The Spiritual Life of the Present in Relationship to the Anthroposophical Movement
CW 239 Esoteric Observations of Karmic Relationships in 6 Volumes, Vol. 5
CW 240 Esoteric Observations of Karmic Relationships in 6 Volumes, Vol. 6
CW 243 The Consciousness of the Initiate
CW 245 Instructions for an Esoteric Schooling
CW 250 The Building-Up of the Anthroposophical Society. From the Beginning to the Outbreak of the First World War
CW 251 The History of the Goetheanum Building-Association
CW 252 Life in the Anthroposophical Society from the First World War to the Burning of the First Goetheanum
CW 253 The Problems of Living Together in the Anthroposophical Society. On the Dornach Crisis of 1915. With Highlights on Swedenborg's Clairvoyance, the Views of Freudian Psychoanalysts, and the Concept of Love in Relation to Mysticism
CW 254 The Occult Movement in the 19th Century and Its Relationship to World Culture. Significant Points from the Exoteric Cultural Life around the Middle of the 19th Century
CW 255 Rudolf Steiner during the First World War
CW 255a Anthroposophy and the Reformation of Society. On the History of the Threefold Movement
CW 255b Anthroposophy and Its Opponents, 1919-1921
CW 256 How Can the Anthroposophical Movement Be Financed?
CW 256a Futurum, Inc. / International Laboratories, Inc.
CW 256b The Coming Day, Inc.
CW 257 Anthroposophical Community-Building
CW 258 The History of and Conditions for the Anthroposophical Movement in Relationship to the Anthroposophical Society. A Stimulus to Self-Contemplation
CW 259 The Year of Destiny 1923 in the History of the Anthroposophical

Society. From the Burning of the Goetheanum to the Christmas Conference

CW 260 The Christmas Conference for the Founding of the General Anthroposophical Society

CW 260a The Constitution of the General Anthroposophical Society and the School for Spiritual Science. The Rebuilding of the Goetheanum

CW 261 Our Dead. Addresses, Words of Remembrance, and Meditative Verses, 1906-1924

CW 262 Rudolf Steiner and Marie Steiner-von Sivers: Correspondence and Documents, 1901-1925

CW 263/1 Rudolf Steiner and Edith Maryon: Correspondence: Letters, Verses, Sketches, 1912-1924

CW 264 On the History and the Contents of the First Section of the Esoteric School from 1904 to 1914. Letters, Newsletters, Documents, Lectures

CW 265 On the History and from the Contents of the Ritual-Knowledge Section of the Esoteric School from 1904 to 1914. Documents, and Lectures from the Years 1906 to 1914, as Well as on New Approaches to Ritual-Knowledge Work in the Years 1921-1924

CW 266/1 From the Contents of the Esoteric Lessons. Volume 1: 1904-1909. Notes from Memory of Participants. Meditation texts from the notes of Rudolf Steiner

CW 266/2 From the Contents of the Esoteric Lessons. Volume 2: 1910-1912. Notes from Memory of Participants

CW 266/3 From the Contents of the Esoteric Lessons. Volume 3: 1913, 1914 and 1920-1923. Notes from Memory of Participants. Meditation texts from the notes of Rudolf Steiner

CW 267 Soul-Exercises: Vol. 1: Exercises with Word and Image Meditations for the Methodological Development of Higher Powers of Knowledge, 1904-1924

CW 268 Soul-Exercises: Vol. 2: Mantric Verses, 1903-1925

CW 269 Ritual Texts for the Celebration of the Free Christian Religious Instruction. The Collected Verses for Teachers and Students of the Waldorf School

CW 270 Esoteric Instructions for the First Class of the School for Spiritual Science at the Goetheanum 1924, 4 Volumes

CW 271 Art and Knowledge of Art. Foundations of a New Aesthetic

CW 272 Spiritual-Scientific Commentary on Goethe's "Faust" in Two Volumes. Vol. 1: Faust, the Striving Human Being

CW 273 Spiritual-Scientific Commentary on Goethe's "Faust" in Two Volumes. Vol. 2: The Faust-Problem

CW 274 Addresses for the Christmas Plays from the Old Folk Traditions

CW 275 Art in the Light of Mystery-Wisdom

CW 276 The Artistic in Its Mission in the World. The Genius of

Language. The World of Self-Revealing Radiant Appearances – Anthroposophy and Art. Anthroposophy and Poetry
CW 277 Eurythmy. The Revelation of the Speaking Soul
CW 277a The Origin and Development of Eurythmy
CW 278 Eurythmy as Visible Song
CW 279 Eurythmy as Visible Speech
CW 280 The Method and Nature of Speech Formation
CW 281 The Art of Recitation and Declamation
CW 282 Speech Formation and Dramatic Art
CW 283 The Nature of Things Musical and the Experience of Tone in the Human Being
CW 284/285 Images of Occult Seals and Pillars. The Munich Congress of Whitsun 1907 and Its Consequences
CW 286 Paths to a New Style of Architecture. "And the Building Becomes Human"
CW 287 The Building at Dornach as a Symbol of Historical Becoming and an Artistic Transformation Impulse
CW 288 Style-Forms in the Living Organic
CW 289 The Building-Idea of the Goetheanum: Lectures with Slides from the Years 1920-1921
CW 290 The Building-Idea of the Goetheanum: Lectures with Slides from the Years 1920-1921
CW 291 The Nature of Colors
CW 291a Knowledge of Colors. Supplementary Volume to "The Nature of Colors"
CW 292 Art History as Image of Inner Spiritual Impulses
CW 293 General Knowledge of the Human Being as the Foundation of Pedagogy
CW 294 The Art of Education, Methodology and Didactics
CW 295 The Art of Education: Seminar Discussions and Lectures on Lesson Planning
CW 296 The Question of Education as a Social Question
CW 297 The Idea and Practice of the Waldorf School
CW 297a Education for Life: Self-Education and the Practice of Pedagogy
CW 298 Rudolf Steiner in the Waldorf School
CW 299 Spiritual-Scientific Observations on Speech
CW 300a Conferences with the Teachers of the Free Waldorf School in Stuttgart, 1919 to 1924, in 3 Volumes, Vol. 1
CW 300b Conferences with the Teachers of the Free Waldorf School in Stuttgart, 1919 to 1924, in 3 Volumes, Vol. 2
CW 300c Conferences with the Teachers of the Free Waldorf School in Stuttgart, 1919 to 1924, in 3 Volumes, Vol. 3
CW 301 The Renewal of Pedagogical-Didactical Art through Spiritual Science

CW 302 Knowledge of the Human Being and the Forming of Class Lessons
CW 302a Education and Teaching from a Knowledge of the Human Being
CW 303 The Healthy Development of the Human Being
CW 304 Methods of Education and Teaching Based on Anthroposophy
CW 304a Anthroposophical Knowledge of the Human Being and Pedagogy
CW 305 The Soul-Spiritual Foundational Forces of the Art of Education. Spiritual Values in Education and Social Life
CW 306 Pedagogical Praxis from the Viewpoint of a Spiritual-Scientific Knowledge of the Human Being. The Education of the Child and Young Human Beings
CW 307 The Spiritual Life of the Present and Education
CW 308 The Method of Teaching and the Life-Requirements for Teaching
CW 309 Anthroposophical Pedagogy and Its Prerequisites
CW 310 The Pedagogical Value of a Knowledge of the Human Being and the Cultural Value of Pedagogy
CW 311 The Art of Education from an Understanding of the Being of Humanity
CW 312 Spiritual Science and Medicine
CW 313 Spiritual-Scientific Viewpoints on Therapy
CW 314 Physiology and Therapy Based on Spiritual Science
CW 315 Curative Eurythmy
CW 316 Meditative Observations and Instructions for a Deepening of the Art of Healing
CW 317 The Curative Education Course
CW 318 The Working Together of Doctors and Pastors
CW 319 Anthroposophical Knowledge of the Human Being and Medicine
CW 320 Spiritual-Scientific Impulses for the Development of Physics 1: The First Natural-Scientific Course: Light, Color, Tone, Mass, Electricity, Magnetism
CW 321 Spiritual-Scientific Impulses for the Development of Physics 2: The Second Natural-Scientific Course: Warmth at the Border of Positive and Negative Materiality
CW 322 The Borders of the Knowledge of Nature
CW 323 The Relationship of the various Natural-Scientific Fields to Astronomy
CW 324 Nature Observation, Mathematics, and Scientific Experimentation and Results from the Viewpoint of Anthroposophy
CW 324a The Fourth Dimension in Mathematics and Reality
CW 325 Natural Science and the World-Historical Development of Humanity since Ancient Times
CW 326 The Moment of the Coming Into Being of Natural Science in World History and Its Development Since Then
CW 327 Spiritual-Scientific Foundations for Success in Farming. The Agricultural Course

CW 328	The Social Question
CW 329	The Liberation of the Human Being as the Foundation for a New Social Form
CW 330	The Renewal of the Social Organism
CW 331	Work-Council and Socialization
CW 332	The Alliance for Threefolding and the Total Reform of Society. The Council on Culture and the Liberation of the Spiritual Life
CW 332a	The Social Future
CW 333	Freedom of Thought and Social Forces
CW 334	From the Unified State to the Threefold Social Organism
CW 335	The Crisis of the Present and the Path to Healthy Thinking
CW 336	The Great Questions of the Times and Anthroposophical Spiritual Knowledge
CW 337a	Social Ideas, Social Reality, Social Practice, Vol. 1: Question-and-Answer Evenings and Study Evenings of the Alliance for the Threefold Social Organism in Stuttgart, 1919-1920
CW 337b	Social Ideas, Social Realities, Social Practice, Vol. 2: Discussion Evenings of the Swiss Alliance for the Threefold Social Organism
CW 338	How Does One Work on Behalf of the Impulse for the Threefold Social Organism?
CW 339	Anthroposophy, Threefold Social Organism, and the Art of Public Speaking
CW 340	The National-Economics Course. The Tasks of a New Science of Economics, Volume 1
CW 341	The National-Economics Seminar. The Tasks of a New Science of Economics, Volume 2
CW 342	Lectures and Courses on Christian Religious Work, Vol. 1: Anthroposophical Foundations for a Renewed Christian Religious Working
CW 343	Lectures and Courses on Christian Religious Work, Vol. 2: Spiritual Knowledge – Religious Feeling – Cultic Doing
CW 344	Lectures and Courses on Christian Religious Work, Vol. 3: Lectures at the Founding of the Christian Community
CW 345	Lectures and Courses on Christian Religious Work, Vol. 4: Concerning the Nature of the Working Word
CW 346	Lectures and Courses on Christian Religious Work, Vol. 5: The Apocalypse and the Work of the Priest
CW 347	The Knowledge of the Nature of the Human Being According to Body, Soul and Spirit. On Earlier Conditions of the Earth
CW 348	On Health and Illness. Foundations of a Spiritual-Scientific Doctrine of the Senses
CW 349	On the Life of the Human Being and of the Earth. On the Nature of Christianity

CW 350 Rhythms in the Cosmos and in the Human Being. How Does One Come To See the Spiritual World?

CW 351 The Human Being and the World. The Influence of the Spirit in Nature. On the Nature of Bees

CW 352 Nature and the Human Being Observed Spiritual-Scientifically

CW 353 The History of Humanity and the World-Views of the Folk Cultures

CW 354 The Creation of the World and the Human Being. Life on Earth and the Influence of the Stars

SIGNIFICANT EVENTS IN THE LIFE OF RUDOLF STEINER

1829: June 23: birth of Johann Steiner (1829-1910)—Rudolf Steiner's father—in Geras, Lower Austria.

1834: May 8: birth of Franciska Blie (1834-1918)—Rudolf Steiner's mother—in Horn, Lower Austria. "My father and mother were both children of the glorious Lower Austrian forest district north of the Danube."

1860: May 16: marriage of Johann Steiner and Franciska Blie.

1861: February 25: birth of *Rudolf Joseph Lorenz Steiner* in Kraljevec, Croatia, near the border with Hungary, where Johann Steiner works as a telegrapher for the South Austria Railroad. Rudolf Steiner is baptized two days later, February 27, the date usually given as his birthday.

1862: Summer: the family moves to Mödling, Lower Austria.

1863: The family moves to Pottschach, Lower Austria, near the Styrian border, where Johann Steiner becomes stationmaster. "The view stretched to the mountains...majestic peaks in the distance and the sweet charm of nature in the immediate surroundings."

1864: November 15: birth of Rudolf Steiner's sister, Leopoldine (d. November 1, 1927). She will become a seamstress and live with her parents for the rest of her life.

1866: July 28: birth of Rudolf Steiner's deaf-mute brother, Gustav (d. May 1, 1941).

1867: Rudolf Steiner enters the village school. Following a disagreement between his father and the schoolmaster, whose wife falsely accused the boy of causing a commotion, Rudolf Steiner is taken out of school and taught at home.

1868: A critical experience. Unknown to the family, an aunt dies in a distant town. Sitting in the station waiting room, Rudolf Steiner sees her "form," which speaks to him, asking for help. "Beginning with this experience, a new soul life began in the boy, one in which not only the outer trees and mountains spoke to him, but also the worlds that lay behind them. From this moment on, the boy began to live with the spirits of nature...."

1869: The family moves to the peaceful, rural village of Neudorfl, near Wiener-Neustadt in present-day Austria. Rudolf Steiner attends the village school. Because of the "unorthodoxy" of his writing and spelling, he has to do "extra lessons."

1870: Through a book lent to him by his tutor, he discovers geometry: "To grasp something purely in the spirit brought me inner happiness. I know that I first learned happiness through geometry." The same tutor allows him to draw, while other students still struggle with their reading and writing. "An artistic element" thus enters his education.

1871: Though his parents are not religious, Rudolf Steiner becomes a "church child," a favorite of the priest, who was "an exceptional character." "Up to the age of ten or eleven, among those I came to know, he was far and away the most significant." Among other things, he introduces Steiner to Copernican, heliocentric cosmology. As an altar boy, Rudolf Steiner serves at Masses, funerals, and Corpus Christi processions. At year's end, after an incident in which he escapes a thrashing, his father forbids him to go to church.

1872: Rudolf Steiner transfers to grammar school in Wiener-Neustadt, a five-mile walk from home, which must be done in all weathers.

1873-75: Through his teachers and on his own, Rudolf Steiner has many wonderful experiences with science and mathematics. Outside school, he teaches himself analytic geometry, trigonometry, differential equations, and calculus.

1876: Rudolf Steiner begins tutoring other students. He learns bookbinding from his father. He also teaches himself stenography.

1877: Rudolf Steiner discovers Kant's *Critique of Pure Reason*, which he reads and rereads. He also discovers and reads von Rotteck's *World History*.

1878: He studies extensively in contemporary psychology and philosophy.

1879: Rudolf Steiner graduates from high school with honors. His father is transferred to Inzersdorf, near Vienna. He uses his first visit to Vienna "to purchase a great number of philosophy books"—Kant, Fichte, Schelling, and Hegel, as well as numerous histories of philosophy. His aim: to find a path from the "I" to nature.

October 1879-1883: Rudolf Steiner attends the Technical College in Vienna—to study mathematics, chemistry, physics, mineralogy, botany, zoology, biology, geology, and mechanics—with a scholarship. He also attends lectures in history and literature, while avidly reading philosophy on his own. His two favorite professors are Karl Julius Schröer (German language and literature) and Edmund Reitlinger (physics). He also audits lectures by Robert Zimmerman on aesthetics and Franz Brentano on philosophy. During this year he begins his friendship with Moritz Zitter (1861-1921), who will help support him financially when he is in Berlin.

1880: Rudolf Steiner attends lectures on Schiller and Goethe by Karl Julius Schröer, who becomes his mentor. Also "through a remarkable combination of circumstances," he meets Felix Koguzki, a "herb gatherer" and healer, who could "see deeply into the secrets of nature." Rudolf Steiner will meet and study with this "emissary of the Master" throughout his time in Vienna.

1881: January: "... I didn't sleep a wink. I was busy with philosophical problems until about 12:30 a.m. Then, finally, I threw myself down on my couch. All my striving during the previous year had been to research whether the following statement by Schelling was true or not: *Within everyone dwells a secret, marvelous capacity to draw back from the stream of time—out of the self clothed in all that comes to us from outside—into our innermost being and there, in the immutable form of the Eternal, to look into ourselves.* I believe, and I am still quite certain of it, that I discovered this capacity in myself; I had long had an inkling of it. Now the whole of idealist philosophy stood before me in modified form. What's a sleepless night compared to that!"

Rudolf Steiner begins communicating with leading thinkers of the day, who send him books in return, which he reads eagerly.

July: "I am not one of those who dives into the day like an animal in human form. I pursue a quite specific goal, an idealistic aim—knowledge of the truth! This cannot be done offhandedly. It requires the greatest striving in the world, free of all egotism, and equally of all resignation."

August: Steiner puts down on paper for the first time thoughts for a "Philosophy of Freedom." "The striving for the absolute: this human yearning is freedom." He also seeks to outline a "peasant philosophy," describing what the worldview of a "peasant"—one who lives close to the earth and the old ways—really is.

1881-1882: Felix Koguzki, the herb gatherer, reveals himself to be the envoy of another, higher initiatory personality, who instructs Rudolf Steiner to penetrate Fichte's philosophy and to master modern scientific thinking as a preparation for right entry into the spirit. This "Master" also teaches him the double (evolutionary and involutionary) nature of time.

1882: Through the offices of Karl Julius Schröer, Rudolf Steiner is asked by Joseph Kurschner to edit Goethe's scientific works for the *Deutschen National-Literatur* edition. He writes "A Possible Critique of Atomistic Concepts" and sends it to Friedrich Theodore Vischer.

1883: Rudolf Steiner completes his college studies and begins work on the Goethe project.

1884: First volume of Goethe's *Scientific Writings* (CW 1) appears (March). He lectures on Goethe and Lessing, and Goethe's approach to science. In July, he enters the household of Ladislaus and Pauline Specht as tutor to the four Specht boys. He will live there until 1890. At this time, he meets Josef Breuer (1842-1925), the coauthor with Sigmund Freud of *Studies in Hysteria*, who is the Specht family doctor.

1885: While continuing to edit Goethe's writings, Rudolf Steiner reads deeply in contemporary philosophy (Edouard von Hartmann, Johannes Volkelt, and Richard Wahle, among others).

1886: May: Rudolf Steiner sends Kurschner the manuscript of *Outlines of Goethe's Theory of Knowledge* (CW 2), which appears in October, and which he sends out widely. He also meets the poet Marie Eugenie Delle Grazie and writes "Nature and Our Ideals" for her. He attends her salon, where he meets many priests, theologians, and philosophers, who will become his friends. Meanwhile, the director of the Goethe Archive in Weimar requests his collaboration with the *Sophien* edition of Goethe's works, particularly the writings on color.

1887: At the beginning of the year, Rudolf Steiner is very sick. As the year progresses and his health improves, he becomes increasingly "a man of letters," lecturing, writing essays, and taking part in Austrian cultural life. In August-September, the second volume of Goethe's *Scientific Writings* appears.

1888: January-July: Rudolf Steiner assumes editorship of the "German Weekly" (*Deutsche Wochenschrift*). He begins lecturing more intensively, giving, for example, a lecture titled "Goethe as Father of a New Aesthetics." He meets and becomes soul friends with Friedrich Eckstein (1861-1939), a vegetarian, philosopher of symbolism, alchemist, and musician, who will introduce him to various spiritual currents (including Theosophy) and with whom he will meditate and interpret esoteric and alchemical texts.

1889: Rudolf Steiner first reads Nietzsche (*Beyond Good and Evil*). He encounters Theosophy again and learns of Madame Blavatsky in the Theosophical circle around Marie Lang (1858-1934). Here he also meets well-known figures of Austrian life, as well as esoteric figures like the occultist Franz Hartman and Karl Leinigen-Billigen (translator of C.G. Harrison's *The Transcendental Universe.*) During this period, Steiner first reads A.P. Sinnett's *Esoteric Buddhism* and Mabel Collins's *Light on the Path.* He also begins traveling, visiting Budapest, Weimar, and Berlin (where he meets philosopher Edouard von Hartmann).

1890: Rudolf Steiner finishes volume 3 of Goethe's scientific writings. He begins his doctoral dissertation, which will become *Truth and Science* (CW 3). He also meets the poet and feminist Rosa Mayreder (1858-1938), with whom he can exchange his most intimate thoughts. In September, Rudolf Steiner moves to Weimar to work in the Goethe-Schiller Archive.

1891: Volume 3 of the Kurschner edition of Goethe appears. Meanwhile, Rudolf Steiner edits Goethe's studies in mineralogy and scientific writings for the *Sophien* edition. He meets Ludwig Laistner of the Cotta Publishing Company, who asks for a book on the basic question of metaphysics. From this will result, ultimately, *The Philosophy of Freedom* (CW 4), which will be published not by Cotta but by Emil Felber. In October, Rudolf Steiner takes the oral exam for a doctorate in philosophy, mathematics, and mechanics at Rostock University, receiving his doctorate on the twenty-sixth. In November, he gives his first lecture on Goethe's "Fairy Tale" in Vienna.

1892: Rudolf Steiner continues work at the Goethe-Schiller Archive and on his *Philosophy of Freedom. Truth and Science*, his doctoral dissertation, is published. Steiner undertakes to write introductions to books on Schopenhauer and Jean Paul for Cotta. At year's end, he finds lodging with Anna Eunike, née Schulz (1853-1911), a widow with four daughters and a son. He also develops a friendship with Otto Erich Hartleben (1864-1905) with whom he shares literary interests.

1893: Rudolf Steiner begins his habit of producing many reviews and articles. In March, he gives a lecture titled "Hypnotism, with Reference to Spiritism." In September, volume 4 of the Kurschner edition is completed. In November, *The Philosophy of Freedom* appears. This year, too, he meets John Henry Mackay (1864-1933), the anarchist, and Max Stirner, a scholar and biographer.

1894: Rudolf Steiner meets Elisabeth Förster Nietzsche, the philosopher's sister, and begins to read Nietzsche in earnest, beginning with the as yet unpublished *Antichrist*. He also meets Ernst Haeckel (1834-1919). In the fall, he begins to write *Nietzsche, A Fighter against His Time* (CW 5).

1895: May, *Nietzsche, A Fighter against His Time* appears.

1896: January 22: Rudolf Steiner sees Friedrich Nietzsche for the first and only time. Moves between the Nietzsche and the Goethe-Schiller Archives, where he completes his work before year's end. He falls out with Elisabeth Förster Nietzsche, thus ending his association with the Nietzsche Archive.

1897: Rudolf Steiner finishes the manuscript of *Goethe's Worldview* (CW 6). He moves to Berlin with Anna Eunike and begins editorship of the *Magazin fur Literatur*. From now on, Steiner will write countless reviews, literary and philosophical articles, and so on. He begins lecturing at the "Free Literary Society." In September, he attends the Zionist Congress in Basel. He sides with Dreyfus in the Dreyfus affair.

1898: Rudolf Steiner is very active as an editor in the political, artistic, and theatrical life of Berlin. He becomes friendly with John Henry Mackay and poet Ludwig Jacobowski (1868-1900). He joins Jacobowski's circle of writers, artists, and scientists—"The Coming Ones" (*Die Kommenden*)—and contributes lectures to the group until 1903. He also lectures at the "League for College Pedagogy." He writes an article for Goethe's sesquicentennial, "Goethe's Secret Revelation," on the "Fairy Tale of the Green Snake and the Beautiful Lily."

1898-99: "This was a trying time for my soul as I looked at Christianity.... I was able to progress only by contemplating, by means of spiritual perception, the evolution of Christianity .... Conscious knowledge of real Christianity began to dawn in me around the turn of the century. This seed continued to develop. My soul trial occurred shortly before the beginning of the twentieth century. It was decisive for my soul's development that I stood spiritually before the Mystery of Golgotha in a deep and solemn celebration of knowledge."

1899: Rudolf Steiner begins teaching and giving lectures and lecture cycles at the Workers' College, founded by Wilhelm Liebknecht (1826-1900). He will continue to do so until 1904. Writes: *Literature and Spiritual Life in the Nineteenth Century; Individualism in Philosophy*; *Haeckel and His Opponents; Poetry in the Present;* and begins what will become (fifteen years later) *The Riddles of Philosophy* (CW 18). He also meets many artists and writers, including Käthe Kollwitz, Stefan Zweig, and Rainer Maria Rilke. On October 31, he marries Anna Eunike.

1900: "I thought that the turn of the century must bring humanity a new light. It seemed to me that the separation of human thinking and willing from the spirit had peaked. A turn or reversal of direction in human evolution seemed to me a necessity." Rudolf Steiner finishes *World and Life Views in the Nineteenth Century* (the second part of what will become *The Riddles of Philosophy*) and dedicates it to Ernst Haeckel. It is published in March. He continues lecturing at *Die Kommenden*, whose leadership he assumes after the death of Jacobowski. Also, he gives the Gutenberg Jubilee lecture before 7,000 typesetters and printers. In September, Rudolf Steiner is invited by Count and Countess Brockdorff to lecture in the Theosophical Library. His first lecture is on Nietzsche. His second lecture is titled "Goethe's Secret Revelation." October 6, he begins a lecture cycle on the mystics that will become *Mystics after Modernism* (CW 7). November-December: "Marie von Sivers appears in the audience...." Also in November, Steiner gives his first lecture at the Giordano Bruno Bund (where he will continue to lecture until May, 1905). He speaks on Bruno and modern Rome, focusing on the importance of the philosophy of Thomas Aquinas as monism.

1901: In continual financial straits, Rudolf Steiner's early friends Moritz Zitter and Rosa Mayreder help support him. In October, he begins the lecture cycle *Christianity as Mystical Fact* (CW 8) at the Theosophical Library. In November, he gives his first "Theosophical lecture" on Goethe's "Fairy Tale" in Hamburg at the invitation of Wilhelm Hubbe-Schleiden. He also attends a gathering to celebrate the founding of the Theosophical Society at Count and Countess Brockdorff's. He gives a lecture cycle, "From Buddha to Christ," for the circle of the *Kommenden*. November 17, Marie von Sivers asks Rudolf Steiner if Theosophy needs a Western-Christian spiritual movement (to complement Theosophy's Eastern emphasis). "The question was posed. Now, following spiritual laws, I could begin to give an answer...." In December, Rudolf Steiner writes his first article for a Theosophical publication. At year's end, the Brockdorffs and possibly Wilhelm Hubbe-Schleiden ask Rudolf Steiner to join the Theosophical Society and undertake the leadership of the German section. Rudolf Steiner agrees, on the condition that Marie von Sivers (then in Italy) work with him.

1902: Beginning in January, Rudolf Steiner attends the opening of the Workers' School in Spandau with Rosa Luxemberg (1870-1919). January 17, Rudolf Steiner joins the Theosophical Society. In April, he is asked to become general secretary of the German Section of the Theosophical Society, and works on preparations for its founding. In July, he visits London for a Theosophical congress. He meets Bertram Keightly, G.R.S. Mead, A.P. Sinnett, and Annie Besant, among others. In September, *Christianity as Mystical Fact* appears. In October, Rudolf Steiner gives his first public lecture on Theosophy ("Monism and Theosophy") to about three hundred people at the Giordano Bruno Bund. On October 19-21, the German Section of the Theosophical Society has its first meeting; Rudolf Steiner is the general secretary, and Annie Besant attends. Steiner lectures on practical karma studies. On October 23, Annie Besant inducts Rudolf Steiner into the Esoteric School of the Theosophical Society. On October 25, Steiner begins a weekly series of lectures: "The Field of Theosophy." During this year, Rudolf Steiner also first meets Ita Wegman (1876-1943), who will become his close collaborator in his final years.

1903: Rudolf Steiner holds about 300 lectures and seminars. In May, the first issue of the periodical *Luzifer* appears. In June, Rudolf Steiner visits London for the first meeting of the Federation of the European Sections of the Theosophical Society, where he meets Colonel Olcott. He begins to write *Theosophy* (CW 9).

1904: Rudolf Steiner continues lecturing at the Workers' College and elsewhere (about 90 lectures), while lecturing intensively all over Germany among Theosophists (about a 140 lectures). In February, he meets Carl Unger (1878-1929), who will become a member of the board of the Anthroposophical Society (1913). In March, he meets Michael Bauer (1871-1929), a Christian mystic, who will also be on the board. In May, *Theosophy* appears, with the dedication: "To the spirit of Giordano Bruno." Rudolf Steiner and Marie von Sivers visit London for meetings with Annie Besant. June: Rudolf Steiner and Marie von Sivers attend the meeting of the Federation of European Sections of the Theosophical Society in Amsterdam. In July, Steiner begins the articles in *Luzifer-Gnosis* that will become *How to Know Higher Worlds* (CW 10) and *Cosmic Memory* (CW 11). In September, Annie Besant visits Germany. In December, Steiner lectures on Freemasonry. He mentions the High Grade Masonry derived from John Yarker and represented by Theodore Reuss and Karl Kellner as a blank slate "into which a good image could be placed."

1905: This year, Steiner ends his non-Theosophical lecturing activity. Supported by Marie von Sivers, his Theosophical lecturing—both in public and in the Theosophical Society—increases significantly: "The German Theosophical Movement is of exceptional importance." Steiner recommends reading, among others, Fichte, Jacob Boehme, and Angelus Silesius. He begins to introduce Christian themes into Theosophy. He also begins to work with doctors (Felix Peipers and Ludwig Noll). In July, he is in London for the Federation of European Sections, where he attends a lecture by Annie Besant: "I have seldom seen Mrs. Besant speak in so inward and heartfelt a manner...." "Through Mrs. Besant I have found the way to H.P. Blavatsky." September to October, he gives a course of thirty-one lectures for a small group of esoteric students. In October, the annual meeting of the German Section of the Theosophical Society, which still remains very small, takes place. Rudolf Steiner reports membership has risen from 121 to 377 members. In November, seeking to establish esoteric "continuity," Rudolf Steiner and Marie von Sivers participate in a "Memphis-Misraim" Masonic ceremony. They pay forty-five marks for membership. "Yesterday, you saw how little remains of former esoteric institutions." "We are dealing only with a 'framework'... for the present, nothing lies behind it. The occult powers have completely withdrawn."

1906: Expansion of Theosophical work. Rudolf Steiner gives about 245 lectures, only 44 of which take place in Berlin. Cycles are given in Paris, Leipzig,

Stuttgart, and Munich. Esoteric work also intensifies. Rudolf Steiner begins writing *An Outline of Esoteric Science* (CW 13). In January, Rudolf Steiner receives permission (a patent) from the Great Orient of the Scottish A & A Thirty-Three Degree Rite of the Order of the Ancient Freemasons of the Memphis-Misraim Rite to direct a chapter under the name "Mystica Aeterna." This will become the "Cognitive-Ritual Section" (also called "Misraim Service") of the Esoteric School. (See: *Freemasonry and Ritual Work: The Misraim Service* (CW 265). During this time, Steiner also meets Albert Schweitzer. In May, he is in Paris, where he visits Edouard Schuré. Many Russians attend his lectures (including Konstantin Balmont, Dimitri Mereszkovski, Zinaida Hippius, and Maximilian Woloshin). He attends the General Meeting of the European Federation of the Theosophical Society, at which Col. Olcott is present for the last time. He spends the year's end in Venice and Rome, where he writes and works on his translation of H.P. Blavatsky's *Key to Theosophy*.

1907: Further expansion of the German Theosophical Movement according to the Rosicrucian directive to "introduce spirit into the world"—in education, in social questions, in art, and in science. In February, Col. Olcott dies in Adyar. Before he dies, Olcott indicates that "the Masters" wish Annie Besant to succeed him: much politicking ensues. Rudolf Steiner supports Besant's candidacy. April-May: preparations for the Congress of the Federation of European Sections of the Theosophical Society—the great, watershed Whitsun "Munich Congress," attended by Annie Besant and others. Steiner decides to separate Eastern and Western (Christian-Rosicrucian) esoteric schools. He takes his esoteric school out of the Theosophical Society (Besant and Rudolf Steiner are "in harmony" on this). Steiner makes his first lecture tours to Austria and Hungary. That summer, he is in Italy. In September, he visits Edouard Schuré, who will write the introduction to the French edition of *Christianity as Mystical Fact* in Barr, Alsace. Rudolf Steiner writes the autobiographical statement known as the "Barr Document." In *Luzifer–Gnosis*, "The Education of the Child" appears.

1908: The movement grows (membership: 1,150). Lecturing expands. Steiner makes his first extended lecture tour to Holland and Scandinavia, as well as visits to Naples and Sicily. Themes: St. John's Gospel, the Apocalypse, Egypt, science, philosophy, and logic. *Luzifer-Gnosis* ceases publication. In Berlin, Marie von Sivers (with Johanna Mücke (1864-1949) forms the *Philosophisch-Theosophisch* (after 1915 *Philosophisch-Anthroposophisch*) *Verlag* to publish Steiner's work. Steiner gives lecture cycles titled *The Gospel of St. John* (CW 103) and *The Apocalypse* (104).

1909: *An Outline of Esoteric Science* appears. Lecturing and travel continues. Rudolf Steiner's spiritual research expands to include the polarity of Lucifer and Ahriman; the work of great individualities in history; the Maitreya Buddha and the Bodhisattvas; spiritual economy (CW 109); the work of the spiritual hierarchies in heaven and on earth (CW 110). He also deepens and intensifies his research into the Gospels, giving lectures on the Gospel of St. Luke (CW 114) with the first mention of two Jesus children. Meets and becomes friends with Christian Morgenstern (1871-1914). In April, he lays the foundation stone for the Malsch model—the building that will lead to the first Goetheanum. In May, the International Congress of the Federation of European Sections of the Theosophical Society takes place in Budapest. Rudolf Steiner receives the Subba Row medal for *How to Know Higher Worlds*. During this time, Charles W. Leadbeater discovers Jiddu Krishnamurti (1895-1986) and proclaims him the future "world teacher," the bearer of the Maitreya Buddha and the "reappearing Christ." In October, Steiner delivers seminal lectures on "anthroposophy," which he will try, unsuccessfully, to rework over the next years into the unfinished work, *Anthroposophy (A Fragment)* (CW 45).

1910: New themes: *The Reappearance of Christ in the Etheric* (CW 118); *The Fifth Gospel; The Mission of Folk Souls* (CW 121); *Occult History* (CW 126); the evolving development of etheric cognitive capacities. Rudolf Steiner continues his Gospel research with *The Gospel of St. Matthew* (CW 123). In January, his father dies. In April, he takes a month-long trip to Italy, including Rome, Monte Cassino, and Sicily. He also visits Scandinavia again. July-August, he writes the first mystery drama, *The Portal of Initiation* (CW 14). In November, he gives "psychosophy" lectures. In December, he submits "On the Psychological Foundations and Epistemological Framework of Theosophy" to the International Philosophical Congress in Bologna.

1911: The crisis in the Theosophical Society deepens. In January, "The Order of the Rising Sun," which will soon become "The Order of the Star in the East," is founded for the coming world teacher, Krishnamurti. At the same time, Marie von Sivers, Rudolf Steiner's coworker, falls ill. Fewer lectures are given, but important new ground is broken. In Prague, in March, Steiner meets Franz Kafka (1883-1924) and Hugo Bergmann (1883-1975). In April, he delivers his paper to the Philosophical Congress. He writes the second mystery drama, *The Soul's Probation* (CW 14). Also, while Marie von Sivers is convalescing, Rudolf Steiner begins work on *Calendar 1912/1913*, which will contain the "Calendar of the Soul" meditations. On March 19, Anna (Eunike) Steiner dies. In September, Rudolf Steiner visits Einsiedeln, birthplace of Paracelsus. In December, Friedrich Rittelmeyer, future founder of the Christian Community, meets Rudolf Steiner. The *Johannes-Bauverein*, the "building committee," which would lead to the first Goetheanum (first planned for Munich), is also founded, and a preliminary committee for the founding of an independent association is created that, in the following year, will become the Anthroposophical Society. Important lecture cycles include *Occult Physiology* (CW 128); *Wonders of the World* (CW 129); *From Jesus to Christ* (CW 131). Other themes: esoteric Christianity;

Christian Rosenkreutz; the spiritual guidance of humanity; the sense world and the world of the spirit.

1912: Despite the ongoing, now increasing crisis in the Theosophical Society, much is accomplished: *Calendar 1912/1913* is published; eurythmy is created; both the third mystery drama, *The Guardian of the Threshold* (CW 14) and *A Way of Self-Knowledge* (CW 16) are written. New (or renewed) themes included life between death and rebirth and karma and reincarnation. Other lecture cycles: *Spiritual Beings in the Heavenly Bodies and in the Kingdoms of Nature* (CW 136); *The Human Being in the Light of Occultism, Theosophy, and Philosophy* (CW 137); *The Gospel of St. Mark* (CW 139); and *The Bhagavad Gita and the Epistles of Paul* (CW 142). On May 8, Rudolf Steiner celebrates White Lotus Day, H.P. Blavatsky's death day, which he had faithfully observed for the past decade, for the last time. In August, Rudolf Steiner suggests the "independent association" be called the "Anthroposophical Society." In September, the first eurythmy course takes place. In October, Rudolf Steiner declines recognition of a Theosophical Society lodge dedicated to the Star of the East and decides to expel all Theosophical Society members belonging to the order. Also, with Marie von Sivers, he first visits Dornach, near Basel, Switzerland, and they stand on the hill where the Goetheanum will be built. In November, a Theosophical Society lodge is opened by direct mandate from Adyar (Annie Besant). In December, a meeting of the German section occurs at which it is decided that belonging to the Order of the Star of the East is incompatible with membership in the Theosophical Society. December 28: informal founding of the Anthroposophical Society in Berlin.

1913: Expulsion of the German section from the Theosophical Society. February 2-3: Foundation meeting of the Anthroposophical Society. Board members include: Marie von Sivers, Michael Bauer, and Carl Unger. September 20: Laying of the foundation stone for the *Johannes Bau* (Goetheanum) in Dornach. Building begins immediately. The third mystery drama, *The Soul's Awakening* (CW 14), is completed. Also: *The Threshold of the Spiritual World* (CW 147). Lecture cycles include: *The Bhagavad Gita and the Epistles of Paul* and *The Esoteric Meaning of the Bhagavad Gita* (CW 146), which the Russian philosopher Nikolai Berdyaev attends; *The Mysteries of the East and of Christianity* (CW 144); *The Effects of Esoteric Development* (CW 145); and *The Fifth Gospel* (CW 148). In May, Rudolf Steiner is in London and Paris, where anthroposophical work continues.

1914: Building continues on the *Johannes Bau* (Goetheanum) in Dornach, with artists and coworkers from seventeen nations. The general assembly of the Anthroposophical Society takes place. In May, Rudolf Steiner visits Paris, as well as Chartres Cathedral. June 28: assassination in Sarajevo ("Now the catastrophe has happened!"). August 1: War is declared. Rudolf Steiner returns to Germany from Dornach—he will travel back and forth. He writes the last chapter of *The Riddles of Philosophy*. Lecture cycles include: *Human and Cosmic Thought* (CW 151); *Inner Being of Humanity between Death and a New Birth* (CW 153); *Occult Reading and Occult Hearing* (CW 156). December 24: marriage of Rudolf Steiner and Marie von Sivers.

1915: Building continues. Life after death becomes a major theme, also art. Writes: *Thoughts during a Time of War* (CW 24). Lectures include: *The Secret of Death* (CW 159); *The Uniting of Humanity through the Christ Impulse* (CW 165).

1916: Rudolf Steiner begins work with Edith Maryon (1872-1924) on the sculpture "The Representative of Humanity" ("The Group"—Christ, Lucifer, and Ahriman). He also works with the alchemist Alexander von Bernus on the quarterly *Das Reich*. He writes *The Riddle of Humanity* (CW 20). Lectures include: *Necessity and Freedom in World History and Human Action* (CW 166); *Past and Present in the Human Spirit* (CW 167); *The Karma of Vocation* (CW 172); *The Karma of Untruthfulness* (CW 173).

1917: Russian Revolution. The U.S. enters the war. Building continues. Rudolf Steiner delineates the idea of the "threefold nature of the human being" (in a public lecture March 15) and the "threefold nature of the social organism" (hammered out in May-June with the help of Otto von Lerchenfeld and Ludwig Polzer-Hoditz in the form of two documents titled *Memoranda*, which were distributed in high places). August-September: Rudolf Steiner writes *The Riddles of the Soul* (CW 20). Also: commentary on "The Chemical Wedding of Christian Rosenkreutz" for Alexander Bernus (*Das Reich*). Lectures include: *The Karma of Materialism* (CW 176); *The Spiritual Background of the Outer World: The Fall of the Spirits of Darkness* (CW 177).

1918: March 18: peace treaty of Brest-Litovsk—"Now everything will truly enter chaos! What is needed is cultural renewal." June: Rudolf Steiner visits Karlstein (Grail) Castle outside Prague. Lecture cycle: *From Symptom to Reality in Modern History* (CW 185). In mid-November, Emil Molt, of the Waldorf-Astoria Cigarette Company, has the idea of founding a school for his workers' children.

1919: Focus on the threefold social organism: tireless travel, countless lectures, meetings, and publications. At the same time, a new public stage of Anthroposophy emerges as cultural renewal begins. The coming years will see initiatives in pedagogy, medicine, pharmacology, and agriculture. January 27: threefold meeting: " We must first of all, with the money we have, found free schools that can bring people what they need." February: first public eurythmy performance in Zurich. Also: "Appeal to the German People" (CW 24), circulated March 6 as a newspaper insert. In April, *Towards Social Renewal* (CW 23) appears—"perhaps the most widely read of all books on politics appearing since the war." Rudolf Steiner is asked to undertake the "direction and leadership" of the school founded by the Waldorf-Astoria Company. Rudolf Steiner begins to talk about the "renewal" of education. May 30: a building is selected and purchased for the future Waldorf School. August-September, Rudolf Steiner gives a lecture course for Waldorf teachers, *The Foundations of Human Experience (Study of Man)* (CW 293). September 7: Opening of the first Waldorf School. December (into January): first science course, the *Light Course* (CW 320).

1920: The Waldorf School flourishes. New threefold initiatives. Founding of limited companies *Der Kommende Tag* and *Futurum A.G.* to infuse spiritual values into the economic realm. Rudolf Steiner also focuses on the sciences. Lectures: *Introducing Anthroposophical Medicine* (CW 312); *The Warmth Course* (CW 321); *The Boundaries of Natural Science* (CW 322); *The Redemption of Thinking* (CW 74). February: Johannes Werner Klein—later a cofounder of the Christian Community—asks Rudolf Steiner about the possibility of a "religious renewal," a "Johannine church." In March, Rudolf Steiner gives the first course for doctors and medical students. In April, a divinity student asks Rudolf Steiner a second time about the possibility of religious renewal. September 27-October 16: anthroposophical "university course." December: lectures titled *The Search for the New Isis* (CW 202).

1921: Rudolf Steiner continues his intensive work on cultural renewal, including the uphill battle for the threefold social order. "University" arts, scientific, theological, and medical courses include: *The Astronomy Course* (CW 323); *Observation, Mathematics, and Scientific Experiment* (CW 324); the *Second Medical Course* (CW 313); *Color.* In June and September-October, Rudolf Steiner also gives the first two "priests' courses" (CW 342 and 343). The "youth movement" gains momentum. Magazines are founded: *Die Drei* (January), and—under the editorship of Albert Steffen (1884-1963)—the weekly, *Das Goetheanum* (August). In February-March, Rudolf Steiner takes his first trip outside Germany since the war (Holland). On April 7, Steiner receives a letter regarding "religious renewal," and May 22-23, he agrees to address the question in a practical way. In June, the Klinical-Therapeutic Institute opens in Arlesheim under the direction of Dr. Ita Wegman. In August, the Chemical-Pharmaceutical Laboratory opens in Arlesheim (Oskar Schmiedel and Ita Wegman are directors). The Clinical Therapeutic Institute is inaugurated in Stuttgart (Dr. Ludwig Noll is director); also the Research Laboratory in Dornach (Ehrenfried Pfeiffer and Gunther Wachsmuth are directors). In November-December, Rudolf Steiner visits Norway.

1922: The first half of the year involves very active public lecturing (thousands attend); in the second half, Rudolf Steiner begins to withdraw and turn toward the Society—"The Society is asleep." It is "too weak" to do what is asked of it. The businesses—*Der Kommende Tag* and *Futura A.G.*—fail. In January, with the help of an agent, Steiner undertakes a twelve-city German lecture tour, accompanied by eurythmy performances. In two weeks he speaks to more than 2,000 people. In April, he gives a "university course" in The Hague. He also visits England. In June, he is in Vienna for the East-West Congress. In August-September, he is back in England for the Oxford Conference on Education. Returning to Dornach, he gives the lectures *Philosophy, Cosmology, and Religion* (CW 215), and gives the third priests' course (CW 344). On September 16, The Christian Community is founded. In October-November, Steiner is in Holland and England. He also speaks to the youth: *The Youth Course* (CW 217). In December, Steiner gives lectures titled *The Origins of Natural Science* (CW 326), and *Humanity and the World of Stars: The Spiritual Communion of Humanity* (CW 219). December 31: Fire at the Goetheanum, which is destroyed.

1923: Despite the fire, Rudolf Steiner continues his work unabated. A very hard year. Internal dispersion, dissension, and apathy abound. There is conflict—between old and new visions—within the society. A wake-up call is needed, and Rudolf Steiner responds with renewed lecturing vitality. His focus: the spiritual context of human life; initiation science; the course of the year; and community building. As a foundation for an artistic school, he creates a series of pastel sketches. Lecture cycles: *The Anthroposophical Movement; Initiation Science* (CW 227) (in England at the Penmaenmawr Summer School); *The Four Seasons and the Archangels* (CW 229); *Harmony of the Creative Word* (CW 230); *The Supersensible Human* (CW 231), given in Holland for the founding of the Dutch society. On November 10, in response to the failed Hitler-Ludendorf putsch in Munich, Steiner closes his Berlin residence and moves the *Philosophisch-Anthroposophisch Verlag* (Press) to Dornach. On December 9, Steiner begins the serialization of his *Autobiography: The Course of My Life* (CW 28) in *Das Goetheanum.* It will continue to appear weekly, without a break, until his death. Late December-early January: Rudolf Steiner refounds the Anthroposophical Society (about 12,000 members internationally) and takes over its leadership. The new board members are: Marie Steiner, Ita Wegman, Albert Steffen, Elizabeth Vreede, and Guenther Wachsmuth. (See *The Christmas Meeting for the Founding of the General Anthroposophical Society* (CW 260). Accompanying lectures: *Mystery Knowledge and Mystery Centers* (CW 232); *World History in the Light of Anthroposophy* (CW 233). December 25: the Foundation Stone is laid (in the hearts of members) in the form of the "Foundation Stone Meditation."

1924: January 1: having founded the Anthroposophical Society and taken over its leadership, Rudolf Steiner has the task of "reforming" it. The process begins with a weekly newssheet ("What's Happening in the Anthroposophical Society") in which Rudolf Steiner's "Letters to Members" and "Anthroposophical Leading Thoughts" appear (CW 26). The next step is the creation of a new esoteric class, the "first class" of the "University of Spiritual Science" (which was to have been followed, had Rudolf Steiner lived longer, by two more advanced classes). Then comes a new language for Anthroposophy—practical, phenomenological, and direct; and Rudolf Steiner creates the model for the second Goetheanum. He begins the series of extensive "karma" lectures (CW 235-40); and finally, responding to needs, he creates two new initiatives: biodynamic agriculture and curative education. After the middle of the year, rumors begin to circulate regarding Steiner's health. Lectures: January-February, *Anthroposophy* (CW 234); February: *Tone Eurythmy* (CW 278); June: *The Agriculture Course* (CW 327); June-July: Speech [?] Eurythmy (CW 279); *Curative Education* (CW 317); August: (England, "Second International Summer School"), *Initiation Consciousness: True and False Paths in Spiritual Investigation* (CW 243); September: *Pastoral Medicine* (CW 318). On September 26, for the first time, Rudolf Steiner cancels a lecture. On September 28, he gives his last lecture. On September 29, he withdraws to his studio in the carpenter's shop; now he is definitively ill. Cared for by Ita Wegman, he continues working, however, and writing the weekly installments of his *Autobiography* and *Letters to the Members/Leading Thoughts* (CW 26).

1925: Rudolf Steiner, while continuing to work, continues to weaken. He finishes *Extending Practical Medicine* (CW 27) with Ita Wegman.
On March 30, around ten in the morning, Rudolf Steiner dies.

INDEX